Psychology

a dictionary of the mind, brain and behaviour

Arrow Reference Series

General Editor: Chris Cook

Other books in the series:

Basic Economics
A dictionary of terms, concepts and ideas
Tim Congdon and Douglas McWilliams

Computing
A dictionary of terms, concepts and ideas
Anthony Hyman

Earth Resources
A dictionary of terms and concepts
David Dineley, Donald Hawkes, Paul Hancock, and Brian Williams

The Environment
A dictionary of the world around us
Geoffrey Holister and Andrew Porteous

Astronomy
A dictionary of space and the universe
Iain Nicolson

Photography
A dictionary of photographers, terms and techniques
Jorge Lewinski

Psychology

a dictionary of the mind, brain and behaviour

Dr Chris Evans

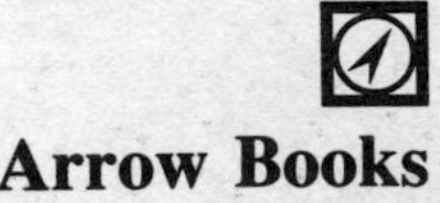

Arrow Books Ltd
3 Fitzroy Square, London W1P 6JD

An imprint of the Hutchinson Publishing Group

London Melbourne Sydney Auckland
Wellington Johannesburg and agencies
throughout the world

First published Arrow Books Ltd 1978
Arrow edition

Set in VIP Times by Input Typesetting Ltd
Made and printed in Great Britain by
The Anchor Press Ltd, Tiptree, Essex.

ISBN 0 09 918070 7

Introduction

Know then *thyself*
Presume not God to scan,
The proper study of Mankind is Man.

ALEXANDER POPE

It's impossible to resist the temptation to offer the first few lines of this dictionary of psychology to the poet Alexander Pope. This cautionary fragment of verse, written over 250 years ago, preserves its message with undiminished strength today. The universe is full of mystery, and thousands of years of scientific endeavour might well pass before we understand the half of it. But in our flush of enthusiasm for unravelling the secrets of the galaxies, harnessing the power of the sun, controlling weather masses and exploring the elusive worlds of subatomic physics, we should remember that in the long run the most interesting – and certainly the most relevant – mystery in the universe is man himself. If that does not make psychology the Queen of sciences today, it certainly ought to at some time in the future, for only by understanding ourselves can we hope to understand the complex interpersonal relationships that exist within human societies, and which at present divide rather than unite mankind. Perhaps before spending many more billions on the exploration of outer space, we should decide to invest just a fraction of that capital into looking at the fabulous, limitless universe inside our own heads.

Psychology can be defined in a number of different ways, and even psychologists themselves do not agree on how to state its goals and subject matter. Its literal definition is 'the study of the spirit', which with an easy transition becomes 'the study of the mind'. In the early part of this century, with the rise of Pavlovian behaviourism, the word mind became first unfashionable and then positively taboo, and most psychologists switched to describing their field as 'the study of behaviour'. At the most extreme phase of this movement it was even argued that the principal target for psychologists' investigations should be animals rather than humans. This was partly because rats and pigeons could be more readily examined under experimental conditions, but also because it was felt that as animals didn't have 'personalities', prejudices, the capacity to think, or 'minds' of any kind, they therefore constituted purer and less ambiguous material for the study of the essence of behaviour. But the pendulum has, fortunately, swung back a bit and today, even if psychology has not returned to its vaguely mystical, philosophical beginnings, it no longer denies the reality of man's personal, powerful, individualistic mental life and experience and, what is perhaps more important, it believes that these are suitable and realistic topics for experiment and theory.

Today, if one had to offer a general definition, one might say that psychology was the study of the mind, brain and behaviour of individual human beings, a study which of course has to be approached and viewed from a number of different angles. A catalogue of these gives a fairly comprehensive, if somewhat daunting, picture of the breadth and scope of this emerging science. All the topics listed below receive coverage, to greater or lesser extent, in the dictionary, and while most can be considered as aspects of psychology in their own right, they also have themes or features overlapping other items on the list.

1. *The brain and nervous system*: strongly rooted in anatomy and physiology, this approach is concerned with the hard facts of how the brain and nervous system are constructed; what are the main components; how are they put together; and what are the main principles of operation?

2. *Sensory physiology*: the study of the senses – vision, audition, taste, smell, touch and the mechanism of balance. In other words, the devices by which the brain gathers information from the outside world. It also studies the nature of the neurone (nerve cell) and its mode of action.

3. *Experimental psychology*: how the psychologist attempts to study his chosen subject matter; the essence of the experimental method, its virtues and its pitfalls; how to design experiments and ensure proper controls, and how to interpret data once gathered; and statistical methods and theory.

4. *Animal psychology*: what is known about the brain and behaviour of non-human members of the animal kingdom? In what ways are the 'higher' animals – in particular the mammals and primates – similar to ourselves, and in what ways do they differ? The relevance of ethology (the study of animal behaviour in its natural environment) to psychology; when are experimental studies of animal behaviour essential, and when are they likely to be unhelpful, or even misleading?

5. *Perception*: the distinction between sensation (receipt of information in the brain) and perception (the interpretation or integration of sensory information by the brain). The history of perceptual research and theory, including the contribution of Gestalt psychology, and current trends of both research and theory.

6. *Learning and memory*: traditionally one of the most important topics, and one of the earliest, to be studied experimentally. Once

information has entered the nervous system, how is it stored (learning)? How much is stored, and how is it extracted (memory)? Why is one thing apparently stored and another apparently not?

7. *Cognition*: in some ways the central topic of psychology, the study of 'knowing', thinking, reasoning and conscious intellectual processes. Why is it also one of the toughest aspects of psychology, both experimentally and theoretically?

8. *Motivation*: what is it that leads an animal or human to do one thing rather than another? The concepts of need, drive and goal. What is meant by reward, and what is its relevance to motivation, and also to learning and memory?

9. *Brain and nervous system in action*: emotion and arousal; what is known about the way in which the brain coordinates and integrates its activity? Sleep and wakefulness; psychomotor activity; the difference between reflex activity and voluntary responses.

10. *Maturation and early development*: how the brain evolves from its embryonic state; the importance of adequate nutrition to the growing brain; the effects of sensory and environmental deprivation in early life.

11. *Developmental psychology*: the application of psychological techniques and expertise to ensuring optimum intellectual and emotional development in childhood and beyond. What is known about the relative influences of heredity and environment? Child psychology and the theories of Piaget.

12. *Applied psychology*: what can the psychologist contribute to the problems of society, to education methods, to work efficiency, job motivation, etc.?

13. *The psychology of communication*: the development and use of spoken language; unconscious communication between individuals (body language, etc.); interpersonal communication within groups; techniques of persuasion; hypnosis; the development of the science of psycholinguistics and its relevance to psychology.

14. *Social psychology*: the study of human behaviour in groups, and the relationship between the individual and the society of which he is a part; theories of small group behaviour, concepts of leadership and role; the relationship of social psychology to sociology.

15. *Abnormal and clinical psychology*: the concept of normality and abnormality; clinical testing and diagnosis; the role of the clinical psychologist; theories of psychoanalysis; behaviour therapy; and assessing and defining intelligence.

16. *The relationship of psychology to other disciplines*: neurophysiology; medicine; pharmacology; biochemistry, etc. Philosophical approaches to psychology; and the status of parapsychology.

The considerable spread of these topics, many of them clearly of great and obvious relevance to man's understanding of himself and his society, may come as a surprise to any reader who makes the common assumption that psychology is merely concerned with some single topic, say, the treatment of mental illness. Of course no psychologist, no matter how well trained or qualified, could consider himself to have an expert knowledge of all or even the majority of these areas, but it is true to say that anyone contemplating psychology as a career will need to provide him or herself with a fairly comprehensive understanding of them, and of the way they interrelate.

The topic is so vast that an impartial overview is almost impossible to achieve; therefore the reader will soon find that the contents of the dictionary reflect many of the author's interests and enthusiasms. If this serves to make the subject more approachable I hope this bias will be forgiven.

Using this Dictionary

Not all the terms defined in this dictionary are cross-referenced to one another each time they occur. Only when the understanding of a term used in an entry adds to the reader's comprehension of the particular area under discussion will the term be marked in small capitals, thus:

Furor. An attack of intense anger, sometimes occurring in EPILEPSY.

A single arrow has been used for 'See'; double arrows for 'See also'.

A guide to further reading may be found at the back of the book.

Abbreviations

16PF sixteen factor test
AA Alcoholics Anonymous; achievement age
ACH acetylcholine
ACTH adrenocorticotrophic hormones
AD average deviation
AL absolute limen or threshold
ANS autonomic nervous system
AQ achievement quotient
ARAS ascending reticular activating system
ASL American Sign Language
BMR basal metabolic rate
C constant; controlled variable
CA chronological age
CE constant error
CFF critical flicker frequency
CNS central nervous system
CR conditioned response; critical ratio
CS conditioned stimulus
Cs conscious
D symbol for drive
dB decibel
DL difference limen or threshold
DNA deoxyribonucleic acid
DOPA dihydroxyphenylanaline
DOT Dictionary of Occupational Titles
DTs delirium tremens
E experimenter; environment
EA educational age
ECG electrocardiogram (ph)
ECT electroconvulsive therapy
EDR electrodermal response (➧ GSR)
EEG electroencephalogram (ph)
EFT embedded figure test
EKG electrocardiogram (ph)
EMG electroymogram (ph)

EOG electroculogram (ph)
EPI Eysenck Personality Inventory
EQ educational quotient
ERG electroretinogram (ph)
ESP extra-sensory perception
f frequency
G symbol for gaol
GABA gamma-amino-butyric acid
GAS general adaptation syndrome
GPI general paralysis of the insane
GSR galvanic skin response
Hz hertz
ICD International Classification System of Diseases
IQ intelligence quotient
IRM innate releasing mechanism
IU interval of uncertainty
jnd just noticeable difference
k mathematical symbol for any constant
L limen or threshold
LSD lysergic acid diethylamide
LTM long-term memory
M mean (but more commonly $\bar{X}$)
MA mental age
MAO monoamine oxidase
MMPI Minnesota Multiphasic Personality Inventory
MPI Maudsley Personality Inventory
N number of observations; symbol for need
n number of cases in subcategory; number of variables
O observer; organism
OOBE out-of-the-body experience
OT occupational therapy
P probability
Pcs preconscious
PE probable error
PGR psychogalvanic reflex
PI proactive inhibition
PK psychokinesis
PKU phenylketonuria
PSE point of subjective equality
PTC phenylthiocarbamide
Q quartile deviation
r symbol for correlation
r product-moment correlation coefficient
RAS reticular activating system
REM rapid eye movements

RI	retroactive inhibition
RL	absolute threshold
RNA	ribonucleic acid
ROC	receiver operating characteristic
S	subject; stimulus
SAT	Scholastic Aptitude Test
SD	standard deviation
SE	standard error
S-O-R	Stimulus-Organism-Response
S-R	Stimulus-Response
STM	short-term memory
SU	sensation unit
SK	skewness
t	time passed
T	total; total amount of time spent in responding to all inkblots in a Rorschach test
TAT	Thematic Apperception Test
TE	trial-and-error learning; time error in psychophysical judgements
TM	transcendental meditation
Ucs	unconscious
UR, UCR	unconditioned response
US, UCS	unconditioned stimulus
VTE	vicarious trial and error
W	word fluency; a weight
WAIS	Wechsler Adult Intelligence Scale
WISC	Wechsler Intelligence Scale for Children
X	a raw score; a dependent variable
$\bar{X}$	the arithmetic mean
z	a standard score

A

Abandonment. The practice of deserting sick, elderly or other unproductive individuals when the survival of the group to which they belong is threatened.

Abasia. Lack of ability to walk caused by poor psychomotor coordination and without any obvious organic cause.

Abdomen. The part of the body between the chest and the pelvis. It contains most of the digestive system.

Abduscent nerve. The sixth cranial nerve which controls the external rectus muscle of the eye.

Aberration. Anything that differs notably from the normal, especially psychological maladjustment. In optics aberrations refer to deviations in light rays as they pass through some distorting medium. (♦ CHROMATIC ABERRATION; SPHERICAL ABERRATION.)

Ability. The capacity to do something and in particular to do it *now*. Contrast APTITUDE, which means a latent ability that could be developed through training. (♦♦ SKILL.)

Ablation. Removal of some part of the body or brain through surgery.

Ablution. Ritual washing which forms part of religious exercises aimed at symbolic or spiritual cleansing. This varies from the ceremonial bathing of Hindus in the Ganges to the Christian practice of baptism.

Abnormal. A difficult word to define because it assumes an understanding of the concept of normality. What, for example, is 'normal' height or weight? Psychologists tend to fall back on statistical definitions in the last resort, but while these will do when numerical measures are available this approach breaks down when it comes to assessing mental or social behaviour. In the long run behaviour is classed as 'abnormal' if it noticeably troubles the individual, his family or society.

Abnormal psychology. That branch of psychology which relates itself to the study of abnormalities or deviations of human behaviour, their diagnosis and treatment. Despite the fact that to the lay person this is generally considered to be the only form of psychology, it is but part of a major scientific discipline which includes educational, animal, experimental psychology, etc. A number of different disciplines are involved in the field of abnormal psychology, including psychiatry, psychoanalysis and clinical psychology.

Abortion. Expulsion of the foetus before it is mature enough to survive outside the uterus.

Abraham, Karl (1877–1925). German psychoanalyst and early disciple of FREUD. Abraham did pioneering work on dream symbolism and was one of the first people to attempt the treatment of psychoses through psychoanalysis.

Abreaction. The dramatic relief of tension which often follows a patient's recollection of a repressed traumatic incident. Once an important part of psychoanalytic treatment, its therapeutic significance has now been somewhat downgraded. It is almost identical in meaning to CATHARSIS.

Abscissa. The horizontal axis or base line of a graph.

Absence. A brief loss of consciousness, typical of *petit mal* EPILEPSY.

Absolute. Independent of other things; not relative.

Absolute judgement. Any judgement made without reference to a COMPARISON STIMULUS.

Absolute pitch. An ability some people have to identify, with great accuracy, individual tones or musical notes without comparing them against others.

Absolute threshold. The lowest value of a stimulus which will just be capable of causing a response 50 per cent of the time.

Abstract. Something not concrete or specific; e.g. honesty.

Abstract thinking. Human beings have the ability to form concepts and to consider events and objects as classes and in relation to other events and objects of the same kind. This capacity to get away from the specific is known as abstract thinking. (◆◆ DEVELOPMENTAL PSYCHOLOGY.)

Absurdity test. A simple test suitable for children and people with a very low IQ or schizophrenic tendencies. The subject is shown a picture with a rather obvious absurdity and asked to point it out.

Abulia. Lack of ability to make decisions.

Acalculia. A form of aphasia in which most mental functions remain unimpaired but the individual is incapable of performing very simple arithmetic. Its most common cause is local brain damage due to a stroke.

Acarophobia. Abnormal fear of tiny animals such as ants, mites, etc.

Accessory nerve. The eleventh cranial nerve which works in association with or as an accessory to the tenth nerve, the vagus.

Accident proneness. The supposed tendency of some people to be abnormally liable to accidents. In many cases this is due to poor psychomotor coordination, but psychiatrists occasionally find patients prone to self-damaging incidents which may vary from falling downstairs to getting drugs and their doses mixed up. It is sometimes suggested that these patients have an unconscious wish to harm themselves or alternatively to gain sympathy and attention.

Accommodation. The change in the shape of the lens of the eye when the focus is shifted to objects at different distances. The term is sometimes used within the context of sociology to refer to those changes in habits and customs which take place in individuals and groups in response to interaction with other individuals or groups. In Piagetian theory the term is used to refer to the process by which schemas are modified in the light of experience.

Acculturation. The process by which customs, beliefs, ideas and patterns of behaviour transfer from one culture to another as two previously independent social groups meet and merge.

Acetylcholine. Important chemical compound released at certain nerve endings and believed to assist the transmission of the electric impulse across synaptic junctions. (➧➧ SYNAPSE.)

Acetylsalicylic acid. The chemical name for aspirin, one of the most widely used and effective drugs known to man.

Achievement age. A child's level of achievement as measured against the standards expected for his particular age group.

Achievement drive. ➧ ACHIEVEMENT MOTIVE.

Achievement motive. Most people feel some sense of urgency to strive for success in various aspects of their life, and this general push has been called an achievement motive. The concept, however, has more value to psychoanalytic theories – in particular that of ADLER – than to physiology.

Achievement quotient (AQ). The ratio between the level of achievement expected from a child on the basis of his age and the actual achievement as measured by a standardized test. (➧➧ INTELLIGENCE QUOTIENT.)

Achondroplasia. An hereditary disorder of the cartilage cells which occurs in infancy and prevents bones from developing normally. It is a common cause of the condition known as dwarfism.

Achromatic. Lacking in colour or hue. Achromatism is the name given to the very rare condition of total COLOUR BLINDNESS, generally due to the total absence of colour-sensitive cones or pigments in the retina. People suffering from this condition perceive the world as a series of greys, differing only in brightness.

Acoustics. The scientific study of sound and hearing. The term also refers to the special properties of a room which affect the detection or judgement of sound inside it.

Acquired characteristics. Any change which takes place in the structure or behaviour of a living organism as the result of its activity or interaction with the environment. The simplest example would be the development of muscles following exercise, but it could also apply to a learned skill such as driving and reading. Acquired characteristics are discriminated from those which are innate or built in at birth. An argument has persisted for centuries as to whether characteristics acquired by an animal in its lifetime can be passed on to its successors, presumably through modification of the genetic structure. (➧ LAMARKIANISM; EVOLUTION.)

Acquired drive. Primary drives – hunger, thirst, sex – are normally assumed to be innate and inherited. Some drives, however, can be learned, often as the result of becoming associated with some more basic drive. A possible example would be alcohol addiction.

Acromegaly. A condition caused by abnormal activity of the PITUITARY and which leads to weird growth and deformity in the extremities of the body – hands, face, etc. The condition is almost non-existent today because of the ease with which hyperpituitarism can be treated.

Acrophobia. Abnormal fear of heights.

Action potential. The brief electrical impulse which follows the stimulation of a NEURONE and sets the main nervous impulse in motion.

Activation. The state of preparing an organ, the body or the CENTRAL NERVOUS SYSTEM for action. In the case of the central nervous system control is exercised by the reticular formation or RETICULAR ACTIVATING SYSTEM (RAS).

Active vocabulary. The total number of words a person can use as opposed to merely understand.

Activity cage. A device for measuring or counting the number of movements which an animal makes over a given period.

Activity cycle. A pattern of behaviour detected in all humans and animals featuring alternating high and low output of energy. In man there is a striking diurnal cycle, but in animals the alternation may be measured in minutes or even months. Compare CIRCADIAN RHYTHM.

Activity drive. The tendency, supposedly present in all humans and animals, to perform activity 'for its own sake' – i.e. when one is not attempting to satisfy any of the basic drives such as hunger, thirst or sex. It is an important concept in some behaviourist theories.

Acuity. Literally sharpness, in particular the ability of the eye or ear to detect fine detail. (⧫⧫ VISUAL ACUITY.)

Acupuncture. An ancient Chinese medical system supposed to relieve pain and treat disease. Fine gold needles are inserted in particular parts of the body according to maps or charts which appear to have no anatomical or physiological significance. The method is still employed on a limited and declining basis in present-day China, though with far less dramatic results than popular accounts would suggest. Not all patients may be operated on and even those who are selected are normally sedated with supporting drugs. Acupuncture does not work with children, nor with animals unless they are strapped firmly down. There is increasing evidence that suggestive techniques play a major role in making acupuncture work (where it does) though it is not clear why such an apparently superstitious practice is promoted and publicized by orthodox Chinese medicine.

Acute. Of short duration, not the same as 'intense'. Contrast CHRONIC.

Acute chorea. ⧫ ST VITUS'S DANCE.

Adaptation. The process by which animals change their state in order to adjust themselves to new conditions in their environment. Adaptation may be physiological, as when our muscles develop, our skin tans or we become resistant to disease, but man is also capable of considerable psychological adaptation by employing mechanisms of learning and memory. (⧫⧫ ADJUSTMENT; ACCOMMODATION.)

Addiction. The condition in which the body has, as the result of continual exposure to a drug or other foreign substance, changed its state so that the drug-based existence becomes the 'normal' and the drug-free condition the 'abnormal'. Addiction is in fact a special kind of adaptation, and it is characterized by a dominating drive on the part of the animal to acquire the substance which its body now requires to maintain its 'normal' state.

Addison's disease. A serious degenerative condition known to be caused by a breakdown in the function of the ADRENAL CORTEX.

Adequate stimulus. Stimulus which is strong enough to activate an appropriate receptor.

Adjustment. The changes made by an animal allowing it to deal with alterations in the world around it. Adjustment should be contrasted with ADAPTATION, which refers to changes *in* an organism rather than *by* it.

Adler, Alfred (1870–1937). An early supporter of FREUD and also the first major disciple to break with him. Adler left the Viennese Psychoanalytic Society in 1911, convinced that Freud was wrong in his view that sexual conflicts lay at the root of all neuroses. He emigrated to the USA and founded his own psychoanalytic school, individual psychology, proposing that the fundamental motivating force was not sexual libido but rather a drive for power. Adler's ideas are somewhat out of fashion today, but his concept of the INFERIORITY COMPLEX has had staying power, as has his work on the effect of birth order in the family.

Adolescence. An important transitional period of life whose onset and duration tends to vary from culture to culture, but is normally held to begin with the age of puberty (twelve or thereabouts) and conclude when pubescent growth ceases (twenty or twenty-one). From a biological point of view adolescence is a critical period because, with the emergence of the secondary sex characteristics and the onset of menstruation in the female, the individual finds him or herself equipped with a 'new body'. From a psychological point of view problems arise which involve an awareness of one's growing sexual needs and also the control or channelling of sexual drives, which tend to be blocked or frustrated in modern societies. From a social point of view, adolescence is important because the individual, by seeking independence, has to sever most parental ties and at the same time adjust to the much wider pattern of stimulation provided by the larger society of which he or she is now a part. Studies of the problems of adolescence and the identity crisis which is often experienced in this period form part of the field known as DEVELOPMENTAL PSYCHOLOGY.

Adrenal cortex. The outer portion of the ADRENAL GLANDS which secretes steroids and helps control some metabolic and sexual functions.

Adrenal glands. Pair of glands near the kidneys which secrete adrenalin and steroids and which help control stress reactions, metabolic and sexual functions. The two major parts of the gland are known as the ADRENAL CORTEX and the ADRENAL MEDULLA.

Adrenalin (or epinephrine). Hormone with an alerting function secreted by the ADRENAL MEDULLA. It releases sugar from the liver, increases heart rate and blood supply and cuts back on digestive processes.

Adrenal medulla. The centre of the ADRENAL GLANDS and the source of ADRENALIN and NORADRENALIN.

Adrenergic. Having an action equivalent to that of ADRENALIN.

Adrenocorticotropic hormones (ACTH). Hormones secreted by the pituitary which regulate the activity of the ADRENAL CORTEX.

Adult intelligence. Intellectual power or, to be more exact, intellectual capacity, is supposed to be unchanged with age – at least until the brain begins to show signs of senile decline. However, the development of a child's brain leads to effective changes in intellectual power which will continue until maturity. Clearly, different approaches to the measurement of intelligence are required for the evolving capabilities of the child and the relatively stable ones of the adult. For this reason psychologists choose to discriminate between adult and child intelligence, and take this into account in devising and scoring their tests. (➧ INTELLIGENCE-QUOTIENT; INTELLIGENCE.)

Adventitious deafness. Loss of hearing brought on by accident or disease, as opposed to deafness inherited or present at birth.

Adynamia. Loss of strength or a general weakness, normally of a neurotic origin. It is also known as neurasthenia or 'nervous debility'.

Aero-acrophobia. A specialized PHOBIA in which the individual has a dread of both high *and* open places.

Aerophagia. Swallowing of air. This common neurotic habit can lead to stomach pains and general discomfort.

Aerophobia. Abnormal fear of draughts or winds.

Aesthesiometer. A device used for measuring skin sensitivity or TWOœ POINT DISCRIMINATION.

Aesthetics. In psychology the experimental and theoretical study of pleasant sensations, including visual beauty, musical appreciation, poetic quality, etc. One might ask why some shapes – such as a circle – seem to be basically more 'satisfying' or 'pleasing' than others – say, jagged or angular figures. Are these preferences culturally determined, or are they, as Gestalt psychologists believed, based on fundamental properties of the brain and visual system? (➧➧ GESTALT PSYCHOLOGY.)

Aetiology. The scientific study of the causes and origins of disease and illness.

Affect. A word with special meaning in psychology where it refers to feelings, moods and emotions. An object or person may be said to have 'affect' for someone when it provokes a strong emotion in him.

Affective psychosis. Any major mental disorder characterized by major changes in mood, such as in manic-depressive psychoses or involutional melancholia.

Affectivity. Tendency to react in an emotional way.

Afferent fibres. Nerves or neurones which carry information into the brain, e.g. from the eyes or some other sense organ. Their counterparts, which carry information outwards from the brain (e.g. to the muscles), are known as EFFERENT fibres.

Affiliation. The formation of social contacts; the need to cooperate, please and form friendships. (⧫⧫ ATTACHMENT.)

Afterdischarge. Nerves continue to transmit a weak signal for a short period after the original stimulus has been withdrawn. This trace is known as the afterdischarge.

After-image. When a bright light stimulates the retina some of the pigment in the receptive cells is bleached and this bleaching, or rather the conversion of the pigments from chemical to electrical energy, induces the visual signal which in turn is transmitted to the appropriate areas of the brain. After the original stimulus has been removed, the pigment begins regenerating and this also sends a signal to the brain, though a much weaker one. The result is the after-image, most commonly seen when the eyes are closed after fixating on a very bright light.

Age-equivalence scale ⧫ YEAR SCALING.

Age-grade. A sociological term which refers to the division of society into groups of individuals, bound together roughly according to age. The transition of an individual from one age-grade to another is marked in some societies by a formal ritual or ceremony, e.g. *rites de passage*.

Agent. In biochemistry, a substance which takes an active part in a chemical reaction; in psychotherapy, an individual who plays a deliberately dominant role in group therapy sessions; in parapsychology, the person who attempts to transmit signals in an ESP test.

Aggression. Hostility, whether physical or psychological, to any person or thing. There is a strong and natural aggressive component in the make-up of all human beings which conflicts in many ways with the conformist demands made on people by society. A lot of attention is paid to frustrated aggression in psychoanalysis and ADLER even argued that aggression was the most important single human drive. Aggression is also an important concept in social learning theory.

Aggression centre. Hypothetical area of the brain from which aggressive impulses are presumed to originate. By implanting electrodes in the hypothalamus of experimental animals and 'switching anger on and off', physiologists claim to have identified this particular organ as an 'aggression centre'.

Aging. The changes that take place in an individual between the period of maturity and death. The topic is of interest to psychologists because of the effects of aging on an individual's personality, behaviour and social effectiveness. The most easily identified changes are that short-term memory deteriorates and so does reaction or response time. Creativity is not, however, measurably affected, though outstanding contributions in, for example, mathematical topics are rarely made after the early thirties. From a social point of view aging may be important because of personality changes that occur in later life which, when severe, are often due to pathological alterations in the brain itself.

Agitated depression. Severe depressive condition in which a patient feels depressed but at the same time restless and physically agitated. It is more common in older patients.

Agnosia. The condition, most commonly brought about by brain damage, in which everyday objects and images seem meaningless or cannot be recognized. Agnosia is generally selective to a particular sense or area, e.g. one may be able to recognize pictures and yet not know the names for them.

Agoraphobia. An abnormal fear of open spaces, and one of the most common and debilitating PHOBIAS.

Agrammaphasia. Disorder of speech in which individual words can be spoken correctly but grammatical rules are more or less totally lost.

Agraphia. Inability to communicate in writing.

Aha reaction. A phrase coined by Wolfgang KÖHLER to describe the curious moment when the mind suddenly seems to grasp the solution of a previously elusive problem or puzzle. Köhler's observation of an apparent 'aha reaction' in his chimpanzee Sultan is now a piece of classic psychology folklore. The ape, after unsuccessfully struggling to get a banana some distance beyond the bars of his cage, roamed about vaguely for a while and then, in a determined and apparently purposeful way, fitted together two sticks and pulled the banana in. (⧫⧫ INSIGHT.)

Ailurophobia. Abnormal fear of cats.

Alalia. Complete inability to speak.

Alarm function. A reaction of the brain, particularly the RETICULAR ACTIVATING SYSTEM, to stress or an alerting stimulus.

Albedo. The reflectance of an object, i.e. the proportion of light reaching its surface which is thrown back from it.

Albinism. A condition in which melanin and other dark pigments of the hair, skin, eyes, etc., are deficient or absent from birth.

Alchemy. Quasi-scientific forerunner to chemistry in which the basic aim was the transmutation of cheap metals such as lead into expensive ones such as gold.

Alcohol. An organic chemical compound which acts as a depressant on central nervous system activity. Alcohol is a potentially addictive drug.

Alcoholic. Someone addicted to the drug alcohol. The true alcoholic suffers severe withdrawal symptoms when he is deprived of the drug, but unfortunately there is no simple test to distinguish between people who are dependent in the psychological sense on the drug and those who are addicted to it. (⧫⧫ DIPSOMANIA.)

Alcoholics Anonymous (AA). A voluntary organization which has achieved some genuine measure of success in bringing about a socially based treatment for alcoholism. Founded in 1936 by former alcoholics, it educates the addict into realizing that he has become totally overcome by his addiction and is helpless in fighting it on his own. The organization sets out to give sustained and sympathetic support to the sufferer and an apparently important sense of *camaraderie*.

Alexia. Sometimes known as word blindness, this is the loss of the ability to read caused by brain damage in the temporal lobe. Compare DYSLEXIA.

Algesia. Sensitivity to pain.

Algolagnia. The tendency to become sexually aroused through pain. The term includes, of course, SADISM and MASOCHISM.

Algorithm. A set of fixed steps used in solving a particular problem. Once an algorithm has been developed it can be applied to solve any other similar problem.

Alienation. Broadly speaking psychological or physical isolation from other people, but the term has acquired special significance in sociology. Its first use in this context seems to have been by Karl Marx, who stated that the average worker in a capitalist society is 'alienated' because he cannot identify with the work he is doing and is not justly rewarded for the labour he puts in. The psychoanalyst Erich Fromm expanded this point, arguing that this form of alienation was responsible for many of the sicknesses of man and society. Unfortunately the word appears in sociological literature in a number of different contexts, of which that of Marx and Fromm is only one. The most direct attempt at defining these came from Sleeman, who identified six basic usages:

1. Powerlessness: roughly Marx's usage.
2. Meaninglessness: the lack of a feeling of purpose to life.
3. Normlessness: lack of commitment to most social goals.
4. Cultural estrangement: sense of isolation from established values.
5. Social isolation: feeling of loneliness in social relationships.

6. Self-estrangement: feeling of conflict within one's self, e.g. roughly the psychoanalytic usage.

Alienist. The legal term used to refer to a psychiatrist or other expert in the field of personality disorders. Its use is more common in the USA than in the UK.

Alimentary canal. The long and tortuous passageway that runs from the mouth to the anus.

Allaesthesia. Misjudgement of the location of a stimulus which has touched the skin.

Allaterality. ➧ MIXED CEREBRAL DOMINANCE.

Allergy. A special type of hypersensitivity or over-reaction by the body to a foreign substance. The body has a natural capacity to react and adapt itself to any alien substance and its defence mechanism largely consists of the formation of antibodies. Occasionally too many may be formed. The symptoms of an allergy are in fact evidence of the body's over-enthusiastic marshalling of its defence mechanisms.

Alloeroticism. Sexual excitement involving oneself and another individual, as in sexual intercourse. This contrasts with autoerotic behaviour, such as MASTURBATION.

Allopreening. The term used in ethology to refer to the way in which a bird or other animal will preen another in response to a ritual 'invitation'. It is a basic form of courtship behaviour.

All-or-none law. Neural activity is assumed to be binary, a nerve having only two states of existence, active or non-active. Any stimulus strong enough to activate a NEURONE will therefore cause it to fire to its maximum extent. This is known as the all-or-none law. Physiologists have long been interested in the possibility that some neurones might be able to provide 'graded' responses, firing with a strength which was proportional to the intensity of the original stimulus, but there is at present no clear evidence that such neurones exist. The intensity of a stimulus therefore is signalled to the brain by the total number of neurones being fired and also the frequency of their response.

Allport, Gordon W. (1897–1967). American psychologist whose special interest was the development of tests to assess and measure PERSONALITY.

Allport-Vernon-Lindzey study. ➧ STUDY OF VALUES.

Alpha rhythm. Waves of electrical activity with a frequency of between 8 and 12 Hz, and most easily recorded from the back or occipital region of the skull. The rhythm disappears when the subject concentrates on something and reappears when in a relaxed and dreamy state.

When it was first discovered by Berger half a century ago hopes were high that other waves associated with a wide variety of mental activity would turn up, but the alpha rhythm has remained the most interesting of all the electrical patterns recorded from the brain. Its real significance is still uncertain and it cannot be detected in almost 10 per cent of otherwise normal individuals. Personal control of the alpha rhythm is an important feature of the currently fashionable experiments in BIOFEEDBACK. (♦ ELECTROENCEPHALOGRAPH.)

Alternating psychosis. Obsolete term for MANIC-DEPRESSIVE PSYCHOSIS.

Altruism. Selfless as opposed to selfish activity. (♦♦ RECIPROCAL ALTRUISM.)

Amacrine cells. Cells which link the second order or BIPOLAR-NEURONES in the retina. The amacrine cells seem to have no axon, but are richly endowed with dendrites.

Ambidextrous. Capable of performing equally well with both hands and both sides of the body.

Ambiguous figure. Visual pattern with at least two perceptual states which tend to alternate when the figure is looked at for any length of

Figure 1. Ambiguous figure: the young wife or old hag. The hat of the young wife is the scarf of the old woman; the jaw, the nose; the neck, the mouth.

time. Although physiologically identical signals are presumably sent up from the retina, these can trigger any one of two or more perceptual recognition systems. The rate of alternation of ambiguous figures tends to speed up with prolonged inspection and may be altered by drugs, conscious effort and, most effective of all, a change in fixation. (⧫⧫ FIGURE-GROUND PHENOMENON; REVERSIBLE PERSPECTIVE.)

Ambisexual. Showing no dominance of male or female sexual characteristics.

Ambivalence. Tendency to alternate between different opinions, emotions or modes of action. The concept is important in psychoanalysis when it is often assumed to denote an unconscious conflict of some kind.

Ambiversion. A state which is neither introversion nor extraversion but a happy balance of both.

Amblyopia. Poor vision which appears to have no specific physical cause. It is often associated with excessive drinking or drug taking.

Amenorrhea. Stoppage or marked reduction of MENSTRUATION for emotional or psychological reasons. It is sometimes associated with a 'false pregnancy'.

Amentia. Failure to develop intellectually. Contrast DEMENTIA.

American Sign Language (ASL). A method of verbal communication for the deaf and dumb using hand and arm gestures.

Ames Room. A distorted room used as a demonstration by the psychologist Adelbert Ames and designed to show how conflicting information can disrupt perceptual mechanisms. In its classic form the facing wall of the room (which is looked at through a small hole) appears to be parallel to the viewer and to have two windows of equal size. In fact the wall slopes away sharply and the two windows are at different distances, though the further one has been appropriately enlarged. The brain holds to its original hunch that the windows are of identical size and when two people are introduced into the room they appear as giant or dwarfish figures, depending on which window they are seen against. (⧫ TRANSACTIONAL THEORY.)

Amino acids. Organic compounds which are constituents of proteins and are used by the body extensively in metabolic processes.

Amnesia. Loss of or lack of memory. This generally has a physical cause, such as brain damage or excessive doses of alcohol or other drugs. When caused by accident it may be retrograde (involving events before the injury) or anterograde (for events following the injury), though the former is more common. Periods of amnesia without obvious physical causes occur from time to time in people under great stress or during a

NERVOUS BREAKDOWN. Events that take place in these conditions are often recalled later, thus distinguishing them from physical amnesia where the memory traces apparently no longer exist.

Amoral. ➧ IMMORAL.

Amphetamines. A class of potentially addictive drugs, including benzedrine and dexedrine, which act as stimulants to the central nervous system.

Ampulla. Part of the semicircular canals in the inner ear, containing hair cells which detect changes in the acceleration and deceleration of head movements.

Amusia. The more or less total inability to recognize or reproduce melodies; a severe form of TONE DEAFNESS.

Amygdala. Clump of cells, forming an almond-like structure, located in the temporal lobe and believed to control most emotional and motivational states. Some tranquillizing drugs act by damping amygdaloid activity.

Anabolism. The process concerned with the conversion and adaptation of food for use by body tissues. Part of the total process known as METABOLISM.

Anaesthesia. Loss of responsiveness to sensory stimulation which may be local (through nerve damage or neural blocking) or general, when consciousness is lost.

Anaglyph. Stereoscopic picture, generally printed in red and green, with the coloured images slightly off-set. When viewed through spectacles with one red and one green filter a striking perception of depth occurs.

Anal character. FREUD believed that the sexual impulse was diffuse at birth but gradually evolved through three phases – oral, anal and genital. In the normal adult genital sexuality predominates but because of conflict, family or social factors a person might become fixated partially or totally on one of the earlier stages. An anal type is a person whose sexual pleasure is concentrated heavily on anal stimulation and secondary pleasures such as defaecation. The personality is identifiable by the so-called 'anal triad' – the characteristics of obstinacy, miserliness and an obsession with tidiness. (➧➧ ORAL CHARACTER; GENITAL CHARACTER.)

Analgesia. Lack of responsiveness to or awareness of pain.

Analog. Something similar or parallel.

Analog computer. Computer which stores and processes information on a continuous rather than a step-by-step basis with the numbers represented by some physical quantity, e.g. electrical voltage. Compare DIGITAL COMPUTER.

Analysand. A person undergoing PSYCHOANALYSIS.

Analysis. A process of examination of a complicated set of circumstances. In psychology it is often used as an abbreviation for *psycho*analysis.

Analytical psychology. The name given by Carl JUNG to the system of psychoanalysis which he developed when he broke away from FREUD in 1912. The main change of emphasis was his rejection of sexual energy as the primary motivating force behind human nature.

Anaphia. Loss of the sense of touch.

Anaphrodisiac. Something which reduces sexual responsiveness.

Anchoring of ego. Psychoanalytic term referring to the way in which one individual identifies with another to provide a sense of psychological security. (➧➧ IDENTIFICATION.)

Androgens. Hormones which cause the development of male sexual characteristics.

Androgyneity. Anthropological term referring to the belief of many primitive societies that all young people have an equal share of male and female sexual potential. Conversion to one or other sex comes about as the result of a tribal ritual such as *rites de passage*.

Android. A man-like being created by man, e.g. Frankenstein's monster. Androids are biological automata, whereas robots are made of inorganic materials.

Anechoic room. A room with sound-absorbing walls and ceilings, used in ACOUSTIC studies.

Anencephaly. Lacking a brain at birth.

Anger. Vigorous short-term emotional state in which the autonomic nervous system assumes temporary command of the body, and the individual is put in the optimum state for aggressive action. It is difficult to distinguish, physiologically, anger from FEAR.

Angular gyrus. Fold of tissue in the parietal cortex believed to be important to speech function.

Anhedonia. Lack of normal ability to feel pleasure of any kind. It is a psychological rather than a physiological deficiency.

Anima. Important concept in Jungian psychology, but carrying two shades of meaning. At first it was used to refer to the unconscious side of the personality, roughly equivalent to the ID in Freudian terms. Later

Jung used it to refer to the feminine component of the male personality, when it contrasts with the ANIMUS.

Animal. Any living organism, simple or complex, which does not rely on photosynthesis for its life support. The word is generally reserved for all living things (other than plants) which are not human.

Animal magnetism. Obsolete term for hypnosis. It was originally employed in the late eighteenth century by MESMER who believed that hypnotic phenomena were caused by some physical emanation roughly equivalent to magnetism. When this hypothesis was disproved the name mesmerism was adopted. (♦ HYPNOSIS.)

Animal psychology. The study of the behaviour of animals in an experimental or laboratory setting. The study of animal behaviour in *natural* surroundings is generally given the name ETHOLOGY.

Animatism. The belief, common in primitive societies, that all *natural* objects, including stone, water, fire, etc., are living or animate things.

Animism. The belief that the universe contains spiritual or 'life' forces which are separate or distinct from physical matter.

Animus. Jungian term for the male component of the female personality. (♦♦ ANIMA.)

Aniseikonia. A condition, sometimes caused by a defect in a lens, which causes the retinal image in the two eyes to be different in size and shape.

Annoyer. Used by THORNDIKE as synonymous with punishment. Contrast SATISFIER.

Anomaly. Deviation from the normal which does not have any known pathological background.

Anomie. The term used by the sociologist Durkheim to refer to any state where group norms are unclear, poorly integrated or in conflict. (♦♦ ALIENATION.)

Anorexia nervosa. Compulsive fasting which may lead to physical illness or even death. It is common in teenage girls who become obsessed with a weight problem and, despite the evidence of their mirror, believe themselves to be grotesquely fat.

Anosmia. Lack of the sense of smell.

Anoxia. Severe shortage of oxygen in the blood or brain. The first symptoms of anoxia are dizziness, euphoria and loss of psychomotor skill.

Antabuse. A drug used as an aid to treating alcoholism. When present in the body it causes violent physiological reaction when alcohol is taken. Its use is a highly effective therapy, provided that the alcoholic can be relied upon to take the Antabuse regularly.

Antagonist. Anything with a counteracting effect. The term may refer to muscles, to a substance which blocks the action of a drug or to complementary colours.

Anterograde amnesia. Loss of memory for events which *follow* the onset of AMNESIA.

Anthropoid. Like man. The term is used to refer to the higher apes.

Anthropology. The study of man as a social animal, including his origins, physique, culture and racial characteristics. (◆◆ SOCIAL ANTHROPOLOGY.)

Anthropometry. The measurement of the shape and proportions of the body in relation to sexual and racial differences.

Anthropomorphism. A tendency to see human-like motives or qualities in animals or even non-living objects, such as rivers, storms, fire. Compare ZOOMORPHISM.

Antibodies. Organic chemical substances created by the body to fight and destroy invading alien substances.

Anti-conformity. Refers to the situation where the individual, whilst not adhering to the usual norms of society, nevertheless adheres to the norms of another group.

Anvil. One of the AUDITORY OSSICLES of the middle ear: a tiny, anvil-shaped bone sometimes known as the incus.

Anxiety. State of stress with or without an identifiable cause. Anxiety is almost always accompanied by disturbances in the autonomic nervous system and corresponding uneasiness in the stomach.

Anxiety neurosis. Chronic or long-term anxiety state caused by persistent stress or conflict situations, and featuring a wide range of symptoms which vary from sleeplessness to obsessive compulsive behaviour.

Apathy. Lack of normal or appropriate emotional response.

Aphasia. A blanket term used to cover a wide range of disruptions of language, caused by damage to the brain and which may involve loss of speech, word memory or reading ability.

Aphonia. Any loss of speech not brought on by cerebral damage.

Aphrasia. Loss of ability to speak or understand phrases or sentences.

Aphrodisiac. Something which induces sexual excitement. No drug is known to act directly as an aphrodisiac, but alcohol, marijuana and similar drugs may affect sexual mood indirectly by removing psychological inhibitions.

Apollonian. Relating to the intellect rather than the emotions. Contrast DIONYSIAN.

Apopathetic behaviour. Behaviour influenced by the presence of other people in a group, though not directly involving them. In particular it refers to 'showing off' or exhibitionism. ➧➧ SOCIAL FACILITATION.

Apoplexy. A fit or seizure brought on by a sudden disruption of the blood supply to the brain.

A posteriori. Refers to inductive reasoning; attempting to establish the cause of something by the careful observation of a set of facts. The term contrasts with *a priori*.

Apparent movement. Movement which is inferred by the brain, even when conflicting evidence is presented to it from the senses. For example, if two lights are switched on and off briefly in sequence, and they are not too far apart, the brain sees a single light apparently jumping across the gap. This particular example is known as the phi phenomenon and is the basis for 'moving' illuminated advertising signs.

Apperception. The final stage of perception, often involving the recognition of a specific object.

Appetite. A drive or motivational state arising from some basic physiological need – including hunger, thirst, sex and even such biological functions as the need to exercise.

Applied psychology. The practical application of what is known about the mind, brain and behaviour as a result of theoretical and experimental psychology.

Apport. Something transported 'supernaturally' from one place to another.

Apprehension. Awareness of something. Also anxious awareness of some *future* happening.

Apprehension span. The amount of information that can be grasped and absorbed by the brain following a brief exposure to the senses. The classic psychological experiment involves presenting a field of objects in a TACHISTOSCOPE and noting the maximum number that can be identified or counted correctly.

Approach-avoidance conflict. A state of psychological uncertainty when an animal or human wishes to do something and yet has powerful reasons counteracting the positive ones. For example, in an experiment an animal may only be fed at a place where it also receives an electric shock. (⧫⧫ EXPERIMENTAL NEUROSIS.)

Apraxia. Loss of ability to carry out purposeful movements due to brain damage.

A priori. Refers to deductive reasoning; working out from known principles what should take place in an experimental situation. Contrast A POSTERIORI.

Aptitude. The potential to do something, generally after training. Contrast ABILITY, which is the capacity to do something *now*.

Aqueous humour. The transparent fluid which fills the front part of the eye, between the cornea and the lens.

Arachnophobia. Abnormal fear of spiders.

Arachoid. ⧫ MENINGES.

Archetype. An important concept in Jungian psychology. JUNG believed that all human beings share a common set of deep-seated motivational and behaviour patterns carried over from generation to generation and part of our evolutionary heritage. Though part of the unconscious mind, and therefore vaguely similar to Freud's concept of the ID, some of these might come to dominate the personality and cause neurosis. These subsystems of the mind he called archetypes and claimed that their presence could occasionally be detected in dreams and, less directly, in symbolism and works of art.

Aristotle's illusion. When the first and second fingers are crossed and rubbed against the nose, one 'feels' two noses rather than one.

Arithmetical mean. The simplest approximation to 'average'; the sum of a set of values divided by their number. The conventional mathematical symbol is $\bar{X}$. (⧫⧫ GEOMETRIC MEAN.)

Army Alpha Test. One of the first attempts at mass screening for intellectual ability. It was used by the American Army in the First World War to sort its vast number of recruits, but because it was heavy on verbal skills it was a less satisfactory measure of intelligence than had been hoped. (⧫ INTELLIGENCE TEST.)

Arousal. A state in which the cerebral cortex is alerted to a high degree of activity, set in motion by impulses directed upwards from the reticular activating system.

Arteriosclerosis. Thickening of the arteries with consequent reduction of blood supply to the brain.

Articulation. Speech which features clear production of the consonants.

Artificialism. A word used by PIAGET to describe the way in which children believe that natural phenomena, such as sunshine or thunder, are caused by some living being.

Ascendant behaviour. Tendency for a person or animal to dominate or control the behaviour of others in a group. Compare with DOMINANCE.

Ascending reticular activating system (ARAS). An important section of the brain's arousing and alerting centre (known as the reticular activating system or reticular formation).

Asemia. ➧ ASYMBOLIA.

Asexual. Method of reproduction, used by the simplest living organisms, not involving the union of male and female cells.

Asocial. Paying no attention to social needs, but not usually antisocial.

Asonia. Lack of pitch sensitivity.

Aspiration level. The mental goal which the individual sets for himself and is disappointed if he does not achieve.

Aspirin. A highly effective drug which reduces pain, temperature and inflammation. It is the proprietary name for acetylsalicylic acid.

Assimilation. The absorption or blending of one thing into another. In psychology the term tends to refer to learning processes and was first used in this context by Thorndike to describe the way in which information learned in a previous situation will be carried over when the organism is confronted with a new but somewhat similar situation. In the Piagetian sense it refers to the way in which a child acquires or absorbs perceptual or cognitive information from his or her environment.

Association areas. Segments of the cortex which do not appear to have a direct sensory function. They were so named because it was once thought that they acted to bridge ideas and sensations. The best guess at present is that they are concerned with language and integrative functions such as perception and decision making.

Association fibres. NEURONES which act to link sensory and motor nerves or separate centres in the brain. Compare COMMISSURAL and PROJECTION FIBRES.

Association laws. The earliest attempts at explaining learning and memory were based on principles of association, i.e. that certain things, by their nature or perhaps because of the way in which the brain or mind operates, are more likely to be bonded together in the memory. Aristotle suggested the three laws of SIMILARITY, CONTINUITY (or contiguity) and CONTRAST – things which are similar, close together in time or contrast with each other are more likely to be subsequently associated in the mind. A number of other 'laws' – such as CAUSALITY – have been formulated and a major school of philosophical psychology, springing from Aristotle's ideas and elaborated by Berkeley, Hume and Mill, reached its peak in the nineteenth century. There is clearly something in associationism, but it is no longer considered to offer any real explanation for many of the facets of memory. Just to say that *similar* things somehow become glued together does not help one to see how this can occur in physiological terms.

Assonance. Similarity in vowel sounds.

Assumed mean. ➧ GUESSED MEAN.

Astasia. Inability to stand when there is no obvious organic cause. It is an hysterical condition.

Astereognosis. Loss of power to recognize things by touching them.

Asthenia. Lack of strength or vitality.

Asthenic type. ➧ KRETSCHMER.

Astigmatism. Error in refraction due to distortion of the cornea.

Astraphobia. Abnormal fear of thunder, lightning and other spectacular celestial events.

Astrology. Pseudoscientific forerunner of astronomy in which the future of individual humans and even societies is supposed to be predictable from a knowledge of celestial patterns.

Asylum. A place of refuge; obsolete term for a mental hospital.

Asymbolia. Loss of the ability to understand or use symbols in communication; generally caused by brain damage.

Asymptote. The theoretical limit of a statistical curve.

Ataraxy. A calm and relaxed state of mind; hence ataractic drugs or TRANQUILLIZERS.

Atavism. A throwback to the past. In genetics, the term refers to the reappearance of a trait after it has apparently vanished for generations. In psychoanalysis it refers to a tendency to behave in an infantile way.

Ataxia. Lack of brain and muscle coordination due to organic damage.

Athletic type. ➧ KRETSCHMER.

Atomism. An approach to psychology (or any other science) which attempts to reduce complex events to their individual components and argues that this is the only way to achieve total and true understanding.

Atrophy. The withering away of an organ or muscle, generally as a result of disease.

Atropine. Drug used to depress activity of parasympathetic system.

Attachment. An emotional link or psychological bond between two people, but especially between mother and child (or parent and child), assumed by some schools of psychology to be of paramount importance in bringing up a stable and non-neurotic adult. The bond is increasingly believed to be important in perceptual, social, linguistic, cognitive and emotional development. A characteristic of an attachment bond is that it endures over space and time. The notion is based on some early clinical observations by Bowlby, to the effect that a high proportion of juvenile delinquents were deprived of maternal affection and contact as infants, and has been popularly advocated by writers such as Benjamin Spock. (➧➧ DEVELOPMENTAL PSYCHOLOGY; AFFILIATION.)

Attensity. A word used by Titchener to refer to clarity of vision or any other sense.

Attention. A focusing of consciousness or alternatively a restriction of sensory input from unwanted aspects of the environment. The precise mechanism of attention is not understood, but whereas at one time it was believed that all sensory stimulation was received by the brain and sorted or 'attended' to after it had arrived, more recent experiments seem to imply that unwanted information can be sealed off at the sense organs themselves. For example, when an animal is looking at its prey, irrelevant sounds may be blocked in the ear itself and thus would not travel up the auditory nerve. The ALPHA RHYTHM recorded from the occipital cortex disappears during attentive states, but whether this is of any significance to understanding attention mechanisms is uncertain.

Attenuation. A reduction in the strength of something, particularly a nervous or electrical impulse.

Attitude. In its simplest definition, a tendency to behave or think in a particular way. Attitudes arise because the human mind or brain is faced with such a wide range of experiences, all subtly and minutely different, that in the interests of efficiency it must classify and group them to some degree, and thus also group the responses to them. Attitudes are assumed to have three components:

1. Cognitive, which concerns the *beliefs* one has about something.
2. Affective, which concerns how one *feels* about it.
3. Conative, which concerns what one *does* as the result of the previous two components.

In attempting to measure attitudes, the direction (good or bad feelings) and strength (strong or weak fellings) are the two parameters normally taken into account. Much effort in sociology has gone into attitude research, for a number of reasons ranging from the purely commercial to the overtly political. Nevertheless, despite some fairly vigorous research dating back to Thurstone's attitude scales in the late 1920s, progress has been rather slow, and controversy still surrounds most techniques for attitude assessment and (perhaps fortunately) attitude modification and control. (➧➧ OPINION; BELIEF; PREJUDICE.)

Attribute. A basic property of something.

Aubert phenomenon. If one looks at a single vertical line with the head tilted slightly to one side, the line appears to be slightly tilted in the other direction.

Audience. Group of individuals, assembled either casually or intentionally, with a common purpose although not necessarily interacting.

Audile. A person with a strong inclination to auditory as opposed to visual imagery in thinking. Compare VISILE.

Audiogenic seizure. A kind of epileptic fit which can be induced by high frequency sounds. Rats, for example, may be thrown into convulsions by the repeated jingling of keys.

Audiometer. A device used for measuring the sensitivity of the human ear.

Audition. The sense of hearing. The detection capability of the human ear is in the range 15 to 20 000 Hz.

Auditory nerve. The eighth cranial nerve which serves audition and the vestibular senses.

Auditory ossicles. In mammals three tiny bones known as the hammer, anvil and stirrup located in the middle ear, and also known as the malleus, incus and stapes. Their function is to carry sound waves from the eardrum to the cochlea or inner ear. (➧ EAR.)

Auditory projection area. Part of the temporal lobe of the cortex which receives fibres from the ear and where sound perception takes place.

Auditory tube. ➧ EUSTACHIAN TUBE.

Aura. Curious sensation, such as a sense of detachment or anxiety, an unusual sound or smell, which is often the forerunner of an epileptic attack. Sufferers from EPILEPSY make use of the aura as a convenient early warning system.

Aural. Relating to the ear.

Authoritarianism. In the political sense, refers to government by an individual or small group which requires the absolute submission of the vast majority of the society. In psychology, the term refers to a particular form of personality marked by a desire for submission from all who are considered to be lower in status or power. Key factors of the authoritarian personality include a great respect for authority figures and a low tolerance for ambiguity and uncertainty. It has been claimed that certain sub-traits are strongly characteristic of this personality type, including conventionalism, superstition, cynicism and even an unusual preoccupation with sexual matters.

Authoritarian personality. Someone who easily accepts the idea and practice of controlling human behaviour by command and personal authority. This personality type may be either dominant or submissive.

Autism. A special kind of self-centred thinking. In its most extreme case the individual becomes oblivious to the world around and preoccupied with fantasy. Progressive withdrawing into one's own inner world, which is often a characteristic of autistic children, was once considered to be one of the symptoms of schizophrenia, but ◆◆ KANNER'S SYNDROME.

Autochthonous. Tending to originate from inside the individual and unlikely to be modified by external stimuli.

Autocracy. A group or society with an actively dominant leader who is personally responsible for the group or society's activities.

Autoerotic. Directing one's sexuality back on oneself; masturbation.

Autogenic. Self-originating.

Autohypnosis. The supposed capacity of some people to put themselves into an hypnotic trance.

Autokinesis. Self-moving.

Autokinetic effect. A compelling phenomenon in which a small spot of light in a completely dark room appears to wander and drift of its own accord. The effect is destroyed as soon as any frame of reference is supplied.

Automatism. Any kind of behaviour in which the individual appears to be performing relatively complex tasks not under conscious control. Sleepwalking is a good example, as also are some of the peculiar spiritualistic activities such as automatic writing.

Automaton. A man-like robot or alternatively a human being who behaves like a robot.

Autonomic. Self-regulating.

Autonomic nervous system. One of the main functional sections of the NERVOUS SYSTEM, and principally concerned with the control of 'housekeeping' functions in the body organs. It is itself divided into the sympathetic and parasympathetic systems, the former coming into action in all emergencies and bringing on an increase in heart rate, surge of adrenalin, inhibition of digestion, etc. The parasympathetic system is more concerned with the non-emergency functions such as the digestive and sexual processes.

Autosuggestion. Self-suggestion; a conscious attempt at producing modification of a personal behaviour pattern.

Average. A word vaguely used to refer to a number of ways of measuring a central tendency in data. The most common of these measures are the MEAN, MEDIAN and MODE.

Aversion therapy. The attempt to eliminate undesirable habits, such as alcoholism or homosexuality, by behaviourist methods – an alcoholic may be given a drug, such as ANTABUSE, which immediately makes him vomit when he takes alcohol. (➧ BEHAVIOUR THERAPY.)

Avoidance learning, Used in experimental psychology to refer to a situation where an animal learns the 'correct' response because it escapes punishment by making it. (➧➧ ESCAPE LEARNING.)

Axiom. A self-evident truth.

Axon. The main extended trunk of a NEURONE, down which impulses flow from the cell body itself.

B

Babinski reflex. A reflex, present in infants up to the age of two, which causes the toes to curl upwards when the sole of the foot is stroked. In due course it is replaced by the plantar reflex in which the toes curl down. When the Babinski reflex occurs in adults it is a sign of neurological disease.

Bacillophobia. Abnormal fear of germs. The condition is often seen in obsessive-compulsive neuroses.

Backwardness. Mild intellectual deficiency, particularly that caused by poor education. (⧫⧫ REMEDIAL; RETARDATION.)

Ball-and-field test. An item in the Stanford-Binet IQ test in which a child is asked to demonstrate the strategy he or she would adopt in looking for a ball lost in a field.

Bandwagon effect. Sociological term used to describe human beings' apparent need to associate themselves with any expanding popular movement or belief.

Baraesthesia. The sense of pressure.

Barbiturates. A group of central nervous system depressants derived from barbituric acid. Highly effective, they are also markedly addictive.

Bar chart. A common method of plotting scores or values as a series of columns of different heights. Another name is histogram.

Bard-Cannon theory. A theory which proposed that the hypothalamus was the seat of emotions, *triggering off* alerting responses in other centres of the brain and in the stomach, etc. It is generally contrasted with the JAMES-LANGE THEORY, which argued that the awareness of emotion *followed* automatic alerting responses in the heart, viscera, etc.

Baroreceptors. Receptors in various parts of the body which can detect local changes in pressure.

Barrier. Term used by LEWIN to refer to factors which prevent behaviour from being directed towards a particular goal. Contrast VECœ TOR.

Barykinetic type. ⧫ KRETSCHMER.

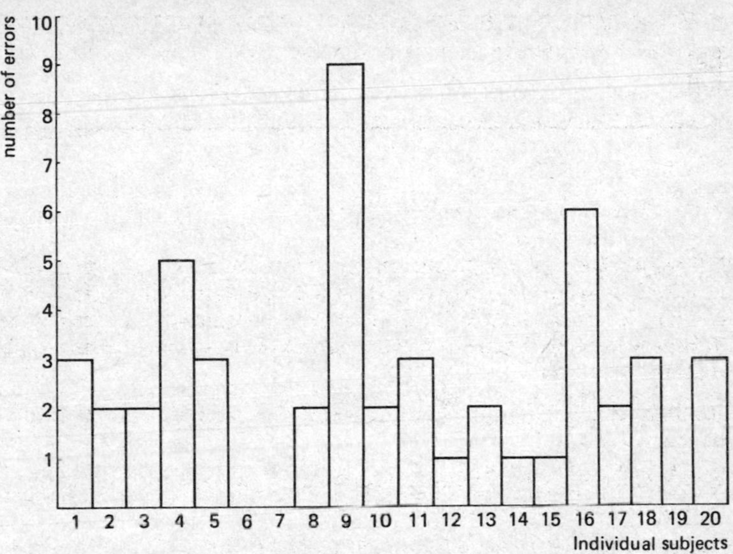

Figure 2. Bar chart. How one would plot the results of a hypothetic experiment featuring the number of errors each subject made in a learning test.

Barylalia. Mumbling, slurry speech, often associated with brain damage.

Basal. Literally at the base of, but also taken to mean lowest normal.

Basal ganglia. A large mass of neurones located deep in the cerebral hemispheres and important in muscular coordination.

Basal metabolic rate. The lowest amount of energy used when the normal body is at total rest, but not asleep.

Basic anxiety. Psychoanalytic term for the fundamental insecurity of the neurotic individual, who seeks relief by demanding attention, affection or power, or by withdrawing emotionally.

Basic need. One of the vital NEEDS, such as hunger, thirst or sex. Such needs are generally supposed to be instinctive and are sometimes known as physiological needs.

Basic skills. The 'Three Rs' – reading, writing and arithmetic – without some knowledge of which educational development cannot begin.

Basilar membrane. A delicate membrane in the COCHLEA which transmits mechanical signals caused by sound waves to the organ of Corti. In the organ of Corti these mechanical signals are converted to electrical energy and transmitted up the auditory nerve to the brain.

Battery test. A group of tests designed to be administered in sequence, and whose results may later be pooled.

Battle fatigue. A state of shock, extreme nervous tension or even psychosis, induced by the noise and tumult of modern warfare. It is generally of short-term duration.

Bedlam. The slang name for the old London Hospital of St Mary of Bethlehem – one of the world's first insane asylums. From this is derived its present use to indicate any wild or frenzied state.

Behaviour. Any response or set of responses made by a living animal. The word has come to be treated as the true or basic subject matter of psychology, with the result that critics have tended to dismiss psychology as the study of animals or humans making muscular responses, whether learned or inherited. The term behaviour, however, should include *any* response of an organism, including those that take place in the brain – language, thoughts, dreams, wishes, etc. – and thus the whole of mental as well as physical activity. However, because muscular responses are so easy to study objectively and mental ones so elusive, there has been an understandable tendency for psychologists to concentrate on the former. (➧ BEHAVIOURISM.)

Behavioural pattern. A complex act, such as driving a car, which is itself made up of a number of simpler skills and reflexes.

Behavioural sciences. The group of sciences which attempt the experimental study of the behaviour of man and animals. The most notable are psychology and sociology.

Behaviour disorder. Any type of abnormal behaviour which is not due to physical illness or to any psychotic condition, but which is assumed to be a reaction to environmental factors. At the simplest and most common level it includes nail-biting, thumb-sucking, etc., and at the more extreme level includes vandalism, alcoholism, persistent delinquency, etc.

Behaviourism. A school of psychology founded by the American J. B. WATSON in 1913, under a banner which declared that the only true and meaningful subject matter of psychology was the observable behaviour of men and animals. Watson was much influenced by PAVLOV's work on the conditioned reflex, which at the time seemed to suggest that all human and animal activity could in the long run be reduced to a complex collection of individual refiexes, some instinctive and some learned or conditioned. In many ways the behaviouristic thesis parallels the Victorian physicists' view of the universe as a gigantic collection of molecular billiard balls. While it was an equally gallant attempt at producing a 'simple' explanation of its subject matter, it was equally doomed to failure as the brain, like the universe, revealed its limitless subtleties.

Behaviourism's weak point was its more or less total rejection of mental life and thought processes. Modern behaviourists, such as the great American psychologist Skinner, take a far more sophisticated view, but still hold that the only tactic guaranteed to succeed in the end is the study of an animal or human's *responses* in carefully controlled experimental situations. (▸ NEOBEHAVIOURISM; SKINNERIAN PSYCHOLOGY; CONDITIONING.)

Behaviour therapy. An approach to psychotherapy in which it is assumed that an individual's problems, whatever form they take, arise because he has at some time learned inappropriate responses to particular situations. Behaviour therapy seeks to 'unlearn' these responses and replace them with alternative, more appropriate patterns of behaviour, normally using the technique of conditioning first developed by PAVLOV. The approach may be crudely straightforward, say administering electric shocks when bedwetting takes place, or more subtle and gradual, as when a compulsive thief is rewarded whenever he shows signs of accepting other individuals' rights to ownership. (▸ CONDITIONING; ▸▸ DECONDITIONING.)

Belief. The holding of a particular view, without necessarily having conclusive evidence that the view is correct. A belief is generally somewhat more specific than an attitude – i.e. it concentrates on a rather smaller aspect of an individual's life-space. (▸▸ ATTITUDE; OPINION; PREJUDICE.)

Belief system. The set of beliefs accepted by any society, group or individual. Compare VALUE SYSTEM.

Bell curve. The 'normal distribution curve' in which the plot of scores of a group falls evenly away on either side of the mean in a rough bell-shape.

Bender-Gestalt Test. A test for brain damage in which the patient is asked to copy simple patterns.

Benham's top. A disc with black and white sectors and marked with black rings, which when rotated gives the illusion of colours. (▸▸ PECHNER'S COLOURS.)

Benign. Refers to any illness which is essentially treatable and will not lead to progressive deterioration.

Benzedrine. A trade name for amphetamine, a drug which stimulates the central nervous system.

Benzodiazepines. Common tranquillizing drugs, including librium and valium, which promote muscle relaxation and apparently suppress activity in the arousal centre of the brain, the reticular activating system.

Berdache. The name given by American Indians to any man who does a woman's work. It is now used in psychology to refer to a transvestite.

Berger rhythm. Obsolete name for the ALPHA RHYTHM, and named after its discoverer, R. J. Berger.

Bergson, Henri (1859 – 1941). French philosopher, particularly interested in the nature of the mind. A strong anti-materialist, he supported the notion that living things were possessed with a unique and totally non-physical force, the *élan vital*.

Bernard, Claude (1813 – 78). French physiologist with a strong materialistic bias. He was the first to demonstrate the importance of hormones in controlling mood and behaviour.

Bernreuter Personality Inventory. Introduced in the early 1930s, and one of the first tests designed to segregate personality into a number of specific factors.

Best fit. Statistical term more commonly known as GOODNESS OF FIT.

Bestiality. Any kind of objectionable, animal-like behaviour, but in particular sexual intercourse with animals.

Beta movement. A series of lights turned on in sequence giving the illusion of movement. It is one of the most common forms of APPARENT MOVEMENT.

Beta rhythm. Electrical signals recorded from the cerebral cortex which have a slightly higher frequency and lower amplitude than the ALPHA RHYTHM. They are associated with mental activity rather than relaxation. (➧ ELECTROENCEPHALOGRAPH.)

Betz cells. Unusually large pyramid-shaped cells found in a particular part of the motor cortex.

Betzold-Brücke effect. ➧ PURKINJE EFFECT.

Bias. A tendency to make particular errors, or a systematic distortion in experimental data. (➧➧ EXPERIMENTER BIAS; RESPONSE BIAS.)

Bibliokleptomania. Compulsive desire to steal books.

Bibliotherapy. A planned course of reading as an aid to treating neurotic conditions.

Bidwell's ghost. ➧ PURKINJE AFTER-IMAGE.

Bilateral transfer. Ability to transfer a skill learned on one side of the body to the other side.

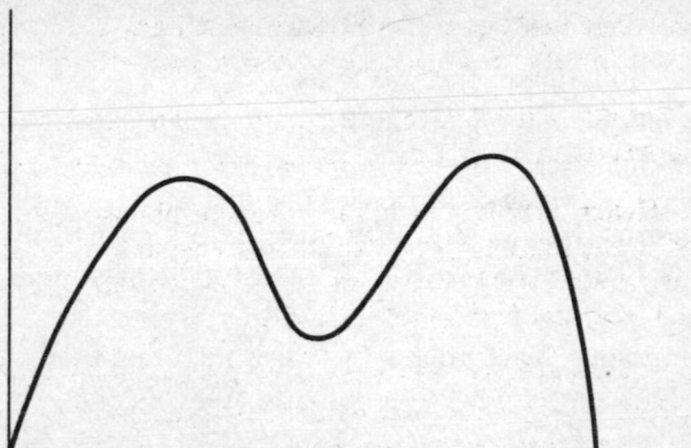

Figure 3. Bimodal distribution.

Bimodal distribution. Statistical concept relating to data which, when plotted on a graph, show two clear peaks.

binary equivalent	0	1	10	11	100	101	110	111	1000	1001	1010
decimal number	0	1	2	3	4	5	6	7	8	9	10

Figure 4. Binary digits.

Binary digit (bit). Unit used in computer science to measure information. (➧ INFORMATION THEORY.)

Binary system. A numbering or counting system using two symbols, 1 and 0, in place of the more familiar ten of the decimal system. All digital computers operate on the binary system, each of their components being either in an 'on' or an 'off' state at any one time. Since neural activity generally operates on a yes/no basis, the brain can also be looked upon as a binary system. (➧➧ DIGITAL COMPUTER; ALL-OR-NONE LAW.)

Binaural. Relating to the two ears.

Binaural shift. When two sounds of slightly different frequency are fed separately into the two ears an apparent change in their intensity is sometimes experienced.

Binet, Alfred (1857–1911). French psychologist who developed what is now generally agreed to have been the first standardized intelligence test. (➧➧ STANFORD-BINET TEST.) He was also responsible for some pioneering studies of personality and developed the first PROJECTIVE TESTS.

Binet-Simon Test. ➧ STANFORD-BINET TEST.

Binocular. Relating to the two eyes.

Binocular disparity. When one fixates a single object with two eyes, slightly different images of the object are cast on to the two retinae. This slight difference, which is due to the fact that the eyes are each viewing the object from a fractionally different angle, is known as disparity and it is one of the fundamental cues in the perception of depth. (➧ DEPTH PERCEPTION.)

Binocular fusion. The process by which the brain blends the slightly disparate images coming from the two eyes into a single perceptual experience.

Binocular rivalry. ➧ RETINAL RIVALRY.

Biochemistry. The study of the chemical components and mechanisms of living things.

Biocybernetics. The study of living organisms from the point of view of the engineering and integrative problems which they pose.

Bioelectrical potential. The electrical properties of living systems, particularly nerve cells.

Biofeedback. A relatively recently coined word which refers to the technique of giving organisms, particularly human beings, information about the state of their internal body or brain processes. The most common application is coupling the electrical activity of the brain to a visual or auditory display so that the subject can observe his own 'brain waves', attempt to modify them and receive instant feedback as to whether the modification has been successful. Biofeedback experts tend to concentrate on control of the ALPHA RHYTHM, the most striking and easily detectable brain rhythm in man. Because of the apparent association between the presence of the alpha rhythm and a relaxed or inattentive state of mind, many claims have been made about the usefulness of this form of alpha control as an aid to relaxation. The topic is a genuine area of scientific study, though interpretation of biofeedback findings is still a matter of controversy. (➧➧ ELECTROENCEPHALOGRAPH.)

Biogenetics. The study of the origins and evolution of life forms.

Biology. The scientific study of living organisms in general. It technically includes human psychology, but for practical purposes most biologists concentrate on the study of the lower animals.

Biometry. The development and use of statistical techniques for studying human and animal behaviour, including group and social activity.

Bionomics. The study of the way in which the external environment affects the development and behaviour of animals.

Biorhythms. The rhythms of life, ranging from short cycles such as the neural cycles recorded in the electroencephalograph, to longer ones such as the menstrual cycle. Compare CIRCADIAN RHYTHMS.

Biosocial. Relating to the study of the effects of environmental factors on the social relationships of a group of living things.

Biosphere. The realm of life including the living things themselves and those parts of the earth which are capable of supporting them.

Bipolar. Having two ends. A bipolar neurone is one with two distinct strands, generally an axon and a dendrite, which reach out in different directions from the cell body.

Birth trauma. The process of birth which features the transition from the protective darkness and warmth of the womb into the noisy instability of the outside world is supposed, according to some psychoanalysts (e.g. Rank and Ferenczi), to lay down a trauma which can persist through life and produce chronic anxieties. Attempting to purge the birth trauma by forcing the patient to come to terms with a realization that he is no longer physically tied to his mother is a special technique employed in some forms of psychoanalysis.

Bisexuality. A state in which an individual has the physical and/or psychological characteristics of both sexes. (➧➧ HERMAPHRODITISM.)

Bit. ➧ BINARY DIGIT.

Bitter. One of the four dimensions of TASTE.

Black box. Expression used in science to indicate any piece of apparatus which works but whose principles of operation are not properly understood. In psychology, the brain is sometimes likened to a black box.

Blacky Pictures. Series of drawings showing dogs in various human-like situations which are used as diagnostic tests for emotionally disturbed children. The child is asked to make up a story about the pictures and the narrative is examined for clues about the child's problems. (➧ PROJECTIVE TESTS.)

Bleuler, Eugen (1857–1939). Swiss psychiatrist who coined the term schizophrenia. One of the first to recognize the potential of FREUD's theory of psychoanalysis.

Blind spot. A small area of the retina, situated on the nasal side of the fovea about 10 degrees off-centre, where the optic nerve leaves the eye. The area is totally insensitive to light.

Block-design test. A test, included in the WECHSLER ADULT INTELLIGENCE SCALE, in which coloured blocks are laid out in a particular pattern and the subject is asked to copy it using other blocks.

Block sampling. The technique of breaking down a population into a number of different groups and then taking a sample from each in the hope that the total sample will give an accurate representation of the population as a whole. (⧫⧫ STRATIFIED SAMPLING.)

Blood-brain barrier. A structure, whose existence has not been demonstrated physically but which many physiologists believe must be present, whose function is to prevent certain substances in the blood from passing into the brain.

Blood group. One of a number of different types of blood cell, differing according to the chemical structure of their membranes. As blood groups (A, B; AB, O, etc.) are known to be genetically determined, they are particularly useful in studying population mixtures and distributions. (⧫⧫ RH FACTOR.)

Blood pressure. The pressure of the blood as pumped into the arteries by the heart.

Blue. The colour perceived when light with a wavelength of about 480 nm strikes the retina.

Blue-yellow blindness. Tritanopia, a rare form of colour blindness in which blues and yellows are confused. (⧫ COLOUR BLINDNESS.)

Body build index. A measure introduced by EYSENCK which attempts to classify body build type according to the relationship between height and chest diameter. The index is the height multiplied by a hundred, divided by the chest diameter multiplied by six. The various types are leptomorph, eurymorph and mesomorph. (⧫ CONSTITUTIONAL THEORIES.)

Body image. The picture built up in the course of one's life as to how one's body appears to other people. It is an important component of SELF-CONCEPT.

Body language. Information given to other people, consciously or unconsciously, by postures or movements of the body. (⧫⧫ NON-VERBAL COMMUNICATION.)

Body type. The classification of the human body according to its physical characteristics. Sheldon's classificatory system is perhaps the best known. (⧫ CONSTITUTIONAL TYPES.)

Bogen test. A test of intelligence in which the subject has to move a ball through a three-dimensional maze.

Bone conduction. The transmission of sound to the inner ear via the bones in the head, used by people who have become deaf as a result of damaged eardrums.

Borderline intelligence. The intellectual level at which the subnormal blends into the 'normal' – roughly speaking, an IQ in the 70s. (➧ MENTAL RETARDATION.)

Boring, Edward G. (1886 – 1968). Prolific American psychologist, experimentalist and historian of the subject.

Brachycephalic. Broad-skulled; having a CEPHALIC INDEX of between 81 and 85.4.

Bradylalia. Unusual slowness of speech.

Braidism. The name given to HYPNOSIS at one time in its history when it was being investigated by the nineteenth-century Scottish surgeon, James Braid.

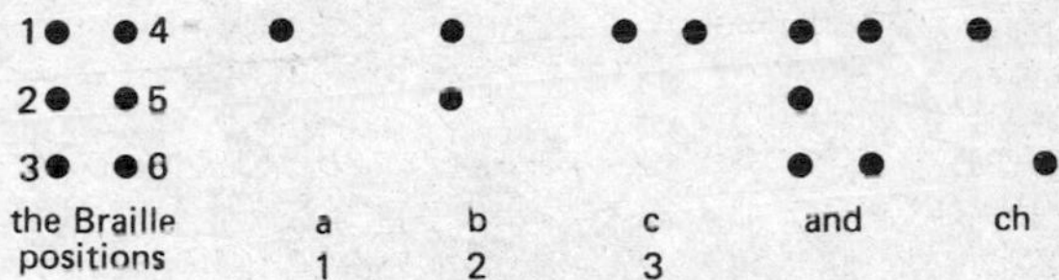

Figure 5. Braille consists of sixty-three characters, each coded by one or more of six raised dots from a six-position matrix. The characters are embossed in lines and read by pressing the fingertip lightly across the page.

Braille. Set of embossed characters, specially coded for fingertip reading by the blind.

Brain. In anatomical terms, the collection of nervous tissue contained inside the skull; in functional terms, the principal organ of the central nervous system which receives, processes and stores information from the outside world, and utilizes this information to control other parts of the nervous system and the organism as a whole. The brain is the most elaborate and complicated organ in the body – in fact it would be more accurate to describe it as a set of organs, all interdependent to some degree – and any attempt at describing it has to err on the side of oversimplification. In addition, there is no absolute agreement among anatomists as to how to break it down into separate parts or units, with some workers concentrating on the physical appearance of different parts, while others lean toward the functional roles. The problem is even further complicated because, despite intensive study lasting over a period of a century, the precise function of some parts of the brain is still not properly understood. One common descriptive approach, however, divides the brain into three main units which, starting from the one closest to the spinal cord, are (1) hindbrain, (2) midbrain, and (3) forebrain.

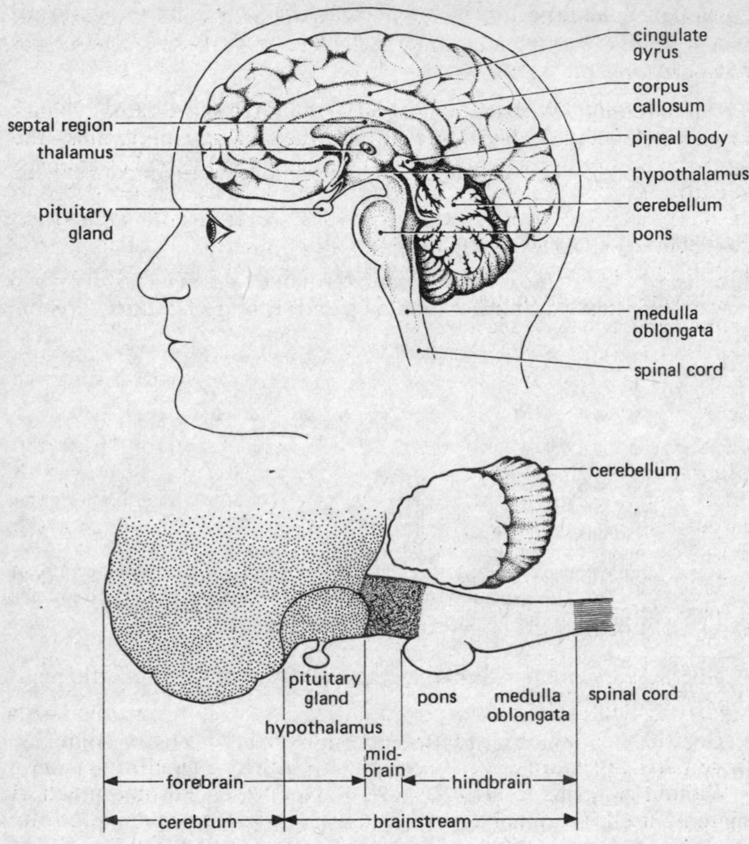

Figure 6. The brain.

1. *The hindbrain*. This is a cluster of structures comprising the medulla, the pons and the cerebellum. The medulla is really a kind of extension of the spinal cord and contains a mass of fibres and nuclei which serve to control the most basic of automatic bodily functions, such as respiration and blood circulation. Just behind it is the cerebellum, sometimes called the 'little brain', which is heavily involved in motor coordination, while above the medulla is the pons which, as its Latin name implies, acts as a bridge between the two halves of the cerebellum. The hindbrain is in many ways an evolutionary primitive structure.

2. *The midbrain*. This is a small structure, directly above the pons and buried deep inside the mass of the brain. It contains a number of

substructures, including the corpora quadragemina and the tegmentum, and its principal role appears to be the control of eye movements and the vestibular system.

3. *The forebrain*. Whereas almost all vertebrates share rather similar structuring of the so-called lower centres – the mid- and hindbrains – the forebrain is enormously enlarged and developed in the higher animals, in particular the mammals. Anatomically the forebrain is divided into the diencephalon (consisting of the thalamus and the hypothalamus) and the telencephalon (which includes the limbic system, the basal ganglia and, most significant of all in primates, the cerebral cortex). The cortex, which is in fact a convoluted layer of neurones covering the surface of the entire telencephalon, plays an important role in sensory and motor functions, though as one ascends the phylogenetic scale a greater and greater proportion of it is given over to integrative and associative functions.

To confuse matters somewhat, a large part of the forebrain and midbrain is also known collectively as the cerebrum, which is itself divided into the right and left hemispheres, connected at the base by the corpus callosum. The chasm separating the hemispheres, which is the most striking single feature of the brain when seen from above, is known as the interhemispherical fissure, while other deep folds include the central and lateral fissures. These fissures tend to be useful to the neurologist in marking out the various lobes of the cerebrum – frontal, temporal, parietal, etc. – and they also tend to constitute boundary lines separating out functionally different areas of the cortex, e.g. those parts concerned with receiving sensory information and those concerned with associative or integratory processes. The remainder of the brain, i.e. those parts which are not the cerebrum, is known as the brain stem.

Without resorting to elaborate drawings, or even to some practical anatomy itself, there is little point in going into greater detail on the structure of the brain, though it is worth emphasizing again that many of its functions are still extremely poorly understood. It is still not entirely clear, for example, just why the cerebrum is divided up into two hemispheres, nor why local damage may sometimes have negligible, sometimes drastic effects. The mechanism of information storage within the brain – learning and memory – is almost totally mysterious, and little is known about the relationship between cortical activity and the 'higher faculties' of reasoning, imagery and consciousness. To some extent the brain appears rather more mysterious now than it did half a century ago, and we will probably do well to prepare ourselves to be still more puzzled before any major advances in understanding cerebral functions come about.

Brain lesion. Physical damage, whether caused by accident or surgery, to tissues within the brain.

Brain localization. A controversial issue in psychology and physiology concerning the question whether particular perceptual experiences or memory traces are located in specific areas of the brain or distributed more generally. (➧ MASSED ACTION; LASHLEY.)

Brain potential. The electrical activity of the brain at any one time.

Brain stem. The so-called 'lower centres' of the brain, i.e. all parts of the brain other than the cerebrum (which includes the cortex) and cerebellum. (➧ BRAIN.)

Brain stimulation. The study of the brain by the electrical stimulation of specific areas in order to observe responses and determine their origins.

Brainwashing. Any attempt to change an individual's personality or system of belief by subjecting the brain to extreme conditions – prolonged sleeplessness, information overload, repetitive conflict situations, etc.

Brain waves. A popular term for the various types of rhythmic electrical activity which can be recorded from the surface of the brain with special electrodes. The most notable is the ALPHA RHYTHM. (➧ ELECTROENCEPHALOGRAPH.)

Breakthrough. A term used in psychotherapy to refer to a sudden and dramatic insight or change of personality on the part of the patient.

Breuer, Josef (1842–1925). Friend and colleague of FREUD whose interest in hysteria and experimental employment of hypnosis in psychotherapy greatly influenced Freud and prepared him for the ultimate development of psychoanalytic theory.

Brightness. The degree of intensity of the perception of illumination.

Bristol Social Adjustment Scale. British counterpart of the VINELAND SOCIAL MATURITY SCALE.

Broca's area. Part of the brain which plays an important role in speech, situated in the left hemisphere of right-handed people. (➧➧ LANGUAGE CENTRES; SPEECH CENTRE.)

Brodmann's areas. Sections of the brain mapped according to the technique of the physiologist Brodmann.

Bruner, Jerome S. (1915 –). American psychologist with a wide range of expertise, including learning, cognition, experimental and educational psychology.

Brunswik ratio. A measure of perceptual constancy which assesses the resistance of the constancy to systematic changes in the environment.

Bruxism. Teeth grinding during sleep.

Buccal. Relating to the cheek and mouth.

Buffoonery psychosis. Quasi-psychotic state in which the individual makes peculiar faces and acts in an eccentric way. Generally this is a sham psychosis, for such behaviour is rarely characteristic of genuine mental disorder.

Bulimia. Abnormal desire for food, associated with some psychoses.

Bunsen-Roscoe law. The rule that the threshold of vision is a function of the *intensity* of a stimulus multiplied by its *duration*.

Burned. One of the six primary smells. (➧ ODOUR PRISM.)

C

C factor. In theories which assume that intelligence is made up of a number of different faculties (learning ability, creative power, etc.) the C factor refers to cleverness or quickness of response.

Cachexia. Severe malnutrition caused by disease and often with subsequent impairment of brain function.

Cachinnation. Absurd or inappropriate laughter, often found in schizophrenic states.

Cacodemonomania. Delusional belief that one is a demon or possessed by one.

Cacogeusia. Hallucination of a foul taste, sometimes the aura preceding an epileptic attack.

Caffeine. Mildly addictive CNS stimulant.

Cainophobia. Abnormal fear of new experiences, new people, etc.

Calvaria. Those parts of the skull other than the facial bones and jaw.

Canalization. A term for the supposed strengthening of a particular neural pathway with repeated use; also the establishment of particular behavioural patterns.

Cancellation test. A test of psychomotor ability in which the subject is presented with an array of different symbols and asked to cancel all those of a particular type as fast as possible.

Cannabis indica. CNS depressant and mild hallucinogen, derived from Indian hemp and also known as hashish. It is not believed to be physiologically addictive.

Cannon, Walter B. (1871–1945). American physiologist whose main contribution was a theory of emotions, which he saw as the body's automatic response to emergencies. In a classic study he showed that stomach contractions (as measured by their effect on an experimentally swallowed balloon) occurred simultaneously with hunger pangs. (➧ BARD-CANNON THEORY; ➧➧ EMERGENCY THEORY; EMOTION.)

Capacity. The full physical and intellectual potential of a person.

Capillary. Tiny blood vessel, a tributary of an artery or vein.

Cardiac neurosis. Obsessive fear of a heart attack when there is no physical danger of one.

Cardiograph. Instrument which records the strength and frequency of the heartbeat.

Cardiovascular. Relating to the heart and the blood vessels.

Carotid arteries. Main source of blood supply to the head and neck.

Case history. All the information about a patient's age, background, medical records, etc., relevant to diagnosis and treatment.

Caspar Hauser. The name of a young German boy found wandering in the street after having been kept in a cellar, supposedly isolated from all social contact for the whole of his life. He was unable to speak, read, write, etc. Caspar Hauser *experiments* involve rearing animals in complete social isolation and studying their development and reactions when released and their capacity to learn to adjust to a complex environment.

Caste. A group isolated from others by marked social or religious barriers.

Castration complex. A term introduced by FREUD to refer to neurotic symptoms brought on by fears of castration originating in childhood. Young boys are supposed to fear the loss of their penis as a punishment, and young girls to believe that they have already lost their penis! According to Freud the child associates the punishment with improper sexual desires, in particular for one of his or her parents. (⧫⧫ PENIS ENVY.)

Catabolism. The metabolic processes concerned with the breakdown of food and its conversion into energy. (⧫⧫ ANABOLISM.)

Catalepsy. State of prolonged muscular rigidity, associated with hypnotic trances or certain schizophrenic conditions. (⧫⧫ WAXY FLEXIBILITY.)

Cataplexy. A tense rigid state brought on by severe shock.

Catarrhines. The 'Old World' monkeys, including baboons and apes. These animals have the same number of teeth as man and downward pointing nostrils. Compare PLATYRRHINES ('New World' monkeys).

Catatonia. An extreme change in behaviour, generally featuring muscular rigidity and stereotyped postures. In catatonic SCHIZOPHRENIA there is often more or less total withdrawal of contact from the environment and a severe disruption of personality.

Catecholamines. A group of hormones secreted by the adrenal medulla during stress, including adrenalin and noradrenalin.

Catharsis. The release of emotional tension or psychical stress, often brought on by some crisis situation or moment of insight in psychotherapy. In the early days of psychoanalysis it was noted that recalling a repressed traumatic incident would frequently bring on a flood of tears or other excitable state, and that this was often followed by a dramatic feeling of relief. (⧫⧫ ABREACTION.)

Cathartic method. The deliberate attempt to relieve neurotic tension by reviving a repressed traumatic memory. This technique was once very fashionable in psychotherapy.

Cathexis. Psychoanalytic term referring to the way in which objects or people are endowed with psychic energy. For example, a place where one has had a deeply emotional experience may have cathectic value for years or decades afterwards, so that whenever one approaches it the emotional state originally associated with it is vividly re-experienced. (⧫⧫ EGO CATHEXIS; OBJECT CATHEXIS.)

Cattell, James McKeen (1860 – 1944). Student of Wundt and Galton and a pioneer of personality and intelligence testing.

Cattell, Raymond B. (1905 –). Influential American psychologist who was a pioneer of personality and intelligence testing.

Caudate nucleus. Small structure of grey matter buried deep in the cerebral cortex next to the thalamus. It is believed to be involved in conscious muscle control.

Causalgia. Unpleasant burning pain caused by injury to a peripheral nerve.

Causality. An important scientific principle based on the assumption that all events in the universe, both physical and psychological, are 'caused' by something. There has been some experimental interest in the theory that the brain *infers* causality wherever and whenever it can, the studies of Michotte being notable in this field. A non-causal theoretical approach has been advanced by Jung and given the name SYNCHRONICITY.

Ceiling. The maximum possible score that can be obtained on a test.

Cell. The smallest structural unit of the body that can have independent life. (⧫ NEURONE.)

Cell assembly. Hypothetical collection of cells in the brain which, because they are repeatedly fired together, come in due course to behave and operate as an independent unit. Although cell assemblies have never been discovered physiologically they form the basis of the influential theory of memory and perception developed by the Canadian psychologist D. O. Hebb. When a cell assembly is activated a complete percept such as that of a straight line, a curve or other unit, is experienced.

Cell body. The main part of the cell, principally containing the nucleus.

Cenotrope. Behaviour pattern exhibited by all individual animals in a biological group. It is believed to be partly learned and partly instinctive.

Censor. Psychoanalytic term for that part of the mind which sifts material existing in the unconscious and prevents it from reaching consciousness and thereby alarming the EGO. The censor is assumed to be partially off-guard during sleep, when repressed material occasionally evades it to come to the surface in the form of DREAMS.

Central conflict. Psychoanalytic term, introduced by HORNEY, for the (largely unconscious) conflict which arises between the demands of a person's true self and his 'ideal' self – i.e. the personality that he believes and wants himself to be.

Central fissure. The deep groove in the cerebral cortex which separates the frontal from the parietal lobes in each hemisphere. (➧ CEREBRAL HEMISPHERES.)

Central inhibition. Blocking or damping down of sensory information by the brain.

Central motive state. A term introduced by early behaviourists referring to hypothetical forces acting within the brain which are self-generating and only partially influenced by environmental changes. The term is roughly equivalent to DRIVES.

Central nervous system (CNS). All the nervous tissue in the brain and spinal cord. The CNS is responsible for all conscious, voluntary and most of the automatic behaviour of animals, and also involved in learning, perceptual and other coordinating activities. (➧ NERVOUS SYSTEM.)

Central processor. That part of a computer which has control and coordinating functions rather similar to those of the brain.

Central tendency. A statistical and psychological term which refers to the tendency of values to cluster around a central point. (➧➧ MEAN; MODE; AVERAGE; MEDIAN; STANDARD DEVIATION.)

Central vision. Vision involving the fovea, the most sensitive and central part of the retina.

Centrifugal. Refers to nerve fibres whose direction of transmission is from the centre outwards. Mainly these are those controlling motor activity.

Centripetal. Referring to nerve fibres whose transmission is from the periphery inwards to the brain – principally sensory nerves.

Cephalic. Relating to the head.

Cephalic index. Measure of the shape of the head, used mainly in physical anthropology. The head breadth is divided by the head length, and multiplied by a hundred.

Cephalization. The tendency for important parts of the nervous system to be clustered in the front or head of the animal.

Cephalocaudal. Relating to the head-tail axis of the body.

Cerebellum. Small but important part of the BRAIN lying underneath the cerebrum and towards the back of the head. Plays a major role in motor coordination.

Cerebral. Relating to any part of the brain or its function.

Cerebral blindness. Loss of vision due to damage to some part of the cerebrum, particularly the cerebral lobes, when neither the eye nor optic nerve is undamaged.

Cerebral cortex. The outer layer of the CEREBRUM and, in evolutionary terms, the 'newest' part of the brain. Only a few millimetres thick, it consists of thousands of millions of intertwined nerve cells of a greyish colour (hence grey matter) which are involved in almost all the higher mental processes – learning, perception, thinking, etc. (➧ BRAIN; ➧➧ GRANULAR LAYER.)

Cerebral dominance. The tendency for one hemisphere of the brain to exercise control over behaviour. The left hemisphere is dominant in most right-handed people, and vice versa.

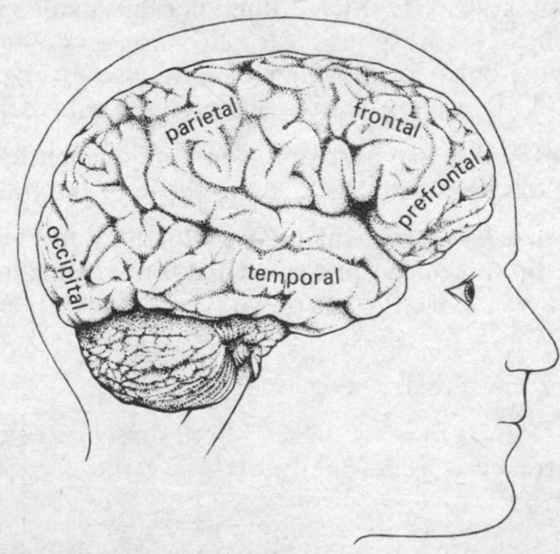

Figure 7. Cerebral hemisphere with lobes.

Cerebral hemispheres. The symmetrical left and right halves of the brain. They are separated at the top by a deep fissure (the interhemispherical fissure), running from front to back and joined lower down by a common body known as the corpus callosum.

Cerebration. Brain activity.

Cerebrospinal fluid. Transparent fluid in which the brain and spinal cord is bathed and which has a nutritive function.

Cerebrotonia. ◆ SHELDONIAN THEORY.

Cerebrum. The largest portion of the brain, largely consisting of the two cerebral hemispheres. It is involved in all voluntary and conscious behaviour and the higher nervous functions. (◆ BRAIN.)

Chain reflex. A collection of individual nervous responses which are linked together so that the completion of one automatically triggers the other.

Chance. An elusive but important concept in science and psychology which refers to the occurrence of something without a cause. Since, however, most scientists and philosophers assume that the universe is causal (◆ CAUSALITY) it is probably better to speak of a chance event as being one whose cause cannot be established or whose occurrence could not have been definitely predicted. The term sometimes refers to randomness, an almost equally elusive concept. (◆◆ STATISTICAL SIGNIFICANCE.)

Change of life. Popular name for the MENOPAUSE.

Channel. A system for transmitting information from one point to another.

Channel capacity. The maximum potential of a communication system, such as a neurone or collection of them, to carry information. The term has filtered into psychology from communication engineers and computer scientists. (◆◆ INFORMATION THEORY.)

Character. Has a double meaning in psychology and may refer either to some special and enduring feature of an individual's personality or the sum of all features, great and small, which when integrated make up his total personality. The word comes from the Greek, meaning something stamped or engraved.

Character analysis. Attempt at treating a personality disorder through psychoanalysis.

Character armour. The front which an individual puts up against the world to protect his EGO and self-esteem. Breaking through the character armour can be a major problem in psychoanalysis.

Character neurosis. A neurotic condition supposed to have its origins in a personality problem developed in childhood. The term was introduced by Horney.

Charcot, Jean-Martin (1825 – 93). French neurologist whose application of HYPNOSIS in psychotherapy attracted the attention of one of his students, Sigmund FREUD.

Chess-board illusion. Slight perception of depth produced by a circular pattern of black and white squares.

Cheyne-Stokes breathing. Alternating periods of very slow and very fast breathing, associated with brain damage or with heart failure.

Chiasma. The junction point in the hypothalamus at which the left and right ptic nerves meet and then separate out again on their journeys to the left and right hemispheres. Fibres from the right halves of the retinae end up in the left hemisphere, and vice versa.

Childhood. The period that lies between infancy and puberty, roughly from four to the early teens. Also refers to the second DEVELOPMENTAL LEVEL.

Child intelligence. The intellectual ability of a child. In practical terms it is often distinguished from ADULT INTELLIGENCE because, while the latter is supposed to be static and therefore amenable to a standard test, the intellectual potential of a child is developing steadily as the brain matures.

Child psychology. The study of the personality of children and the patterning of childhood behaviour, and taking into particular account the problems and development of the maturing brain (➧➧ DEVELOPMENTAL PSYCHOLOGY.)

Chi square. One of the most useful, simple statistical tests used in psychology to determine how and whether experimental results differ from those that would have been expected by chance.

Chlordiazepoxide. The technical name for the drug librium, a relatively new TRANQUILLIZER which appears to be non-addictive.

Chloroform. A potent central nervous system depressant, now rarely used as an anaesthetic in surgery because of its physiological side-effects.

Chlorpromazine. An effective tranquillizing drug with a number of different names, including largactil, thorazine, etc., used widely in the treatment of schizophrenia. (➧ TRANQUILLIZER.)

Choice point. Any decision point in a psychological experiment, commonly a junction in a maze.

Choice reaction time. The delay in a subject's response when the experiment requires that he has to choose between a number of different responses, each induced by a different stimulus. (⧫⧫ COMPOUND REACTION.)

Choleric type. ⧫ TEMPERAMENT.

Cholinergic. Relating to the activity of ACETYLCHOLINE and other associated substances.

Chomsky, Noam (1928 –). American philosopher and linguist whose studies on the structure of language drew the attention of many psychologists to the relevance of this area to their own topic and who pioneered the largely post-war development known as psycholinguistics. By emphasizing the importance of language and the need to study its mechanisms Chomsky, not altogether unwittingly, led an anti-behaviourist wave in psychology which gained strength throughout the 1960s and early 1970s. ⧫ PSYCHOLINGUISTICS; TRANSFORMATIONAL GRAMMAR.)

Chorea. A disorder of the nervous system whose main symptoms are muscular spasms and facial twitches.

Choreomania. Wild or frenzied dancing; the term is sometimes used to describe the 'dancing mania' which swept medieval Europe after the Black Death. It may have been partly due to neurological damage caused by the disease and partly to a religious fad.

Choroid coat. Membranous layer of the eye beneath the outer skin or sclerotic.

Christian Science. A minority religion founded in 1879. Its followers believe that all illness is a manifestation of evil and at the same time illusory. Complete faith in the healing power of God and of the human spirit is believed to banish both the illness and the evil completely.

Chroma. Colour 'depth' or saturation.

Chromaesthesia. The tendency for visual imagery involving particular colours to be associated with particular sounds or passages of music. (⧫⧫ SYNAESTHESIA.)

Chromatic aberration. Error in any optical system caused by the different refraction of the various colours which make up white light.

Chromatics. The scientific study of colour.

Chromatotropism. A tendency on the part of an animal to orientate itself to a particular colour.

Chromosome. Strands in the cell nucleus which carry the genes. In humans there are twenty-two pairs of chromosomes, carrying the main genetic information, plus two singles which are sex determiners – making a total of forty-six.

Chronaxie. A measure of the excitability of a nerve, specifically its reaction time when stimulated by a current twice its threshold.

Chronic. Refers to an illness of long duration. Contrast ACUTE.

Chronological age (CA). Age since birth. CA forms one component in the assessment of IQ.

Ciliary muscles. Tiny muscles which can alter the curvature of the lens of the eye and thus its focal length.

Cingulate gyrus. Fold of tissue in the brain close to the CORPUS CALLOSUM which plays a role in emotional behaviour.

Circadian rhythm. A cyclic biological change taking place in animals and occurring with a rough frequency of twenty-four hours. Compare BIORHYTHM; ACTIVITY CYCLE.

Circular psychosis. Obsolete term for a psychotic condition featuring recurrent extreme changes in mood. The most common is manic-depressive psychosis.

Circumcision. The surgical removal of the foreskin of the penis. This ancient ritual practice is sometimes associated with puberty and may have a certain hygienic value.

Circumvallata papilla. Tiny folds in the surface of the tongue containing chemical receptors.

Clairaudience. The alleged power of spiritualistic mediums to hear the voices of dead people.

Clairvoyance. The alleged ability of spiritualistic mediums to see the forms of dead people. The term has a more specialist meaning in PARAPSYCHOLOGY where it relates to any paranormal ability to know something (such as the order of a shuffled pack of cards) not known to any other person. (♦ EXTRA-SENSORY PERCEPTION.)

Clan. A group of people who need not be direct blood relations but who claim a common ancestor.

Clang association. A particular type of response met in WORD ASœ SOCIATION TESTS when the subject responds with a word of a similar sound to the stimulus, e.g. 'father' – 'lather'.

Class. A group of objects sharing definite characteristics; also a taxonomic classification in zoology (♦ TAXONOMY; ♦♦ SOCIAL CLASS.)

Classical conditioning. CONDITIONING carried out according to the rather tightly prescribed situation of the early Pavlovian experiments.

The animal's environment would be restricted as far as possible so that the response which it was hoped to condition could easily become associated with the already conditioned or instinctive response. Contrast OPERANT CONDITIONING.

Classical psychoanalysis. Psychotherapy carried on in strict accordance with the psychoanalytic principles of FREUD.

Classification test. A test in which the subject has to group or mark things into classes. It is useful in diagnosing brain damage, schizophrenic conditions or mental deficiency. The term can also refer to a task used in studying concept formation.

Claustrophobia. Abnormal fear of being confined in an enclosed space.

Clever Hans. One of a group of specially trained horses from the German town of Elberfeld who were billed as having mathematical ability. In fact the animals had been trained to respond to minute cues given by their owner.

Client-centred therapy. An approach to psychoanalysis developed by Carl Rogers in which little effort is made at diagnosing a patient's condition and the prime aim is to provide an atmosphere of tolerance, reassurance and acceptance. This method, which is gaining in popularity particularly in the USA, is supposed to allow the patient or 'client' to gain confidence to examine himself and rebuild his personality. (➧ NON-DIRECTIVE THERAPY.)

Climacteric. The time of the MENOPAUSE; often associated with depression and emotional disturbance.

Climax. The peak of sexual excitement, generally with ejaculation in the male and vaginal spasms in the female.

Clinic. A place for the diagnosis and treatment of illness, particularly where out-patients may attend.

Clinical psychology. The application of the theory and principles of psychology to the diagnosis and treatment of mental disorders. Technically speaking, the term should cover *all* applications of the science of psychology in a diagnostic or therapeutic setting, but in practice most therapy or treatment of mental disorders is conducted by medically qualified individuals able to prescribe drugs – psychiatrists. The role of the clinical psychologist tends to be to act as a back-up to psychiatric practice, by providing special expertise in administering diagnostic, aptitude, intelligence and personality tests, in counselling and special guidance, and sometimes in psychotherapy using the techniques of psychoanalysis. Clinical psychology as a profession has been making steady headway particularly in the United States, where most large hospitals employ teams of non-medically trained specialists, all of whom deal directly with patients, though without, of course, prescribing drugs or performing surgery.

Clitoral orgasm. Changes which take place in the clitoris which parallel the tumescence and detumescence of the penis of the male in sexual intercourse. The term also refers to sexual climax in a woman achieved by stimulation of the clitoris rather than the inside of the vagina.

Clitoris. Highly sensitive organ in the external genitalia of a woman which is the anatomical equivalent of the male penis.

Cloacal theory. The idea children sometimes have that babies are born through the anal passage or cloaca.

Clonus. Rapid alternating relaxation and contraction of muscles.

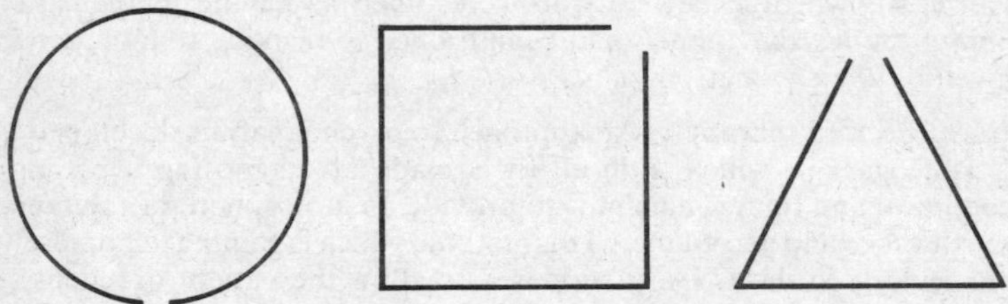

Figure 8. Closure.

Closure. One of the laws of perceptual organization formulated by the Gestalt psychologists. They claimed that the brain attempts to mould sensory experience to suit its own structural principles and the closure law was built on the assumption that the brain 'preferred' a complete to a broken or fragmented figure. Thus if a circle with a small segment missing is exposed briefly or in very dim light, the brain perceives it as complete or closed. (➧ GESTALT PSYCHOLOGY.)

Clouding of consciousness. Vague, somewhat confused state when the individual becomes momentarily uncertain of his identity or surroundings. It is common in psychoses and occasionally experienced prior to an epileptic fit.

Cluttering. Babbled, incoherent speech.

Coacting group. Sociological term for people who work towards a common goal but without necessarily communicating much between themselves.

Cocaine. A local anaesthetic which also acts as a central nervous system stimulant. It is not usually physiologically addictive.

Coccyx. The lowest bone in the vertebral column, representing a vestigial tail in apes and man.

Cochlea. Small portion of the inner ear shaped rather like a snail. It contains the main organ of hearing.

Cochlear canal. The tiny tube inside the cochlea which contains the main hearing mechanism known as the organ of Corti. It is also known as the scala media.

Co-consciousness. A term sometimes used to refer to all information which, while not immediately present in consciousness, can be referred to almost instantaneously without apparently searching the memory.

Codeine. An analgesic derived from morphine.

Coefficient. A statistical term relating to the degree to which a particular characteristic or relationship occurs in a set of values. For example, the coefficient of correlation gives a measure of how closely two variables – say cigarette smoking and lung cancer – are related in a population. The word may also refer to a factor by which a value is multiplied.

Cognition. General term for all processes – one might guardedly use the term 'mental' processes – by which a human being becomes aware of his or her environment. These include perception, reasoning, judging, thinking and so on. Some psychologists like to reserve the term for humans, but it is occasionally used for the reasoning processes some of the higher animals appear to demonstrate. Cognition is always assumed to involve conscious as opposed to unconscious mental processes.

Cognitive consistency. The tendency for an individual's beliefs to be consistent with each other.

Cognitive development. Those progressive changes in intellectual growth which take place from birth to adulthood, and which are assumed to follow a definable sequence. Two main theories of cognitive development dominate DEVELOPMENTAL PSYCHOLOGY at the moment, those of Piaget and Bruner.

Cognitive dissonance. A term coined by Festinger for the state of mind supposed to exist in a person when he finds a severe conflict between his beliefs and the factual evidence put before him. The state is an intolerable one and forces him either to change his original beliefs or disregard and distort the opposing facts.

Cognitive learning theory. Behaviouristic or Pavlovian theories argue that the whole of learning and memory can be explained in terms of direct neural connections between stimulus and response. Cognitive theories propose that a 'reasoning' or 'mental' bridge between the stimulus and the response must be built. (⧓ INTERVENING VARIABLE.)

Cognitive map. Any mental or internal representation of a task or situation which an animal or human may use to assist learning. The creator of the term, the psychologist E. C. Tolman, argued that when a rat learns a fairly complex maze it must build up some kind of a 'cognitive map' inside its brain in the course of doing so.

Cognitive style. A term used to describe an individual's characteristic style of responding to the environment. This characteristic style would be shown in a variety of different situations.

Cohesion law of learning. The principle that events which occur together in time tend to become associated with each other. (➧➧ CONTIGUITY.)

Coincidence. The occurrence together by chance of two events which appear to be significantly or meaningfully related.

Coitus interruptus. The removal of the penis from the vagina prior to ejaculation.

Cold spot. A tiny spot on the skin which is particularly sensitive to cold stimulation.

Colitis. Inflammation of the colon, sometimes associated with emotional problems.

Collateral. A branch which runs off the main stem or axon of a nerve cell.

Collecting instinct. Tendency to hoard things, even if they have little present or foreseeable practical value. Animals *and* humans hoard, but how much of the behaviour is genuinely instinctive and how much socially determined is not clear.

Collective unconscious. A key concept in the psychological theories of JUNG. Through his own observations of the remarkable correspondences between the symbolism of human dreams and artistic imagery in general, Jung argued that man must have available to him not only the information which comes into his brain in the course of his life but also a pool of information bequeathed to him, possibly through the genes, from his ancestorial past. This quasi-mystical notion has never been widely accepted amongst psychologists, even though Jung was not proposing that people shared a 'collective mind' in the popular sense of the word. (➧➧ PERSONAL UNCONSCIOUS.)

Colliculus. A bump or protuberance in the nervous system.

Colligation. A collection of units which, though grouped together, retain their identities and do not fuse into a whole.

Colour. Type of visual sensation, relatively independent of brightness, which is a function of the wavelength of light striking the retina. (➧➧ COLOUR VISION.)

Colour adaptation. Tendency for the hue or saturation of a colour to appear weaker when it is looked at for a long time.

Colour antagonist. A colour which when mixed with another one (red-green, yellow-blue) produces white or grey. The term is roughly equivalent to complementary colour.

Colour blindness. Lack of ability to perceive one or more colours. In the (rare) cases of total colour blindness (ACHROMATISM) all the individual sees is shades of grey. Red-green colour blindness (DEUTERANOPIA and PROTANOPIA) is the most common, occurring in about one in ten males but, curiously, much less often in women. More unusual is blue-yellow colour blindness (TRITANOPIA). (➧➧ ISHIHARA TEST; STILLING TEST.)

Colour constancy. Tendency for coloured surfaces to be perceived as relatively unchanging, even if the light thrown on them alters significantly.

Colour contrast. Phenomenon in which the apparent quality of a colour may be changed dramatically when another colour is placed alongside it. For example, yellow seems yellower when placed alongside blue. This is known as SIMULTANEOUS CONTRAST. *Successive* contrast occurs when one fixates on first one colour and then another. (➧➧ CONTRAST.)

Colour mixture. The combining of colours so as to fuse them. This may be done in a number of ways with slightly different results. In scientific studies coloured lights are normally projected on to a single screen and this process is known as an *additive* mixture. Artists mixing paint produce what is known as a *subtractive* mixture and, because of the ways in which the pigments blend, this produces different sets of fused colours.

Colour pyramid. A three-dimensional map on which can be plotted the relationships of different colours, shades of grey and their different degrees of brightness and saturation. (➧ Fig. 9 on p. 66.)

Colour vision. The process by which the eye and brain discriminate between different wavelengths of light in the range of 400–750 nm. The precise mechanism of colour vision and perception have not been worked out, but the most common theories suggest that the RETINA is equipped with a number – most probably three – of types of receptors sensitive to different colours. In the most famous theory, the Young-Helmholtz, receptors sensitive to red, green and blue are proposed. White light is perceived when all three types are stimulated. The structures most likely to be colour receptors are cones, which are packed into the fovea in central vision, for physiologists have shown that they are

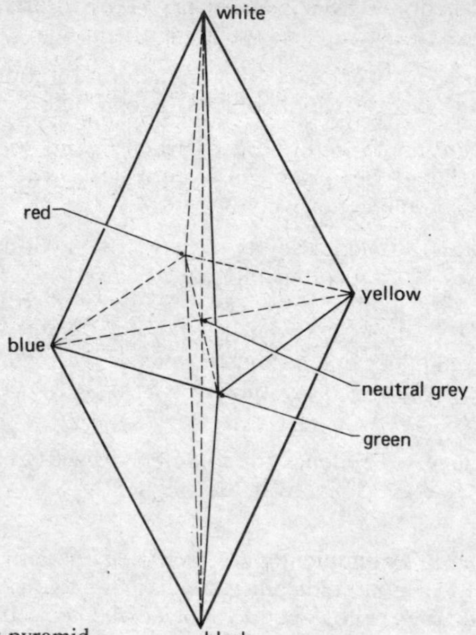

Figure 9. Colour pyramid.

supplied with pigments sensitive to light of different wavelengths. It has also been suggested that the cones act as interference filters, selectively responsive to different types of light. Strictly speaking, one should use the phrase colour vision for the processes by which the eye discriminates between different wavelengths and reserve colour perception for the cerebral processes involved.

Coma. State of deep unconsciousness from which it is impossible to arouse the individual and when many reflexes are suspended.

Combat fatigue. ➧ BATTLE FATIGUE.

Combination tone. A new tone heard when two tones are sounded together. (➧ DIFFERENCE TONE; SUMMATION TONE.)

Commissural fibres. Nerve fibres joining the two hemispheres of the brain (such as via the corpus callosum) or the two sides of the spinal cord. Compare ASSOCIATION FIBRES and PROJECTION FIBRES.

Common fate. One of the Gestalt laws of perceptual organization which states that in a complex field any objects that are moving in the same direction and at the same speed will be perceived 'as a group', even if they are of different shapes, colours or brightness. (➧ GESTALT PSYCHOLOGY.)

Communication. The movement of energy or information from one place to another, and of course including the exchange of information between people and animals. The vast increase in telecommunications in recent years has led to the development of INFORMATION THEORY, which particularly deals with the operation of transmitters and receivers and the capacity and limitations of the channels linking them.

Community. A group of animals or humans living close together and sharing a social organization.

Community catharsis. The elimination of an emotion or feeling, such as guilt or the desire for revenge, which has been shared by a community. Sometimes advanced, admittedly on shaky grounds, as an argument in favour of capital punishment.

Comparative judgement. A judgement made, not on the basis of the absolute value of something (e.g. what weight it is), but on how that thing compares with something else (e.g. is it lighter or heavier?).

Comparative psychology. The study of the similarities and differences in the behaviour patterns of various animal species, including man.

Comparison stimulus. In experimental psychology or psychophysics, any stimulus which is compared in one way or another against a standard one.

Compatibility. Harmonious coexistence.

Compensation. One of the mechanisms, according to psychoanalytic theory, by which an individual protects his personality structure against anxieties and frustration. Compensation is the substituting of one type of activity for another which one would have *liked* to have performed but which is somehow being frustrated or blocked. The idea was seized on most vigorously by ADLER who argued that a physically undersized person might compensate for his lack of strength by aggression and psychologically dominating behaviour. (◆◆ DEFENCE MECHANISM.)

Compensatory movement. An automatic reaction which brings an off-balance system into equilibrium.

Complementary colour. In optics the colour which when mixed with another will produce grey. Confusingly, the term is used in a slightly different sense for pigment mixtures.

Complementary instinct. Psychoanalytic term for two opposing drives in the personality which may end up cancelling each other out.

Complementary probabilities. The PROBABILITY of an event occurring, and of it not occurring. The two probabilities will always add up to 1.

Completion test. Any test in which the subject fills in blanks or gaps in a series.

Complex. A word, often misused in psychology, which technically refers to a collection of associated ideas or factors. In psychoanalysis, it refers to a collection of ideas or beliefs – as in the various states of mind involved in the inferiority complex – which conflict with other facets of the personality. Because of this it has acquired the overtones associated with sickness or maladjustment.

Complex indicator. Any hesitation or peculiarity of response in a word association test which suggests that an area of emotional significance has been approached.

Compliance. A type of conformity where the individual accepts the demands and standards of the group for as long as it is expedient. Contrast PRIVATE ACCEPTANCE.

Complication. A secondary illness, physical or mental, which arises while another illness is running its course.

Complication experiment. ➧ PRIOR ENTRY LAW.

Component instinct. Psychoanalytic term for two or more instincts which have become fused into one. It particularly refers to the numerous sub-instincts (sucking, biting, sadism, etc.) which become absorbed into sexual behaviour.

Composite figure. An important principle in dream interpretation. An individual appearing in a dream may turn out on analysis to be an amalgam of different people.

Compos mentis. Legal term for sanity.

Compound eye. Structurally complex eye with numerous lens and retinae, found in many insects.

Compound reaction. Reaction time experiment in which the subject has to make a decision of some kind (e.g. which of two levers to press) before responding. It is very close in meaning to choice reaction.

Comprehension test. A key item in some early intelligence tests. The subject would be given an hypothetical situation and asked what he would do if faced with it in real life. Also refers to a test which measures a person's understanding of a piece of text.

Compression. More commonly, CONDENSATION.

Compulsion. An overwhelming desire to do something, generally against one's conscious wishes and often without any understanding of its nature.

Compulsive personality. ➧ OBSESSIVE PERSONALITY.

Computer. A device which receives information, analyses it and acts on the analysis in some way. By this definition the brain and modern data processing devices, particularly those equipped with memories and a range of programs so that they can perform lots of different tasks, are equally computers.

Computer language. A set of rules and strategies by which computers may reliably exchange information and through which humans may instruct and modify their behaviour. Common languages are Algol, Fortran, Cobol, Basic, etc.

Computer simulation. Developing a model or hypothesis in such a way that it can be tested by a computer and predictions made about its likely effectiveness in the external world.

Conarium. A hypothetical point where the non-physical mind and the materialistic body meet and interact. Descartes suggested the pineal gland in the brain as the site of this union.

Conation. Dynamic mental activity; willing or striving to meet a goal.

Concept. In its most simple definition, a fairly deep-seated mental process which may later be translated into words, symbols or imagery. More precisely, the word refers to the mental categorization of events or objects on the basis of their having common properties or qualities. This classification may be very specific – for example, many domestic animals have the common property of being covered with dense, soft hair and as such yield the concept 'furriness'. This classification is known as a concrete one. At a more general level, events such as visits to the dentist can be grouped as being 'unpleasant', or jet aircraft may be partly described by the concept 'fast', etc. Concepts of this kind are known as abstract.

The ability to conceptualize is important to any information processing system, whether it be a human brain, animal brain or even a computer, if that system is to cope effectively with an environment which is not only filled with elaborate detail, but which also is in a constant state of flux. Aspects of that environment must be grouped and classified to allow the system both to recognize and respond appropriately to them – if not, one would have to approach each experience as though it were totally new, paying no attention to what one had learned about it in the past. Clearly the process of forming and holding concepts (◆ CONCEPT FORMATION) is tied up, at the first level, with perception and at a higher, more abstract, level with language, symbolization and 'naming'. Man makes great use of linguistic and abstract concepts and there is little doubt that the higher primates (notably chimpanzees) do so to a more limited degree. Even the laboratory rat may apparently learn (with difficulty) the concept of 'triangularity', when this acts as a signal for food. Rudimentary concept formation has been exhibited by computers, or more precisely by computer programs, particularly in such areas as chess playing and pattern recognition.

Concept attainment. Term used by Bruner to refer to the state of having achieved a CONCEPT, the terminal point of CONCEPT FORMATION.

Concept formation. The process by which the brain sorts its experiences into classes or rules. Essentially, this seems to consist of comparing various aspects of a number of different things and ending up with a kind of overview which expresses some relationship between them (➧ CONCEPT). The ability to form abstract concepts is strongly developed in humans and seems to emerge in the young child at roughly the same period as does the acquisition of speech and language. Notable studies in this area have come from the Swiss psychologist Piaget, who holds that the developing brain passes through a series of fairly discrete stages in which concept formation becomes progressively more powerful. (➧ DEVELOPMENTAL PSYCHOLOGY.) Piaget's studies are clinically oriented and have been criticized as being heavily subjective. A more experimental approach has come from Bruner and his colleagues, who see concept formation as a trial and error process, in which the individual generates a set of hunches about the common features of a complex environment and then sets out to test them.

Concept-formation tests. ➧ CONCEPT FORMATION; SORTING TEST; VIGOTSKY TEST; WEIGL-GOLDSTEIN-SCHEERER TEST.

Conception. The process of fertilizing an ovum; in psychology, the initial stages in the formation of an idea.

Conceptual learning. The learning of CONCEPTS and abstract ideas as opposed to the learning of facts or unrelated data.

Conceptual nervous system. Any one of a number of models or theories of the nervous system which allows one to make predictions about its operation.

Concomitant variation. Principle put forward by J. S. Mill that when two events are observed to vary or change together one can infer that they are causally related in some way.

Concrete. Something which is specific or directly observable, as opposed to something which is general, abstract and intangible.

Concrete intelligence. Intellectual behaviour related to the solution of practical problems.

Concrete operational thinking. Piagetian term. (➧ DEVELOPMENTAL PSYCHOLOGY.)

Concrete thinking. Disturbance of thought, common with brain damage, in which the patient becomes obsessed with specific, current facts, is unable to switch from one task to another and seems unable to make judgements about future developments.

Concussion. State, generally involving loss of consciousness and brief disturbances of memory, often associated with a severe blow on the head.

Condensation. Key concept in DREAM INTERPRETATION based on the theory that different events in the latent ('hidden') content of a dream may become fused into a single feature in the manifest content. The puzzling and apparently unidentifiable nature of some dream figures is because they are condensed forms of a number of different personalities. Condensation acts as a partial disguise.

Conditional probability. The likelihood of one event occurring because of the presence of another.

Conditioned reflex. A reflex or response which has been induced through the basic learning process first studied extensively by PAVLOV and known as CONDITIONING.

Conditioned stimulus. A neutral or 'unimportant' stimulus which comes to elicit a particular response because it has been associated with that response in a CONDITIONING experiment.

Conditioning. The mechanism by which animals learn – i.e. receive information, store it and relate subsequent behaviour to this information – is one of the basic problem areas of experimental psychology. Although the precise mechanism of LEARNING is still not understood, a major advance in theory came as the result of the experiments conducted by the great Russian physiologist PAVLOV in the early part of this century into the phenomenon which he called 'conditioning'. In a conditioning experiment an animal is placed in a rather passive situation with a simplified environment and a limited number of things for it to do. In his classic experiments, Pavlov used hungry dogs strapped in harnesses which would, naturally enough, salivate when a bowl of food was brought near them. The automatic reaction *food/salivation* he called a reflex and assumed it to be instinctive or wired into the organism from birth. In the next stage of the experiment he rang a bell at the moment that the food was presented to the dog and after a number of presentations *bell/food/salivation* he found that he could omit the food and get *bell/salivation*. This new link he called the CONDITIONED REFLEX and proposed that it must be the fundamental unit of learning.

In a brilliant series of studies he was able to show the enormously predictable nature of conditioning experiments and plot, in graphical form, the effect of different variables on the conditioning. For example, the bell and the food had to be presented reasonably close together for the conditioned reflex to be set up, and the probability of it being set up was a function of how closely the two stimuli were paired – if the bell preceded the food by too great a margin conditioning would be slow or would not take place at all. He was also able to plot the parameters of *de*conditioning – e.g. how many trials would it take *without* food being presented after the bell before the animal would cease to salivate? This process he called extinction. These experiments and results may seem simple and obvious to us today, but their real and historical significance was the fact that Pavlov had shown that a process such as learning, which had previously tended to be looked upon in a rather mystical way, could not only be studied in the laboratory but could also be shown to follow relatively simple and describable laws.

Pavlov's early results set off a great wave of enthusiasm among physiologists and psychologists in various parts of the world and led to premature hopes that the intricacies of mental behaviour could soon be reduced to elaborate chains of conditioned reflexes. The most notable expansion of his philosophy came from the school of behaviourism under J. B. Watson, which dominated Western psychology for decades and only began to wane slightly in the early 1960s. Russian psychology is still heavily committed to Pavlovian modelling, even though there seems to be little hope that the complexities of thought and language will ever be precisely described in terms of conditioning in the classical sense. (⧫⧫ BEHAVIOURISM; SKINNERIAN PSYCHOLOGY; WATSON; OPERANT CONDITIONING; CLASSICAL CONDITIONING.)

Conduction. The movement of a nervous impulse from one part of the nervous system to another.

Conductivity. One of the three basic properties of living things; the capacity of an organism to transfer information from one part of it to another. (⧫⧫ CONTRACTILITY; IRRITABILITY.)

Cone. One of the two main types of specialized receptor in the RETINA. The cones, which mediate colour and daylight vision, are densely packed in the fovea, the central and most sensitive part of the retina. The periphery of the retina is largely made up of RODS, which take over when luminance falls. (⧫ COLOUR VISION.)

Confabulation. Filling in the blanks in one's memory with a fabricated story. The tendency is commonly observed in patients with amnesia caused by alcoholism or brain damage.

Confession stage. An early stage of psychoanalysis in which the patient 'confesses' his problems – or at least those that are available to consciousness.

Confirmation reaction. The reaction which, presumably, takes place in the brain when an animal has achieved its goal or an expectancy has been met.

Conflict. A state which occurs when two or more drives of roughly equivalent strength oppose each other. The conflict between competitive drives in the unconscious mind or between conscious and unconscious drives is assumed to lie at the root of neurotic behaviour according to the theory of psychoanalysis. In areas of behaviour other than motivational conflict the term DISSONANCE is used. In social psychology it can refer to conflict between norms and roles of two differing groups when an individual is a member of both.

Confluence. Psychoanalytic term for the blending of several motives or wishes into one.

Conformism. Relates to behaviour patterns or states of mind which tend to be moulded by group or social standards.

Conformity. The tendency to behave in accordance with the behaviour patterns or beliefs of the group of which one is a part. Conformity is a powerful social effect and an important aspect of GROUP DYNAMICS. The word may also refer to a particular personality trait – i.e. a tendency to be conformist in one's behaviour. (◆◆ NORM; COMPLIANCE; PRIVATE ACCEPTANCE.)

Congenital. Something present at birth, though not necessarily inherited; also known as INNATE.

Congruence. Term introduced by Carl ROGERS to describe the conscious integration and blending of an individual's life experiences into his personality.

Conjugate movements. Coordinated movements of the two eyes.

Conjunctival reflex. Automatic closing of the eyelid when the cornea is stimulated.

Connate. Present at birth. The term is similar in meaning to CONGENITAL.

Connectionism. A theory originally put forward by THORNDIKE which stated that learning takes place because the neurone handling a stimulus becomes connected to the neurone handling a response through the formation of some physical link – possibly involving a third neurone forming a bridge between the others.

Connector. Any nerve cell which forms a link between one neurone and another.

Connotative meaning. The idiosyncratic or personalized meaning of something. Contrast DENOTATIVE MEANING. (◆◆ SEMANTIC DIFFERENTIAL.)

Consanguinity. The relationship which exists between people descended from a common ancestor.

Conscience. The sum total of an individual's moral values. FREUD made great use of the concept in his personality theory, effectively renaming the conscience as SUPEREGO.

Consciousness. The state of being aware of oneself as a distinct entity, separate from other people or things in one's environment. The awareness is probably present to a varying degree in the higher animals as well as man, and presumably a function of the complexity of the living brain and its integrative power.

Consensual actions. Behaviour not under voluntary control, but of which the individual is aware.

Consistency. The tendency for something to be in agreement with its own principles. In the case of an experiment or test the term may refer to its INTERNAL CONSISTENCY or its consistency with other theories or tests.

Consolidation. The process assumed to take place in the brain after something has been learned and which is roughly equivalent to a 'cementing' of the MEMORY.

Constancy. A phenomenon which plays an important part in perception. The brain has a vested interest in simplifying the world to the maximum reasonable extent, and yet the information presented through the senses can vary wildly from moment to moment. For example, consider a round object held close to the eye, which is then moved a few centimetres, tilted slightly and less brightly illuminated. Quite exceptional changes take place in the retina as the result, and yet the brain still recognizes the same round object and judges or perceives it as being relatively unchanged. Even when the object is moved to twice the distance and its retinal angle halved, it still 'looks' roughly the same size. This tendency to simplify the perceptual world is known as constancy and it operates most strikingly in vision along the parameters of size, shape, brightness and colour.

Constant. An experimental condition which is kept unchanged at all times.

Constant error. Type of error which occurs frequently in psychological experiments and which tends to be consistent in a particular direction. An excellent example is in the MÜLLER-LYER ILLUSION where people consistently over-estimate the length of the line. Compare VARIABLE ERROR.

Constant method. Used as an experimental procedure in psychophysics in which the subject has to judge a series of rather similar stimuli and compare them with a standard (the constant).

Constellation. Psychoanalytic term for a collection of ideas which have all got some emotional significance for the individual.

Constitution. The basic psychological and physiological make-up of a person; the sum of his heredity and acquired characteristics.

Constitutional theories. Various approaches to personality theory which rely on there being some kind of association between an individual's build or physique and his overall psychological mood. The best known is probably that of W. H. Sheldon. (➧ SHELDONIAN THEORY; KRETSCHMER; SOMATOTYPOLOGY; BODY BUILD INDEX.)

Constitutional types. Complexes of physiological and psychological characteristics which are assumed to go together and determine an individual's overall PERSONALITY. This assumption is a fundamental feature of theories such as that of Sheldon, but originate in principle in Hippocrates' notion that certain anatomical characteristics were often associated with a tendency to particular diseases.

Construct. A concept which has been formally 'worked out'; a theory or model of something. The word is acquiring new relevance within the framework of Kelley's REPERTORY GRID theory.

Constructive. Refers to thinking which attempts to build rather than to destroy.

Construct validity. A term used widely in relation to psychological testing. It has a number of slightly different shades of meaning, but roughly speaking refers to the extent to which a test measures the factors which it sets out to test.

Consumer psychology. The application of psychological techniques to the study of the development, marketing and distribution of goods and services. This includes the psychology of advertising and market research.

Consummatory response. The final response in a chain of behaviour which leads to a reward or goal.

Contagion. Used in sociology to refer to the spread of behaviour patterns or ideas through personal or group suggestion.

Contamination. The distortion of results because of faulty experimental method and in particular the personal influence, either conscious or unconscious, of the experimenter in the selection or treatment of his results.

Content. The basic material present in something; may also refer to material present in consciousness.

Content response. Refers to the main image, object or theme reported by a subject when he interprets an inkblot in a RORSCHACH or other projective test.

Context. Anything which surrounds or encompasses some other thing and at the same time influences its perception.

Contiguity law. A principle first put forward by Aristotle that events which occur close to each other in space or time tend to be associated in the brain. (➧ ASSOCIATION LAW.) This would of course apply to stimulus and response and therefore relate to learning. The idea was also taken up by the Gestalt psychologists, who advanced it as one of their 'laws of perception', stating that things which are close together in the visual field tend to be perceived as units. (➧➧ GESTALT PSYCHOLOGY.) A theory of learning based on the principle of contiguity was also formulated by E. R. GUTHRIE. (➧ STATISTICAL LEARNING THEORY.)

Continence. The ability to control bowel and bladder movements; also the ability to abstain from sexual relations.

Contingency. The dependency of one factor upon another. A common statistical measure is known as the contingency coefficient.

Continuity. One of the laws of association first put forward by Aristotle. Things which are continuous – follow each other closely in time or space – tend to be associated together. It is similar in meaning to contiguity. (➧ ASSOCIATION LAWS.)

Continuity-non-continuity theories. When an animal is learning something, say a maze, does it absorb information all the time or just at critical moments, such as at CHOICE POINTS or when confronted by something novel or unusual? A controversy once raged as to which of these two hypotheses was correct but was never experimentally resolved. At its root is the question whether an animal is a passive absorber of information, or selectively attends to its environment in an 'insightful' way.

Contour. A boundary or edge. Contour is vital to perception.

Contractility. One of the three properties normally associated with living organisms, i.e. the ability of tissue to change shape by contraction. The other two properties are CONDUCTIVITY and IRRITABILITY.

Contracture. A muscle's failure to return to its original position after contracting.

Contralateral. The opposite side of the body.

Contrast. When two distinctly different stimuli are placed together, either in space or time, they affect each other's perception, generally by heightening the apparent difference between them. The importance of contrast was first recognized by Aristotle who listed it as one of his laws of association – things which contrast with each other tend to be linked together in memory. (▸ ASSOCIATION LAWS; COLOUR CONTRAST.)

Contrasuggestion. Tendency to resist ideas or arguments put forward by someone else, and even to harden one's original position in the face of suggestion.

Control. An important concept in experimental psychology. In attempting to decide whether one variable has an effect on another – say whether a drug can improve learning ability – one needs at least two experiments. In the first the drug is administered and the effects noted, in the second some neutral substance is administered and the effects of this noted as well. The second experiment acts as a control and allows a base line with which the results of the first experiment can be compared. The important thing about the control study is that it should be identical in all possible respects to the first experiment, with the single exception of the INDEPENDENT VARIABLE – in this example the drug. (▸▸ CONTROL GROUP.)

Control group. A group of people or animals used as a comparison in an experiment, selected because they have the same characteristics as the EXPERIMENTAL GROUP. (▸▸ MATCHED GROUPS.)

Convention. Behaviour pattern considered to be socially normal and acceptable, though not legally binding. Compare MORES.

Convergence. The turning in of the eyes when changing fixation from a far to a near object so that the images fall on the fovea of each retina. Contrast DIVERGENCE. The term refers also to the appearance in taxonomically unrelated animals of similar features as the result of their sharing a common environment – a good example is the whale and the fish.

Convergent thinking. The tendency to look for the conventional, commonsense or safest answer to a problem. Compare DIVERGENT THINKING; LATERAL THINKING.

Conversion. A sudden change of religious belief. In abnormal psychology the term refers to the transfer of psychological problems into physical ones, e.g. hysterical paralysis, neurotic aches and pains, etc.

Conversion hysteria. A neurotic condition in which severe physical symptoms are believed to have their basis in mental conflicts.

Convolution. One of the many folds and wrinkles in the surface of the cerebral cortex.

Convulsion. Series of rapid, involuntary contractions and relaxations of muscles.

Convulsive therapy. A method of treatment in psychiatry, most often used to shorten the duration of a depressive illness. The patient is given an electric shock or some drug such as metrazol, which causes unconsciousness and some convulsive movements. The anti-depressant drugs have partly replaced convulsive therapy. (⧫⧫ ELECTRO-CONVULSIVE THERAPY; INSULIN COMA.)

Coordinate. One of two or more reference points or lines.

Coordination. Effective interaction of parts of the body, most particularly muscles.

Coping behaviour. Any behaviour successful in leading to the achievement of a goal.

Coprolalia. An excessive tendency to use obscene language.

Coprophagia. Desire to eat excrement.

Coprophilia. Abnormal interest in faecal material, often associated with sexual perversion.

Copulation. Sexual intercourse.

Core store. Form of rapid-access computer memory.

Cornea. The window at the front of the eye.

Corneal lens. Tiny contact lens which fits over the cornea.

Corneal reflection method. A technique of measuring and recording eye movements by photographing a spot of light reflected from the cornea.

Corneal reflex. Automatic closing of the eyelid when the cornea is stimulated.

Coronal plane. The axis of the head passing through the two ears.

Corporal. Relating to the body.

Corpora quadrigemina. Two pairs of organs at the back of the mid-brain known as the superior and inferior colliculi, and controlling visual reflexes.

Corpus callosum. Bundle of fibres deep in the BRAIN which links the two cerebral hemispheres.

Corpuscle. A small, specialized cell. Most corpuscles are found in the blood, but some act as sensory nerve endings.

Corpus striatum. Part of the cerebrum, markedly striped; also known as the striate body.

Correlation. The degree of relationship between two variables. It may be positive or negative and can be measured by appropriate statistical techniques.

Correlation coefficient (*r*). Statistical measure of the extent to which two variables are related.

Corresponding points. Segments of the retina of each eye which, when stimulated, lead to a fused, single perceptual image. Contrast DISPARATE RETINAL POINTS.

Cortex. The outer layer of a body. (➧➧ CEREBRAL CORTEX.)

Cortical. Related to the CORTEX.

Cortical blindness. ➧ AGNOSIA.

Cortical grey. The vague grey colour seen when the eye is closed and in total darkness.

Cortical inhibition. Damping of nervous activity by the cortex.

Corticalization. The tendency in evolutionary terms for the CORTEX to become more and more important in the control of behaviour.

Cortical satiation theory. The assumption that the repetition of a stimulus leads to a local failure of the responsiveness of cells in the CORTEX. It was used by Gestalt psychologists in an attempt to explain some visual illusions and perceptual oddities.

Cortisone. A hormone secreted by the adrenal cortex.

Cosmology. The study of the origins and nature of the universe.

Co-twin study. ➧ TWIN STUDY.

Couéism. Once-fashionable approach to personal psychotherapy through autosuggestion, named after its founder, E. Coué. The individual was supposed constantly to repeat such phrases as 'Each day I am getting steadily a little better.'

Counselling. Advice and guidance on personal or psychological problems given by a trained individual, though not necessarily a doctor or psychologist.

Counterego. Psychoanalytic term referring to that part of the unconscious mind which is opposed to the EGO.

Counter-transference. ➧ TRANSFERENCE.

Couvade. Ancient and widespread practice in which the father ritually takes to bed at the time that his child is born.

Covariance. ➧ PRODUCT MOMENT CORRELATION.

Cover memory. More commonly known as SCREEN MEMORY.

Covert. Hidden or concealed. Covert behaviour refers to that which cannot be observed directly though it *may* be inferred by measurement – the pulse, brain waves, gastric motility, etc.

Cranial. Relating to the cranium or brain case.

Cranial capacity. The cubic capacity of the brain case.

Cranial division. The upper part of the cranio-sacral or parasympathetic division of the autonomic nervous system.

Cranial index. ➧ CEPHALIC INDEX.

Cranial nerve. One of the twelve main nerves which originates in the brain and passes out through one of the various holes in the skull.

Craniometry. Measurement of the skull.

Cranio-sacral division. Anatomical name for the parasympathetic nervous system. (➧➧ THORACICO-LUMBAR DIVISION.)

Cranium. The skull, particularly the brain case.

Creativity. The ability of the mind to perceive new relationships or propose new solutions to problems. This definition unfortunately bears little relationship to the phenomena of artistic creativity, which is almost totally undefinable. (➧➧ DIVERGENT THINKING.)

Crespi effect. Sudden jump or spurt in learning which is unrelated to any obvious factors such as increases in reward or motivation.

Cretinism. Mental deficiency caused by a congenitally underactive thyroid.

Criminology. The scientific study of crime and its social origins.

Crisis. A turning point in an individual's life or in a physical or mental illness.

Criterion. A clearly definable factor against which other things can be measured.

Critical flicker frequency (CFF). The frequency at which a flickering light is perceived as fused or continuous.

Critical period. A period of time in the life of an animal or human when it is assumed to be particularly prone to specific influences. A good example is those phases in the life of a young animal when IMPRINTING is supposed to occur.

Critical ratio. A commonly used statistical technique to determine whether there is a significant difference between two means. (➧ STANDARD ERROR.)

Cro-Magnon man. Human species inhabiting Europe about a hundred thousand years ago, and exceedingly similar to modern man.

Cross-correspondence. A term used in psychical research to refer to apparent cooperative effort on the part of dead people to prove their personal survival. Different mediums receive individually meaningless messages which, when combined, make up a meaningful whole.

Cross-cultural psychology. The systematic study of similarities in social and personal behaviour as they appear in different cultures. Such studies are of particular interest in determining how much and what aspects of human behaviour are determined by environmental factors and how much by heredity. The pioneer in this field is generally agreed to have been the anthropologist Margaret Mead, whose studies of child rearing, the cultural conditioning of sexual behaviour and problems of adolescence in primitive Pacific societies are now classics. Cross-cultural psychology can be brought to bear on such divergent topics as the 'rightness or wrongness' of homosexuality or the universality of visual illusions. It may be particularly helpful in predicting the consequences of rapid cultural change – as when an immigrant group has to blend its cultural heritage into that of a larger host society.

Cross-cultural studies. Examination of similarities in social and personal behaviour as they appear in different cultures.

Cross-modal integration. The coordination by the brain of information coming from different senses.

Crowd. A temporary, generally unorganized, group of people united by having some goal or purpose. CROWD BEHAVIOUR was one of the first areas of study in social psychology. (➧ MOB; GANG.)

Crowd behaviour. Behaviour patterns common to a group of people gathered together for a particular purpose.

Crucial experiment. A test which allows the acceptance or rejection of a hypothesis.

Crude score. Experimental data before they have been analysed or processed.

Cryptaesthesia. Unusual sensory ability, sometimes assumed to be the explanation for alleged 'extra-sensory' phenomena; literally, hidden sense.

Cryptomnesia. A memory which is not recognized as such and is sometimes mistaken for a totally new experience or idea. (➧ DÉJÀ VU.)

Cue. Something standing for, or associated with, something else. Most cues are learned.

Cult. A group of people united, generally by a religious belief, and having an identifiable head or leader. (▸▸ RELIGION.)

Cultural deprivation. Anything which prevents an individual or group from participating in the cultural life of his or their own society.

Cultural determinism. The assumption that the principal forces moulding personality and behaviour are cultural (and therefore not inherited). (▸▸ RACE.)

Cultural lag. The delay between the introduction of a new idea, belief or technological development into a society and its widespread acceptance by the society.

Cultural relativism. Theory that what is 'abnormal' in one society may not be in another.

Culture. When one speaks of a culture, one is referring to those aspects of the life of a society which are shared by all members of that society and are normally handed down from generation to generation. In this sense a culture needs to be distinguished from all patterns of behaviour which are inherited in the genetic sense, and obviously it includes all laws, manners, customs, values, methods of education, artistic achievement, etc. At one time it was assumed that man was the only species of animal which could truly be said to have a culture, but a more recent view is that some of the higher primates at least pass down patterns of behaviour – methods of rudimentary communication, simple tool use, etc. – and therefore must be thought of as having at least a primitive culture.

Another intriguing question is the mechanism by which culture spreads from one society to another, and whether common features of geographically separate cultures are due to contact at some time in the past or to spontaneous development within the society. An early view that humans' psychology was so similar that separate cultures would inevitably evolve culturally along similar lines, whether or not there had been significant contact between them, is no longer widely held. For example, there is very little evidence that major inventions have sprung up in different parts of the world – a possible exception being the fire-piston, a primitive fire-making device invented in the Philippines and then, much later and apparently quite independently, in Europe in the early nineteenth century. (▸▸ SOCIETY; RACE.)

Culture epoch theory. The belief that all societies evolve through similar phases of development (nomadism, agriculture, industrialization, etc.).

Culture-free test. Test which, ideally, could be usefully administered to members of any culture. Very few, if any, tests can of course meet this requirement. (▸▸ INTELLIGENCE TESTS.)

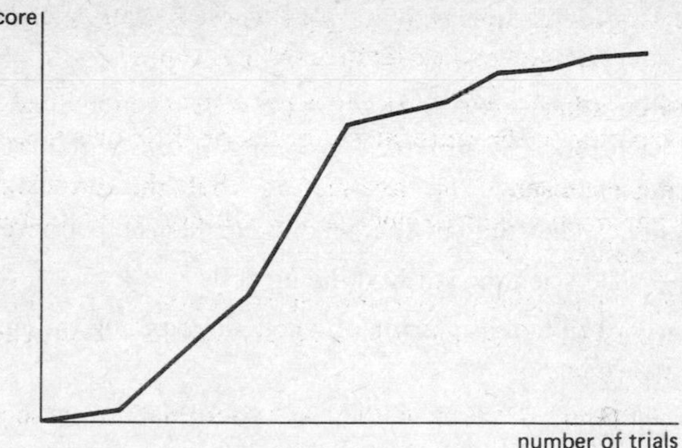

Figure 10. Cumulative distribution.

Cumulative distribution. Rising curve on a graph in which new values are plotted as the sum of themselves and all previous values.

Cunnilingus. Oral stimulation of the female genitals.

Curare. A drug which causes paralysis by preventing the response of muscles to nerve impulses.

Curiosity drive. The supposed instinctive desire of animals to explore their environment for its own sake.

Cursive. Script or handwriting in which the letters are joined together.

Curve fitting. The use of a statistical test to determine a curve which most suitably expresses a collection of data.

Custodial care. Keeping people in hospital without treatment, mainly as a protective measure.

Custom. A behaviour pattern characteristic of a particular society.

Cutaneous. Relating to the skin. The cutaneous senses are touch, pressure, temperature and pain.

Cybernetics. The scientific study of complex systems, particularly those which have controlling or regulating mechanisms built into them. The word, which comes from the Greek meaning roughly 'steermanship', was coined by Norbert Wiener in 1948 and the science grew out of electrical and, in particular, computer engineering. In the 1960s it became highly relevant to psychology as psychologists and engineers alike began to study parallels between the brain and the increasingly powerful and flexible computers which were just beginning to make their presence felt. Cybernetic principles can also be applied to systems such as societies and elaborate business organizations. It includes all attempts at studying human behaviour through mathematical modelling.

Cyclothymia. ➧ KRETSCHMER.

Cytoarchitecture. The structural grouping of cells within an organ or tissue.

Cytogenetics. The study of the genetic mechanisms of heredity.

Cytology. The scientific study of living cells.

Cytoplasm. The liquid interior of a cell surrounding the nucleus.

D

Dactylology. Communication using finger signs.

Daltonism. Obsolete term for protanopia, red-green COLOUR BLINDœ NESS, named after the colour-blind English chemist who was the first to study it scientifically.

Damping. Blocking or reducing something.

Dancing language. Elaborate ritual movements made by bees outside their hive which, according to von Frisch, convey information to other bees about the nature and location of honey supply.

Dancing mania. ➧ CHOREOMANIA.

Dark adaptation. The process by which the eye adapts itself to lowered illumination. The CONES in central vision cease to function, while the sensitivity of the RODS is increased as they become charged with the pigment known as rhodopsin or 'visual purple'. Hours may elapse before the maximum sensitivity point of the dark-adapted eye has been reached.

Darwin, Charles Robert (1809–82). Great English biologist responsible for the theory of EVOLUTION by natural selection.

Data processing. The analysis of factual or numerical material, particularly when carried out by an automatic device such as a COMPUTER.

Day blindness. ➧ HEMERALOPIA.

Daydream. Collection of fantasies or mental images partly under voluntary control and experienced during consciousness.

Day residue. Odd fragments of memories of the day's experiences which, according to FREUD, make up the building blocks of all dreams. It is the structure and integration of these memories, rather than the memories themselves, which give clues to the unconscious processes moulding the dreams. (➧ DREAM WORK.)

Deafferentation. Severing sensory nerves to the spinal cord in a living animal in order to study the activity of the nerves when they are no longer in communication with the brain.

Deaf-mute. Someone who has failed to learn to speak because of severe deafness. The vocal apparatus may be unimpaired.

Death feigning. Rigid posture assumed by some animals when severely frightened.

Death instinct. Supposed unconscious drive towards death. Hypothesized by Freud as an opposing force to the life instinct, Eros, and given the name THANATOS. The idea no longer figures strongly in psychoanalytic theory.

Debility. Weakness or lack of vigour.

Decerebrate. Without a CEREBRUM.

Decerebrate rigidity. A prolonged state of rigidity of the limbs caused by damage to the brain, especially the midbrain.

Decibel (dB). Unit of measurement of the perceived relative intensity of sounds. The dB scale is logarithmic.

Decision-making. The selection and assessment of evidence and the choice of a particular course of action as a result. Decision-making processes are of particular interest in social psychology, where there have been a number of formal studies of how groups arrive at decisions and the various patterns of interaction which lead up to them.

Deconditioning. The process of unlearning or removing unwanted habits or behaviour patterns. (➧ BEHAVIOUR THERAPY; CONDITIONING.)

Decorticate. Without a CORTEX.

Decorticate conditioning. CONDITIONING, in the sense of Pavlov's experimental procedure, taking place in an animal that has no cortex. Only a limited number of conditioned reflexes can be set up in such severely handicapped creatures.

Decrement. A reduction or loss.

Decussation. The crossing over of nerve fibres from one side of the brain to the other.

Deduction. Making an inference from a set of known facts which leads to a further assumption or conclusion. Compare INDUCTION.

Deep structure. ➧ TRANSFORMATIONAL GRAMMAR.

Defective. Failing to reach the norm or average.

Defeminization. Tendency for a woman to assume the SECONDARY SEXUAL CHARACTERISTICS of the male. This may be due to a tumour or hormonal disorder.

Defence mechanism. A term created by FREUD for the various strategies which the ego, or conscious self, employs to protect itself from unwanted, threatening or repressed ideas lying in the unconscious. The central notion of Freudian psychology is that the mind or personality can be divided into three sub-entities, the EGO, the ID and the SUPEREGO. The ego is almost entirely conscious and represents that part of the personality which directly interacts with the external world and is also partly moulded by it. The ego strives to maintain equilibrium and free itself from anxieties, most of which arise from the unconscious as the results of conflicts between the id and the superego. When these conflicts become particularly strong they begin to affect the conscious self, whereupon the ego erects various barriers to prevent them from thrusting to the surface. The main defence mechanisms include REPRESSION, REGRESSION, REACTION-FORMATION, DENIAL, PROJECTION, UNDOING and SUBLIMATION.

Defensiveness. A tendency to be over-susceptible to criticism.

Defloration. The breaking of the hymen at the first complete sexual intercourse.

Degenerate. Someone who has fallen away from a society's moral or social standards; tends to be used for sexual offenders.

déjà vu. Vivid experience of the 'I have been here before' variety. The most likely explanation for the phenomenon is that a similar situation has actually been experienced and, through some confusion in the memory store, the brain assumes that the present and past experiences are identical.

Delayed conditioning. In Pavlovian experiments, when there is a marked pause between the presentation of the conditioned stimulus (e.g. the bell) and the unconditioned stimulus (e.g. food) this is known as delayed conditioning. (➧ CONDITIONING.)

Delayed reaction experiments. In a typical experiment of this kind an animal is shown a series of paths, one of which leads to food, but before it can respond a door is closed so that the paths can no longer be seen. The maximum delay for which the animal can 'hold' an image of the correct path is measured.

Delinquency. Breaking the moral or legal code, particularly by someone under the age of eighteen.

Délire du toucher. Obsolete term for the obsessive-compulsive desire to touch objects.

Delirium. Disturbance of consciousness featuring hallucinations, anxiety states and restlessness.

Delirium tremens (DTs). Agitated hallucinatory state accompanying chronic ALCOHOLISM, most generally seen when the patient is withdrawn from the drug.

Delta movement. Illusion in which an object appears to move slightly when its brightness is suddenly changed.

Delta rhythm. Relatively slow brain waves with a frequency of less than 4 hertz and occurring during sleep. (⧫ ELECTROENCEPHALOGRAPH.)

Delusion. A false belief which cannot be shaken by evidence or reasonable argument.

Delusions of grandeur. Irrational belief by someone that he is a great person, king or even a supernatural being.

Dement, William (1928–). American psychiatrist credited with the remarkable discovery of the association that exists between the RAPID EYE MOVEMENTS and the dream periods of sleep. (⧫ DREAM; DREAM DEPRIVATION.)

Dementia. A reduction or deterioration of mental powers, characteristic of senility, brain damage and certain psychoses. Contrast AMENTIA.

Dementia praecox. Obsolete term for SCHIZOPHRENIA.

Democracy. A group or society whose leader is elected by the group and whose decisions are subject to group approval or disapproval.

Demography. Statistical study of population growth, distribution, etc.

Demonology. The study of the belief in demons and evil spirits and the practices associated with these beliefs.

Demonomania. Abnormal fear of or obsession with demons and evil spirits.

Demophobia. Abnormal fear of crowds.

Demyelination. The loss of the myelin or insulating sheath which surrounds nerve fibres.

Dendrite. One of the trailing branches of a nerve cell which conducts electrical impulses towards the cell body. (⧫ NEURONE.)

Denervation. The surgical removal of the nerve supply to an organ, generally to prevent pain.

Denial. One of the principal mechanisms of EGO DEFENCE according to FREUD. In its simplest form this involves the ego simply refusing to accept that it is being troubled by the anxiety or conflict. (⧫⧫ DEFENCE MECHANISM.)

Denotative meaning. The factual or dictionary meaning. Contrast CONNOTATIVE MEANING. (⧫⧫ SEMANTIC DIFFERENTIAL.)

Density. A vague term sometimes used to refer to the richness or depth of quality of a stimulus.

Dentate nucleus. Collection of cells, looking somewhat like a set of teeth, in the cerebellum.

Dentition. The state of development of the teeth.

Deoxyribonucleic acid (DNA). Biochemical substance present in the nuclei of all living cells, out of which it is believed that the genetic material or 'blueprint' is formed. (⧫⧫ RIBONUCLEIC ACID.)

Dependency. The extent to which one person relies on another individual or on some physical factor, such as a drug. (⧫ DRUG DEPENDENCY.) As a second meaning, in the theory of causality, B is supposed to be *dependent* on A to the extent that A has *caused* B. In social psychology, the term refers to a tendency to look to others for decision-making.

Dependent variable. The variable in an experiment which is affected by the intervention of an experimental or INDEPENDENT VARIABLE. In a study of, say, the effect of a drug on learning, the drug will be the *independent* variable, while the subject's performance in a learning test is the *dependent* variable. Therefore the subject's performance is *dependent* on the independent or experimental variable. (⧫⧫ CONTROL.)

Depersonalization. Disturbance of consciousness in which the individual feels unreal and detached from himself or his surroundings.

Depolarization. Change in the electrical balance of a nerve cell when it is fired.

Depressant. A drug which cuts down the activity of the central nervous system. Noted depressants include alcohol, barbiturates and tranquillizers.

Depression. A state of psychological debility, often accompanied by varying degrees of anxiety or despair. It is one of the most common forms of mental illness which may vary from the minor, when normal life is barely affected, to the severe, when hospitalization may be required. There are three broad theoretical approaches to understanding depression, the first of which assumes it is purely psychogenic and caused by internal mental conflicts, the second which assumes that it is purely physiological and probably due to biochemical change in the body, and the third which assumes that it is a mixture of both. The third is probably the most likely overall explanation, for depression will respond to a variety of treatment, including drugs and psychotherapy.

Depressive reaction. ⧫ REACTIVE DEPRESSION.

Depressor nerve. Nerve which acts to reduce motor or glandular activity.

Deprivation. Removing or severely limiting anything that an organism badly needs. (⧫⧫ SENSORY DEPRIVATION; SLEEP DEPRIVATION.) In *developmental* psychology, the term is used by Bowlby to refer to a situation involving a lack of mothering care for the child (maternal deprivation).

Depth interview. An interview in which a psychologist questions a lay person and attempts to gain information, not only about the other's verbal and conscious statements, but also his unconscious or less clearly expressed feelings. The method is used in some forms of market research and job selection as well as in psychology.

Depth perception. The perceptual awareness of depth or three-dimensionality in the visual world. A number of clues are used by the brain to achieve this, including BINOCULAR DISPARITY, MOTION PARALLAX, the interposition of objects, the degree of ACCOMMODATION of eye muscles, etc. Absolute depth perception requires two functioning eyes. (⧫⧫ STEREOPSIS; PARALLAX.)

Depth psychology. Any attempt to study or explain human behaviour in terms of the activity of the unconscious mind, e.g. psychoanalysis.

Derealization. The feeling that one's environment has lost its reality. Compare ALIENATION; ANOMIE.

Dereistic thinking. Thinking which rejects reality and emphasizes personal needs.

Derived property. A term used in GESTALT PSYCHOLOGY to refer to the parts of an object which can be 'derived' or broken down from the perceptual whole.

Dermal sensitivity. The capacity to respond to the external world through skin senses, such as touch, temperature, etc.

Dermatitis. Inflammation of the skin, sometimes caused by anxiety or stress.

Dermatography. Literally, skin writing; extreme sensitivity of the skin so that marks appear upon it when touched.

Dermis. The main layer of skin lying below the outer covering or epidermis.

Descartes, Réné (1596 – 1650). French philosopher who attempted to resolve the mind–body problem by suggesting that the two substances met and interacted in the pineal gland, a physiologically obscure centre in the brain.

Desensitization. Decreased responsiveness; also the removal of a mental problem after therapy.

Desexualization. Attempting to detach sexual feelings from a particular object, person or situation.

Desire. A conscious and definable need.

Destination. In information theory the place where a message should be received.

Destrudo. Psychoanalytic term for the psychic energy supposedly associated with the DEATH INSTINCT. Contrast MORTIDO.

Desurgency. Term used by CATTELL to describe a personality trait associated with anxiety and seclusiveness. Contrast SURGENCY.

Detached affect. Used in psychoanalytic theory to refer to emotionality or AFFECT which has become separated from its original source-idea, and appears therefore to be neutral or non-threatening to the EGO. Unfortunately, the detached emotional state has to anchor itself to something else and, according to FREUD, it is this relocation of the affect that lies at the root of most obsessions and phobias.

Detachment. In psychoanalytic terms, a neurotic attitude of mind characterized by a lack of feeling for others and incapacity to identify with their problems. In developmental psychology the term is used by Bowlby to refer to the final stage of a child's reaction to maternal deprivation.

Deterioration index. Measure of the progressive loss of mental function which takes place with increasing age.

Determinant. A causal factor.

Determinism. The philosophy that all events have a direct and, in principle, describable cause. Thus if one had enough information one should be able to establish exactly the reasons for any human behaviour. Determinism is at odds with the principle of FREE WILL, for the latter suggests that some human behaviour should be completely unpredictable.

Detour test. Any test of an animal's ability to reach its goal by an indirect route.

Detraction. A weakening of attention, but with no shift in its focus.

Detumescence. Loss of the state of erection in the penis and clitoris following sexual intercourse.

Deuteranomaly. Form of mild COLOUR BLINDNESS featuring relative insensitivity to green.

Deuteranopia. A form of red-green COLOUR BLINDNESS with particular weakness in the green range. It is the most common form of colour blindness.

Development. Systematic changes in an organism which occur throughout its life, but particularly those preceding maturity.

Developmental level. A phase of life. It is usual to refer to five levels: infancy, childhood, adolescence, maturity and old age.

Developmental psychology. One of the fastest growing aspects of modern psychology and in principle, if perhaps not yet in practice, one of the most important. Psychology itself is often criticized on the grounds that it is too 'mechanistic' and that it seems to be contributing very little towards an understanding of human nature. This partly valid criticism reflects the heavy emphasis on behaviouristic studies which guided most research in the first half of this century, and which of necessity made the laboratory animal the main focus of experimental study. In the 1960s, however, a powerful anti-behaviouristic movement, partly led by the growing interest in PSYCHOLINGUISTICS, got under way, and with it studies of such topics as the evolution of human thought processes and the development of mental life became less taboo.

At the heart of developmental psychology lies one great question: how much of human personality, intelligence and creativity is genetically determined and how much conditioned by environmental circumstances – family background, nutrition, education, etc.? (➧➧ RACE.) It is important to remember that most nineteenth-century thinking on the topic heavily favoured the genetic view, i.e. people were born into a class, be it social or intellectual, and once born into it they stayed with it. It was even generally believed that criminal tendencies were handed down in the genes, a belief that was superficially supported by the undoubted tendency for some families to 'go criminal'.

A striking finding which seemed to contradict the genetic view came from the British psychologist John Bowlby, who found in the 1940s that of forty-four juvenile thieves referred to his child guidance clinic, seventeen had been seriously deprived of maternal care in the first five years of their lives. The concept that the development of a 'normal' personality is heavily dependent upon there being a strong unbroken bond of love between mother and infant has not always been backed up by subsequent experimental studies, but it has nevertheless influenced generations of mothers and is exemplified by such books on child rearing as those by Dr Benjamin Spock. But perhaps its main significance, in terms of psychology, has been that it drew attention to the importance of studying the child as a living being, evolving steadily towards adulthood in essentially a pre-programmed way but passing through certain critical periods during which, if the right environmental features are not present, progress will be slowed and perhaps even halted.

At a physiological level this approach is typified by the long-term studies of Tanner, who has been systematically charting the stages of growth of London school children for decades, and also by the work showing that poor diet during pregnancy and in early infancy may lead to the incomplete development of the brain and nervous system. At a psychological level, the work of Jean PIAGET is absolutely paramount. Piaget, whose research was inspired by studying the intellectual development of his own children, argues that the mental evolution of the child moves through four main phases which follow each other in a predetermined order, and each of which is recognizable by particular characteristic behaviour patterns and 'modes of thinking and reasoning'. The first period, from birth to the age of two, is largely concerned with the acquisition of simple sensorimotor skills – learning to use muscles and recognize external objects and events. The second phase (two to about seven) is the most rapid phase of language growth when words and symbols become associated with concrete objects in the external world, and is known as the preoperational period. The third stage (seven to eleven approximately) is known as the concrete operational period and involves a strong adherence to the concrete realities of the child's world. The fourth stage (eleven to sixteen or thereabouts), known as the period of formal operational thinking, involves a strong shift away from the concrete to the abstract in thought processes, with the child becoming aware of logical principles and the formation of hypotheses. The boundaries between the four phases are slightly diffuse, but in Piaget's view one phase must be completed before its successor can begin. He also insists that the speed with which the child passes through the stages is dependent upon the social and cultural richness of its environment.

Piaget's ideas are still counted as controversial but they are enormously influential, and represent the main theoretical thrust in this field at the moment. An alternative, and somewhat more flexible, approach has come from Bruner who, while agreeing that critical periods exist, does not believe that they follow the fixed sequence proposed by Piaget, and claims that cognitive processes are better developed in the infant than has been suspected, and are allowed for, in Piaget's approach. While still relatively weak as far as theories, and to a lesser extent facts, go developmental psychology is attracting steadily more interest as its obvious practical applications are realized. Significantly it attracts the attention of workers in a wide range of non-psychological disciplines, including nutrition, linguistics and even ethology.

Developmental stage. A period in life when particular attitudes, habits or behaviour patterns characteristically emerge.

Developmental task. A skill or level of achievement which it is believed an individual should have reached at a particular age in order to ensure satisfactory social and personal adjustment.

Deviancy. Refers to any behaviour which is not in accord with the values and goals of a particular society and which, at least to some degree, is believed by members of that society to debase these values or hamper the goals. This clearly establishes from the start that deviancy is not an absolute but a relative concept and can only be judged within a framework of knowledge about a particular society. Early theories of deviancy took a vaguely psychoanalytic view and held that a 'deviant' was one who found his internal drives and goals conflicting with those of society and who was unable to effect a satisfactory compromise. Later theories suggest that deviancy occurs when an individual is unable to achieve the goals most prized by a society by legitimate means and resorts to alternative methods. A criminal, therefore, is one who seeks – to give easily the most common example – the Western goal of affluence not by 'hard work' but by theft, fraud or some other illegal means. This approach strongly implies that the principal causes of deviancy are social rather than personal and thus, perhaps rather idealistically, that the elimination of social problems will automatically eliminate deviant behaviour.

Deviate. Someone who violates social, if not legal, standards particularly in sexual matters.

Deviation. Statistical term expressing the degree to which a score differs from the MEAN OR AVERAGE. More generally it refers to any departure from the 'normal'. (➧ DEVIANCY.)

Devolution. Reversal or undoing of an evolving pattern.

Dexterity. Manual skill.

Dextrality. A tendency to use the right hand.

Dextroamphetamine. The technical name for the central nervous system stimulant dexedrine.

Dextrosinistral. A left-handed person who has been trained to use his right hand.

Diabetes insipidus. A disease in which damage to the hypothalamus or underactivity of the pituitary leads to an abnormal thirst.

Diad. ➧ DYAD.

Diagnosis. Judgement about the nature of a disease on the basis of the symptoms presented by the patient.

Dialectic. A process of systematic reasoning.

Diana complex. Psychoanalytic term for the repressed wish of a woman to become a man.

Dianetics. Controversial approach to psychotherapy by an American science fiction author, L. Ron Hubbard, which swept America in the early 1950s. Out of Dianetics grew Scientology, a philosophico-religious system which is now one of the world's minority religions.

Diaphragm. A flexible partition between two organs.

Diastole. The period when the heart dilates and fills with blood.

Diathermy. Use of oscillating, high frequency electric current to heat body tissues.

Diathesis. An inherited tendency to be susceptible to a disease.

Diazepam. The technical name for the tranquillizing drug valium.

Dichotic. Relating to the independent stimulation of the two ears.

Dichotomy. The breaking down of data or units into two definable classes.

Dichromatism. COLOUR BLINDNESS in which only two colours can be perceived.

Didactic analysis. Personal psychoanalysis which all would-be Freudian analysts must undergo as part of their training.

Diencephalon. Part of the forebrain, including the thalamus, hypothalamus and epithalamus. (➧ BRAIN.)

Difference threshold. The minimum difference between stimuli which the subjects can report *as a difference* 50 per cent of the time. It is sometimes known as the jnd or 'just noticeable difference'.

Difference tone. A third tone heard when two notes are played steadily above a certain intensity. (➧ COMBINATION TONE; SUMMATION TONE.)

Differential. Relating to differences. (➧➧ SEMANTIC DIFFERENTIAL.)

Differential diagnosis. Discriminating between two highly similar diseases.

Differential psychology. The study of the differences between humans, animals, groups and societies, and the origins of these differences.

Differential reinforcement. Reinforcing or rewarding one response while failing to reinforce another. For example, one might reinforce a response to light of a particular intensity only. The technique is useful in determining the ability of an animal to discriminate along a sensory continuum.

Difficulty scale. A test with its items arranged in order of difficulty.

Diffraction. The bending of light or sound waves on passing through an obstacle.

Diffuse. Vague or uncertain.

Diffusion. Spread of information in various directions. In anthropology, the spread of ideas from one culture to another.

Digital. Relating to the digits – the numbers from 0 to 9; also, relating to the fingers and toes.

Digital computer. A computer which performs calculations by representing numbers as discrete units, e.g. the number of switches in an 'on' or 'off' state at a particular time. Compare ANALOG COMPUTER.

Digit-span test. Test of short-term memory in which the subject is asked to recall a series of random numbers. Most normal people can manage approximately seven without difficulty.

Dihydroxyphenylanaline (DOPA). A powerful antidepressant.

Diminishing returns law. The more you put into something the less (proportionally) you get out. In psychology, after an initial period of rapid gain in learning, extra practice yields steadily slower progress.

Dimorphic. Having two forms – as with a caterpillar and butterfly.

Dionysian. Relating to the emotions rather than the intellect. Contrast APOLLONIAN.

Diopter. Unit of measurement for the refractive or focusing power of a lens.

Diotic. ➧ DICHOTIC.

Diplegia. Double-sided paralysis.

Diplopia. Double vision.

Dipsomania. Form of ALCOHOLISM in which the individual goes on periodic drinking sprees. This contrasts with chronic alcoholism where there is a daily abnormal consumption.

Directive therapy. The classic form of psychotherapy, including most psychoanalysis, in which the therapist plays a major role in directing the course of treatment and guiding the patient along particular lines of thinking. Contrast NON-DIRECTIVE THERAPY.

Direct vision. Vision involving images projected onto the FOVEA. Compare PERIPHERAL VISION.

Disability. A severe handicap or loss of function, either physical or psychological.

Disaesthesia. The technical name for skin discomfort, such as 'pins and needles'.

Disarranged sentence test. Test of intellectual ability in which the subject has to unscramble a jumbled sentence.

Discharge. The firing of a nerve cell when stimulated; also the reduction of tension or emotional states.

Discharge of affect. Psychoanalytic term for the elimination of an emotional 'charge' associated with a particular person or situation.

Discipline. A field of knowledge; voluntary or externally imposed control.

Discontinuity theory. Also known as non-continuity theory; states that learning takes place as a result of *active* inspection of the environment by an animal, selecting significant features of a situation, rather than as a *passive* state in which all information presented to the senses is stored. (♦ CONTINUITY-NON-CONTINUITY THEORIES.)

Discord. An inharmonious collection of stimuli, particularly sounds.

Discrete. Separate; measurable in units.

Discrimen. A sensory difference, not necessarily perceived as such.

Discriminanda. Things in an environment likely to be perceived by an organism and which can be used to help it make discriminations.

Discriminate. To appreciate differences.

Discrimination tests. Experiments designed to show the capacity of an animal to detect differences between stimuli, e.g. colours, shapes or brightness. Normally these tests involve DIFFERENTIAL REINFORCEMENT so that an animal is taught to respond in one way to one stimulus and in a different way to another.

Disease. Any abnormal state of body or mind.

Disinhibition. Pavlovian term for a curious phenomenon occasionally observed in CONDITIONING studies. If an animal has been conditioned to salivate to the sound of a bell, and then the food reinforcement or reward is withdrawn, in due course the salivatory response will begin to diminish. However, if a buzzer is unexpectedly substituted for the bell, there will be a marked upsurge in the output of saliva for two or three trials. This apparent reactivation of an old decaying reflex by a novel stimulus is known as disinhibition.

Disintegration. A breakdown of an organized system.

Disorder. Disturbance of an organized system.

Disorientation. Loss of the ability to relate oneself in space or time or to persons.

Disparate retinal points. Sections of the two retinae which, when stimulated by the image of a single object, lead to the perception of two objects (double vision). Contrasts with corresponding points – areas which when stimulated lead to a fused or single image.

Disparation. If one fixates on a finger held a few inches in front of the eye and then shifts one's attention (without changing fixation) to another finger at a greater or lesser distance from the eye, the second finger will be seen as double. If one repeats the experiment, but fixating on the second finger and attending to the first, the latter will now be seen double. This phenomenon is known as disparation.

Disparity. Any kind of dissimilarity.

Dispersion. Scatter; used in connection with light and also as a statistical term.

Displaced aggression. Turning anger from one situation to another because its direct expression is blocked for some reason.

Displacement. A word used in psychoanalysis to refer to the shift of the focus of emotion from one situation to another. The word has a special meaning in Freudian interpretation of dreams, where an object of no true significance to the dreamer appears to have tremendous importance. It is assumed that the dream 'censor' is diverting attention from the truly significant aspect of the dream to a trivial or unimportant feature. (➧➧ DRIVE DISPLACEMENT.)

Displacement effect. A term used in PARAPSYCHOLOGY to refer to a supposedly unconscious shift of extra-sensory power from the required target to one close to it. For example, a subject hoping to guess the next card in sequence may 'displace' his focus to the next but one card.

Display. In ethology, elaborate patterns of movement made by an animal as part of courtship or attack ritual.

Disposition. The overall make-up of an individual and the characteristics and personality traits which arise from this. (➧➧ TEMPERAMENT.)

Disseminated sclerosis. ➧ MULTIPLE SCLEROSIS.

Dissimulation. Disguising one's emotions and attitudes.

Dissociation. A splitting up of the personality so that some of its ideas or aspects of thought become apparently detached and no longer interact with the 'main self'. An individual may therefore hold apparently opposing points of view without any feeling of conflict or anxiety. The most dramatic examples of dissociation are the occasional cases of DUAL PERSONALITY or MULTIPLE PERSONALITY.

Dissociative reactions. Behaviour patterns which appear to be not under conscious control or in conscious awareness – memory fugues, sleepwalking, etc.

Dissonance. A collection of stimuli which appear inharmonious and unpleasant when matched with different stimuli. (⧫⧫ COGNITIVE DISSONANCE.)

Dissonance theory. Theory of motivation put forward by Festinger. (⧫ COGNITIVE DISSONANCE.)

Distal. Away from something, particularly the centre of the body; opposite of PROXIMAL.

Distal stimulus. The stimulus as it leaves the source, e.g. light as it is emitted from the lamp. The proximal stimulus is the stimulus when it excites a sensory receptor.

Distance receptor. Sensory receptor designed to detect distant stimuli – visual, auditory, chemical, etc.

Distance vision. Seeing of objects more than six metres away.

Distortion. Psychoanalytic term for the disguising or other modification of DREAM material.

Distributed practice. An approach to learning in which lessons or trials are separated out rather than presented in a mass. It has been shown experimentally to be the more effective of the two methods. (⧫ MASSED PRACTICE.)

Distribution. A graphical or tabular display of scores or values.

Disulfiram. The technical name for the drug ANTABUSE, used in the treatment of alcoholism.

Disuse. Lack of use.

Diuretic. Something which increases the production of urine.

Diurnal. Occurring during the day.

Divagation. Confused or rambling speech.

Divergence. The turning out of the eyes when changing fixation from a near to a distant object so that the images fall on the fovea of each retina. Contrast CONVERGENCE.

Divergent thinking. The capacity to shift one's ideas away from the obvious or the routine. Contrast CONVERGENT THINKING. (⧫⧫ LATERAL THINKING.)

Divination. Attempting to predict the future by some supernatural means.

Divining rod. A device used in attempting to find underground water, etc., by the process known as DOWSING. It is often a springy twig of wood, such as hazel.

Dizygotic twins. Non-identical twins born because of the fertilization of separate eggs.

Doctrine. A teaching, generally of a religious kind.

Dogma. A statement of principle handed down by authority and supposed to be accepted on faith.

Dolichocephalic. Long-headed; with a CEPHALIC INDEX of less than 75.

Domal sampling. Interviewing people or canvassing opinions in their homes.

Dominance. In psychology a personality type characterized by an interest and facility in controlling other people. Cerebral dominance is the tendency for one hemisphere of the brain to control behaviour.

Dominant wavelength. The wavelength of light which, when mixed with white light, will exactly match a particular colour.

Don Juan type. A man excessively concerned with sexual conquests, supposedly to boost his ego.

Dopamine. Substance derived from l-Dopa, which acts to enhance the transmission of the neural impulse across synapses in the corpus striatum.

Doppler effect. Change in frequency of light or sound waves as the source comes closer to or recedes from an observer. The classic example is the change in perception of a whistle or hooter on a fast moving vehicle.

Dora case. One of the first detailed case histories reported by FREUD and used in building his theory of dream interpretation.

Dorsal. Relating to the back; opposite to VENTRAL.

Dorso-ventral. The back-front axis of the body.

Dotting test. Test of psychomotor ability in which the subject has to place dots in the centre of a string of circles which pass before him on a moving strip of paper.

Double alternation problem. Experiment in which an animal is required to make two similar responses in succession, followed by another two of a different kind, then two of the first kind, etc. For example, in a T-maze the animal would have to make two turns to the right, followed by two turns to the left, then to the right, etc., to be rewarded.

Double aspect theory. Spinoza's argument that mind and body are merely different aspects of the same thing.

Double bind hypothesis. Refers to an extreme psychological dilemma where a child or other dependent individual is faced with opposing or conflicting demands from a parent which place him in an impossible position. It was once thought that schizophrenia was caused by intense and unresolvable dilemmas of this kind.

Double-blind experiment. Technique commonly employed in drug experiments which, by denying both experimenter and subject of knowledge as to which are experimental trials and which the CONTROL, guards against conscious or unconscious influencing of the results of their initial analysis. In a single-blind experiment, only the subject is unaware of the relevant details.

Double vision. Also known as diplopia; occurs when the eyes are unable to focus images on to corresponding points in the two retinae.

Down's syndrome. Form of congenital mental subnormality with characteristic facial features, previously known as mongolism. The condition occurs more frequently in the children of older mothers.

Dowsing. Attempt to locate water or some mineral in a hidden place or underground by the use of a twig or gadget such as a pendulum or hanging rod. There are numerous theories of dowsing, some of which assume that the mind and the rod act in concert as detecting mechanisms so that when the required substance is near the rod moves as the result of unconscious signals from the brain. Despite an enormous heritage of folklore about dowsing, scientists have been unable to find any acceptable experimental evidence for its effective reality.

Dramamine. Antihistamine used to relieve travel sickness.

Drama therapy. Also known as PSYCHODRAMA.

Dramatization. Psychoanalytic term for the conversion of ideas and thoughts into symbolic form.

Draw-A-Person Test. A test for young or mentally subnormal children in which the subject is asked to draw a simple figure of a person. The test can also give a gross measure of intellectual ability.

Dream. Experience associated with sleeping or, to be more exact, with momentary interruptions of sleep. The most primitive theories of dreams relied on the assumption that during sleep the mind or spirit moved into some different world and that dreams were fragmentary memories of these adventures. It was assumed that the barriers of space and time came down and the spirit could observe events in different parts of the world or even in the future. The endurance of this belief is obvious when one considers the tremendous frequency with which one hears stories of this kind related today.

The first truly significant theory of dreams, however, came from the work of FREUD who proposed that they must have a dynamic function, reflecting unconscious processes which were bursting to the surface during the sleep state. At the same time he realized that an inspection of the material of dreams could give vital clues as to the true motives, anxieties and conflicts of the individual. From these ideas grew the whole theory of psychoanalysis, since elaborated and refined by numerous other workers.

The next significant development had to await over half a century until Dement's discovery that the strange rapid movements of the eyes (REMs), which occur for up to a fifth of sleeping time in all adult humans, were associated with dreams, thus providing the first behavioural index of the dream state. At the moment theories of the nature and purpose of dreams are in a state of flux, with a growing number of workers arguing that one of the principal functions of sleep may be to allow the dream or REM state to take place. This clearly takes things somewhat beyond the Freudian theory and it is evident that the psychoanalytic approach requires some modification. Nevertheless, Freud's insistence that the dream was dynamic and purposeful rather than a random process seems to have been justified.

Dream content. The raw material of the DREAM. Freud distinguished between the latent content (the true and basic meaning of the dream) and the manifest content (the material as present in the memory of the dreamer or as told to the analyst).

Dream deprivation. Experimental investigation of the function of dreams, made possible by Dement's discovery that periods of dreaming sleep were signalled by easily observable series of RAPID EYE MOVEMENTS (REMs). In early studies Dement selectively deprived people of their REMs and claimed to have found marked psychological disturbances. These early findings have not been replicated in a clear-cut way, but it is still believed by most workers that the dream state is in some way important to the psychological welfare of man and, for that matter, of animals.

Dream interpretation. Any attempt at discovering the true significance or hidden meaning of a dream – in essence, distinguishing between its manifest and latent content. In Freudian psychoanalysis the principal technique employed is FREE ASSOCIATION. Attention is also paid to the occurrence of symbols and their significance. Freud argued that all dreams would sooner or later be revealed as some form of wish fulfilment and therefore must be interpreted in this light.

Dream work. Psychoanalytic term for the process by which unconscious wishes are converted into acceptable form in the material of dreams, using stray memories (which Freud called the day residue) as the building blocks.

Drive. Basically speaking anything which pushes an animal or human into action. Tends to refer to instinctive forces which have great significance to the organism – sex, hunger, thirst, etc. – which when consummated give a sense of relief or pleasure. Compare MOTIVATION, NEED, INSTINCT.

Drive displacement. If an animal is aroused by a particular DRIVE but cannot relieve or gratify it, behaviour appropriate to another drive may appear. A hungry animal which cannot find food may engage in sexual activity, for example.

Drive reduction. The weakening or stopping of behaviour, generally because an appropriate GOAL has been reached and the DRIVE consummated. Various theories of behaviour and learning have been based on drive reduction, in particular those of Thorndike and Hull. According to these, *all* behaviour arises from specific drives and learning *only* takes place when a particular pattern of behaviour is accompanied by some degree of drive reduction.

Drug. In modern usage, any chemical compound used in the diagnosis, treatment or prevention of disease. The word is also used of narcotics.

Drug addiction. ➧ ADDICTION.

Drug dependency. Used sometimes to refer to a state of psychological rather than physical need for a drug; the boundaries between drug dependency and drug addiction are not clear.

D-state. The period of sleep when the brain is assumed to be dreaming, and often associated with the presence of RAPID EYE MOVEMENTS.

Dualism. The theory that there are two separate and distinct components to human beings, a non-physical mind and a material brain. The description of human personality as being a 'ghost in a machine' aptly sums up the dualistic position.

Dual personality. Dissociated state in which an individual may have two markedly different aspects to his personality, seemingly at odds with each other or acting independently and apparently unaware of the other's presence. The state is usually held to be of an hysterical nature. (➧➧ DISSOCIATION; MULTIPLE PERSONALITY.)

Ductless gland. ➧ ENDOCRINE GLAND.

Dull. Flat, lacking in sharpness. The phrase dull normal is used for people whose IQ lies between 70 and 90. (➧ MENTAL RETARDATION.)

Duodenum. The upper part of the small intestine where it joins the stomach.

Duplicity theory. Theory, now widely accepted, that vision involves two mechanisms, one for daylight (cone or photopic) and one for night (rod or scotopic) vision.

Dura mater. ➧ MENINGES.

Dwarfism. Underdevelopment of the body which may be due to severe dietary deficiencies in infancy or to a primary deficit in the pituitary or thyroid glands.

Dyad. Sociological term for a group of two people.

Dyanamometer. A device for measuring muscular strength.

Dynamic. Relating to life, activity, movement and purpose.

Dynamic equilibrium. State of a complex system in which the distribution of energy remains balanced; if energy is expended in one part of the system it will be withdrawn from another part to maintain the balance. The phrase is also used in Piagetian terms. (➧ EQUILIBRATION.)

Dysbulia. Inability to attend or concentrate one's thoughts; abnormal lack of 'will power'.

Dyscalculia. ➧ ACALCULIA.

Dysgraphia. Inability to convert thoughts into writing; often associated with brain damage.

Dyslalia. Defective speech.

Dyslexia. Disorder of word perception, not solely concerned with reading, when not due to a deficiency in intelligence. There are various and subtle shades of dyslexia, e.g. some people have auditory confusions, some visual and some both.

Dysmenorrhea. Disturbance of MENSTRUATION with an assumed psychological origin.

Dyspareunia. Lack of ability to enjoy sexual intercourse; painful or difficult intercourse.

Dysphasia. Breakdown in speech process, commonly associated with brain damage.

Dysphoria. An anxious, depressed state.

Dyspraxia. A loss of psychomotor skill.

Dystrophy. Muscular atrophy, generally caused by malnutrition due to intestinal disorders.

E

Ear. The organ of hearing equipped with the physiological mechanisms to detect sound vibrations in the range 15 to 20 000 Hz in man. It is convenient to divide the ear into three main parts – the outer, middle and inner ears. The outer includes the fleshy protuberance on the side of the head (pinna), which acts as a sound catcher and direction indicator, and the auditory channel (external auditory meatus) as far as the eardrum. The middle ear includes the three auditory ossicles (hammer, anvil and stirrup), which transmit vibrations from the eardrums to the cochlea deep in the inner ear. The cochlea itself is the main feature of the inner ear and contains special cells (located on the organ of Corti) which translate physical vibrations into electrical energy for transmission up the auditory nerve to the brain. Other important features of the inner ear are the semicircular canals which, together with the utricle, assist in the sense of balance and the perception of body movement.

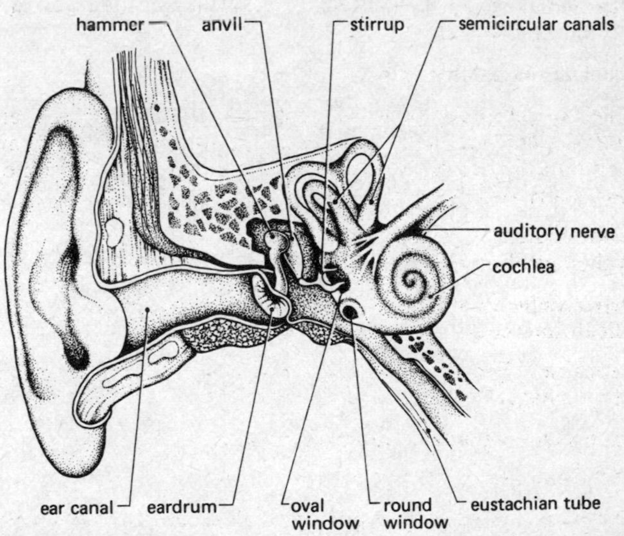

Figure 11. The ear.

Eardrum. The membrane which separates the auditory canal from the middle ear. Vibrations of the drum caused by sound waves are transmitted to structures deeper in the ear.

Early infantile autism. ➧ KANNER'S SYNDROME.

Ebbinghaus, Hermann (1850 – 1909). German psychologist who did some of the first systematic experiments of human learning. He invented the NONSENSE SYLLABLE.

Eccentric. Clearly deviating from the 'normal' but not to the point of being harmful or seriously troublesome.

Eccentric paranoia. Obsolete term for a psychosis featuring hallucinations and extreme distortions of thinking; also known as religious mania.

Eccentric projection. Locating perception at the position of the stimulus itself rather than in the sense organ which is stimulated. It is common to distance receptors, e.g. we locate the perception of the sun in the sun itself and not in the eye, whereas the sense of touch is related to a point on the skin.

Eccles, John Carew (1903 –). Australian physiologist who received a Nobel Prize for his work on the mechanism of synaptic transmission (➧ SYNAPSE.)

Echolalia. Meaningless repetition of words or phrases spoken by another person. It is a symptom of severe brain damage or mental deficiency.

Echolocation. Ability to locate objects in space by detecting the pattern of sounds reflected from them. It was once known as facial vision and sometimes advanced as evidence for extra-sensory perception. The faculty is often well developed in blind people, who may be unaware of the nature of their remarkable skill. Echolocation is of course particularly effectively employed by animals such as bats.

Echopathy. Meaningless repetition of movements or gestures made by others. This may be a symptom of brain damage or mental deficiency.

Eclampsia. Epileptoid convulsions and coma occurring during pregnancy or after childbirth.

Eclecticism. Attempting to produce a theory by selecting material from a large number of different sources not necessarily related to each other or strictly compatible.

Ecmnesia. Also known as ANTEROGRADE AMNESIA.

Ecology. The scientific study of living organisms and in particular their relationship to their environments.

Ecomania. A syndrome featuring abnormal behaviour or attitudes directed specifically to one's own family.

Economics. Used in psychoanalytic theory to refer to an individual's capacity for producing and preserving PSYCHIC ENERGY.

Ecouteur. Someone whose main sexual pleasure comes from listening to accounts of the sexual activity of others; auditory equivalent to VOYEUR.

Ecphoria. Obsolete term for the reactivation of a MEMORY TRACE.

Ecstasy. An extreme and vivid emotional state in which all perception is focused on one particular sensation or idea.

Ecto-. Prefix meaning outer. For example, ectodermal: relating to the outer layer of the embryo.

Ectomorphy. ➧ SHELDONIAN THEORY

Ectoplasm. In physiology the outer layer of a cell. In psychical research the word means a mysterious substance exuded from the body of Spiritualist mediums and supposedly used to produce the materialized forms of dead people.

Eczema. Skin inflammation, sometimes assumed to be psychogenic in origin.

Educability. The capacity to benefit from formal teaching. A minimum IQ of 50 is assumed to be necessary.

Education. Teaching and training carried out according to formal principles. (➧➧ SOCIALIZATION.)

Educational age. ➧ ACHIEVEMENT AGE.

Educational guidance. The exploration of a child's intellectual potential in an attempt to highlight those features – good or bad – most likely to benefit from special education.

Educational psychology. The scientific study of the principles and methods of formal training; also deals with the problems, intellectual and behavioural, concerned with education.

Educational quotient. ➧ ACHIEVEMENT QUOTIENT.

Eduction. Thinking which involves the perception of new relationships between things.

Effect. The end product of a cause. (➧➧ LAW OF EFFECT.)

Effective-habit strength. A term used in HULL's attempt at a mathematical theory of behaviour to refer to the strength of a particular learned response as a function of the number of reinforcements.

Effective stimulus. A stimulus which succeeds in producing a response.

Effector. That part of a muscle or gland which responds to stimulation from an efferent neurone.

Effeminacy. Tendency for female characteristics, psychological or physiological, to be noticeably present in a male.

Efferent. Refers to neurones or fibres which carry nervous impulses away from the central nervous system and down towards muscles and glands. Contrast AFFERENT.

Efficiency. The relationship between work done and energy consumed.

Effluvium. Body odour; may also refer to the shedding of hair.

Effort. Increased output of work to solve problems; also refers to the sensations experienced with increased work.

Effort syndrome. Neurotic disturbance, typically featuring breathlessness or palpitations, and often associated with ANXIETY states.

Egersis. Abnormal wakefulness.

Ego. An important concept in the Freudian theory of personality. The ego or self is supposed to be formed in early childhood as the instinctive forces, with which all human beings are endowed at birth and which FREUD termed the ID, come into contact with the external world and are subsequently moulded and structured by it. The ego or conscious self 'believes itself' to be in control of all behaviour. It is also the scene of a battle between the unconscious, instinctive forces of the id and the corrective, restrictive forces of the 'conscience' which Freud named the SUPEREGO. According to psychoanalytic theory, all neuroses represent disturbances of the ego brought about by these id-superego battles. (◆◆ DEFENCE MECHANISM; PSYCHOANALYSIS; SELF-CONCEPT.)

Ego analysis. Investigation, using the techniques of psychoanalysis, of the motives and conflicts of the EGO. Concerns itself largely with conscious factors and little account is taken of the problems and conflicts of the ID – as there would be in complete psychoanalysis.

Ego anxiety. Psychoanalytic term for a disturbance of the personality, mild or severe, caused by unresolved conflicts between the three facets of the mind – EGO, ID and SUPEREGO.

Ego block. Anything preventing the development of the EGO.

Ego cathexis. Psychoanalytic term referring to the satisfactory channelling of instinctive desires and wishes into activity which does not threaten or disturb the EGO. Sublimation is a good example, as when a sexually frustrated person relieves tension by engaging in creative work. (⧫⧫ CATHEXIS.)

Egocentricity. Extreme interest in one's own wishes and problems to the exclusion of the needs and feelings of others. In Piagetian psychology, the term refers to speech and thinking which is almost exclusively directed by the individual's needs or beliefs.

Ego defence. Protection of the EGO from the threat of undesirable impulses from the unconscious. According to psychoanalytic theory, this is achieved by a number of strategies known as DEFENCE MECHANISMS.

Ego development. The process, taking place in early childhood, by which the EGO or conscious self is formed. According to FREUD, the ego normally develops as ID forces interact with the realities of the external world and are subsequently modified or moulded by them.

Ego-eroticism. The concentration of sexual energy on oneself rather than on others; 'selfish' sexual behaviour.

Ego function. Activities of the EGO as opposed to those of the ID and SUPEREGO.

Ego ideal. Early Freudian term for the SUPEREGO. The term was later used to refer to that part of the superego concerned with parental admiration.

Ego instincts. All instincts related to self-preservation and associated with the individual's conscious need to protect himself from danger.

Ego involvement. Concentration on a task or idea to such an extent that one totally identifies with it.

Egoist. Someone dominated by selfish and personal motives. Compare EGOCENTRICITY.

Ego neurosis. Disturbance of the EGO caused by failure to adjust to the demands of the ID or SUPEREGO.

Ego resistance. Occurs in the course of psychoanalysis at the point when the EGO recognizes that unpleasant ideas are being dredged up from the unconscious. The ego responds to this threat by attempting to repress or deny them even more vigorously. (⧫⧫ DEFENCE MECHANISM.)

Ego strength. The basic power of the EGO; when fully operational, the individual is supposed to be free from emotional disturbance.

Eidetic imagery. Brilliantly clear visual, and occasionally auditory, imagery which allows vivid and accurate recall of something previously observed. It is supposedly common in young children and (sometimes) mental deficients.

Einstellung. Obsolete term for attitude, SET or expectancy.

Ejaculatio praecox. Premature ejaculation during sexual intercourse.

Élan vital. The 'life force'. According to the philosopher Bergson, this is a dynamic non-physical power which motivates all living things.

Elation. Extreme good humour and pleasant excitement.

Elberfeld horses. ➧ CLEVER HANS.

Electra complex. According to psychoanalytic theory, the desire, largely unconscious, that all daughters have for sexual relationships with their fathers. It is the female equivalent of the OEDIPUS COMPLEX.

Electrocardiograph (ECG). Device used for recording the electrical activity of the heart muscles.

Electroconvulsive theory (ECT). A technique used in the treatment of severe depression and other mental disorders, in which an electrical current is passed through the brain for a short duration. The shock is strong enough to produce unconsciousness, and also a brief period of amnesia. For some reason, not properly understood, it helps to lift depression and relieve mental confusion. Patients these days are given a general anaesthetic and muscle relaxants before the shock is administered and the muscle convulsions, previously a rather dramatic and aesthetically unpleasant feature of the treatment, are markedly reduced.

Electroculograph (EOG). Device for recording and measuring eye movements electrically. There is an electrical potential between the retina and the front of the eye which changes as the eyes move. By placing electrodes appropriately it is possible to record this change.

Electrode. Any device used to apply an electric current to tissue, or record electrical activity present in tissue.

Electrodermal response (EDR). More commonly known as the GALVANIC SKIN RESPONSE.

Electroencephalograph (EEG). Device used for recording the minute changes in electrical activity which are constantly taking place in the nervous tissue of the brain. In most cases electrodes are attached to the outside of the scalp and the signals recorded from within the skull, after passing through an amplifier, are recorded on an oscilloscope or moving paper strip. Early experiments with the EEG were conducted by Adrian and Berger in the 1920s and 30s, and at one stage it was hoped that they had uncovered a powerful tool for investigating and classifying mental processes. One of the first discoveries was that much of the brain's electrical activity was clearly rhythmic, the ALPHA RHYTHM, running at about 10 Hz, being the most clear-cut. Today, most researchers feel that the EEG has not lived up to its early promise, though electrical recordings made from electrodes implanted in the nervous tissue of the brain itself have yielded vital information about mechanisms of perception. Neurophysiologists are in fact not much further forward today in their understanding of the function of the various brain rhythms than they were fifty years ago. In clinical medicine the EEG has, however, turned out to be useful in locating epileptic lesions, brain tumours and the like, and the EEG has also been useful in the study of brain activity during sleep.

Electromyograph (EMG). Device for recording the electrical activity of muscles.

Electronarcosis. Period of unconsciousness or coma produced by passing an electrical current through the brain by electrodes placed on the temples. (➧ ELECTROCONVULSIVE THERAPY.)

Electrophysiology. The study of the electrical activity of nervous tissue.

Electroretinogram (ERG). A record of the minute electrical changes which take place in the retina when it is excited by light.

Electroshock therapy. Alternative term for ELECTROCONVULSIVE THERAPY.

Electrotonus. Change in the state of a nerve or muscle when it is stimulated by an electric current.

Elementarism. The belief that mental processes are best understood by analysing them and breaking them down in their basic constituents. (➧ ATOMISM.)

Elgin list. Checklist of psychotic-type behaviour patterns used in psychiatric diagnosis.

Elimination. The expulsion of urine and faeces.

Ellipsis. The deliberate suppression of, or refusal to speak, particular words or phrases in the course of FREE ASSOCIATION during psychoanalysis. Such omissions are counted as being important clues to the repressed material.

Emancipation. Freedom from control, physical or mental. The term may also refer to the resolution of the OEDIPUS COMPLEX.

Emasculation. The destruction of sexuality by physical or psychological means.

Embedded figure. A pattern or picture carefully drawn so that it is concealed in a more complex pattern. Such figures are of relevance to theories of perception because once they have been spotted they are almost impossible to ignore. (➧ GOTTSCHALDT FIGURES.)

Embolism. Blockage of a blood vessel by a clot or air bubble.

Embryo. The first phase of development after conception, lasting approximately eight weeks in humans.

Embryology. The study of the development of organisms from conception to birth.

Emergency theory. Relating to theories of the emotions which rely on the assumption that their role is to prepare the organism for short-term states of high activity associated with fear, rage, etc. The two main emergency theories are those put forward by W. B. Cannon and, more recently, by Hans Selye in his stress hypothesis. (⧫⧫ STRESS; BARD-CANNON THEORY.)

Emission. Discharge of semen; also refers to a response which cannot be identified with a particular stimulus.

Emmert's law. Emmert's law states that the apparent size of an after-image is a function of the distance of the ground or visual scene against which it is projected – if one looks at the horizon, for example, the after-image appears enormous.

Emmetropia. Normal vision in which there is no error of refraction by the eye.

Emotion. A complex reaction taking place within the body, often featuring considerable involvement of the autonomic nervous system and generally accompanied by distinct and powerful psychological states. It is a characteristic of emotions, whether pleasant or unpleasant, that they are directed towards achieving a particular goal and that the state of tension or excitement accompanying them is reduced when the goal is achieved. In this way they may appear to be similar to drives such as hunger, but they are usually much more intense and the 'goals' more general – e.g. flight in the case of fear, or attack in the case of rage. Most theories of emotions see them as reflecting emergency states and try to discriminate between emotion itself, which is the physiological state of alertness or excitement, and 'feelings', which are the psychological response or mental awareness of these physiological states. (⧫⧫ EMERGENCY THEORY.)

Emotional blockage. Disruption of thought processes brought on by a strong emotional state.

Emotional disorder. A mental condition in which the characteristic symptom is inappropriate or excessive emotional reaction.

Emotional immaturity. Tendency to be dominated by emotional behaviour patterns more suitable to a younger age.

Emotionality. The degree to which a person exhibits emotional responses.

Emotional maturity. Tendency to produce emotional responses appropriate for one's age and the society one lives in.

Emotional release. More commonly known as CATHARSIS.

Emotional stability. The capacity to control one's emotional responses so that they do not disturb or handicap one.

Emotive. Relating to things which produce emotional responses.

Empathy. The capacity to respond to and understand other people's feelings. Compare SYMPATHY.

Empirical. Based on facts, observation and experience as opposed to theory or 'hunch'.

Empirical test. A study using systematic experimentation.

Empirical validity. The power of a test to measure what it was designed to measure.

Empiricism. The philosophy that the only source of knowledge is personal experience. This rules out 'revelation', 'inspiration', etc. The term also has a special meaning in psychology when it relates to those aspects of personality and behaviour which are influenced by the environment and experience as opposed to those which are inherited.

Emulation. Deliberately copying or imitating something.

Encephalitis. Inflammation of the brain, sometimes accompanied by personality disorders.

Encephalitis lethargica. Technical name for 'sleepy sickness', a virus infection rampant in the years following the First World War.

Encephalization. Long-term evolutionary process in the course of which the brain becomes progressively more complex and important.

Encephalomyelitis. Inflammation of both brain and spinal cord.

Encephalon. Technical name for the complete BRAIN.

Encoding. The conversion of messages into signals suitable for transmission down an information channel.

Encopresis. Inability to control bowel function when this is not caused by organic factors; symptom of emotional disturbance.

Encounter groups. ➧ SENSITIVITY TRAINING.

Enculturation. The process by which an individual adapts to a new culture or society. Compare SOCIALIZATION.

End brain. ➧ TELENCEPHALON.

End brush. A cluster of tiny fibres or branches at the end of a neuronal axon.

End button. Thickening of the fibres at the end of an end brush where they come in contact with fibres from other cells.

Endo-. Prefix meaning inside. Contrast ECTO-.

Endocathection. Extreme preoccupation with one's own thoughts.

Endocrine gland. Any one of the glands (such as the thyroid) whose products seep through into the blood stream by osmosis. For this reason they are known as ductless glands. (➧ GLAND.)

Endocrinology. Study of the ENDOCRINE GLANDS and the effect of hormones on behaviour.

Endogamy. Anthropological term for the practice of preventing an individual from marrying outside his own social group.

Endogenous. Relating to something that develops *within* a system.

Endolymph. The fluid in the ducts of the inner ear and within the semicircular canals.

Endomorph. ➧ SHELDONIAN THEORY.

Endophasia. Silent speech; forming words or phrases in one's mind.

Endopsychic. Relates to processes going on in the mind, particularly those which are unconscious.

Endowment. Innate or inherited potential.

End plate. Flattened end of a motor neurone at the point where it touches a muscle cell; the flattening is assumed to increase surface contact.

End pleasure. Psychoanalytic term for the satisfaction which takes place when a physical drive is reduced, in particular that associated with orgasm.

End spurt. Rise in performance occurring as the end of a task is approached.

Enelicomorphism. Attributing adult motives and ideas to children.

Energy. The capacity to work.

Enervate. To weaken or reduce energy. The term can also refer to the removal of neurones by surgery.

Engineering psychology. Alternative name for ERGONOMICS.

Engram. When learning takes place some physical change must occur in the nervous system which corresponds to the MEMORY. Engram is the name given for this hypothetical trace, whatever form it may take.

Entelechy. The condition of completing or perfecting something; also has the meaning of an immaterial thing (such as the soul) which controls something material (such as the body).

Enteroceptor. A sense organ which detects changes taking place inside the body, e.g. visceral processes.

Entity. Something which exists and has some control over its own activity.

Entomophobia. Abnormal fear of insects.

Entopic. Relating to visual processes which have their origin within the eye.

Entropy. Concept whose understanding is complicated because of the various shades of meaning which surround it in different disciplines. In mathematics and information theory it refers to the degree of 'disorder' or, to some extent, 'unpredictability' in a system. In psychoanalysis it relates to the extent to which PSYCHIC ENERGY cannot be transferred from an object once it has been invested in it.

Enucleation. Removal of a complete organ, such as the eye, by surgery.

Enuresis. Technical name for bedwetting; also known as nocturnal enuresis.

Environment. All external factors which can influence and modify the behaviour of an organism. The term internal environment refers to all processes taking place *inside* the body which serve to modify that organism's behaviour; this includes various processes from thinking to digestion.

Enzyme. Organic substances which assist metabolic processes by catalysis.

Enzyme blocks. Substances which prevent ENZYMES from working.

Eoanthropus. ➧ PILTDOWN MAN.

Eonism. Equivalent to TRANSVESTISM.

Ependyma. Interior lining of central canal of the spinal cord and the brain ventricles.

Epicritic. Referring to nerve fibres in the skin that serve the fine perception of touch and temperature.

Epidemic. A disease or social phenomenon which spreads with extreme rapidity.

Epidemiology. The scientific study of the spread and control of disease.

Epidermis. The outer layer of the skin.

Epigastric. Relating to the middle region of the abdomen.

Epigenesis. The theory that in the course of its development the embryo is moulded and modified by environmental forces and that the mature embryo is therefore equipped with characteristics which were not present in the fertilized egg. At its most extreme the theory holds that a mother's reading habits during pregnancy will affect her child's intellectual development.

Epilepsy. Group name for a variety of brain disturbances which are characterized in their more severe manifestations by seizures and convulsions. Their cause is not understood but is known to be associated with disharmony in the electrical activity of nerve cells and sometimes with local brain damage due to injury or disease. Epileptic seizures are classified as *grand mal*, which are accompanied by loss of consciousness and convulsions, and *petit mal*, which may produce few symptoms other than mild dizziness or disorientation. *Grand mal* epilepsy in its most spectacular form is not frequently seen these days thanks to the development of anticonvulsant drugs.

Epileptic furor. A wild attack made on another person following an epileptic seizure, and for which there is afterwards total amnesia.

Epileptic stupor. Coma-like state which may follow a *grand mal* attack.

Epileptiform. Relates to seizures of an epileptic type which can be traced directly to physical brain disorders.

Epileptiform patterns. Disturbances of brain rhythm, as recorded on the EEG, characteristic of epileptic seizures.

Epinephrine. Alternative name for ADRENALIN.

Epinosis. The practice of simulating illness in order to gain rewards of some kind.

Epiphenomenalism. The theory that 'mind' and 'consciousness' are not separate non-physical entities but have arisen naturally as a consequence of the stupendous complexity of the living brain.

Epiphenomenon. Something which accompanies something else but is not caused by it.

Epiphysis. The PINEAL GLAND.

Episcotister. Simple device used for studying stimuli for brief exposures. A disc with a 'window' in it revolves at the required speed, giving the observer a brief glimpse of a target behind it. An early version of the TACHISTOSCOPE, it may also be used in FLICKER PHOTOMETRY.

Epistemology. That part of philosophy which deals with the origins and nature of knowledge.

Epithalamus. Small part of the brain near the thalamus and including the pineal gland.

Epithelium. Fine membrane coating the surfaces, interior and exterior of all body organs.

Epsilon movement. Apparent movement observed when a white figure on a black ground is replaced by a black figure on a white ground.

Equality law. One of the Gestalt laws of perceptual organization which states that those parts of a pattern which are equal tend to be perceived as a unit. (➧ GESTALT PSYCHOLOGY.)

Equally noticeable difference. More commonly known as JUST NOTICEABLE DIFFERENCE (jnd).

Equal-sense differences method. ➧ MEAN GRADATION METHOD.

Equated scores. Scores taken from different tests which have been corrected, weighted or balanced so that they can be easily compared.

Equilibration. Adjusting a measuring instrument so that it agrees with a standard. It is also a Piagetian term for the process whereby a child achieves a balance between ASSIMILATION and ACCOMMODATION.

Equilibrium. State of balance in any physical, psychological or social system; roughly equivalent to HOMEOSTASIS.

Equipotentiality. Literally, equivalent in power. In physiology it refers to the theory that different parts of the brain, particularly the cerebral cortex, can be trained to handle a wide variety of tasks. When brain damage occurs non-damaged areas seem to be able to take over the function of those parts which have been destroyed.

Equivalence test. When an animal is conditioned to respond to a particular stimulus, say a buzzer of a certain frequency, to what extent can one change the frequency and yet still elicit the conditioned response? Any stimuli which continue to elicit the response are taken as being equivalent to the animal.

Erection. Swelling of tissue, such as the penis, clitoris, nipples, through the accumulation of blood.

Erethism. Abnormal sensitivity in any part of the body.

Ergasia. General term for the sum total of activity and behaviour taking place within an organism.

Ergasiomania. Abnormal desire to work and keep active.

Ergic. Relating to work, in particular to work with a purpose.

Ergograph. Any device used for measuring the type, amount or pattern of working activity.

Ergonomics. The scientific study of work. The term is used somewhat more broadly to refer to all kinds of working interactions between human beings, and in particular between human beings and machines.

Ergot. A fungus used for treating MIGRAINE.

Erogenous zones. Parts of the body which give rise to sexual pleasure and excitement when stimulated.

Eros. Used by FREUD in his later theories to refer to the drive for life. Contrast THANATOS.

Erotic. Relating to sexual pleasure or love.

Eroticism. In psychoanalysis, refers to an unusual preoccupation with sexual matters.

Erotization. Psychoanalytic term for the process by which a part of the body or some other person or thing becomes associated with sexual pleasure.

Erotomania. Abnormally heightened interest in sex; satyriasis in the male, nymphomania in the female.

Error. Any kind of deviation from the truth, facts or agreed and established rules.

Error of expectation. Common occurrence in psychophysical experiments where an individual makes an incorrect guess or judgement because he has been anticipating a different stimulus on the basis of the preceding sequence of stimuli.

Error of refraction. Difficulty in focusing images on the retina because of imperfections in the cornea, lens or shape of the eyeball.

Erythrophobia. Abnormal fear of the colour red, and in particular blood.

Escape learning. Learning which occurs when an animal has to solve a problem in order to escape from an unpleasant situation. (⧫⧫ AVOIDANCE LEARNING.)

Esoteric. Anything understandable only to a select or privileged group.

Esprit de corps. Community spirit or morale.

Essential hypertension. High blood pressure occurring without discoverable organic disorder.

Estes' theory. An approach to learning theory based on statistical and probabilistic models developed by the American psychologist W. K. Estes. The significance of the model is that it attempts to account for learning without evoking the traditional principle of reinforcement. (⧫ STATISTICAL LEARNING THEORY.)

Estimate. Rough rather than exact judgement.

Estrogen. ⧫ OESTROGEN.

Ethereal. One of the primary odours – typically smells produced by highly volatile substances such as ether and chloroform. (⧫ ODOUR PRISM.)

Ethics. The study of morals and ideals.

Ethnic. Relating to major social or cultural divisions.

Ethnocentrism. The belief that one's own social or cultural group is intrinsically superior and different to any other.

Ethnology. The study of races and major social groups, their origins, distribution and culture.

Ethnopsychology. The study of the comparative psychology of different ETHNIC groups.

Ethology. Once used to refer to the study of ETHICS, but more recently has come to mean the study of animal behaviour and the interactions between animals and their natural environment. (⧫⧫ ANIMAL PSYCHOLOGY.)

Ethos. Literally spirit; refers more particularly to the overall mood and feeling associated with something, or the spirit and group characteristics of a society.

Etiology. ⧫ AETIOLOGY.

Eugenics. The systematic attempt to relate knowledge about the principles of heredity and genetic mechanisms to improving the lot of man on earth, and in particular to raising the physical and psychological qualities of the human race. The first eugenic ideas were advanced by Plato and also argued vigorously in the nineteenth century by Galton. The topic embraces the study of birth control and the elimination of disease, mental deficiency, etc., by selective breeding.

Euglena. Tiny single-celled organism which is remarkable in that it exhibits both animal and plant characteristics.

Eunuch. A male who has been castrated, especially if before puberty.

Euparenia. Sexual intercourse which leads to ORGASM.

Euphoria. A generally sustained mood of extreme optimism and good humour.

Eurhythmia. Smoothly coordinated body movements.

Eurotophobia. Abnormal fear of the female genitals.

Eurymorph. Someone with a stocky, heavy build. (▶▶ BODY BUILD INDEX.)

Eustachian tube. Tiny opening which links the middle ear and the inside of the mouth. It serves to equalize internal and external pressure and can be felt popping in elevators and aeroplanes as it opens or closes. It is also called the auditory tube.

Euthanasia. Mercy killing.

Euthenics. Attempts at improving the welfare and happiness of man by changing his environment to suit him.

Euthymia. A happy and contented state of mind.

Evaluation. Checking the importance or validity of something.

Event. Something which occurs and has a measurable beginning and end.

Eviration. Belief by a man that he is turning into a woman or acquiring female characteristics.

Evoked potential. An electrical process taking place in the brain which can be measured using an EEG and which can be induced reliably by an experimental stimulus such as a flash of light.

Evolution. The principle which explains the enormous diversity of animal life by assuming a gradual process of change in genetic blueprints so that life forms continually adapt to meet changes in the world around them. The most powerful theory of evolution is that put forward by DARWIN, which argues that genetic change is itself a random process, but that those mutations which are best fitted to survive will do so.

Exacerbation. Increase in the severity of the symptoms of a disease or other abnormality.

Exaltation. Extreme good humour or optimism; also, abnormal increase in degree of functioning of an organ.

Exceptional. Used to denote extreme deviations from the normal, particularly on the positive side. The term is mostly used to describe unusually gifted children, but sometimes, confusingly, to include backward or otherwise handicapped children.

Excitability. Readiness to react to stimuli.

Excitation. The process of firing a nerve cell or set of cells. PAVLOV used the term to refer to a spread of activity from one part of the brain to another.

Excitatory potential. Term used by HULL in his mathematical theory of behaviour. It refers, rather generally, to the likelihood of a particular response occurring.

Excitement. Psychiatric term for a highly active, agitated or anxious state, characteristic of certain psychoses.

Executive area. Section of the cortex supposed to exercise a general integrative control over other parts of the cortex.

Exercise. In psychology refers to practice in the process of learning.

Exhaustion. State in which energy resources have been used up and responsiveness is reduced to a minimum.

Exhibitionism. Abnormal and compulsive desire to expose one's genitals in public. It may also refer to the tendency of some individuals to go to unusual lengths to draw attention to themselves.

Existentialism. Philosophical movement which states that the main goal of philosophy and science should be to work out the riddle of man's existence, the nature of ideals such as freedom, and the meaning of life.

Existential psychiatry. Movement, largely pioneered by the Scottish psychiatrist R.D. Laing in the 1960s, which attempted to move concepts of mental illness and their treatment away from the physically based approach using drugs, ECT, surgery, etc., towards a concentration on conscious processes and a detailed analysis of the SELF. Laing's ideas have made considerable headway but, like all innovations in psychiatry, they require lengthy evaluation before one can assess the quality of their contribution.

Existential psychology. Psychological movement which holds that the essential subject matter of psychology is consciousness and the 'higher forms' of mental life. There has been a great revival of interest in these ideas in the past decade, acting in some ways as a counter-movement to the dominant behaviouristic schools. Not many people realize, however, that existential psychology has its roots in the pioneering work of WUNDT a century ago.

Exocathection. Term used by MURRAY to refer to a tendency to be concerned with external rather than internal matters.

Exocrine glands. The ducted as opposed to the ductless (endocrine) glands. (➧ GLAND).

Exogamy. Anthropological term for the practice of prohibiting individuals from marrying inside their own social group.

Exogenous. Relating to something which originates outside the organism.

Exophoria. Muscular disturbance which causes the eyes to turn outward.

Exophthalmic goitre. Thyroid disease causing restless energy and marked protuberance of the eyeballs.

Exoteric. Material or ideas available to the world at large. Contrast ESOTERIC.

Expansiveness. Personality type characterized by extraversion, good humour and talkativeness.

Expectancy. In statistics, the probability that something will occur; in general psychology an attitude of mind (SET) which prepares the individual for one set of circumstances rather than another. (➧➧ PREPERCEPTION.)

Experience. Familiarity with something; also used, more rarely, for conscious awareness. The word is, incidentally, French for experiment.

Experiment. Knowledge about the universe can, in the main, only be gained by observing it in action (the exception is where laws, rules, principles and deductions may be arrived at by logical or mathematical methods). Straight observation is effective when the phenomenon to be studied is common, frequently repeated and relatively isolated from other phenomena, but this approach is lengthy and inefficient in the long run. A more direct approach is the *experimental method* in which some aspects of the phenomenon to be studied are 'trapped' by the scientist and, as it were, run specially for his benefit. This has the advantage that they can be observed at a time to suit the observer, and also that having made the observation he may repeat it (to see if it follows its previous course), and then perhaps alter some component or introduce some new variable to study the effects.

The gains in efficiency that come from experimentation rather than passive observation are considerable, but the principal penalty is that by constraining the universe to meet the requirements of his experimental set-up, the scientist risks, subtly or grossly, changing the nature of the phenomenon he is studying. This problem is particularly dangerous in psychology where one's subject matter is human or animal behaviour, physical and mental, and the likelihood of it being altered by a laboratory setting is considerable. In social psychology, where communication between people is the main focus of interest, the problem is compounded for the presence of the experimenter may itself alter the nature of the group under study. One of the main difficulties in social psychology, therefore, is to ensure the observer's detachment from the experiment itself – a task which has been greatly facilitated by technological developments such as film and videotape, which allow social behaviour to be discreetly recorded and subsequently replayed. Where opinions rather than factual observations are sought, sophisticated techniques of interviewing, sampling and questionnaire analysis have been developed. (⧫⧫ CONTROL; METHODOLOGY.)

Experimental group. A group of subjects, humans or animals, tested in an experiment to determine the effect of an INDEPENDENT VARIABLE (a drug, learning task, etc.) on their behaviour. After the independent variable has been introduced, the experimental group is compared with a CONTROL GROUP who has *not* been subjected to the variable. (⧫⧫ MATCHED GROUP.)

Experimental method. The formal technique employed in scientific experiments. (⧫ EXPERIMENT.)

Experimental neurosis. A state of extreme tension or disturbed behaviour induced in an animal under experimental conditions, mainly by forcing it to try to solve an impossible problem. In the classic experiments of PAVLOV a dog was trained to respond positively to a circle and negatively to an ellipse, and in a series of subsequent trials the circle was made progressively more elliptic and the ellipse more circular. Animals exhibited 'neurotic behaviour' as this discrimination became steadily more difficult.

Experimental variable. ⧫ INDEPENDENT VARIABLE.

Experimenter bias. Distortion of the results of an experiment caused by the experimenter, consciously or unconsciously, influencing the data or their analysis in accordance with his own attitudes. (⧫⧫ BIAS; RESPONSE BIAS.)

Explicit behaviour. Any activity which can easily be seen or detected.

Exploratory drive. The supposed instinctive tendency for animals to investigate their environment. Animals not motivated by any of the physical needs – hunger, thirst, sex, etc. – will still investigate their environment. For example, rats will cross an electrified grid in order to explore a new and, presumably, 'interesting' cage. (➧➧ CURIOSITY DRIVE; ORIENTATING REFLEX.)

Exponent. Number written as a superscript which indicates to what power the main number is to be raised (e.g. in 3^4, '4' is the exponent).

Expression. A physical sign, such as movement of one part of the body (particularly the face), which denotes a particular internal state, whether physiological or psychological.

Expressive aphasia. Loss of the ability to speak or write.

Expressive therapy. Psychotherapy which concentrates on encouraging the patient to express his feelings in an uninhibited way.

Extended family. ➧ FAMILY.

Extensor. A muscle which contracts and by doing so straightens a limb.

External auditory meatus. The channel of the outer ear which leads to the eardrum.

External inhibition. Term coined by PAVLOV for the weakening of a conditioned response which occurs when an 'external' stimulus is presented simultaneously with the conditioned stimulus. For example, if a dog has been conditioned to produce salivation at the sound of a bell, the flashing of a light when the bell is rung will inhibit the flow of salivation.

Externalization. The process of projecting one's thoughts and feelings on to the outside world; also refers to the gradual separation of the self from the external world which takes place throughout childhood. In Freudian terms, it means the process of EGO formation.

External rectus. Muscle which rotates the eyeball outwards.

Exteroceptor. A sensory receptor which responds to physical changes outside the body. Contrast ENTEROCEPTOR.

Extinction. The gradual weakening of a conditioned response when reinforcement is withheld. (➧ CONDITIONING.)

Extirpation. The surgical removal of an organ or part of it.

Extraception. One of MURRAY's personality dimensions, characterized by scepticism and factual accuracy.

Extrajection. Psychoanalytic term more frequently known as PROJECTION.

Extrapolation. The process of inferring something beyond the data available.

Extrapunitive. Relating to frustrated behaviour which is channelled into aggression towards the frustrating object.

Extra-sensory perception (ESP). The supposed capacity of human beings and animals to acquire information about some aspects of the world without the use of the known senses. Whether or not ESP exists is still an open question, though on balance most scientists do not believe that it has been satisfactorily demonstrated. Parapsychologists tend to classify ESP into a number of subheadings, including TELEPATHY, CLAIRVOYANCE; PRECOGNITION and PSYCHOKINESIS. (➧➧ PARAPSYCHOLOGY.)

Extraspectral. Relating to a colour not found in the spectrum, e.g. purple.

Extraversion. One of the major personality types, first proposed by JUNG and now generally agreed as a valid classification of human personality by clinical psychologists and psychiatrists. The extravert is sociable, active and generally confident. Contrast INTROVERSION.

Extrinsic behaviour. ➧ INTRINSIC BEHAVIOUR.

Extrinsic motivation. Performing a task because one gains something particular from it, over and above the pleasure of the activity simply for itself. The latter is called INTRINSIC MOTIVATION.

Extrinsic muscles. The external muscles of the eye which are attached to the outside of the eyeball and which control its movement.

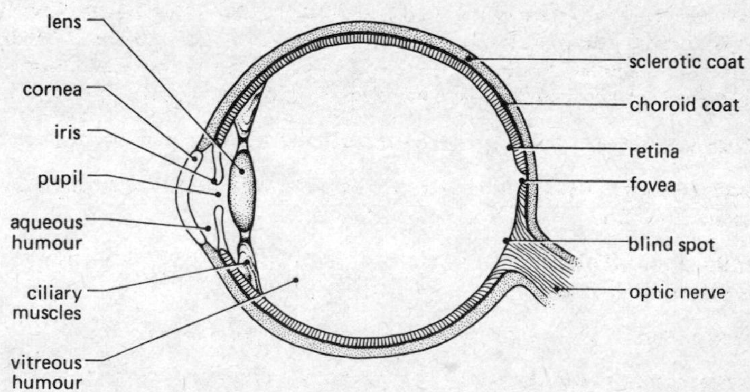

Figure 12. The eye.

Eye. The organ of vision. In man it detects light rays of wavelengths between approximately 400 and 750 nm. At the front of the eye is the cornea, a transparent window, through which light passes to the sensitive layer at the back, the RETINA. The amount of light entering the eye is controlled by the expansion and contraction of a ring muscle, the iris, and rays are focused on the retina by a lens lying between iris and retina. The retina itself is made up of many millions of cells of two general types, RODS and CONES. (▶▶ VISUAL ACUITY; COLOUR VISION.)

Eye dominance. Tendency for one EYE to be used in preference to the other in fixating objects.

Eye movement. The EYE has a wide range of movements, most of which are used in the processes of fixation and scanning and which are under voluntary control. In addition to these main movements, there is also a FINE TREMOR, not detectable without special equipment and *not* under voluntary control, which is believed to play a role in enhancing image quality and VISUAL ACUITY.

Eysenck, Hans J. (1916 –). British psychologist who has made a major contribution to personality theory and testing. He is also known for his outspoken criticism of psychoanalysis as a therapeutic method.

Eysenck Personality Inventory. An up-date of the Maudsley Personality Inventory, featuring a test of neuroticism and extraversion.

F

Fables test. Test for children or adults of low IQ in which the subject is asked to interpret a simple fable; it may be part of either an IQ or a projective test.

Fabulation. An imaginary story or lie.

Face-to-face group. A primary group. (➧ GROUP.)

Face validity. Whether a test is relevant to the variable being measured.

Facial nerve. The seventh cranial nerve which serves face muscles, the tongue and taste.

Facial vision. ➧ ECHOLOCATION.

Facilitation. In psychology, anything which improves performance. (➧➧ SOCIAL FACILITATION.) In physiology anything which helps neural transmission.

Factor. A thing which brings something about or causes it to happen.

Factor analysis. Statistical technique which allows one to analyse complex data and discriminate between the various factors playing a role in the situation under study, and to establish the degree of correlation or interaction between them. Early factor analysis grew out of the work of SPEARMAN, who was interested in determining whether intelligence (as measured by IQ tests) was a single factor or an elaborate combination of a series of subfactors, e.g. cleverness, mathematical ability, verbal skill, etc. Modern computing methods allow extremely powerful factor analyses to be performed very rapidly on great masses of data.

Factor theory. Any theory which attempts to break down a concept such as personality, intelligence or learning, into a series of components which have been highlighted by the use of FACTOR ANALYSIS on relevant data.

Faculty. An ability or characteristic.

Faculty psychology. Any attempt to form a theory of psychology based on the splintering of cerebral processes into a number of distinct faculties. In its early and most extreme form, phrenology, the brain was seen as the origin of a finite number of independent qualities or abilities, each of which could be clearly localized and even identified by appropriate bumps on the skull.

Faeces. Waste material expelled from the bowel.

Faith. Belief in something not supported by direct observation, though occasionally influenced by the testimony of another individual.

Faith healing. A term used rather loosely to refer to any technique which seeks to alleviate or cure illness without the use of drugs or established medical techniques. The practice in countries with a Christian tradition has its roots in the early Christian belief that faith in Jesus Christ would be sufficient to bring about recovery from sickness, and it is employed today by a variety of religious groups, including the Christian Scientists, Spiritualists and many Fundamentalist sects. There is fairly clear evidence that faith healing is effective in some psycho-neurotic conditions, but more spectacular claims, such as cancer cures, are probably based on original faulty diagnosis or on spontaneous remission.

Fallacy. An error in reasoning leading to a false but plausible conclusion.

Falling sickness. Obsolete term for EPILEPSY.

Familial. Relating to the family.

Family. A group of people related to each other by close blood ties. The size of what is considered to be the 'basic family' varies from society to society, but the term nuclear family is generally used to refer to a father, mother, children and any relations living permanently together. The nuclear family therefore is considered to be a continuously independent group. Families connected by blood or marriage but geographically separated are known as extended families.

The term is also a taxonomic classification in zoology. (◆ TAXONOMY.)

Family-centred therapy. Form of group psychotherapy which attempts to treat the individual in his family setting, when it appears that his problems have been caused by his relationships with the family group. (◆◆ MILIEU THERAPY.)

Family constellation. Term used by ADLER to refer to the complex relationships that exist within a family and which he believed were amongst the most important factors affecting an individual's psychological development.

Fanaticism. Excessive preoccupation with a cause and which takes little account of the feelings or attitudes of others not associated with the cause.

Fantasy. The deliberate and conscious experiencing of the imagination to create images and ideas. The word is also sometimes used to refer to dream or drug-induced imagery.

Far point. The most distance point of clear vision without the use of optical aids.

Far sightedness. Poor vision for close objects while distance vision is unaffected.

Fascicle. A small bundle of nerves fibres found in the spinal cord and elsewhere; also bundles of muscles or tendon fibres.

Fatalism. The philosophy that all events are predetermined; implies that free will is illusory.

Father complex. ➧ ELECTRA COMPLEX.

Father figure. Someone who stands in the place of one's father; any one with an authoritarian role.

Father fixation. Abnormal preoccupation with one's father, either of a positive or negative kind.

Fatigue. State of relative immobility or unresponsiveness produced by a depletion of energy. In physiological terms cells are said to be fatigued in the period after prolonged stimulation before they have recovered their capacity to fire again.

Faxen psychosis. ➧ BUFFOONERY PSYCHOSIS.

Fear. One of the most intense emotional states, accompanied by major changes in the activity of the autonomic nervous system, primarily geared to preparing the individual for flight.

Fear of failure. A term used to refer to the negative emotional anticipations which are aroused when the individual is faced with an achievement-oriented task. It is sometimes used as the complement to ACHIEVEMENT MOTIVE.

Feature profile test. Performance test in which the patient must assemble blocks in the shape of a head or profile.

Febrile. Feverish or delirious.

Fechner, Gustav Theodor (1801–87). German philosopher who performed pioneering work in experimental psychology and psychophysics.

Fechner's colours. Colours seen when a disc with black and white sectors on it is rotated at particular speeds.

Fechner's law. It is an interesting principle that the intensity or 'strength' of perception (e.g. the brightness of a light) is proportional to the logarithm of the physical stimulus – in other words substantial increases in stimulus intensity produce proportional (but much smaller) increases in *perceived* intensity. This law was first formulated by Weber and expressed mathematically by Fechner, and it appears to apply to all sensory modalities in humans. It is sometimes known as the Weber-Fechner law, but do not confuse with WEBER'S LAW.

Fechner's paradox. The name given to the observation that something viewed binocularly seems to increase in brightness when one eye is closed.

Feeble-minded. Obsolete term. It was used in America for mental retardation; and in Britain for individuals with an IQ in the range 50–70. (➧ MENTAL RETARDATION.)

Feedback. A word drawn from engineering technology and cybernetics with increasing applications in psychology. Broadly speaking it refers to any process by which the input to a system is regulated by connecting it to the output. In the classic example – the governor on a steam engine – increased speed closes the valve supplying steam to the cylinder, thus reducing the speed. The term is sometimes used to refer to information given to an individual as to how well he is performing in a task (KNOWLEDGE OF RESULTS). (➧➧ BIOFEEDBACK; POSITIVE AND NEGATIVE FEEDBACK.)

Feeling. In its most common usage, any conscious sensation or experience; also relates to an emotional state or AFFECT. (➧➧ EMOTION.)

Feeling type. ➧ RATIONAL TYPE.

Fellatio. Oral stimulation of the penis during sexual intercourse.

Felt need. A need or desire that is consciously experienced.

Femininity. The state of possessing the psychological and physical characteristics of women.

Feminism. Movement whose aims are the elimination of the social divisions traditionally existing between men and women.

Feminization. The process of acquiring feminine sex characteristics, physical or psychological.

Fenestration. Making an opening in something by surgical means.

Feral child. Any child partially or totally reared by animals. A few cases of feral children have been reported but little is known about them. While it is conceivable that a child might escape from his or her family and come to live amongst noncarnivorous animals, it is extremely doubtful whether any human infants have ever been suckled and reared by them.

Fere phenomenon. More commonly known as the GALVANIC SKIN RESPONSE.

Ferry-Porter law. The frequency at which a flickering light appears fused increases in logarithmic relationship to the brightness of the stimulus.

Fertility. The capacity to produce offspring.

Festinger, Leon (1919 –). American psychologist best known for his theory of COGNITIVE DISSONANCE.

Fetishism. In anthropological terms an object revered or worshipped because it is believed to have magical powers. The word has become incorporated into abnormal psychology where it refers to the practice of associating objects belonging to members of the opposite sex with the sexual act, and in some cases transferring a primary sexual drive to the objects rather than to the person. Typical fetishes include clothing such as underwear, stockings, shoes, etc., and the hair or particular limbs such as the foot. In the most extreme form of fetishism the individual is unable to become sexually aroused unless the fetish is present.

Fibre. A single nerve cell or one of the extended processes of a nerve cell, such as an axon or dendrite.

Fibril. A long thread found running through nerve cells, passing out to the axons and dendrites to form nerve fibres or neurofibrils.

Fiction. Word used by ADLER to refer to the lifestyle or sets of attitudes developed by an individual to assist him to overcome any feelings of inferiority or which satisfy his need for power.

Fiducial limits. Points on either side of a mean value beyond which it is considered to be extremely unlikely that a value will be found.

Field. An area of some kind, generally with describable or definable boundaries.

Field of attention. The sum total of things or events to which an individual is attending at any particular time.

Field of regard. All the visual space that an individual can scan when moving his eyes but not his head. Compare VISUAL FIELD.

Field theories. General term for psychological theories which stress that conscious experiences, learning, memory, perception, etc., need to be studied as wholes rather than parts. Any event therefore – say a particular act of perception – can only really be understood if it is seen as part of a larger, integrative brain process. The most famous theory of this kind is undoubtedly that of the Gestalt psychologists who leaned heavily on the notion that the brain operated as a field rather than as a collection of more or less independent neural units. (➧ GESTALT PSYCHOLOGY.) Another important field theory, which grew partly out of the Gestalt ideas, was put forward by Kurt Lewin who attempted to take his ideas a step beyond the Gestaltists and to quantify his theory in mathematical terms.

Field work. Any study of human or animal behaviour undertaken in the 'real world' as opposed to the laboratory environment.

Figural after-effect. When a pattern is fixated for a long period, and the gaze is then shifted to a different pattern, peculiar distortions in the second figure appear. Figural after-effects were used by Gestalt psychologists to support their ideas on FIELD THEORIES and the brain.

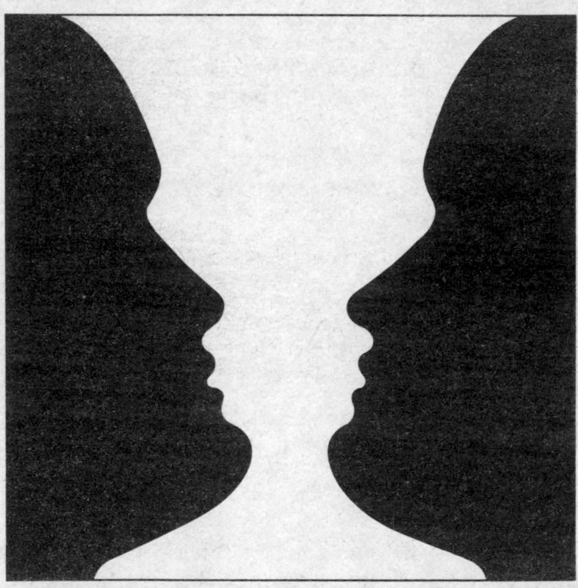

Figure 13. Figure-ground phenomenon. When the setting or 'ground' is not clearly defined, figure and ground alternate. Hence this may be seen as a white vase or two faces.

Figure-ground phenomenon. The visual world appears to be made up of 'figures' which are seen to be standing out against a 'ground', and normally one can concentrate only on one aspect at a time. Characteristically any detail observed in the visual field and any contours are always ascribed to figure rather than to ground. (➧➧ AMBIGUOUS FIGURES; REVERSIBLE PERSPECTIVE.)

Filial regression. Bright parents tend to have bright children and dull parents dull children, but the overall trend after a number of generations is for all offspring to revert towards the average. This law was first put forward by GALTON. It is also called the 'regression toward the mean'.

Film colour. Colour as it is perceived when not apparently on the surface of some object – e.g. the texture-free blue of the sky. Contrast SURFACE COLOUR and VOLUME COLOUR.

Final common path. A bundle of fibres consisting of a large number of motor neurones, upon which converge all the neural connections from higher centres.

Finalism. Any theory which attempts to explain mental processes or life in general in terms of purposes and goals. It is also known as teleology.

Fine tremor. Tiny movements of the eyes occurring with a frequency of about 10 Hz and detectable only with special instrumentation. They are believed to assist VISUAL ACUITY. The phrase also has a meaning in neurology when it is used in contrast with coarse tremor – say of the limbs.

Finger painting. Giving depressed or withdrawn patients the opportunity to express themselves by painting with their fingers instead of brushes. The technique is also used to promote self-expression in children.

Finger spelling. Using the hands and fingers to communicate, as in deaf and dumb language.

Finger-thumb opposal. Use of the finger and thumb to pick up objects – a skill which appears in the second year in the normal child.

Firing. The triggering of electrical activity in a cell.

Fission. Splitting or dividing.

Fissure. A deep groove or channel in the surface of the cortex.

Fistula. An opening into the interior of the body produced by a wound, abscess or surgery.

Fit. Seizure or convulsion; also refers, in a quite different sense, in statistics to the way in which data match what is expected of them.

Fixation. In physiology the process of directing the eye towards an object so that the image of it is projected onto the FOVEA. In psychoanalysis the term refers to the tendency for an individual's psychodynamic growth to be arrested at a particular stage of development or on a particular person or thing associated with that stage – e.g. oral fixation when sensual pleasures concentrate on sucking, biting, etc.

Fixed alternative. Relates to tests of the multiple choice variety.

Flaccid. Spongy, flabby.

Flagellation. Beating or whipping oneself or others in order to gain sexual excitement.

Flattened affect. An inappropriately weak emotional response.

Flatworms. The platyhelminthes: worms with a rudimentary nervous system which are capable of simple learning and have been used in the controversial 'transfer of learning' experiments.

Flavour. A dimension of taste experience.

Flexibilitas cerea. More commonly known as WAXY FLEXIBILITY.

Flexibility. Pliability and, in psychological terms, readiness to accept new ideas.

Flexion. The bending of a limb at a joint.

Flexor. Muscle whose function it is to bend a limb.

Flicker. A rapid on-off alternation of a perceived stimulus.

Flicker-fusion frequency. The frequency at which a flickering light is seen to be continuous or fused. The term is synonymous with CRITICAL FLICKER FREQUENCY.

Flicker photometry. The brighter a light the higher the frequency of flickering before fusion takes place. Using this fact the relative brightness of two fields of colours can be determined by comparing their flicker fusion points.

Flight of colours. The sequence of different colours observed in an after-image of a bright light.

Flight of ideas. Rapid, rather jumbled sequence of ideas or thoughts, generally incomplete; sometimes induced by drugs or mental illness.

Floccillation. Plucking bedding or clothing while in a delirious state.

Fluctuation. Oscillation or change, not necessarily rhythmic.

Fluctuation of attention. Irregular shifts in the clarity with which an object can be perceived, even when one is attempting complete concentration.

Fluency. Mastery of any skill, but in particular verbal skills.

Fluid. Readily changing.

Focal epilepsy. A form of EPILEPSY with no loss of consciousness and in which a limited area of the body is involved in the convulsions.

Focal length. The distance from a lens to the point at which it brings parallel light rays into focus.

Foliate papilla. Set of folds or leaf-like structures on the surface of the tongue.

Folie à deux. The sharing of a delusion by two people, mainly due to the dominating personality of the basically deluded individual. It is most commonly seen in husband and wife.

Folklore. Traditions and beliefs which have survived from a previous culture.

Folk psychology. Study of the beliefs, etc., of primitive, non-literate peoples.

Folkways. Those patterns of behaviour which are traditional in a particular group or society.

Following reaction. A term used in ethology to refer to the way in which a young animal will follow any other living thing it sees during the critical period of early life (➧ IMPRINTING).

Fontanelle. The opening in the top of an infant's skull.

Foramen magnum. The hole in the base of the skull through which the spinal cord passes to the brain.

Forced fantasy. A fantasy suggested to a patient by the psychoanalyst as an aid to the progress of the analysis.

Forebrain. ➧ BRAIN.

Foreconscious. More commonly known as the PRECONSCIOUS.

Forensic psychology. Psychology as it relates to legal matters and including expert testimony in court.

Foreperiod. The time between the 'ready' signal and the onset of the stimulus in a test or experiment.

Forepleasure. Sexual pleasure associated with stimulation of an erogenous zone, prior to intercourse.

Foreshortening. The illusion of shortening that occurs when a line is viewed lengthwise. (➧ HORIZONTAL-VERTICAL ILLUSION.)

Forgetting. Loss of the ability to recall data from the memory store. Early theories of forgetting assumed that the information became destroyed or 'faded away' through disuse or with the passage of time.

Current views tend to the theory that information placed in store is never totally lost (except through brain damage) and that forgetting is more a matter of breakdown in the mechanism of extraction or information retrieval.

Form. The shape or nature of something.

Formal. Relating to anything with agreed rules.

Formal discipline. The theory, no longer accepted, that certain academic subjects should be studied not for the knowledge inherent in them, but because the act of studying them assists all other types of study. The most common example was the belief that the study of Latin 'trained the mind'. (⧫⧫ LEARNING TO LEARN.)

Formalism. Any attempt at systematizing knowledge.

Formal operational thinking. Piagetian term. (⧫ DEVELOPMENTAL PSYCHOLOGY.)

Formant. The quality of diction or timbre which makes one vowel sound different from another.

Formatio reticularis. ⧫ RETICULAR ACTIVATING SYSTEM.

Formboard. Test in which the subject has to fit a variety of shapes into the appropriate holes in a board.

Form quality. Term used in GESTALT PSYCHOLOGY for the properties or characteristics of a shape or pattern which are specific to the complete form and which cannot be analysed or explained in terms of the constituent parts.

Form response. The most common type of response given by patients in a RORSCHACH TEST – e.g. the inkblot is described in terms of its shape, 'a butterfly', 'a face', etc.

Fornix. Collection of nerve fibres linking the hypothalamus and hippocampus.

Fourier's law. The mathematical principle that any complex wave can, by appropriate analysis, be broken down into a series of simpler sine waves.

Fovea (centralis). Small area in the centre of the RETINA which provides the sharpest and clearest vision. The fovea is colour sensitive and almost entirely made up of CONES.

Foveal vision. Vision involving stimulation of the fovea as the result of central fixation of an object.

Fractional antedating goal response. A response which is one of a chain leading to the reaching of a goal but which begins to appear ahead of its time. For example, in running a maze, at the end of which an animal has become accustomed to being fed, salivation may appear progressively earlier and earlier along the pathway.

Fractionation. The hypothesis that in a neural system repeated firing will ultimately lead to certain cells 'dropping out' from the system. The concept is important to ideas such as Hebb's cell assembly theory. (➧➧ RECRUITMENT.)

Fragrant. One of the 'basic' smells – flowery. (➧ ODOUR PRISM.)

Frame of reference. A background or setting, whether physical or conceptual, against which other things can be compared or judged.

Fraternal twins. ➧ DIZYGOTIC TWINS.

Free association. An important technique employed in psychoanalysis in an attempt to break down the DEFENCE MECHANISMS which the conscious self puts up against unwanted impulses and ideas from the unconscious mind. In free association the patient is invited to talk openly, spontaneously and without censoring his thoughts, thus providing the analyst with a chain of material, some of which it is hoped will give clues to the nature of the raw material of the unconscious.

Free association test. ➧ WORD ASSOCIATION TEST.

Free-floating anxiety. State of underlying chronic anxiety not attached to any identifiable objects or events.

Free nerve endings. Nerve endings, not equipped with any obvious receptor devices or mechanism, found in many sections of the skin. At one time they were believed to be associated with pain detection.

Free will. Relates to the assumption that man has absolute control and decision-making powers in at least some aspects of his life. Contrast DETERMINISM.

Frenzy. A wild and uncontrolled emotional state.

Frequency. The rate at which a wave, vibration or similar event repeats itself, traditionally measured in cycles per second (hertz); in statistics, it refers to the number of occurrences of a particular thing in a given sample.

Frequency curve. A plot of the distribution of various values according to the frequency with which they occur in particular groupings. There are a number of other ways of graphically representing frequencies, including histograms and even three-dimensional solids.

Frequency theory. The attempt to explain the principles of hearing by assuming that the basilar membrane in the ear responds to differences in pitch, as does the diaphragm of a telephone, and transmits stimuli to the brain for analysis. The theory is not capable of accounting for the dimension of loudness. (⧫⧫ HEARING THEORIES.)

Freud, Sigmund (1856 – 1939). Viennese physician whose revolutionary theories of the mind, its principles of operation and the roots of its abnormalities had a deep impact on Western philosophy, morals, art and literature. Although Freud was a thinker of immense subtlety and can be credited with a number of major insights, the essence of his contribution can be summed up under two headings. The first was a realization that man is controlled by powerful unconscious forces, of whose existence he is unlikely to be aware, which frequently conflict with the demands of his conscious mind and are rarely subject to conscious command. The second was the superb insight that many of the whims and desires of the UNCONSCIOUS and the conflicts they produce can be revealed in DREAMS. His structural subdivision of the mind into three parts, EGO, ID and SUPEREGO, and his personal system for understanding and treating most forms of mental illness – PSYCHOANALYSIS – are still matters of controversy today. His ideas on the unconscious and the nature of dreams, however, remain unrivalled. (⧫ PSYCHOANALYSIS; GENITAL CHARACTER; OEDIPUS COMPLEX; *et al. passim.*)

Freudian slip. Slip of the tongue or error of phraseology which FREUD believed pointed to the existence of an area of unconscious conflict.

Frigidity. A female's inability to participate fully in and enjoy sexual intercourse. It is the equivalent of impotence in the male.

Fringe of consciousness. Term used by William James for those items not in direct conscious awareness, but which nevertheless contribute to the overall perceptual experience. The concept is sometimes known as marginal consciousness.

Fromm, Erich (1900 –). Psychoanalyst who has drawn heavily on the theories of both Freud and Marx and attempted to develop a culturally and socially based psychological theory.

Frontal lobes. Those parts of the cerebral hemispheres which lie in front of what is known as the central or Rolandic fissure. They are assumed to play a major role in controlling purposeful, rational behaviour. (⧫ CEREBRAL HEMISPHERES.)

Frontal lobotomy. Severing the connections or removal of the frontal lobes from the main structure of the brain. The operation tends to be performed as a last ditch resort in cases of severe and chronic depression, anxiety states or intractable pain. Fashionable in the 1940s and 1950s, but currently under attack – more on aesthetic and moral than practical grounds.

Frottage. The practice of rubbing up against other people in crowds, etc., in order to gain sexual pleasure. The term also refers to sexual pleasure gained by rubbing oneself against another's clothing.

Frustration. The blocking of any drive, desire or pathway to a goal, whether conscious or unconscious.

Frustration-aggression hypothesis. A theory advanced by Dollard and Miller, and supported by some experimental evidence with animals and humans, which states that frustration will always lead to aggression, and that when aggression is present a source of frustration must always exist.

Frustration tolerance. Term used for the ability to tolerate tension arising when an instinctive need is persistently frustrated.

Fugue. A longish period of AMNESIA in which an individual may leave his home and job and commence a new life in apparent ignorance of his old one. It is characteristic of fugues that when they end the earlier life is recalled and the intervening experiences apparently forgotten.

Function. May refer to an activity, purpose or role; or in statistics a value that changes as another value does. It may also refer to something dependent on another thing.

Functional disorders. Disorders which cannot be traced to any physical, biochemical or organic cause. Neuroses are assumed to be functional disorders, whereas the current view is that psychoses are organically based. (➧ NEUROSIS; PSYCHOSIS.)

Functional fixedness. Mental inflexibility, particularly the maintenance of behaviour patterns even when they are no longer seen to be appropriate.

Functionalism. School of psychology which developed in the nineteenth century on the premise that the *functions* of the mind were more suitable and important for study than mental processes themselves. The rival and alternative school of the period was known as STRUCTURALISM.

Functional psychosis. Any psychosis which is assumed not to have an organic cause.

Function engram. Term introduced by JUNG to refer to an inherited neural structure which serves as the physiological basis of an archetypal memory or symbolic image.

Fundamental colour. Hues which are supposed to be important because they form the basis of a theory of colour vision.

Furor. An attack of intense anger, sometimes occurring in EPILEPSY.

Fusion. The combining of different stimuli to one perceptual whole. (➧ BINOCULAR FUSION.)

G

G factor. Hypothetical 'general' ability assumed to be the key factor in intelligence and therefore measured in some way by all intelligence tests. The term was introduced by Spearman. (➧ TWO-FACTOR THEORY.)

Gallup, George Horace (1901–). Psychologist/journalist who developed the first strategies for sampling public opinion by mass interviewing.

Galton bar. Graded rod used in psychophysical experiments on judging visual distance.

Galton, Francis (1822–1911). Remarkable British scientist with a pioneering interest in psychology, statistics and heredity.

Galton whistle. High-pitched whistle used to detect the upper limits of hearing.

Galvanic. Relates to any direct as opposed to alternating current.

Galvanic skin response (GSR). During states of excitement and arousal a small but rapid change takes place in the electrical conductivity of the skin which can be measured using suitable electrodes. As the response is autonomic and not under conscious control, the GSR is incorporated in 'polygraph' lie detector systems. (➧➧ LIE DETECTOR.)

Galvanometer. Device for measuring the strength of an electric current.

Gambler's fallacy. Naive gamblers believe they can 'beat the system' by withholding their bets until particular sequences have been completed. For example, they will wait until five reds have come up in sequence at roulette and will then start betting on black. The essence of the fallacy is the belief that there is a causal relationship between past and future sequences. In fact, *each* turn at the tables represents a random independent event.

Gamete. A sex cell which combines with another to form a zygote, initiating the process of reproduction.

Game theory. The formal study of the rules and tactics of games. Basically a mathematical approach to decision-making behaviour.

Gamma-amino-butyric acid (GABA). A chemical present in the brain believed to damp cortical activity.

Gamma movement. Form of APPARENT MOVEMENT in which an object appears to change size with a change in illumination.

Gang. Sociological term for a group bound together by a common purpose. (◆◆ CROWD.)

Ganglion. A cluster of nerve cells.

Ganser syndrome. Tendency to give ludicrous answers to simple questions, and to perform absurd acts. These transparent tactics are sometimes used by people feigning mental illness. (◆◆ PRISON PSYCHOSIS.)

Ganzfeld. A featureless, evenly illuminated field. It is used in experiments on visual perception and sensory deprivation.

Gargoylism. Disfigurement of the bones of the head and face caused by genetic metabolic disorder. DWARFISM and MENTAL RETARDATION may also be present.

Gating. Blocking of one sensory nerve by another – e.g. when one attends to something in vision, auditory input may be gated.

Gatophobia. Abnormal fear of cats.

Gaussian curve. The bell-shaped, normal distribution curve.

Genes. The packets of information distributed along the CHROMOSOMES and which carry the messages of heredity.

General ability. The ability which is supposed to lie at the heart of intelligence – the so-called G FACTOR. (◆ TWO-FACTOR THEORY.)

General adaptation syndrome (GAS). ◆ STRESS.

General Aptitude Test. A battery of tests widely used in America to determine vocational aptitude, measuring a number of factors related to intelligence, including verbal and numerical ability, psychomotor coordination, etc.

Generalization. Making a judgement which has widespread and general relevance; also refers to a rather broad scientific principle or law.

Generalization gradient. In studies of CONDITIONING and LEARNING it is frequently noted that an animal will react to a stimulus which is rather similar to the original conditioned stimulus, but by making a weaker response. The greater the dissimilarity between the stimuli, the feebler the second response, this relationship being known as the generalization gradient. (◆◆ STIMULUS GENERALIZATION; RESPONSE GENERALISATION.)

General paralysis of the insane (GPI). Obsolete term for psychosis caused by syphilitic infection of the nervous system, also sometimes known as general paresis.

General psychology. The study of the broad rules governing mental life and behaviour as contrasted with the specific study of individuals. Contrast INDIVIDUAL PSYCHOLOGY, DIFFERENTIAL PSYCHOLOGY.

General semantics. The study of symbols of all kinds, and human use of them. The term was also used by the mathematician Alfred Korzybski for his controversial philosophy which rejected Aristotelian principles.

Generation. The average time period in a species between birth and the beginning of reproduction.

Generic. Relates to something present in all members of the biological classificatory group known as a GENUS.

Genesis. The process of creating or coming into being.

Genetics. The scientific study of the biological mechanisms of HEREDITY.

Geniculate bodies. Two clumps of nervous tissue forming part of the thalamus. The *lateral* geniculate body is known to act as a junction box for visual nerve fibres en route to the cortex.

Genital. Relating to the reproductive organs.

Genital character. Psychoanalytic term for an individual whose sexual evolution is, in psychological terms, complete. People reaching the so-called genital stage get their main sexual gratification from stimulation of the genital organs. Where this evolution has not taken place fully, a person is said to be fixated on anal or oral stages. (➧➧ ANAL CHARACTER; ORAL CHARACTER; PHALLIC PHASE.)

Genius. Someone with extremely high intelligence. People scoring over 150 on special IQ tests are generally assumed to lie in the genius class. They represent about two or three people in every thousand of the population. The word tends to be used also to indicate an individual of immense creative ability.

Genotype. The inherited characteristics common to a particular biological group. Contrast PHENOTYPE.

Gens. Anthropological term for a family group tracing their relationship through the male line.

Genus. One level in the classification of living things; usually a number of rather similar species. (➧ TAXONOMY.)

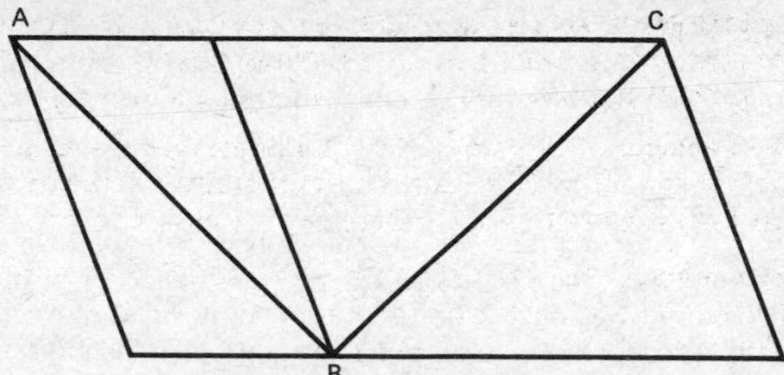

Figure 14. Geometrial illusion. In this figure, AB appears shorter than BC.

Geometrical illusions. Classic visual illusions in which lines or shapes are subject to perceptual distortion by some process in the brain. (➧➧ OPTICAL ILLUSION; ILLUSION.)

Geometric mean. Measure of CENTRAL TENDENCY used in preference to the ARITHMETIC MEAN where the logarithms of the measures are to be averaged (e.g. if one wishes to average a number of means which differ greatly but whose standard deviations are highly similar). It measures the mean ratio instead of the mean value.

Geotropism. Orienting response made by an animal as a result of gravity.

Geriatrics. The study of the diseases associated with old age.

Gerontology. The scientific study of all aspects of old age.

Gestalt. A completed form or figure; something which has unity.

Gestalt psychology. School or movement in psychology which arose in the first half of the twentieth century as a rival to the dominant Pavlovian behaviourist approach. The Gestalt school was founded by Wertheimer, Köhler and Koffka after experiments in visual perception had convinced them that perceptual phenomena were too complex and too subtle to be explained in terms of stimulus-response psychology.

Central to the school was their famous statement that 'the whole is something more than the sum of its parts'. For example, a collection of points of light will cause appropriate stimulation on the retinae and finally be perceived by the brain as a collection of light sources. But when these are arrayed in particular ways the brain perceives them as making up a square, a circle or whatever, although the *squareness* or *circularity* is not present in the dots themselves. The extra dimension – squareness, circularity – is clearly added by the brain, which seems to be striving to force some kind of order on the sensory input. In a series of brilliant experiments the Gestalt psychologists demonstrated time and time again that the brain is not a passive receiver of information (as behaviouristic psychology at the time assumed) but performed dynamic structuring of all input according to fairly definite, apparently universal rules.

Their contribution in this respect has never been challenged; but the weak point was their speculative theorizing on the nature of the mechanisms behind the brain's cohesive powers. Köhler and his colleagues were in fact strongly influenced by ideas from physics and hence they proposed the notion of electrical fields present in cortical nervous tissue which would act to mould sensory input along predictably physical lines. These FIELD THEORIES have now become unfashionable and, in any case, were exploded completely by the experimental work of LASHLEY. The most significant figure among the Gestaltists was probably Wolfgang KÖHLER, who extended Gestalt ideas into the field of learning and is particularly noted for his experiments on problem solving and insight in apes.

Gestaltqualität. That characteristic which gives a figure its unitary quality.

Gestation. The period between conception and birth.

Ghost. The supposed visual trace of a dead person. Victorian pioneers of psychical research made great efforts at photographing ghosts but the most likely explanation for honest reports of their existence lies in hallucinations and waking dreams.

Gifted. Refers to anyone with a high IQ at genius or near-genius level. The term is particularly used in connection with exceedingly bright children. Compare TALENT, SKILL and APTITUDE.

Gigantism. Abnormal growth of bones caused by an overactive pituitary.

Gland. Body organ which discharges substances either into the body (endocrine) or outside it (exocrine) – in this context 'outside' includes into the digestive tract. Endocrine glands control body chemistry in various ways, e.g. by pumping hormones into the blood stream at appropriate times. They are also known as ductless glands. The exocrine glands secrete material such as the tears, protective grease for the skin, digestive juices, etc.

Glans. The sensitive end of the penis or clitoris.

Glaucoma. Disease featuring a marked increase of pressure of the fluid within the eyeball; a major cause of blindness.

Glial cells. Cells found in enormous numbers in the brain and spinal column whose function may be related to the transmission of biochemical information. They are also called neuroglial cells.

Glioma. A brain tumour composed of GLIAL CELLS and one of the most common forms of brain tumour.

Global. Total; embracing a complete field.

Globus hystericus. Psychosomatic symptom in which the patient complains of a constriction or lump in the throat.

Glossolalia. Babbling in an imaginary or nonsense language; 'speaking in tongues', as in certain religious sects.

Glossopharyngeal nerve. The ninth cranial nerve, serving the tongue and upper part of the throat.

Glottis. The opening between the larynx and the vocal cords.

Glove anaesthesia. Loss of sensation in the hand and wrist, but not in any part of the forearm. The distribution of nerves is such that if sensation is lost in any part of the hand due to nerve damage anaesthesia must also extend to some part or parts of the forearm, and glove anaesthesia is an hysterical symptom.

Goal. Anything towards which an organism is striving. A goal may be purely physical and practical, such as food, or conceptual, such as the thought of food or some even more complex idea. Most psychological theories assume that all behaviour is goal-directed, either at the physical or ideational levels. (➧➧ DRIVE.)

Goal-directed behaviour. Any behaviour of an animal which can only be understood on the assumption that it is directed to a definable goal. (➧➧ MEANS-END EXPECTANCY.)

Goal gradient. Term used by HULL to describe the observation that an animal speeds up its activity as it nears a goal; also refers to the observation that when an animal is learning a goal-directed sequence, those aspects closest to the goal are the first learned.

Goal response. The response made which brings about the achievement of a goal – e.g. pressing a bar to receive a food pellet.

Golden section. If one divides up a symmetrical figure, an area or even a line, into two parts so that the ratio of the small to the larger is the same as the ratio of the larger to the *whole*, the effect is somehow aesthetically pleasing. This principle is known as the golden section.

Golem. Fictional clay monster brought to life by magic and which destroyed its creator. The word sometimes denotes a malevolent robot.

Golgi apparatus. Minute structures inside nerve cells containing RIBONUCLEIC ACID and believed to be important in cell maintenance.

Golgi-Mazzoni corpuscle. A specialized nerve ending believed to be sensitive to touch and pressure.

Gonads. The sex glands: testes in male and ovaries in females.

Gonadotropic hormone. Pituitary hormone stimulating the development of the GONADS.

Goniometer. Device for measuring angles or deviations from the upright.

Good continuation. Gestalt concept applying to any line which has 'continuity' even if it is part of a more complex or jumbled figure.

Good Gestalt. Any simple, 'neat' stable figure.

Goodness of figure. Principle formulated by the Gestalt psychologists which holds that a pattern will be perceived by the brain in the most stable and simple way possible. This is based on the typical observation that when a slightly irregular or distorted circle is viewed briefly or in poor illumination it is likely to be perceived or reported as a perfect circle. (⧫⧫ PRÄGNANZ.)

Goodness of fit. Statistical measure of how well a set of values correspond to their expected distribution. For example, the plot of IQ scores in a large population should resemble the bell-shaped NORMAL DISTRIBUTION CURVE. A goodness of fit test would measure how closely a particular sample of IQ scores matched the theoretical distribution.

Figure 15. Gottschaldt figures.

Gottschaldt figures. Simple patterns concealed in more complex ones, used in experiments on shape recognition, visual memory, etc. (⧫⧫ EMBEDDED FIGURES.)

Gradation methods. Methods used in psychophysics which rely on judgements made in equal steps; includes the METHOD OF LIMITS and JUST NOTICEABLE DIFFERENCE judgements.

Grade norm. An educational term referring to the average score expected in any particular class or grade.

Gradient. A regular change in variables, or on a measurement scale.

Gradient of effect. Refers to the observation made in studies of CONDITIONING and animal learning that any responses which are close in time to reward or reinforcement have a greater probability of occurring on subsequent occasions than those made more distant in time.

Gradient of reinforcement. The closer in time a particular response is to reward or reinforcement, the stronger or more durable such a response is likely to be.

Gradient of response generalization. After a particular response has been learned to a stimulus, that stimulus will also occasionally elicit somewhat different responses, though these will occur with a lower frequency; the most probable responses, however, are those which are more similar to the original response.

Gradient of stimulus generalization. When an animal has learned to respond to a particular stimulus, he will also make responses to rather similar stimuli; the strongest, most vigorous responses, however, will be those elicited by those stimuli most similar to the original.

Grammar. A set of rules which express the relationship between spoken or written words. The word is now acquiring special varieties of meaning within the context of PSYCHOLINGUISTICS.

Grand mal. Major epileptic seizure, involving loss of consciousness and muscular spasms.

Granular layer. The cerebral cortex consists of three layers of cells – the outer, molecular layer; a middle layer which contains the cell bodies of the Purkinje cells; and an inner layer, the granular layer, formed from medullated nerve fibres which pass from the grey matter to the central white matter, on which the granular layer rests.

Graphic language. Any communication using visual symbols. (⧫⧫ NON-VERBAL COMMUNICATION.)

Graphic method. ⧫ SCOPIC METHOD.

Graphology. The detailed study of handwriting in an attempt to deduce the writer's personality.

Graphomania. Abnormal urge to write, sometimes a characteristic of paranoid schizophrenia.

Grasping reflex. Automatic tendency for the fingers or toes to curl inwards when the palm or sole is touched. After about the fourth month of life these reflexes are abnormal.

Graves's disease. More commonly known as EXOPHTHALMIC GOITRE.

Green. The colour perceived when the retina is stimulated with light of approximately 500–550 nm wavelength.

Gregariousness. Tendency, apparently inherited, for animals to flock together and human beings to live in groups.

Grey. The transitional zone between black and white. The greys do not have hue, and differ only along the dimension of brightness. The word is sometimes used in neurophysiology as an abbreviation for the cerebral cortex (grey matter).

Grey matter. Masses of neurones in the brain and spinal cord with a characteristic grey colour.

Grey-out. Partial loss of consciousness caused by ANOXIA in which the visual field becomes grey.

Griselda complex. Psychoanalytic term for a father's wish to prevent his daughter from marrying and leaving him. (➧ JOCASTA COMPLEX.)

Grooming. Apparently instinctive behaviour patterns by which animals clean themselves or examine the fur or skin of others. Such behaviour has a practical function in removing parasites, but also plays a role in socialization and courtship behaviour.

Gross score. More commonly known as RAW SCORE.

Ground. Any visual pattern tends to be categorized by the brain into two components, the figure, which 'stands out' and is most easily memorized, and the ground, which has an identity but is more diffuse and less definable. (➧ FIGURE-GROUND PHENOMENON.)

Group. Two or more people united either by some common characteristic or purpose. The study of groups is, in fact, the essential subject matter of social psychology and sociology, and it is based on a number of fundamental observations of which the following are good examples:

1. An individual is likely to behave in a different way when he is a member of a group than when he is on his own.
2. A group is something more than simply the sum of its parts – in other words it has motives, goals, strategies, etc., which only appear once the group has been formed.

It is hard to establish who first drew attention to the importance of studying groups as entities in their own right and not simply as accumulations of people, but the American sociologist C. H. Cooley was a particularly influential pioneer. Cooley introduced the important distinction between 'primary' and 'secondary' groups. The former – sometimes called face-to-face groups – consist of individuals who have more or less continuous direct communication and interaction with each other, or at least the potential for this. The most fundamental primary group is of course the family, with small clubs, fraternities and so on being other examples. Larger groups in which communication between all members is intermittent at best are secondary groups.

Cooley's categorization is useful but of course limited, and much theory in this field has been devoted to establishing other methods of classification. These include, for example, membership and reference groups. The former, perhaps rather obviously, refers to a group of which an individual is a member; the second to a group whose aims, goals or ideals the individual may aspire to even if he is not a member of it. Groups may also be organized or unorganized, structured or unstructured and, most obvious of all, large or small.

Large groups, perhaps because they tend to be diffuse, are extremely difficult to study continuously and carefully, and very little is known about their dynamics of interaction. Consequently the small group has tended to be the focus of most twentieth-century sociology (small groups, incidentally, correspond fairly closely to Cooley's primary groups, the main conditions of their existence being that members must have the opportunity to communicate with each other and that they must be bound by some common objective or ideal). While the early work of Levine on small group dynamics held out much promise in the 1930s, there is a general feeling today that progress has been a little disappointing. However, small group study has drawn attention to the importance of such factors as leadership and thrown up such concepts as NORM, ROLE, status, conflict, etc. There have also been many useful studies on the advantages and disadvantages of group as opposed to individual attempts at problem solving.

Group behaviour. Activities or behaviour patterns which characteristically appear in a group of people but which are less frequently observed in individual members of the group.

Group cohesiveness. The tendency for a group to resist, by one means or another, forces which seek to disintegrate it.

Group dynamics. The principles that govern the behaviour of groups, the interaction between its members and in particular such factors as its goals and leadership. Compare SOCIAL DYNAMICS.

Group experiment. An experimental study involving a large number of subjects in which individual results are generally totalled and averaged.

Group mind. Concept once used to explain the peculiar unitary behaviour of crowds and in particular flocks of birds, armies of ants, etc. The term has now been largely discarded by psychologists and ethologists.

Group norm. ➧ NORM.

Group test. Any test designed to be administered simultaneously to a large number of people. The first intelligence tests were designed for group administration.

Group therapy. Any attempt at psychotherapy of a group of patients together, usually with one or more therapists as group leaders. Behind the theory of group therapy lies the assumption that hearing other patients detail their problems may have a cathartic effect. (⧫⧫ SENSITIVITY TRAINING.)

Growth curve. A graph of the rate at which something grows, plotted against time.

Guessed mean. A rough and ready method for establishing the MEAN of a set of values by picking the one closest to the middle of the distribution.

Guidance. In psychology, any attempt at moulding another person's behaviour along generally acceptable lines, e.g. offering advice on jobs, child rearing, marriage difficulties, etc.

Guiding fiction. Term used by ADLER to refer to an individual's concept of himself, which serves to determine his conduct and behaviour. In the normal person the guiding fiction is close to reality, but in the neurotic and psychotic the real and idealized selves are separated.

Guilt. An emotional state occurring when an individual believes that he has violated some important moral or social law. In psychoanalysis it is supposed to arise as the result of a conflict between the SUPEREGO and the EGO, with the former punishing the latter as the result.

Gustation. The sense of taste.

Guthrie, Edwin R. (1886 – 1959). American behaviourist who attempted to develop a theory of learning which was independent of the traditional principles of reward or reinforcement. His ideas served as a basis for later statistical or 'probabilistic' models. (⧫ STATISTICAL LEARNING THEORY.)

Guttural. Relating to sounds made by the throat.

Gynandromorphism. Hermaphroditism; bisexuality.

Gynandry. Tendency for a female to have male physical characteristics.

Gynephobia. Abnormal fear of women.

Gyrus. A fold on the surface of the cerebral cortex.

H

Haab's reflex. Simultaneous contraction of the pupils when a light is fixated in a dark room.

Habit. In its simplest form, a learned response; may also mean a learned drive such as in drug addiction.

Habitat. The natural environment of a plant or animal.

Habit deterioration. Childish or infantile behaviour which sometimes occurs in deteriorating psychoses.

Habit family hierarchy. A phrase coined by HULL to refer to the mechanism by which animals select one response in preference to another when in a complex environment. The most likely response in any situation will be the one that heads the 'habit family hierarchy'; if this is blocked, number two in the hierarchy is elicited, etc.

Habit pattern. A collection of different habits which together constitute a more elaborate but coordinated 'super habit'.

Habit strength. Phrase used by HULL to refer to the extent to which a particular habit had been learned.

Habituation. When an animal is repeatedly exposed to a stimulus which normally elicits a response – say an eyeblink to a flashing light – after frequent exposures to the stimulus the response will become progressively weaker and may vanish. This is known as habituation and, while clearly a form of learning, is discriminated from it because its effects are less permanent. For example, the eyeblink will return in due course if the subject has a period when he is not exposed to the light flash. The term drug habituation refers to the condition resulting from repeated consumption of a drug with little or no tendency to increase the dose, although there is a desire to continue taking it.

Habromania. Abnormal elation or gaiety.

Haemotophobia. Abnormal fear of blood.

Hair aesthesiometer. Device, normally a hair on the end of a spring, used to test sensitivity on various points of the skin. The amount of compression of the spring before pressure or pain is felt is used as a measure of sensitivity.

Hair cells. Sensory cells with hair-like endings found in the inner ear, where they may act as sound receptors, or in the SEMICIRCULAR CANALS, where they may act as motion detectors.

Hallucination. Vivid experience, predominantly visual but which may occur in any sensory mode, which does not have any obvious eliciting stimuli or trigger points in the external world. Hallucinations may be so vivid as to be mistaken for objective 'reality'. (⧫⧫ ILLUSION; HYPNAGOGIC IMAGE.)

Hallucinogen. A drug such as LSD or mescaline which acts on the central nervous system in such a way as to promote hallucinations.

Hallucinosis. A chronic illness or disease featuring frequent hallucinations. The most common examples are certain schizophrenic psychoses and alcoholic hallucinosis.

Halo. A luminous ring around something; a light radiating from the head denoting spiritual power.

Halo effect. Sociological term for a common error in interviewing and job selection. If a candidate gives an extremely satisfactory answer to his first question or has one outstanding trait, the interviewers tend to be unreasonably biased towards him in subsequent questions. On the other hand, if the first answer is extremely unsatisfactory one gets what is known as the reverse halo effect. Compare INTERVIEWER BIAS.

Hammer. One of the tiny bones (or AUDITORY OSSICLES) in the middle ear, also known as the malleus.

Hampton Court Maze. Famous bushy maze at Hampton Court Palace. The first mazes designed to test rat learning ability were scaled-down copies of it. (⧫ MAZE.)

Handedness. Tendency to use one hand rather than another.

Handicap. Any deficiency, mental or physical, which makes it difficult for an individual to compete with others of his age.

Handwriting scales. Special tests, not particularly successful, which attempt to determine measurable personality characteristics by a coded analysis of handwriting.

Haphalgesia. Abnormal tendency to feel pain when the skin is touched gently.

Haploid. Refers to cells with half the standard number of CHROMOSOMES, in particular the sperm and ovum cells.

Haptic. Relating to the tactile sensitivity of the body surface.

Haptometer. Device for measuring cutaneous sensitivity to touch.

Hard colours. Reds and yellows. They are called hard because they are subjectively the most sharply discriminated from greys of equal brightness.

Harmonic. Relating to the combination of tones into chords. The term also refers to an overtone whose frequency is a multiple of the basic tone.

Harmonic analysis. The breakdown, by some technique such as Fourier analysis, of a complex wave pattern into simpler components.

Harmony. A collection of things or events which blend into an aesthetically satisfying whole.

Harp theory. ➧ RESONANCE THEORY.

Hartley, David (1705–57). British philosopher who founded the Associationism movement and made a determined attempt to employ physiological data in his theorizing.

Hashish. The narcotic drug Indian hemp or *Cannabis sativa*. The word is the Arabic for herb. (➧➧ MARIJUANA.)

Hauser, Caspar. ➧ CASPAR HAUSER.

Hawthorne effect. Memorable sociological study performed at the Hawthorne Electrical Works which showed that workers increased their output, largely unconsciously, when they were being studied. (➧➧ SOCIAL FACILITATION.)

Headship. ➧ LEADERSHIP.

Healy Picture Test. Test suitable for young children in which a partial picture must be completed by selecting from a number of possible shapes.

Hearing theories. A number of attempts have been made at providing theoretical explanations for human hearing, all of which have something useful to say but none of which are totally satisfactory. As a general rule they can be categorized into three groups, with the best known in each case given in brackets:

1. Resonance (Helmholtz) (➧ RESONANCE THEORY).
2. Frequency (Rutherford) (➧ FREQUENCY THEORY).
3. Volley (Wever and Bray) (➧ VOLLEY THEORY).

A more recent, HYDRAULIC THEORY has been put forward by Max Meyer.

Heat. Not the same as warmth. Technically heat is only experienced when both warm *and* cold receptors fire simultaneously and the sensation might be likened to warmth with a degree of pain.

Hebb, D. O. (1904 –). Outstanding Canadian psychologist whose major influential work is the book *Organization of Behaviour*. Published in 1949, this work introduced a hypothetical neural model which showed that the gap between the observations and theories of the Gestalt and Behaviourist schools could, in principle, be bridged. (➧FRACTIONATION; RECRUITMENT; PHASE SEQUENCE; CELL ASSEMBLY.)

Hebephrenia. A common form of SCHIZOPHRENIA which usually starts before the age of twenty. It is characterized by thought disorders, emotional disturbances and behaviour caricaturing that of some adolescents, such as silliness, unpredictable giggling and posturing.

Hebetic. Relating to PUBERTY or ADOLESCENCE.

Hedonic. Relating to pleasure.

Hedonism. Philosophy which argues that the prime purpose of life is the pursuit of pleasure and the avoidance of pain. Compare PLEASURE PRINCIPLE.

Heidegger, Martin (1889 –). German philosopher largely responsible for the evolution of existential psychology. He taught that man can only achieve real happiness when he comes to terms with the inevitability of his own death.

Helicotrema. Opening in the basilar membrane of the cochlea of the inner ear where the scala tympani and the scala vestibuli meet.

Heliotropism. Tendency for an organism to orient itself in response to a light source, especially the sun. It is synonymous with PHOTOTROPISM.

Helix. The curved outline of the outer ear.

Heller's disease. Degeneration of cerebral neurones in infants of three to four years old, leading to loss of speech. It is also known as dementia infantilis.

Helmholtz, Hermann von (1821–94). Remarkable German physiologist and physicist who applied his great talents to the study of the human sensory system and who developed sophisticated theories of colour vision and auditory perception. (➧ YOUNG-HELMHOLTZ THEORY; RESONANCE THEORY.)

Hemeralopia. Word which, unfortunately, has come to mean both day and night blindness. It should technically refer to day blindness, a condition, generally caused by deficiencies in the cones, when the eyes see poorly in the light but reasonably well in the dark. Compare NIGHT BLINDNESS.

Hemi-. As a prefix means half or one-sided.

Hemianaesthesia. Loss of sensation on one side of the body.

Hemianopia. Loss of vision in one half of the visual field. It is generally caused by brain damage.

Hemiplegia. Paralysis of one side of the body.

Hemisphere. One of the two symmetrical lateral halves of the CEREBRUM or of the CEREBELLUM.

Hemispherical dominance. ➧ CEREBRAL DOMINANCE.

Hepatic. Relating to the liver.

Heredity. The process by which characteristics present in parents are combined in the course of reproduction and transmitted in 'shuffled form' to the offspring.

Hering after-image. When a light is flashed briefly and the eyes are closed one perceives a brief visual sensation of the same colour and brightness as the original. The Hering after-image is followed by the PURKINJE AFTER-IMAGE.

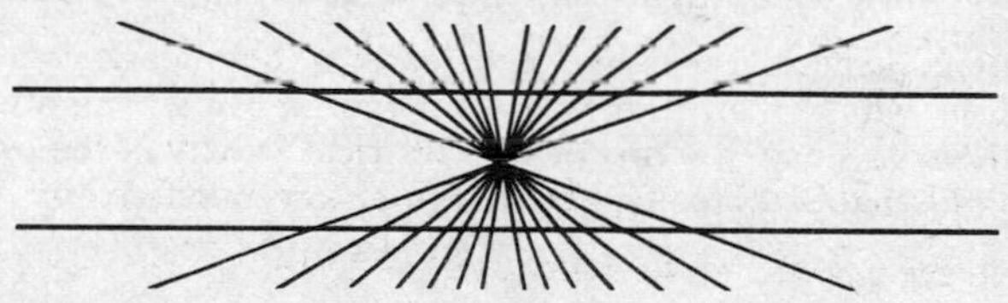

Figure 16. Hering illusion.

Hering illusion. Classic OPTICAL ILLUSION in which two parallel lines are seen as curved when they are interposed over a series of radiating lines.

Hering's theory. Attempt by the physiologist Edward Hering to explain COLOUR VISION in terms of three types of receptors – red/green, blue/yellow and black/white.

Heritage. All biological characteristics transmitted by parents to their offspring. The term also refers to cultural factors retained over a long period within a society.

Hermaphrodite. An individual possessing both the male and female sex organs.

Heroin. Extremely addictive narcotic derived from morphine.

Herpes zoster. Inflammation or lesion of the skin associated with a virus infection of particular nerves. It is popularly known as shingles.

Hertz (Hz). Internationally agreed term for cycles per second.

Hetero-. As a prefix, means other, different.

Heterodox. Concerning opinions and beliefs differing from the normal or standard.

Heterogeneous. Made up of lots of different components. Contrast HOMOGENEOUS.

Heteromorphic. Differing from the normal in shape.

Heteronymous. Directed or ruled by some other person or thing.

Heterosexual. Relating to sexual attraction for the opposite sex.

Heterotropia. ➧ STRABISMUS; squint.

Heuristic thinking. Relates to mental processes which are directed at problem solving, particularly by attempting to develop novel or original strategies. By this definition human beings are capable of heuristic thought, as presumably are some of the higher animals.

Heymans' law. The threshold for a particular stimulus goes up in proportion to the intensity of any simultaneous inhibiting stimulus.

Hibernation. Special sleep-like state featuring a dramatically reduced metabolism which many animals undergo in winter months. The similarities with sleep in terms of the electrical activity of the brain are few and hibernation is really a period of enforced inactivity.

Hidden figure. ➧ EMBEDDED FIGURE.

Hierarchy. Any organization in which control spreads downwards with all lower levels being subordinate to the ones above. The term is also used in behaviour therapy to describe a set of gradually increasing fear-provoking stimuli.

Hieroglyphics. Picture writing.

Higher brain centres. A vague term which may either refer to the cerebrum and its numerous control centres or to those centres in the brain dealing with the 'higher' functions, such as learning, thinking, memory, etc.

Higher mental processes. Group term for cerebral functions involving thinking, memory, etc., rather than those involving muscular control, autonomic activity, etc. (➧➧ COGNITION.)

Higher-order conditioning. Special type of CLASSICAL CONDITIONING in which the conditioned stimulus in one set of trials becomes the unconditioned stimulus in another. For example, when a dog is trained to salivate to a buzzer (conditioned stimulus), if a light is then flashed at the same time as the buzzer is sounded without any further reward or reinforcement, the light on its own will come to induce salivation. This 'cross-conditioning' link was called higher-order conditioning.

Higher response unit. A complex unitary act (say typing a letter) which is itself made up of a number of lesser acts.

High-grade defective. Obsolete American term for a person of low IQ (in the range 50–70) who can nevertheless perform simple tasks without much supervision. (➧ MENTAL RETARDATION.)

Hilgard, Ernest R. (1904 –). American psychologist interested in educational methods and learning. He is the author of a noted introductory textbook on psychology.

Hindbrain. The cerebellum, the pons and the medulla. (➧ BRAIN.)

Hippocampus. A neural bundle deep in the cerebrum, vaguely shaped like a seahorse. It is believed to be concerned with the sense of smell.

Hippus. Major oscillations of the pupil.

Hirsutism. Abnormal growth of body hair.

Histamine. Substance found in animal tissue which causes dilation of blood vessels and smooth muscle contraction.

Histogram. ➧ BAR CHART.

Histology. The study of the structure of biological tissue.

Hobbes, Thomas (1588 – 1679). Great English philosopher who realized that mental life is largely made up of sensory experience.

Holergasia. A severe psychosis which involves the whole personality, for example schizophrenia.

Holism. The belief that it is meaningless to attempt to explain behaviour in terms of a series of simple, discrete acts. It generally contrasts with the behaviourist view. (➧➧ GESTALT PSYCHOLOGY.)

Holmgren test. Test for COLOUR BLINDNESS in which the subject has to compare different threads of wool.

Holography. Intriguing optical development in which three-dimensional images can be created by passing light from a laser through photographic film. It is a curious feature of holograms that they can be recreated in whole – though with a slight loss of definition – when only a section of the original film is activated by the laser. Possible parallels with the memory system of the brain have led to recent attempts at developing holographic theories of memory.

Homeopathy. Ancient but now outdated medical system which relies on the principle that 'like treats like'. Treatment involves administering microscopic doses of a substance which, in greater doses, would cause symptoms similar to those of the disease to be treated.

Homeostasis. The maintenance of balance or equilibrium within a complex system. The body is a system which strives to maintain a constant state and contains a number of homeostatic subsystems, e.g. the mechanism of temperature control.

Homing. The tendency for an animal to seek out and return to its home. Many animals, such as pigeons, exhibit unusual homing powers which were once thought to provide evidence for some form of extra-sensory perception. In the past decade homing mechanisms have become more clearly understood and few ethologists now feel the need to consider ESP in this context.

Homogamy. In-breeding in an isolated population group.

Homogeneity. Tendency for similar qualities to appear amongst individual members of a group. In statistics the term also means the extent to which a single variable is measured by a test.

Homolateral. On or of the same side; ipsilateral.

Homologous. In anatomy refers to organs which have a rather similar structure but which perform a different function, e.g. a bat's wing and a man's hand.

Homosexuality. Sexual behaviour with a member of the same sex.

Homozygous. Containing two GENES of the same type.

Honi effect. The fact that the AMES ROOM and similar illusions lose their effect when the human in the picture is known to the viewer.

Horde. Sociological term for a large group which stays together over a longish period.

Horizontal group. People drawn from the same stratum of society but who may occupy different positions. Compare VERTICAL GROUP.

Horizontal-vertical illusion. OPTICAL ILLUSION in which a vertical line seems to be longer than a horizontal line of objectively the same length. It is also known as the T-illusion.

Hormic psychology. Any theory which leans on the notion of PURPOSE in explaining behaviour. The most powerful protagonist of such theories was William MCDOUGALL.

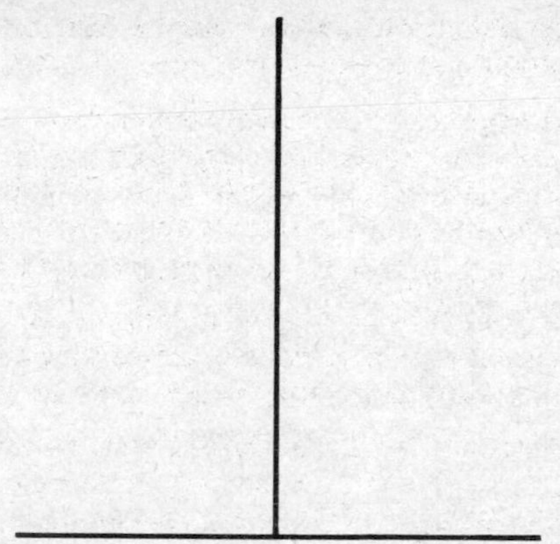

Figure 17. Horizontal-vertical illusion.

Hormone. Chemical released into the blood by an ENDOCRINE GLAND to increase or damp down activity in another part of the body.

Horner's law. States that red-green COLOUR BLINDNESS is transmitted from male to male through the female.

Horney, Karen (1885–1952). Leading psychoanalyst who developed her own modification of FREUD's theories, and in particular rejected his emphasis on the significance of disordered sexuality in determining neuroses.

Horopter. Elusive concept in optics. It amounts to an imaginary map of those sections of the visual field which, when fixated by the two eyes, stimulate CORRESPONDING POINTS in the two retinae.

Horoscope. The position of the planets, stars, etc., at the moment of someone's birth. It is the key point in the pseudoscience of ASTROLOGY.

Hue. Perceived colour; determined by the wavelength of light striking the retinae.

Hull, Clark L. (1884 – 1952). Influential American behaviourist who attempted to describe and predict animal behaviour in terms of simple equations and postulates. Central to his theory was the idea of habit strength (${}_{s}H_{r}$), which was a measure of the degree to which a stimulus response connection had been learned. This was supposed to be a mathematical product of the number of reinforcements, the extent to which a drive had been reduced at the time the task was learned, etc. Hull's system looked superficially complicated but it was actually over-simple and in retrospect can be looked upon as a gallant rather than a useful attempt at providing a mathematical explanation of behaviour.

Human engineering. The study of man and his work environment. (➧ ERGONOMICS.)

Humanistic psychology. Current trend in psychology, much influenced by Carl ROGERS, which stresses that the central goal of psychology should be for man to achieve an understanding of himself. Psychoanalysis and behaviourism are assumed to have become too academic and detached from real human problems. Quite recently the movement has been pressing psychologists to take a more active role in politics and in instigating social change.

Hume, David (1711–76). Scottish philosopher whose *Treatise on Human Nature* put forward the revolutionary view that mind has no reality outside memory, sensation and emotion.

Hunger. Craving for something that one is deprived of.

Huntington's chorea. Progressive and degenerative hereditary disease of the nervous system.

Hybrid. The offspring of parents of different species.

Hydraulic theory. Meyer's theory which attempts to explain hearing on the basis that different tones are produced by the activation of different lengths of the basilar membrane. (➧➧ HEARING THEORIES.)

Hydrocephalus. Abnormal collection of cerebrospinal fluid within the skull, often accompanied by enlargement of the skull. It may involve permanent mental retardation.

Hydrophobia. The disease rabies; literally, fear of water.

Hydrotherapy. Any treatment involving water, but generally prolonged hot or cold baths.

Hydroxytryptamine. More commonly known as SEROTONIN.

Hygiene. Establishing and implementing rules for preventing sickness.

Hyoid. Bone near the larynx to which the tongue muscles are attached.

Hypacusia. Reduced sensitivity to sound.

Hyper-. As a prefix means increased, above, beyond or excessive: e.g. hyperalgesia – increased sensitivity to pain.

Hyperaesthesia. Increased responsiveness of the senses.

Hyperglycaemia. Excessive blood sugar, generally caused by diabetes.

Hyperkinetic. Relating to abnormal muscular activity or motor restlessness.

Hypermania. An extremely excited state characteristic of the peak of a manic-depressive psychosis.

Hypermnesia. Abnormally good memory.

Hyperopia. Far-sightedness; contrast PRESBYOPIA.

Hyperphagia. Excessive eating.

Hyperpituitarism. Abnormal activity of the pituitary gland leading to various diseases including GIGANTISM and ACROMEGALY.

Hyperplasia. Abnormal increase in number of cells.

Hyperpnoea. Excessive, deep and rapid breathing.

Hyperprosexia. Inability to shift one's attention from a particular stimulus or thought.

Hypersexuality. Exaggerated sexual activity.

Hypersomnia. Abnormal desire to sleep.

Hypertension. Abnormally high blood pressure.

Hyperthymia. Excessive emotionality, a feature of some mental illnesses.

Hyperthyroidism. ➧ EXOPHTHALMIC GOITRE.

Hypertonia. Abnormal muscle tension.

Hypertrophy. Abnormal growth of a body organ.

Hypnagogic image. Vivid visual or auditory image, amounting almost to an hallucination, which occurs on the point of falling asleep. Such images are probably caused when the dream mechanism is activated before sleep has been fully established. (➧➧ HYPNOPOMPIC.)

Hypnic. Relating to or causing sleep.

Hypnoanalysis. Form of psychoanalysis in which HYPNOSIS is used as an aid to removing defence mechanisms.

Hypnogenic. Sleep-inducing.

Hypnoidal. Relates to a state which resembles the hypnotic trance.

Hypnopaedia. The technical name for sleep learning. Despite a good deal of enthusiasm for the idea of sleep learning, generally based on the assumption that sleep is a 'waste period' when the brain may as well be put to useful work, the experimental evidence that information can be usefully stored during anything other than the shallowest stages of sleep is questionable.

Hypnopompic. Relates to the dreamy half-state following sleep before full awakening. (➧➧ HYPNAGOGIC IMAGE.)

Hypnosis. A major topic of interest and also controversy in psychology. Hypnosis was originally assumed to be a force which was the biological equivalent of electro-magnetism and was largely brought to public attention by the work of MESMER and later Charcot. Freud was also deeply interested in the curious, apparently detached mental state of hypnotized patients and at one time believed that it might offer the key to the elimination of many mental disorders.

Despite the fact that no one has ever properly defined hypnosis, hypnotic techniques have been employed in a great array of applications, including surgery without general anaesthesia, therapy in anxiety states or minor mental disorders and, at the most bizarre and pseudoscientific level, in 'age regression' studies supposedly providing evidence for pre-natal memory or even reincarnation.

Although hypnosis is a legitimate medical and psychological phenomenon, it is still surrounded by much superstition and ignorance. At the present time the topic, which has been bathed in the glow of scientific approval for the past few decades, is now attracting critical and sceptical attention again. It is pointed out, for example, that the electroencephalogram of someone in a hypnotic trance bears little relationship to that of the EEG of a sleeping individual, which raises the question as to whether hypnosis is anything more than a peculiar state of attention, in which the hypnotized subject concentrates intently on the hypnotist's voice (to the exclusion of other stimuli) and shows an extreme readiness to obey his commands and play any role that he requires. It is possible that the next few years may see a major reappraisal of the mechanisms of hypnosis, leading to a more realistic assessment of its usefulness as a scientific tool rather than as a psychological curiosity. (◆◆ MESMER.)

Hypnotherapy. Approach to psychotherapy which features various hypnotic techniques.

Hypnotic. Anything inducing sleep, including sleep-inducing drugs.

Hypo-. As a prefix, means diminished or lowered. For example, hypoglycaemia is a condition of low blood sugar.

Hypochondria. Unusual concern about one's health.

Hypoglossal. The twelfth cranial nerve controlling the tongue muscles.

Hypomania. A mildly manic or excited condition.

Hypophysis. The PITUITARY.

Hypothalamus. Body lying just below the thalamus largely concerned with the regulation of temperature and various autonomic states.

Hypothesis. A theory which is sufficiently clearly stated to allow experimental testing.

Hypothetico-deductive method. A basic approach to science involving the observation of facts, the construction of a theory to explain them and the subsequent testing of the theory. Hypothetico-deductive thinking is sometimes used in the Piagetian sense of formal operational thinking. (➧ DEVELOPMENTAL PSYCHOLOGY.)

Hypothyroidism. Diminished activity of the thyroid producing cretinism in children and a lowered metabolism or myxoedema in adults.

Hysteria. A rather vague term used to denote neurotic conditions varying from the moderate to the severe, but not verging on psychosis. In the nineteenth century it was assumed to be exclusively a female condition, due to a malfunction of the womb (hysterus). In psychiatric theory there are a number of varieties of the illness, including anxiety, conversion and fixation hysteria. Psychoanalysts believe that all hysterical conditions are caused by unconscious mental conflicts.

Hysterical blindness. Loss of vision with no physical cause.

Hysterical paralysis. Partial or total paralysis with no obvious organic cause and assumed to be due to psychoneurotic conflict.

Hysteriform. Resembling hysteria.

I

Iatrogenic neurosis. An 'imaginary' illness brought on as the result of a doctor's suggestion or diagnosis.

Ich. German for EGO.

Icon. An image, idol or cherished idea.

Ictus. A stroke or epileptic fit.

Id. Term used by FREUD to denote one of the three major divisions of personality according to his theory of the mind. The id is almost exclusively unconscious and in simplified terminology consists of all the instincts and basic 'animal' desires present at birth. Id drives are purely concerned with self-gratification and are difficult to block or eliminate, particularly because they have no representation in consciousness. According to Freudian theory, mental disorders are largely caused by the conflicting demands of the id and the SUPEREGO, the latter being the various rules and regulations built into the mind by society and parental influence. (➧➧ EGO; PSYCHOANALYSIS.)

Idea. Thought or mental concept not necessarily triggered off by sensory experience.

Idealism. Philosophy that mind is more real and essentially superior to matter; also refers to the practice of working towards high standards.

Idealized image. Also known as 'idealized self'; a psychoanalytic term for the image that one has of oneself, which tends towards what one would like oneself to be rather than what one actually is.

Ideas of reference. Characteristic symptom of schizophrenia in which the patients assume that totally unrelated phenomena have some significance to them. For example, a peculiar cloud formation might be assumed to be a message from God.

Ideation. The forming of ideas.

Ideational learning. Learning in which there is a high measure of conscious comprehension of the topic to be learned; contrast ROTE LEARNING.

Idée fixe. Obsessive notion which persists despite evidence to the contrary.

Idée force. The principle that ideas are the starting point of any chain of action and themselves rise spontaneously.

Identical points. More commonly known as CORRESPONDING POINTS (in the retina).

Identical twins. Twins born as the result of the splitting of a fertilized ovum; also known as monozygotic twins. They are particularly interesting to psychologists because they share a common heredity. (➧ TWIN STUDIES.)

Identification. Recognition. In psychoanalysis the word has a special meaning when it refers to the DEFENCE MECHANISM by which an individual identifies with, empathizes with or copies another person with whom he has a strong emotional relationship. In social psychology identification with the nurturant figure is known as anaclitic identification, and when with a threatening figure is known as aggressive identification.

Identification test. Simple verbal test in which an object is pointed to and the subject asked to name it.

Identity. The self or personality.

Identity hypothesis. More commonly known as DOUBLE ASPECT THEORY.

Ideogram. A figure or symbol which represents an object or idea.

Ideokinetic apraxia. Disorder in which one is unable to carry out a *sequence* of movements, even though the individual actions are possible.

Ideological attitude level. Concept referring to the basic philosophy underlying any set of attitudes.

Ideology. An elaborate and detailed belief system.

Ideomotor. Relates to a response set in motion by an idea.

Idio-. As a prefix, implies individuality or personal possession.

Idiodynamics. The principle that human beings only relate or attend to those things in the environment which affect their personality.

Idioglossia. Unintelligble speech.

Idiographic. Relating to individuals, individual laws or unique events. Compare NOMOTHETIC.

Idiolalia. Invented speech.

Idiopathic. Relates to disorders which develop within the body and have no discernible external cause.

Idioretinal light. The vague grey sensation perceived even in total darkness and due to spontaneous retinal or optic nerve firing.

Idiosyncrasy. Unusual behaviour characteristic of an individual.

Idiot. Obsolete term for someone having an IQ of less than 25. Idiots would be incapable of learning and unable to look after themselves. The term is approximately equivalent to 'profound mental retardation'. (➧ MENTAL RETARDATION.)

Idiot savant. Someone who appears to be of subnormal intelligence in some respects and yet extremely superior in others. Most idiot savants are of basically subnormal intelligence but have learned a few impressive 'tricks' of memory. It is possible that many idiot savants of the past were really undiagnosed autistic individuals.

I/E ratio. The ratio of inspiration to expiration which changes during emotional states and is sometimes built in as a measure in polygraph LIE DETECTORS.

Illiteracy. Inability to read and write in someone over about the age of ten when not caused by mental deficiency.

Illumination. The amount of light falling on a surface; normally measured in units known as lux.

Illusion. A mistake in perception caused either by insufficient information being presented to the brain, or by conflicting cues being provided. All illusions have their trigger points in the external world, and can thus be discriminated from HALLUCINATIONS, which are errors of perception triggered by something within the individual. (➧➧ OPTICAL ILLUSION.)

Image. An internal mental experience associated with some previous perception or with memory. The term may also refer to a pattern of light projected through a lens on to a surface.

Imageless thought. Refers to any thought processes not apparently associated with sensation. There was considerable controversy in the nineteenth century as to whether true imageless thought could ever occur.

Imagery. All thought processes involving IMAGES.

Imagination. The process of creating novel thoughts or ideas.

Imago. Psychoanalytic concept referring to the idealistic memory that one has of some highly significant figure in one's past, such as a dead parent, which still exercises control over one's thoughts and feelings.

Imbecile. Obsolete term for someone with an IQ lying between 25 and 50. Imbeciles can rarely look after themselves. The term now more generally used is 'moderate mental retardation'. (➧ MENTAL RETARDATION.)

Imipramine. Anti-depressant drug.

Imitation. Copying of someone else's actions, whether deliberately or unconsciously.

Immaturity. Any state in which complete physical or psychological development has not been achieved.

Immediate memory. More commonly, SHORT-TERM MEMORY.

Immobility. In sociology refers to the state of being resistant to social pressures and change.

Immoral. Relates to anything transgressing moral codes. It is not the same as amoral, which is something outside the framework of reference of morality.

Impedance. The characteristics of an electric circuit which reduce the strength of a current in it.

Imperceptible. Relates to any discrimination which is below threshold.

Implantation. The attachment of the fertilized egg to the wall of the uterus.

Implicit behaviour. Any behaviour which cannot be observed directly or without instruments.

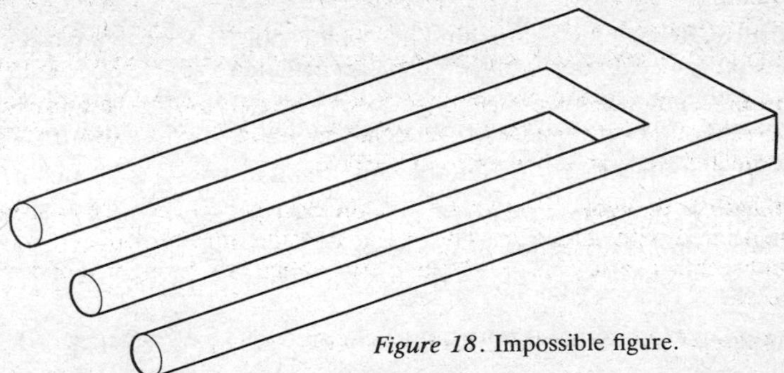

Figure 18. Impossible figure.

Impossible figure. A sketch or drawing which obeys graphic rules but which provides an impossible or contradictory perception. Compare NONSENSE FIGURE.

Impotence. Inability of the male to perform a complete sex act.

Impression. A general sensation or judgement; any mental response to a stimulus.

Imprinting. Phenomenon of great interest to ethologists, which features extremely rapid learning on the part of a very young animal. Imprinting is supposed to take place only during certain critical periods, to be related to some highly significant factor, such as the recognition of the mother, and once established to be irreversible. (◆◆ CRITICAL PERIOD.)

Impulse. A natural or instinctive act. Psychoanalysts use the word to refer to any behaviour initiated by the ID. The word also refers to the electrical activity of a nerve cell.

Impulsiveness. Tendency to act suddenly and without sufficient planning.

Impulsive neurosis. Mental disorder featuring powerful desires to perform particular acts; more commonly known as OBSESSIVE-COMPULSIVE NEUROSIS.

Impunitive type. Someone who tends to respond to frustration by rationalization or by denying that the frustration exists.

Inaccessibility. State of more or less complete lack of responsiveness occurring in the depths of some schizophrenic illnesses and in autistic states.

Inadequacy. General inability to cope. An inadequate personality generally refers to a social failure or misfit.

Inadequate stimulus. A stimulus which is not relevant to a particular receptor or sense organ but which is nevertheless capable of exciting it. For example, one can squeeze the eyeball and, by increasing intraocular pressure, cause retinal receptors to fire and give the sensation of light.

Inappropriate affect. Unsuitable emotional response, e.g. laughing at a tragedy.

Inattention. Fluctuation in the focus of attention.

Inborn. More commonly, INNATE.

Incantation. Verbal or musical ritual assumed to have a magical effect.

Incentive. Something acting outside the organism which serves to increase drive or focus effort towards achieving a particular goal.

Incest. Legal/social term referring to sexual relationships between people with close blood ties.

Incest barrier. Psychoanalytic name for the various taboos which prevent one from having sexual relationships with close members of one's family, particularly parents, and which ultimately lead to the direction of sexual attention to the 'outside' world.

Incest dream. Relatively common dream in which one is having sexual relationships with a member of one's family; considered to be highly important in psychoanalytic terms.

Incest taboo. Most societies prohibit, either by law or by moral sanction, sexual relationships between close members of a family – indeed in most societies the mere discussion of incestual relationships is considered to be improper. This group attitude is known as INCEST BARRIER.

Incidental learning. Learning which takes place without intention, and even without awareness that it is taking place. Arguments about the role of incidental learning were central to the famous CONTINUITY-NON-CONTINUITY controversy. It is similar to LATENT LEARNING.

Incidental stimulus. A stimulus which creeps into an otherwise controlled experiment and which may influence the interpretation of results.

Incipient. About to occur; related to the beginning of something.

Incoherence. State of being confused or disorganized. The term is used especially of speech.

Incommensurable. Relating to items which cannot be compared or measured by the same scale.

Incompatible. Not consistent; unable to work in harmony with something or someone else.

Incompatible response. A response which may be made at the same time but is not consistent with another response.

Incompetence. Legal term for someone mentally disturbed to the extent that they cannot be held legally responsible for their actions.

Incomplete-sentence test. Simple test of intelligence in which the subject has to fill in the missing words in a sentence. It is also a technique used in attitude assessment and personality assessment where subjects complete the end of a sentence.

Incongruous. Relates to something which jars with its surroundings. The term is also used for the dichotomy between the emotion and speech of some schizophrenics.

Incontinence. Lacking the power to prevent defaecation or urination; may also refer to lack of control of sexual impulses.

Incoordination. Lack of smooth control and balance, particularly in muscular movement.

Incorrigible. Incapable of correction.

Increment. When something is changing progressively, the rate of change is expressed in increments of some kind.

Incremental learning theory. Any theory which argues that learning takes place in a relatively smooth or gradual fashion rather than in a series of jumps or insights.

Incubation. Period of apparent mental inactivity when unconscious information processing is in fact taking place. (⧫⧫ INSIGHT.)

Incubus. A sexual nightmare. An incubus is a male demon who has sexual relations with the sleeper, sapping her strength as the result. The female equivalent is a succubus.

Incus. One of the auditory ossicles, more commonly known as the ANVIL.

Indecency. Behaviour, not necessarily sexual, which violates moral or social conventions.

Independence. Situation prevailing when two variables are apparently unrelated in any causal way. It is also used in social psychology to refer to a tendency not to rely on others for decision-making. Contrast DEPENDENCE.

Independent variable. The variable in an experiment which is controlled by the experimenter and introduced to study its effect on something else. In a study of the effect of a drug on learning, the drug is the *independent* or experimental variable, while the subject's performance on a learning test is the DEPENDENT VARIABLE. (⧫⧫ CONTROL.)

Indeterminism. Philosophy that humans are capable of independent action not determined by preceding circumstances. Contrast DETERMINISM.

Index. A sign or number used to mark a change or to denote some particular fact or value.

Indifference point. The moment when one sensation – such as heat – becomes indistinguishable from an opposing sensation – such as cold.

Indifferent stimulus. A stimulus, such as the buzzer in a conditioning experiment, *before* it has been converted into the conditioned stimulus; also known as neutral stimulus.

Indigo. The colour perceived when the retina is stimulated with light of approximately 440 nm wavelength.

Indirect vision. The generally indistinct vision which occurs when images are projected outside the fovea; also known as peripheral vision.

Individualism. The philosophy that argues that the individual is more important than society.

Individual psychology. May refer to that aspect of psychology which deals with the study of differences between individuals. More commonly it refers to the system of psychology developed by ADLER when he broke away from Freud, rejecting his emphasis on sexuality as the main spring of human motivation and replacing it with the notion of the drive to power.

Individual response. A rare or unusual response given in a WORD ASSOCIATION TEST.

Individual test. Test designed for administering to a single person, as opposed to a group.

Individuation. The process by which a unit fragments into independent parts. The word has a special meaning in Jungian psychology where it refers to the evolution of individual segments of the personality, such as archetypes, out of the vague, amorphous whole which is all that exists at birth.

Indoctrination. Any teaching devoted to implanting an idea without critical understanding. In contrast education stresses the comprehension and critical appraisal of learned material.

Induced colour. A perceived colour will often change in quality quite noticeably when another colour is placed alongside it, or when there are other changes in a neighbouring visual field. (◆◆ COLOUR CONTRAST.)

Induction. In physiology, neural activity set in motion by stimulation in a different part of the nervous system. In logic, the term refers to the process of inferring a likely conclusion after considering a set of observations or possibilities. Compare DEDUCTION.

Induction test. Form of intelligence test in which the subject is given a number of facts and invited to draw a conclusion from them.

Industrial psychology. The scientific study of man and his working environment; sometimes called occupational psychology. The first systematic investigations in this area began in the United States in the early part of this century, with the prime goal of increasing productivity. Later other goals, such as raising job satisfaction and improving communication between management and labour, came into being.

The first contributions of industrial psychologists included taking such 'obvious' steps as adjusting factory temperature to suit the workers, improving the design of tools, modifying shift systems and introducing rest breaks. They had dramatic effects on production – so dramatic in fact that staff cuts and lay-offs inevitably followed. The memory of these efficiency purges has lasted till the present day and has somewhat handicapped the industrial psychologist, who often has to face the suspicion of the workers whose output he is studying.

The topic has made relatively peaceful progress on a number of fronts, however, and can usefully be broken down under a number of sub-headings. These include *vocational guidance* (advising people on which jobs their particular abilities are most suited for), *personnel selection* (choosing, placing and training job applicants), *environmental modification* (optimizing shift lengths, working hours, lighting, temperature, background noise, etc.), *machine design and work study* (often known as ergonomics) and *social relationships* (worker/management cooperation, leadership choice, methods of supervision and so on).

Inertia. Resistance to change. In physiology the term relates to the lag that occurs in the response of a neural system to a stimulus.

Infancy. The first of the five DEVELOPMENTAL LEVELS, generally supposed to end with the acquisition of speech. The other four periods are childhood, adolescence, maturity and old age.

Infantile. Characteristic of infancy; any immature characteristics in an adult.

Infantile amnesia. People appear to have only limited memories of their life during infancy and psychoanalysts argue that this is because these memories are particularly prone to REPRESSION. It may also be argued that conscious memories only begin to be laid down with the acquisition of speech.

Infantile birth theories. The various strange theories that children develop about their birth, e.g. that they are born through the anus, the navel, etc.

Infantile paralysis. ➧ POLIOMYELITIS.

Infantile sexuality. Theory that infants and young children are capable of experiencing sexual pleasure. FREUD was heavily and emotionally criticized when he first put forward this proposition. He did not, of course, argue that children were capable of sexual behaviour characteristic of mature adults, but merely that diffuse sexuality, in particular the capacity to feel pleasure when erogenous zones were stimulated, was present at birth.

Infantilism. A reversion to infantile behaviour on the part of an older child or adult. The term sometimes refers to individuals who fail to mature physically.

Inference. Drawing a conclusion as the result of considering a number of previous conclusions.

Inferior. Markedly less than average. In anatomy, the term refers to the lower part of the body or of an organ.

Inferiority complex. A phrase coined by ADLER to refer to the condition associated with a personality which believes itself to be inadequate, unsuccessful or unable to cope with life. The complex does not arise when the individual realizes he is inferior, but as soon as his inferiority feelings make him begin to withdraw from the world in order to protect himself from further failures or evidence of his inadequacy.

Inferior oblique. A muscle which turns the eyeball upwards and outwards.

Infertility. Inability to produce live offspring.

Inflection. A modification of voice pitch.

Information. Facts, ideas or other data capable of collection and analysis.

Information theory. Attempt to quantify the concept of information and its applications which became important when scientists first began to tackle the problems of complex information processing devices, such as electronic computers. Information theory, which is highly mathematical in form, employs as its basic unit the chunk of information known as a bit, the latter being the amount of information required to state which of two equally likely events has taken place. Although the pioneers of information theory were engineers and mathematicians (Wiener, Shannon, Von Neumann, etc.) many of their ideas, such as signal-to-noise ratio, channel capacity, etc., have obvious application in the brain sciences.

Infra-. As a prefix, means below or lower.

Infraconscious. Obsolete expression for the UNCONSCIOUS.

Infrared. Refers to light with a wavelength greater than 760 nm.

In-group. A group of people sharing some common interest and resisting the intrusion of ideas or individuals from outside. Compare OUT-GROUP.

Inherent. Permanently present from the beginning; innate or instinctive.

Inheritance. Heredity; the characteristics passed on either through the genetic mechanism or through cultural systems.

Inhibition. Has a number of meanings in physiology and psychology, but generally refers to the blockage of one function by something else. In psychoanalysis, it specifically refers to the blockage, by the SUPEREGO, of 'unwanted' desires or impulses from emerging out of the unconscious into consciousness.

Inhibition of inhibition. More commonly, DISINHIBITION.

Inhibitory potential. Term introduced by HULL and represented in his mathematical system by $_{S}I_{R}$. This is a brief change in the state of an organism which occurs immediately after a response has been made and which acts to reduce the likelihood of the response being made again.

Initial spurt. The typical high level of output which occurs at the beginning of a phase of work or learning.

Initiation rite. Sociological term for any ritual or ceremony which is used to mark the transition of an individual from one phase of life to another. Anthropologists use the term *rites de passage*, and in this class circumcision ceremonies are particularly significant.

Initiative. Something which sets an act in motion.

Ink blot test. More commonly known as RORSCHACH TEST.

Innate. Present in an animal at birth. Innate behaviour patterns may not *develop* until, say, puberty, but the mechanism which ensures that they will occur at the appropriate time *is* present at birth. Congenital has the same meaning.

Innate releasing mechanism (IRM). Concept of importance in the study of animal behaviour. Ethologists have observed that animals will frequently make an automatic response when presented with a specific stimulus. For example, sparrows will exhibit characteristic flight and defence responses when shown the silhouette of a hawk or bird of prey. Such a response is supposed to be evidence of instinctive behaviour or an IRM. In the example above, the RELEASER setting the chain in motion is the silhouette.

Inner ear. The internal structure of the ear, including in particular the cochlea and the semicircular canals. (➧ EAR.)

Innervation. Neural input to something.

Input. Information or energy fed into a system.

Insanity. Legal rather than psychological term referring to a state of mental disorder so grave that the person cannot be held to be responsible for his actions.

Insensible. Unresponsive to stimuli.

Insight. Achieving a sudden, apparently instantaneous solution to a problem, characterized by perceiving relationships between different parts of the problem which had not been perceived before. Insight is a common subjective experience amongst humans, but there has been a good deal of controversy over whether animals were capable of it. Köhler's observations of insightful behaviour in chimpanzees (➧ AHA REACTION) seemed to demonstrate that it is not peculiar to humans and there is little controversy on the matter today. At one stage, however, the notion of insightful behaviour in animals was rejected by behaviourists because it seemed not to fit with Pavlov-Watson-type models of behaviour.

Insight therapy. Any approach to psychotherapy which holds that once the patient has gained an understanding of the true nature of his problems and the source of any conflicts, he has a significantly increased chance of becoming cured.

Insomnia. Chronic, rather than occasional, inability to sleep.

Inspiration. Technically the drawing of air into the lungs. The term also refers to the solution of a problem which comes instantaneously and apparently without effort.

Instability. Any behaviour which deviates unpredictably and significantly from the average or desired.

Instinct. A pattern of behaviour which does not have to be learned, the mechanism for which is supposed to be present at birth and which also appears in every individual member of a species. Delayed instincts are behaviour patterns not actually present at birth *as behaviour patterns*, but which reliably appear later in life after the appropriate maturation has taken place.

Instinctual. Impulsive. In psychoanalytic terms it refers to behaviour determined by forces stemming from the ID.

Institutionalization. The process of placing an individual in a special institution for therapeutic or corrective purposes.

Instruction. Teaching in a formal and systematized manner.

Instrumental learning. Learning in which the subject, by a particular act or behaviour pattern, directly brings about the reward or reinforcement. (➧ OPERANT CONDITIONING.)

Insula. ➧ ISLAND OF REIL.

Insulin. Hormone secreted in the pancreas which assists in the metabolism of carbohydrates. It is deficient in diabetics.

Insulin coma. Unconsciousness brought on by excessive insulin. The condition is sometimes deliberately induced in the treatment known as insulin shock therapy when it can, for reasons not clearly understood, relieve depression. ELECTROCONVULSIVE THERAPY is the much more common treatment. (⧫⧫ CONVULSIVE THERAPY.)

Integral. Related, in a meaningful way, to a complex whole. In mathematics an integral is the result of any integrative process.

Integration. The process of combining a series of different events or systems into a complex and organized whole. In psychoanalysis the terms primary and secondary integration refer to important phases in the evolution of the EGO.

Intellect. Broadly speaking the sum total of all the higher mental processes such as thinking, reasoning, perceiving relationships, etc.

Intellectualism. An approach to psychology which attempts to explain as many aspects of mental life as possible in terms of conscious cognitive processes and as few as possible in terms of emotional or instinctive behaviour.

Intellectualization. According to psychoanalysis, one of the mechanisms of ego defence in which individuals deny conflict situations by analysing them in cool, 'intellectual' terms.

Intelligence. One of the most important concepts in psychology and at the same time one of the least understood. The fact that all human beings differ from each other in terms of what might, very crudely, be described as 'brain power' is fairly obvious. Also, because of the wide range of tasks needed to run the world and the fact that some of these require more brain power than others, there has been much interest in measuring whatever it is that makes up this brain power. Hence INTELLIGENCE TESTS.

At the present moment intelligence is generally assumed to be a combination of a number of different aspects of the brain's computing powers, most, and possibly all, of which are present in undeveloped form at birth. How fully their potential is developed and exploited then depends upon the various environmental factors – nutrition, social background, education, etc. – which arise in the course of life. (⧫⧫ RACE.) A number of attempts have been made to establish these individual factors without a great deal of common agreement being achieved. It does, however, seem as though the essence of intelligence is a quickness of response to changes in the environment, the ability to scan a variety of solutions to any problem, and in particular the capacity to perceive new relationships between various aspects of any problem. It should be clear from this, incidentally, that intelligence, which might be summed up as 'versatility of adjustment', is something which is not only present in human beings but in varying degrees among any living beings capable of performing anything other than purely instinctive responses. (⧫⧫ INTELLIGENCE QUOTIENT.)

Intelligence quotient (IQ). IQ tests are attempts at measuring some of those rather ill-defined mental abilities which are assumed to be at least partly innate in the human brain. An IQ score is obtained by dividing the individual's MENTAL AGE (as measured by the tests) by his chronological age and multiplying the result by 100. The average IQ in a Western population is arbitrarily assumed to be 100 and the majority of individuals are found, on testing, to have IQs between 90 and 110. (⧫INTELLIGENCE; INTELLIGENCE TEST.)

Intelligence test. Test which attempts to assess human abilities in relation to their intellectual power. Such tests have purely practical goals and are geared on the whole to assessing those aspects of human mental ability that tend to be useful in society. Early tests were heavily biased towards cultural and verbal factors – reading ability, general knowledge, etc. Nowadays they tend to concentrate more on the ability to perceive relationships, the capacity for abstract thought and for finding novel solutions to problems. (⧫ NONVERBAL INTELLIGENCE.) IQ tests for children are generally rather different from those for adults as they deal with mental abilities which have only partially evolved. (⧫⧫ INTELLIGENCE QUOTIENT; INTELLIGENCE; ADULT INTELLIGENCE.)

Intelligible. Comprehensible; easy to understand.

Intensity. The strength of a subjective experience of some kind, whether it be of a light perceived, an emotion felt or an idea or belief held. It is not necessarily related directly to the strength of a stimulus at its source.

Intentional forgetting. Forgetting brought on by repression in the psychoanalytic sense or by a deliberate desire to push the thought from memory.

Intentionality. The aspect of consciousness which is itself conscious of something, or is directed towards some other thing.

Intentional meaning. ⧫ CONNOTATIVE MEANING.

Intentional movement. A brief movement of a tentative kind which often comes at the start of an elaborate set of movements.

Interactionism. Theory which holds that human behaviour can best be explained in terms of a two-way interaction between mind and body. It does not necessarily imply that mind and body are separate and distinct elements. (⧫ DUALISM.)

Interbrain. The DIENCEPHALON.

Intercalation. Automatic insertion of a word or sound in between other words to assist the flow of speech.

Intercourse. Two-way interaction between individuals or groups.

Interest. The act of maintaining attention on a particular problem or situation.

Interest inventory. Type of test often employed for vocational guidance which attempts to assess the subject's latent and manifest areas of interest, e.g. Strong Vocational Interest Blank.

Interference. Has two main meanings in psychology. Most commonly it refers to any aspects of a learning task which interfere with a previously learned task or disturb memories previously established. The term also refers to the change which takes place in the perception of sound or light when two waves of stimulation occur out of phase.

Interference tube. Conducting tube with numerous closed branches and tunnels used to produce pure tones out of a complex sound. The branching tubes eliminate the unwanted sounds by interference.

Interhemispherical fissure. The chasm separating the right and left hemispheres, a most striking single feature of the brain when seen from above.

Interjection theory. The theory that speech evolved out of simple automatic sounds such as grunts and cries.

Intermittence tone. More commonly known as INTERRUPTION TONE.

Intermittent reinforcement. ➧ PARTIAL REINFORCEMENT.

Internal consistency. A measure of the extent to which different parts of a test 'agree' with each other – i.e. are measuring the same variable. (➧➧ RELIABILITY.)

Internal environment. ➧ ENVIRONMENT.

Internal inhibition. Concept introduced by PAVLOV to account for the gradual reduction in the strength of a conditioned response which occurs once reinforcement or reward stops. He assumed a basic inhibitory process which always battles to prevent any permanent change within the nervous system.

Internalization. According to FREUD, the human personality is essentially divided into three parts, ID, EGO and SUPEREGO, only the former being present at birth. The superego is formed as the result of the incorporation into the personality of external motives, attitudes, rules and regulations. These stem from the outside world but are drawn into the personality and the process by which they move from the outside to the inside world is known as internalization.

Internal rectus. Extrinsic eye muscle which roates the eyeball inwards.

Internal reinforcement. Any change in bodily state which acts as a reward and assists learning.

Internal secretion gland. ➧ ENDOCRINE GLAND.

Internal senses. The senses involved in balance and muscular control.

Interneurone. Neurone connecting sensory and motor cells in the spinal cord.

Internal speech. Reading or speaking words 'in one's mind'.

Interoceptor. ➧ ENTEROCEPTOR.

Interocular distance. The distance between the pupils of the eyes.

Interpretation. In psychoanalysis, an attempt to explain the relevance and meaning of dreams and free associated ideas.

Interpretive therapy. An approach to psychotherapy in which the patient's difficulties and problems are explained to him and specific guidance given. Contrast NON-DIRECTIVE THERAPY.

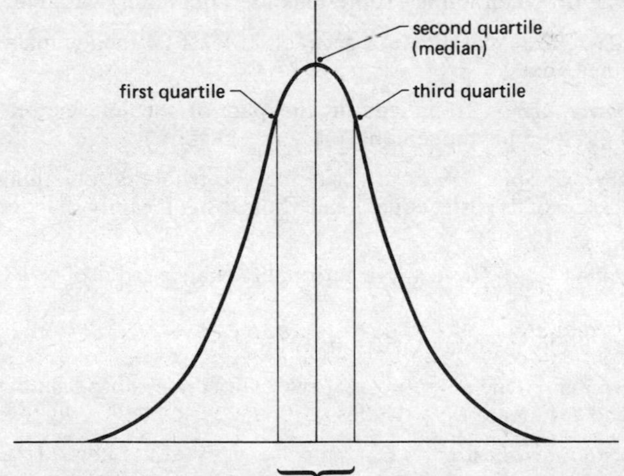

Figure 19. Interquartile range.

Interquartile range. Used as a measure of spread. Data plotted on graphs or tables are frequently divided into four quartiles, one quarter of the plotted values lying in each quartile. The interquartile range covers the territory of the second and third quartiles, comprising the central half of the distribution.

Interruption tone. Characteristic beat or wave sound heard when a tone of constant pitch is rhythmically interrupted. Sirens are a particularly good example.

Intersexuality. Possessing the characteristics of two sexes.

Interval. The space between two events or objects.

Interval of uncertainty (IU). The range of stimuli which fall between upper and lower thresholds established in a series of psychophysical trials.

Interval reinforcement. Reinforcement or reward presented according to a fixed or rhythmic schedule.

Interval scale. A scale commonly used in psychology which has no zero point but whose intervals are equal. (◆◆ RATIO SCALE; ORDINAL SCALES.)

Intervening variable. Hypothetical variable introduced in an attempt to explain what happens between STIMULUS and RESPONSE. For example, when an animal is presented with a repetitive situation as in a conditioning experiment and changes its behaviour as a result, the 'learning' or 'conditioning' represents the intervening variable.

Interview. Personal meeting between at least two individuals with a predefined goal.

Interviewer bias. Prejudices on the part of the interviewer which mould or cloud his judgement. (◆◆ HALO EFFECT.)

Intimacy principle. A GESTALT term. The whole is something more than the sum of its parts; equally the whole is significantly changed if any of its parts are altered.

Intoxication. Any detectable personality change induced by a drug or poison.

Intra-. Prefix meaning inside or within.

Intraception. One of MURRAY's personality dimensions, characterized by friendly, humanistic attitudes.

Intraocular modification. Distortions of a visual stimulus on the retina caused by the physical structure of the eye.

Intrapsychic. Refers to events taking place within the mind or personality, especially conflicts.

Intraserial learning. The learning of associations between items on a list.

Intrinsic behaviour. Behaviour specific to a particular organ or muscle, e.g. the eyeblink. It contrasts with EXTRINSIC behaviour, which can be performed in a variety of different ways, e.g. a ball may be moved with the hands or the feet.

Intrinsic eye muscles. The iris and the ciliary muscles.

Intrinsic motivation. Doing something because one enjoys it (e.g. solving a puzzle) rather than because of the end result. Contrast EXTRINSIC MOTIVATION.

Introception. The process by which an individual accepts and absorbs the goals and standards of a group. Compare CONFORMITY.

Introjection. In psychoanalysis the process of absorbing other people's ideas or personality traits and building them into one's own personality. Compare PROJECTION. The term also refers to the tendency to give inanimate objects some of the characteristics of living things, e.g. having pet names for cars.

Intropunitive behaviour. Self blame, punishment or feelings of guilt aroused in response to frustration. Contrast EXTRAPUNITIVE.

Introspection. The process of looking into one's own mind or personality.

Introspectionism. Approach to psychology which holds that the best strategy for studying the mind is introspection.

Introversion. One of the major personality types first proposed by JUNG and now generally agreed by clinical psychologists and psychiatrists to be a valid classification of human personality. The introvert tends to withdraw from social contacts, may lack self-confidence and is of a relatively passive disposition. The theory that introversion and extraversion constitute a major continuum of the personality has recently been elaborated by EYSENCK.

Introversion/extraversion test. Common and generally reliable questionnaire designed to classify people as introverts or extraverts. (➧ EYSENKL PERSONALITY INVENTORY.)

Intuition. Arriving at a solution without apparently thinking about it or preprocessing information. This is not a helpful psychological concept since it suggests that the solution has come from nowhere.

Intuitive stage. A subdivision of the pre-operational period in Piaget's theory of cognitive development, covering the period from four to seven years. (➧ DEVELOPMENTAL PSYCHOLOGY.)

Intuitive type. ➧ RATIONAL TYPE.

Invagination. A bend or fold in a surface, forming a sheath-like depression.

Invalid. Refers to a conclusion which does not follow logically from its premises. Psychological tests are said to be invalid when they fail to measure what they set out to.

Invariable colour. A colour which does not appear to change its quality when luminance is altered.

Invariance. Any resistance to change. The term also refers to the way in which an after-image appears constant in size no matter what background it is seen against.

Inventory test. A detailed test of the various factors making up a complex area such as personality or scholastic achievement. Through the test a 'profile' of a number of factors emerges.

Inverse square law. Energy falls off in proportion to the square of the distance of the receiver from the source.

Invert. A HOMOSEXUAL.

Investment. Psychoanalytic term for the process of charging a person or thing with emotional feeling or AFFECT.

Inviolacy motive. According to MURRAY, a basic human need to preserve a favourable image of oneself.

Involuntary. Relating to anything not wished or consciously felt.

Involuntary muscle. ➧ SMOOTH MUSCLE.

Involution. Technically the opposite of evolution; a step backwards in physical or psychological terms.

Involutional melancholia. Severe depression, accompanied by agitation and anxiety state, which can accompany the menopause or onset of middle age.

Iproniazid. A widely prescribed anti-depressant drug, withdrawn in the early 1960s because of its physiological side-effects.

Ipsilateral. On the same side.

Iris. The ring-like muscle around the pupil of the eye which contracts or expands in response to changes in light.

Irradiation. Spread of energy from one part of a system to another. There have been a number of attempts to explain the phenomena of learning and perception in terms of irradiation of nervous impulses from one part of the brain to another. The term may also refer to the exposure of tissue to radiation.

Irrational. Lacking a logical structure.

Irrational type. ➧ RATIONAL TYPE.

Irresponsibility. Legal term to describe the condition of an individual who cannot be found guilty because of his disturbed mental state.

Irreversibility. Principle that the neural message cannot travel 'backwards', i.e. from dendrite to axon.

Irritability. One of the three most basic characteristics of life forms – the capacity to react to stimuli. The other two are CONDUCTIVITY and CONTRACTILITY.

Ishihara test. Highly effective test for the most common forms of COLOUR BLINDNESS. The subject has to pick out a number against a complex background, where both figure and ground offer the same brightness and differ only in hue. Colour blind individuals learn, unconsciously, to name colours in terms of their brightness and are completely misled by the Ishihara pictures.

Island of Reil. Fold in the CEREBRAL CORTEX.

Islands of hearing. ➧ TONAL ISLANDS.

Islands of Langerhans. Insulin-secreting cells in the pancreas.

Iso-. As a prefix, means same or equal.

Isochronal. Equal in rate or frequency.

Isocortex. ➧ NEOCORTEX.

Isolation. The condition of being cut off from social contact. (➧➧ ALIENATION.) In psychoanalysis the term refers to the process of deliberately cutting off or denying a troublesome memory.

Isolation effect. Refers to the fact that an item in a series which is isolated or somehow different is often the best remembered in a learning task.

Isomorphism. Concept in GESTALT PSYCHOLOGY which held that there was a one-to-one correspondence between a stimulus and the perceptual fields it generated in the cerebral cortex. The concept was not particularly well-defined even by the Gestalt psychologists themselves and its usefulness today is arguable.

Isophilia. Pleasant emotions towards people of one's own sex.

Isotropic. A term used in optics to describe a transparent substance which transmits or refracts light in the same way at any point on its surface. More generally it means anything which has the same properties in whatever direction it goes.

Item difficulty. The difficulty of a particular feature of a test as measured by how often the feature is passed or failed.

Item validity. The accuracy with which a particular feature of a test measures what it is designed to.

J

Jacksonian epilepsy. Epilepsy in which convulsions are confined to one limb or on one side of the body, although they sometimes spread further.

Jackson's law. The principle that when disease attacks intellectual functions, the 'higher' or more 'advanced' are the first to be affected.

Jactation. Unusual restlessness or excessive body movement.

James-Lange theory. An approach to the understanding of emotions which is in fact a fusion of two independent theories put forward by the philosopher William James and the physiologist C. G. Lange. The argument is that emotions represent awareness of the body's automatic defence or arousal mechanisms. Technically therefore one should not say 'I run because I am afraid', but rather 'I am afraid because I run'. Contrast BARD-CANNON THEORY.

James, William (1842 – 1910). American psychologist and philosopher, particularly interested in emotion and the nature of consciousness. In 1890 he wrote *Principles of Psychology*, one of the first basic textbooks on the subject.

Janet, Pierre (1859 – 1947). Student of Charcot who became interested in hypnosis, hysteria, multiple personality and the like. He was a contemporary of FREUD, who was much influenced by their association.

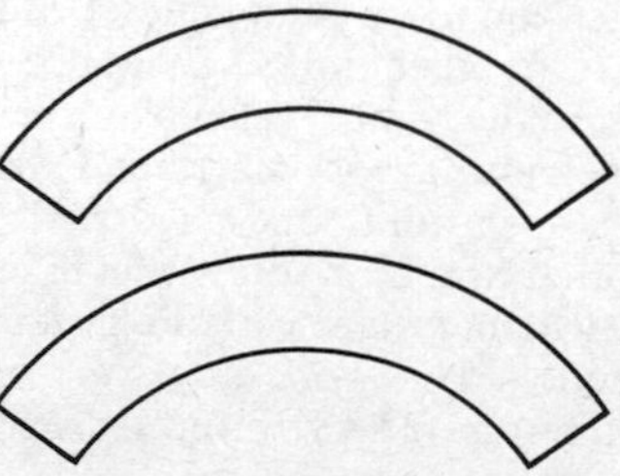

Figure 20. Jastrow illusion.

Jastrow illusion. When two identical ring sectors are placed one above the other, the upper appears smaller.

Java man. Early variety of fossil man found in Java, once known as *Pithecanthropus erectus* and now known as *Homo erectus*.

Job analysis. ➧ INDUSTRIAL PSYCHOLOGY.

Jocasta complex. Abnormal love of a mother for her son. (➧➧ GRISELDA COMPLEX.)

Jones, Ernest (1879–1958). British psychiatrist. He was a student and biographer of FREUD.

Jost's law. In learning where two associations of equal strength are reinforced, the older is more greatly affected by the reinforcement than the younger.

Judgement. The deliberate comparison of objects or events in order to perceive their relationship. The power to judge or make judgements is generally assumed to be one of the main features of any cognitive system, be it animal, man or machine.

Jukes family. Fictitious name given to an American family who were remarkable because of the high proportion of feeble-minded individuals amongst their blood kin. (➧➧ KALLIKAK FAMILY.)

Jung, Carl Gustav (1875–1961). Swiss psychiatrist who was an early colleague of FREUD, but who broke away in 1913 to form his own school of psychoanalysis – ANALYTICAL PSYCHOLOGY. Jung's ideas were far-reaching and controversial and are frequently attacked because of their supposedly mystical nature, but much of this criticism has been caused by a misreading or misinterpretation of his ideas. The concept of the COLLECTIVE UNCONSCIOUS is a particularly good example of a Jungian idea which is widely misunderstood. Jung was not proposing a 'group mind' in the metaphysical sense of the word, but simply pointing out that human behaviour, conscious and unconscious, is strongly affected by our evolutionary past and racial experience – in other words that instincts may deal with subtler and more fundamental collective behaviour patterns than eyeblinks or knee jerks. Evidence of these 'intellectual instincts' can be seen in the archetypal imagery revealed through artistic experience, dreams, hallucinatory states and the like. (➧ ARCHETYPE; SYMBOLISM.) Jung's open-mindedness led him to take an interest in almost every odd corner of human study from flying saucers to astrology, but it is hard to say whether these catholic tastes blunted or sharpened his overall contribution. His work however is currently enjoying a marked revival of interest. (➧➧ SYNCHRONICITY; RATIONAL TYPE.)

Just noticeable difference (jnd). The minimum difference between stimuli which a subject can report 'as a difference' 50 per cent of the time.

Juvenile. Relating to youth, and particularly to someone of school age. In legal terms a person is a juvenile until he or she attains the age of majority.

K

Kallikak family. Fictitious name for an American family, remarkable because of its two branches, one of which had a high average IQ and a record of good citizenship, while the other tended towards mental deficiency and criminality. (⧫⧫ JUKES FAMILY.)

Kanner's syndrome. Also known as early infantile autism. It is a syndrome generally present at birth in which the child, while physically healthy and apparently intellectually normal (or even above), is in fact abnormally unresponsive and physically withdrawn from others. Language development is severely retarded, though signs of high intelligence – in particular well-developed psychomotor skills and an advanced interest in music – are present. The cause of this syndrome, often classed as a psychosis, is unknown. The prognosis seems to be highly dependent on whether the child can be induced to master speech by his or her fifth or sixth year.

Kappa effect. ⧫ TAU EFFECT.

Keeler polygraph. Commercial lie detector. (⧫⧫ POLYGRAPH.)

Kent-Rosanoff test. Free association test featuring 100 stimulus words and a table of the most frequently observed responses to them.

Keratoscope. Device for measuring the curvature of the cornea and assessing ASTIGMATISM.

Kernel of truth hypothesis. Concept in the study of prejudice and stereotyping. This hypothesis seems to suggest that many prejudicial judgements had at one time a factual basis which has been lost.

Key. System for coding or decoding a test.

Kierkegaard, Sören (1813–55). Danish philosopher considered to have been the founder of EXISTENTIALISM.

Kinaesthesis. The sense or senses involved in the perception of muscle position and movement. The term can also include the sense of balance mediated by the inner ear mechanisms.

Kine-. As a prefix, denotes movement of some kind.

Kinephantom. Any ILLUSION in which moving shadows are seen. The most common example is the apparent 'backwards rotation' of the spokes of a wheel when seen on a movie film.

Kingdom. ➧ TAXONOMY.

Kinsey report. One of the first serious sociological studies of human sexual behaviour.

Kinship. Anthropological term for family relationship.

Kjersted-Robinson law. The amount of information learned in equal fractions of learning time is constant for different lengths of material.

Klang association. ➧ CLANG ASSOCIATION.

Klein, Melanie (1882–1960). One of the major figures in the modern psychoanalytic movement. She was a pioneer of child psychoanalysis and play therapy.

Kleptolagnia. Sexual excitement gained from stealing.

Kleptomania. Compulsive desire to steal.

Klinefelter's syndrome. Disease caused by the individual having an extra CHROMOSONE – forty-seven instead of the normal forty-six – and featuring changes in the primary sex characteristics. Contrast TURNER'S SYNDROME.

Klüver-Bucy syndrome. Psychic blindness, or failure to recognize common objects. The condition was first described in monkeys who had suffered damage to the temporal lobes. The complete syndrome also includes loss of fear and rage reactions and hypersexuality.

Knowledge of results. Information given to a subject in an experiment indicating whether his response is correct or incorrect. This is known to facilitate learning. (➧➧ FEEDBACK.)

Knox Cube Test. Test for mental deficiency or brain damage in which the subject has to tap a series of cubes in a particular sequence.

Koffka, Kurt (1886 – 1941). One of the pioneers of the Gestalt movement and author of *Principles of Gestalt Psychology*. (➧ GESTALT PSYCHOLOGY.)

Köhler, Wolfgang (1887–1967). One of the major figures in twentieth-century psychology and a pioneer of the Gestalt movement. Köhler is particularly well-known for his experiments in visual perception and also for his studies of the intellectual processes of primates. His book *The Mentality of Apes* aroused considerable controversy when he argued that chimpanzees have 'insightful' behaviour. (➧➧ AHA REACTION.) He also performed a number of imaginative neurophysiological experiments in an attempt to demonstrate the presence of cortical electrical fields – a prime postulate of Gestalt theory. (➧ GESTALT-PSYCHOLOGY.)

König cylinders. Metal cylinders emitting very high frequency tones used in pitch determination experiments.

Korsakov's syndrome/psychosis. A disorder of memory and consciousness, most commonly induced by chronic ALCOHOLISM.

Korte's laws. Laws relating to the perception of APPARENT MOVEMENT and in particular the phi phenomenon.

Kraepelin, Emil (1856 – 1926). Psychiatrist and one-time student of WUNDT. He was one of the first people to formulate a classification of the psychoses.

Krafft-Ebing, Richard (1840 – 1903). German psychiatrist and a pioneer in the scientific study of sexual behaviour.

Krause end bulb. Anatomically distinct nerve ending believed to be involved in the detection of cold stimuli.

Kretschmer, Ernst B. (1888 – 1964). German psychiatrist who attempted to trace a relationship between personality characteristics and body type, classifying individuals as schizothymic/asthenic, cyclothmic/pyknic and barykinetic/athletic. The classificatory system had a passing vogue in psychiatry, but as with most other CONSTITUTIONAL THEORIES (e.g. SHELDONIAN THEORY) its influence has waned.

Kundt's rules. The principles that (a) divided distances seem greater than undivided ones, and (b) when attempting to bisect a horizontal line in monocular vision, one tends to place the bisecting point too close to the nasal side of the eye.

Kurtosis. The degree of flatness of a frequency curve near the modal point.

Kymograph. A rotating drum used as a recording device in psychological experiments.

L

Labile. Free and flexible.

Laboratory experiment. An EXPERIMENT conducted in a controlled environment, at a time to suit the experimenter and to conditions determined by him. It generally contrasts with FIELD STUDIES or with 'informal experiments.'

Labyrinth. The part of the inner ear containing the cochlea, the vestibule and the semicircular canals.

Labyrinthine sense. The sense of head position and body movement.

Lacuna. A brief gap in memory or consciousness.

Ladd-Franklin theory. Theory of colour vision based on four primaries, red, green, yellow and blue.

Lag. The period between the cessation of a stimulus and the cessation of its effect.

Laing, Ronald D. (1927 –). A controversial figure in the 'new psychiatry' movement of the 1960s. Attacking traditional psychiatric methods and ideology, Laing's work has ranged from the experimental use of LSD in psychotherapy to a questioning of various long-held assumptions about the nature of mental illness. (◆◆ EXISTENTIAL PSYCHIATRY.)

Laissez-faire group. Sociological term for a group with a passive, non-dominant leader.

Lallation. Infantile, or unintelligible speech.

Lamarckianism. A theory of evolution which holds that characteristics acquired in an animal's life can be transmitted through the genetic structure to its offspring. Lamarckianism was almost totally overthrown by the alternative Darwinian approach. (◆ ACQUIRED CHARACTERISTICS.)

Lambert. A unit of brightness of reflected light.

Lambert's law. The intensity of a reflected light varies in accordance with the cosine of the angle of the rays perpendicular to the surface.

Land effect. Demonstration of full colour perception using only red and white light. The demonstration requires photographing a scene with a red and then with a green filter, and then projecting the two pictures through red and 'white' filters to form a fused image. The interest of the effect lies in the fact that it is not easily explained by the more common theories of COLOUR VISION.

Landolt circles. Circles with small gaps in them used as tests of visual acuity.

Language. In its widest sense, any set of symbols used for communication purposes. Traditionally, the word refers to verbal and written communication, and in this sense is assumed to be specific to human beings. But this usage ignores other important areas such as communication between animals – the so-called 'food dance' of the bees being a good example – and more recently, communication between man and computer or even computer and computer. What does distinguish human language from animal language (if not from computer languages) is that it seems to be almost infinitely variable and that there appear to be no aspects of human life which cannot be described or expressed in human language or some modification of it. Animal languages (such as the bees' dance) in contrast, tend to be specific to a particular topic or very limited domain. Again, there may be exceptions to this rule, for recent experiments in the United States suggest that chimpanzees may be able to learn and even build up a very 'human-like' general-purpose language using, for example, AMERICAN SIGN LANGUAGE as a basis.

Among the most interesting aspects of language is the question regarding its development in children. No human being inherits the ability to speak any individual language but all humans inherit the capacity, and even apparently a *drive*, to learn one. Babbling sounds occur in all normal infants within the first few months of life, the first meaningful word normally coming at about one year and brief sentences between eighteen months and two years. Theories of the origins of the universal acquisition of a spoken language began with the assumption – widely held in the nineteenth century – that there was a universal grammar underlying all human speech and that individual differences were due to national or cultural factors. These ideas fell out of favour as being vaguely mystical but have been revived unexpectedly, largely due to the work of the philosopher Noam CHOMSKY, who argues powerfully that *all* human languages have a common deep structure, the essence of which is innate. Chomsky's theories are still a matter of controversy, but they have attracted increasing support since their first exposure in the 1950s. (➧➧ NONVERBAL COMMUNICATION.)

Language centres. Sections of the cortex concerned with all language function, of which the best known is probably Broca's speech centre.

Language universal. Structural property common to all natural languages – e.g. every language has some way of expressing a question or implying a negative. (➧ PSYCHOLINGUISTICS.)

Laplacian curve. ➧ NORMAL DISTRIBUTION curve.

Lapsus linguae. A slip of the tongue.

Largactil. ➧ CHLORPROMAZINE.

Laryngograph. Device for recording movements of the larynx during speech.

Larynx. The organ containing the vocal cords.

Lashley, Karl Spencer (1890 – 1958). American psychologist with a brilliant experimental record. He is perhaps best known for his studies of perception and learning in the rat and in particular for his finding that a learned habit was not located in any particular segment of the cortex but appeared to be distributed evenly throughout it. (➧ MASS ACTION.) His paper 'In search of the engram', which gives an account of his fruitless attempts to identify any physiological MEMORY TRACE, is a highly readable classic.

Latency. The period between the onset of a stimulus and the onset of a response.

Latency period. Psychoanalytic term for the phase of life between infancy and puberty when there is supposed to be little if any interest in sex.

Latent. Hidden or dormant.

Latent content. Term used by FREUD to refer to the hidden or true material of a dream, as opposed to the manifest content, which relates to the describable 'obvious' aspects of a dream. The latent content is supposed only to be revealed through one of the techniques of psychoanalysis. (➧ DREAM INTERPRETATION.)

Latent learning. Learning which takes place incidentally to a task, and which is not at first detectable in performance terms. For example, animals trained to perform a particular task in a particular situation absorb stray information about the situation which they can later put to use if and when it becomes relevant. There was a good deal of surprise among experimentalists when latent learning was first demonstrated, but it would in fact be surprising if it did *not* occur. The term is similar in meaning to INCIDENTAL LEARNING.

Lateral. Relating to the side of something.

Lateral dominance. Tendency for one side of the brain to be dominant.

Lateral fissure. Also known as the Sylvian fissure; a deep cleft which divides the temporal lobe from the frontal and parietal lobes. (➧ CEREBRAL HEMISPHERES.)

Lateral geniculate body. ➧ GENICULATE BODIES.

Laterality. Sidedness.

Lateral thinking. A term introduced by Edward de Bono to refer to any attempt at problem solving which deliberately rejects the normal, direct pathway. The method is successful because it frequently leads to a restatement of the problem, thus allowing a solution which would previously have been considered to be inapplicable. Compare DIVERGENT, CONVERGENT THINKING.

Latin square. Standardized experimental design providing a specific trial for each experimental condition, each subject being exposed to every condition and in a different order.

Law of effect. THORNDIKE's principle which states that a stimulus response connection is weakened when the consequences are unpleasant and strengthened when they are pleasant. The circularity of the law of effect becomes apparent if it is examined closely.

Law of exercise. Principle put forward by THORNDIKE that if an act is repeated it is more likely to be learned than one which is not – all other things being equal.

Law of recency. Other things being equal, the best remembered items or events are those most recently experienced. Compare PRIMACY LAW.

Lay analysis. Psychoanalysis practised by someone not medically qualified. Freud always argued that the prime qualification for a psychoanalyst was a thorough training in the principles of the analytic method itself.

Leader. Someone who takes authority within a social group. The attributes of leaders, the mechanism by which they assume their role and the reaction of other members to their authoritarian control are part of the study of GROUP DYNAMICS. A good leader is, of course, not merely someone capable of ordering other people around but rather should first be able to understand the goals of the group he is to command, secondly be able to convince the group that he does understand these goals, and thirdly be able to channel the group's efforts into achieving them.

Leadership. An important role in any group is that of leader. Leadership is the performance of those acts which help the group to achieve its preferred outcomes. Not to be confused with *headship*, where the 'guiding hand' is imposed from outside the group.

Learning. The acquisition and subsequent storage of information by an animal in a way that allows it to modify its behaviour in the future. Learning needs to be distinguished from MEMORY, which is the *act* of storage or the storage mechanism itself, and REMEMBERING, which is the process of bringing the learned information out of store. All animals with any degree of complexity in their nervous system are capable of learning, and in the case of mammals, and primates in particular, the learning powers are sufficiently developed to allow enormous flexibility and adaptability of behaviour. Learning is one of the major areas of investigation in modern psychology and is the centre of a good deal of theoretical controversy. The simplest theories of learning are those based on Pavlovian conditioning, but modern approaches emphasize cognition and invoke cybernetic and mathematical models of considerable sophistication.

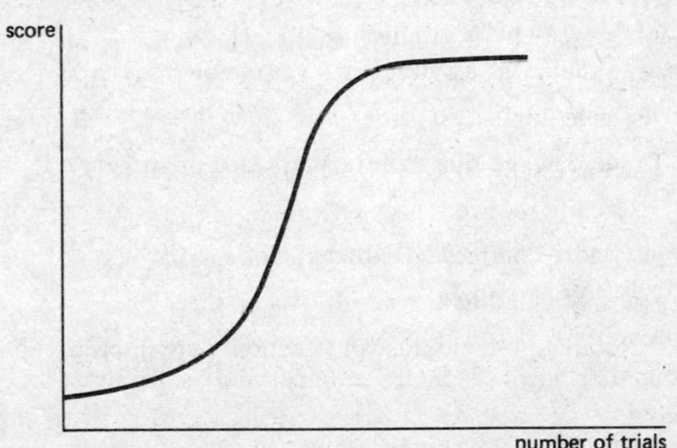

Figure 21. Learning curve.

Learning curve. The characteristic curve revealed when performance in a learning task is plotted against time. The most common form is S-shaped (ogive), denoting a slow improvement in early trials, followed by a notable acceleration, which is in turn replaced by a flattening of the curve or 'plateau'.

Learning theory. Any approach to formulating the rules or principles of learning in man and animals.

Learning to learn. The acquisition of skills which themselves seem to facilitate subsequent learning. (♦♦ FORMAL DISCIPLINE.)

Learning types. Individuals characterized by their different approaches to learning, some being dominated by visual imagery, others by verbal skills, etc.

Least effort principle. States that animals tend to follow the easiest possible path to a goal.

Least noticeable difference. More commonly JUST NOTICEABLE DIFFERENCE.

Least squares method. Mathematical formula for finding the best fitting curve of a given kind for a set of data.

Leiter Performance Test. Nonverbal test for intelligence using colour, picture matching, etc., and supposed to be valid for people from different cultures.

Lens. The flexible transparent structure in the front of the eye which, by changing its convexity, can bring an image into sharp focus on the RETINA.

Leptomorph. ➧ BODY BUILD INDEX.

Leptosome. Someone of slender build. The term is also used in KRETSCHMER's theory as a synonym for asthenic body type.

Lesbian. Female homosexual.

Lesion. Tissue damage due to injury, disease or surgery.

Lethargy. Greatly reduced activity.

Leucotomy. More commonly FRONTAL LOBOTOMY.

Level. A rank attained as the result of a test.

Levellers. Refers to individuals who generally are unprepared to tolerate ambiguities, inconsistencies or uncertainties. Contrast SHARPENERS.

Levelling. The tendency for memories to become simplified with the passage of time.

Levelling effect. When a repeated series of measurements are made of a particular phenomenon or experiment, individual peculiarities and extremes tend to drop out – as a result of practice or some other factor – and the measurements become clustered around the MEAN.

Level of aspiration. The general GOALS which an individual sets himself in life.

Levitation. The apparent raising of objects or people into the air by supernatural means.

Lewin, Kurt (1890 – 1947). American psychologist best known for his work on child psychology and for his attempt to develop a Gestalt-type field theory of motivation and learning. (➧ FIELD THEORIES.)

Libidinal development. The growth and evolution of the LIBIDO which passes through the phases of oral, anal and genital eroticism. It is a Freudian concept.

Libidinal object. The focus of attention of the LIBIDO: may be an object or person.

Libido. A word of considerable significance to psychoanalytic theory which has acquired subtle shades of meaning because of the way it has been used by different theoreticians. FREUD originally used it to refer to sexual energy which he took to be the main driving force of human nature. He later expanded its scope to cover all kinds of psychic energy, but its most common usage today is to denote sexuality. Both JUNG and ADLER disagreed with Freud on the significance of the libido and developed rival concepts of motivation.

Libido damming. Blocking the evolution and development of the LIBIDO.

Librium. A common tranquillizing drug promoting muscle relaxation.

Lie detector. Device for monitoring one or more aspects of the action of the autonomic nervous system – heart rate, respiration, electrical resistance of the skin, etc. Marked changes take place in such activity during emotional states, including the moment when a 'significant' lie is being told. (♦ POLYGRAPH; GALVANIC SKIN RESPONSE.)

Life. Property shared by plants and animals and marked by three main characteristics – IRRITABILITY, CONDUCTIVITY and CONTRACTILITY.

Life goal. A term introduced by ADLER to refer to the need to overcome feelings of inferiority which he believed to be the primary motivating force in human behaviour, and which he offered as an alternative to the Freudian concept of libidinal energy.

Life instinct. In psychoanalysis, the desire to preserve and reproduce oneself. It is also known as Eros. Contrast DEATH INSTINCT.

Life lie. Adlerian term for any 'excuse' or rationalization offered up by an individual to account for his general failure to succeed in life. (♦♦ DEFENCE MECHANISM.)

Life plan. Adlerian term. Humans wish to succeed in everything that they do but there must inevitably be some failures. To prevent these from damaging the ego or personality they construct an elaborate set of DEFENCE MECHANISMS to excuse or deny evidence of the failure.

Life space. A term used by LEWIN to refer to all forces, psychological or physical, acting on an individual at any one time. (➧➧ FIELD THEORIES.)

Light adaptation. The DAMPING response made by the eye to increased illumination. It includes narrowing of the pupil and increased activity of the cones.

Light induction. When one part of the retina is stimulated by light, simultaneous changes may occur in other sections of the retina or even in the other eye. These in turn may affect perception.

Likert scale. A test in which the subject indicates whether he agrees or disagrees with particular attitudes or statements using a three or five point scale.

Limbic system. Important group of structures within the cerebrum believed to be involved in generating emotional states and basic drives.

Limen. A THRESHOLD.

Liminal. Relating to a threshold; at or above a threshold.

Liminal sensitivity. The lower limits of sensory acuity.

Liminal stimulus. A stimulus just capable of provoking a relevant response.

Limits method. ➧ METHOD OF LIMITS.

Linear. Relating to a straight line or continuous processes.

Linear correlation. When the relationship between values on a graph can easily be represented by a straight line, this is called a linear correlation. The degree of correlation is measured by the coefficient of correlation (r).

Linear operational model. A statistical theory which attempts to explain the learning process as representing a series of random samplings of the environment by an organism. A learned pattern of behaviour gradually builds up with repeated samplings. (➧ STATISTICAL LEARNING THEORY.)

Linear perspective. The apparent differences in the perceived size of objects at various distances.

Linear regression. A relationship between two variables whose values produce a straight line when plotted on a graph.

Linear system. Any system in which input and output have a more or less direct relationship.

Line of direction. The line of sight from an object to the nodal points of the eyes viewing it.

Line of regard. The straight line from the centre of the viewing eye to an object being viewed.

Lingual papilla. Tiny folds or protuberances on the tongue containing the taste buds.

Linguistic relativity. Refers to the theoretical view that the language we speak in fact colours our perceptions of the world around us.

Linguistics. The study of language.

Linkage. The tendency for specific characteristics to be linked together in the genetic mechanism.

Lipids. Fatty acids and other fat-soluble substances which are a major chemical component of the brain.

Lip key. Device for detecting lip movements and thus voice reaction time.

Lissajou's figures. Closed figures which are produced when a beam of light is reflected off mirrors attached to the prongs of two tuning forks vibrating in perpendicular planes to each other.

Little Albert. Young boy, experimental subject of J. B. Watson, in whom a phobia of white rats was induced by CLASSICAL CONDITIONING, and subsequently eliminated by similar techniques.

Little Hans. A child patient whom FREUD cured of a phobia of horses through psychoanalysis.

Lloyd Morgan's law. In interpreting the behaviour of an animal one should first seek to explain it in terms of lower functions before proceeding to higher ones. For example, before suggesting telepathic powers as an explanation for pigeons' homing abilities, one should first eliminate the possibility of more simple navigational skills. The principle is also known as Morgan's canon. (⧫⧫ OCCAM'S RAZOR.)

Loading. The degree to which a test correlates with a factor.

Lobe. The round part of any organ and in particular a major protuberance of the brain.

Lobectomy. Removing a lobe of any organ or gland.

Lobotomy. ⧫ FRONTAL LOBOTOMY.

Local excitatory state. The initial response when a neurone is stimulated, consisting of an increased negative potential on the neural membrane.

Localization. Identifying the source or origin of something; in neurophysiology, attempting to identify which parts of the brain perform which functions.

Local sign. Whatever it is that allows one to be able to distinguish one sensory experience from another in space.

Locke, John (1632–1704). English philosopher who put forward the suggestion that the mind of a newborn babe was a blank tablet (*tabula rasa*) and thus devoid of all sensory experience. Until his proposal it was generally assumed that most ideas and thoughts were innate.

Locomotor ataxia. *Tabes dorsalis*: a disease of the spinal cord with resulting loss of the ability to walk.

Locus. Place or position.

Logarithmic curve. Curve in which every value of one coordinate is the log of the value of the other coordinate.

Logarithmic mean. More commonly GEOMETRIC MEAN.

Logarithmic scale. A scale in which the units are measured in logarithms rather than the basic numbers.

Logic. The study of the rules of correct thinking and reasoning.

Logical positivism. An important school of philosophy which rejects all metaphysical statements and argues that one can only study what one can define operationally. In psychology, the behaviouristic school has been influenced by the logical positivist approach.

Logomania. ➧ LOGORRHEA.

Logorrhea. Excessive and generally rambling speech, associated with some psychoses.

Lolopathy. Any speech disorder.

Long-term memory. Permanent as opposed to temporary or SHORT-TERM MEMORY.

Longitudinal study. Observations of individual or group behaviour over an extended period of time.

Looking-glass self. A term particularly used by Cooley to indicate one's self-image as based on the opinions and reactions of other people. (➧➧ SELF-IMAGE.)

Lordosis. Concave or hollow back. The term also refers to the automatic arching of the back in female animals when sexually stimulated.

Lorenz, Konrad (1903 –). Pioneer ethologist who introduced and popularized the concepts of IMPRINTING and INNATE RELEASING MECHANISMS.

Loss. Has a special meaning in social psychology where it refers to the psychological shock or sense of unease felt when a child is deprived of regular maternal contact. (➧ ATTACHMENT.)

Loudness. The intensity of a sound.

Low-grade defective. American term for a mentally subnormal person requiring institutionalization and with an IQ of less than 50. (➧ MENTAL RETARDATION.)

Lucidity. Mental clarity; also refers to a period of clear thinking on the part of a usually mentally disturbed person.

Lumbar. Relating to the middle region of the back.

Lumbar puncture. Tapping cerebrospinal fluid from around the spinal cord in the lumbar region.

Lumen. The unit of LUMINOUS FLUX.

Luminance. Transmitted light energy.

Luminosity. The relative brightness of a light source – not the same as LUMINANCE.

Luminous flux. The perceived flow of light past an observer.

Lunacy. Obsolete term for insanity.

Luria, A. R. (1902 – 1977). Leading Soviet psychologist well-known for his work on the development of the brain and the effects of brain damage.

Lustprinzip. The PLEASURE PRINCIPLE – Freudian term.

Lux. The unit of illumination or the amount of light thrown on to a surface.

Lycanthropy. The superstitious belief that a man can change himself into a wolf.

Lymph. Body fluid derived from the blood and containing substantial amounts of protein. Lymph flows through lymphatic ducts, eventually reaching the venous blood circulation.

Lymphatic temperament. Obsolete term for someone of sluggish mood and disposition.

Lysergic acid diethylamide (LSD). An hallucinogenic drug producing bizarre mental symptoms in many ways comparable to those experienced in psychoses. It is a PSYCHOTOMIMETIC drug.

M

Mach, Ernest (1838 – 1916). Austrian philosopher, physicist and experimental psychologist who was also a pioneer of the logical positivist movement.

Machiavellism. Personality trait characterized by ruthless pursuit of personal goals, if necessary at the expense of other members of society.

Machine language. Set of symbols – normally in a binary or 'machine code' – used to act as instructions or programs for computers.

Machine theory. Any theory which attempts to explain the general principles of machine operation, but in particular one which considers human and animal behaviour in mechanistic terms.

Macrocephaly. Having an extremely large head. This is a congenital condition caused by excessive cerebrospinal fluid, and usually accompanied by mental deficiency. Contrast MICROCEPHALY.

Macrocosm. The universe or society viewed 'as a whole'.

Macropsia. Tendency to see objects as larger than they should be, due to some physical disorder of the eye.

Macroscopic. Viewed 'as a whole'.

Macrosplanchnic. Body build featuring an unusually large trunk in proportion to limb size.

Macula acoustica. Tiny cluster of hair cells found in the utricle and saccule in the inner ear, whose function is not properly understood but which is probably related to sense of balance.

Macula lutea. The central portion of the human retina, largely made up of the FOVEA. It is also known as the yellow spot.

Maddox rod. Device used for testing muscular imbalance of the eye.

Magic. Any attempt to understand or control the universe by the use of supernatural powers or formulae. Magical theories may be logically self-consistent but themselves at odds with scientific knowledge. Compare SUPERSTITION, RELIGION.

Magical thinking. Refers to childlike beliefs that there is a direct causal link between one's wishes and the world around one. Magical thinking is seen in children and psychotics.

Magna Mater. Jungian term for the ARCHETYPE image of the universal mother.

Magnetropism. Tendency for an animal to orientate itself towards a magnetic field.

Main score. The score based on the initial responses made in a RORSCHACH TEST and disregarding the free associations which follow.

Maintaining stimulus. A term used in ethology to refer to any stimulus which elicits a behaviour pattern in an animal as long as it is present.

Maintenance level. The point in an animal's life cycle when physical development ceases.

Major solution. Psychoanalytic term for the repression of a basic neurotic trend in order to resolve a conflict.

Make-A-Picture-Story Test. A test in which the patients are invited to construct a picture out of standard basic elements and tell a story about it. The themes of the narrative are then analysed for significance. (➧ PROJECTIVE TEST.)

Maladjustment. Failure of an individual to adjust to the pressures and problems which arise in his life.

Malaise. A vague feeling of being unwell.

Malevolence. A feeling of profound ill-will for someone else.

Malfunction. Failure to work properly.

Malignant. Referring to a disease highly resistant to treatment.

Malingering. Faking illness for gain.

Malleus. One of the three auditory ossicles, often known as the HAMMER.

Malleus Maleficarum. Medieval book devoted to the detection and punishment of witches.

Malpractice. Unprofessional behaviour.

Malthus, Thomas Robert (1766 – 1834). English economist who warned that population would inevitably outgrow food supply and as a result proposed a world-wide reduction in family size. Malthusianism was at one time synonymous with birth control.

Mammalia. Warm-blooded animals which suckle their young.

Mammary gland. The gland secreting milk in the female.

Mammillary bodies. Two tiny protuberances on the HYPOTHALAMUS.

Mana. Mystical power or life force.

Management psychology. The study of the methods employed in successful management; part of INDUSTRIAL PSYCHOLOGY.

Mand. Skinnerian term for a brisk sound or word of command effective in eliciting behaviour.

Mandala. A symbol or aid to meditation, normally a closed figure or repetitive sound. JUNG used the concept in his own theories to refer to man's striving for unity within himself.

Mania. Highly excitable or uncontrolled behaviour; also an obsolescent term or insanity or madness.

Mania a potu. Alcohol-induced excitement, sometimes with violence.

Maniaphobia. Fear of going mad.

Mania senilis. Insanity associated with old age.

Manic. Referring to an excitable or restless condition.

Manic-depressive psychosis. A condition in which the individual suffers from extreme cycles of agitated elated behaviour and periods of deep, sometimes suicidal depression. There are very strong suggestions that this psychosis has a biochemical origin, and of course mild manic-depressive swings occur from time to time in the normal individual.

Manifest. Obvious, open to study.

Manifest anxiety. Anxiety which in psychoanalysis is taken as symptomatic of an underlying (latent) mental conflict.

Manifest content. The obvious, easily memorable and describable content of a dream. Compare with the LATENT CONTENT, which Freud argued to be the true but hidden or disguised message of the dream.

Manifold. Collection of objects or ideas sharing a common feature.

Manikin test. Test in which the subject has to assemble the parts of a small wooden model of a person.

Man-machine system. A man and a machine acting together as a complex unit.

Mannerism. Something characteristic of an individual; also refers to movements or gestures characteristic of certain types of mental illness.

Mann-Whitney test. Statistical method which allows one to compare the CENTRAL TENDENCY of two distributions of data.

Manometer. Device for measuring the pressure of a fluid.

Manoptoscope. Device for testing eye dominance.

Man-to-man rating scale. One of the first attempts at a standardized rating or scaling test. It was used in the First World War for officer selection.

Manual method. Any sign language for the deaf and dumb, e.g. AMERICAN SIGN LANGUAGE.

Marginal consciousness. ➧ FRINGE OF CONSCIOUSNESS.

Marginal contrast. A heightened contrast effect which appears near any boundary in the visual field.

Marginal intelligence. ➧ BORDERLINE INTELLIGENCE.

Marijuana. A narcotic, mildly hallucinogenic drug prepared from the hemp plant.

Marketing psychology. ➧ CONSUMER PSYCHOLOGY.

Market research. Detailed and systematic studies of product acceptability and consumer buying habits.

Markov process. A statistical model concerned with conditional probabilities and used in some approaches to learning theory.

Masculine protest. A term used by ADLER to refer to a particular form of the will to achieve power. It may also refer to a woman's desire to be male in order to achieve power.

Masculinism. Tendency for a female to show male characteristics.

Masked epilepsy. Relatively mild form of EPILEPSY in which vague disturbances of consciousness take place but there are no motor convulsions. There is generally amnesia of the attack.

Masking. Blocking one sensory process by another.

Masochism. Pleasure, generally sexual, achieved through suffering pain. Psychoanalysts see this as an example of the individual turning his death or destructive instincts on to himself. Contrast SADISM.

Mass action. The principle put forward by K. S. LASHLEY, as the result of his experiments, that learning must be a property of the whole cerebral cortex. Lashley taught a large number of rats to run a maze and then removed different chunks of the cortex from each animal. He found that no individual rat appeared to be seriously affected in this maze running by surgery – in other words the information about the maze had not been stored in any of the chunks of cortex removed. He did find, however, that if he removed larger chunks from each animal, the maze habit was interfered with in direct proportion to the amount of cortex removed and not to its location. He thus concluded that the maze habit must be one of mass action, involving the cortex as a whole. Such evidence as exists on the location of complex skills in the human cerebral cortex – one can only study the problem in people suffering from accidental brain damage for obvious reasons – does not on the whole support the mass action hypothesis and it may be that it relates to animals with a less complex cortex than man.

Massed practice. Learning a task by carrying out a long series of trials in sequence and without a break. It has been shown to be less effective than distributed practice, where the trials are spaced out.

Mass media. Communication systems, such as radio and TV stations, newspapers and magazines, which can contact larger numbers of people at the same time. A study of the media is of great interest to sociologists because of the persuasive influence such channels can have on public opinion.

Mass method. Studies of individuals in groups, particularly large groups.

Mass observation. Sampling behaviour or opinion on a large scale as with public opinion polls.

Mass reflex. Widespread reflex reaction induced by a single stimulus, e.g. the startle reaction.

Masson disc. White disc with a series of black squares on it. When rotated the black segments are seen as bands of grey and the device was originally used in measuring brightness difference thresholds. It is now usually employed to study fluctuations of attention.

Mastery. The state of having developed a skill to a point of near perfection.

Masturbation. Gaining sexual pleasure by manipulating the sex organs. Once clouded with social taboos, the practice is no longer assumed to be physiologically or psychologically harmful.

Matched groups. Groups of subjects who have been selected because they do not deviate from each other in any obvious way. Matched groups are employed in experiments, allowing a meaningful comparison between the EXPERIMENTAL GROUP and CONTROL GROUP to be made.

Matched sample. A sample believed to be identical to all intents and purposes with another sample.

Matching test. Test which requires the subject to match items occurring in different lists.

Mate. A stable sexual partner.

Materialism. Any theory which attempts to explain the phenomena of life and the universe as a whole in physical terms.

Materialization. The appearance of the physical form of a ghost or spirit. This is alleged to occur at spiritualistic seances.

Maternal behaviour. The complex behaviour patterns by which a mother cares for her young.

Maternal drive. The apparent need that a mother has to feed her infants and ensure their survival. Some aspects of the maternal drive appear to be instinctive, others are learned.

Mathematical model. Any attempt to understand or predict animal behaviour which employs the techniques of mathematics, in particular the development and use of special equations. Some aspects of mathematical modelling are exceedingly simple, such as WEBER'S LAW $\left(\frac{\Delta I}{I} = K\right)$ Others may be more elaborate, such as the system put forward by HULL. Others again, such as those models drawn from INFORMATION THEORY and CYBERNETICS, involve considerable mathematical sophistication.

Mathematico-deductive system. A theory which employs mathematical notation or principles to clarify its argument or allow formal deductions to be made.

Mating behaviour. Those behaviour patterns, many of them instinctive and some involving elaborate courtship rituals, which precede and include the sex act.

Matriarchy. A female-dominated social group. Contrast PATRIARCHY.

Matrilineal. Anthropological term for a society where descent and inheritance follow through the female line.

Matrix. The context in which something is set. In mathematics the term refers to a set of numbers so arrayed in a two-way table that they can be subjected to mathematical procedures or computation.

Maturation. Refers to the general processes of development which occur in the normal individual from birth (or possibly conception) to the point of psychological maturity. These processes, which include the development of body organs and the cerebral cortex, follow near-identical lines in all members of a particular species, and they proceed more or less independently of external influences. The evolution of intelligence is supposed to be a maturational process and independent of learning.

Maturation theory. The belief that a large number of behaviour patterns are determined by heredity, but can only be triggered into action when the appropriate level of physical maturity has been reached.

Maturity. A state in which development, whether physical or psychological, has reached its optimum level. It also refers to the fourth DEVELOPMENTAL LEVEL lasting from approximately from the age of twenty-one to sixty-five.

Maudsley Personality Inventory (MPI). Test of neuroticism and extraversion, now replaced by the EYSENCK PERSONALITY INVENTORY.

Maximal sensation. The upper limit of intensity of a sensation.

Maxwell discs. Interleaved coloured discs which when rotated give a variety of mixtures of hues.

Maxwell's demon. A concept introduced by Clerk Maxwell to allow one to visualize various processes in physics. The 'demons' are imaginary beings who assist physical processes, instigating chemical reactions, distributing gas molecules evenly around a container, etc.

Maze. An unpredictable path or set of paths to a goal. Used especially in studying human and animal learning, mazes may vary from simple T-junctions where only a right or left turn has to be performed and which worms, insects, etc. can learn, to exceedingly complex three-dimensional labyrinths used to test humans of superior intelligence.

McDougall, William (1871 – 1938). Prodigious writer and experimental psychologist who believed that all life was purposive and vigorously rejected the Pavlovian/behaviouristic approaches. He was instrumental in setting up the world-famous Parapsychology Laboratory at Duke University in North Carolina. (⧫⧫ PARAPSYCHOLOGY; HORMIC PSYCHOLOGY.)

Mead, Margaret (1901 –). American anthropologist noted for her studies of Oceanic societies, and in particular for her observations of childhood, adolescence and the emergence of sexuality in these cultures. (⧫⧫ CROSS-CULTURAL PSYCHOLOGY.)

Mean ($\bar{X}$ or M). One of the most common measures of central tendency. It is the arithmetic average of a set of values obtained by summing the values and dividing by the total number in the sample.

Mean deviation. An estimate of the degree to which individual values are scattered around their MEAN. (⧫⧫ STANDARD DEVIATION.)

Mean gradation method. Psychophysical method, also known as the equal-sense differences method, in which the subject has to find the halfway point between two sensory stimuli.

Meaning. Whatever it is that a particular symbol stands for. Meaning implies an observer and some mechanism for interpreting whatever is observed. (⧫⧫ CONNOTATIVE MEANING; DENOTATIVE MEANING.)

Means-end capacity. A concept introduced by the psychologist E. C. TOLMAN who argued that one could only hope to understand an animal's behaviour by accepting that it sets itself goals and is aware of the 'significance' and relevance of particular stimuli acting as signs for these goals. This ability is the means-end capacity.

Means-end expectancy. TOLMAN's phrase describing the state of expectation supposedly set up in an animal once it has identified a goal. Tolman used similar concepts – means-end learning, means-end readiness, etc. – in his theory of motivation and behaviour. (⧫⧫ GOAL-DIRECTED BEHAVIOUR.)

Mean variation. Average variation of individual measurements about their MEAN.

Measure. A judgement based on a standard of some kind.

Meatus. A canal or passage.

Mechanical stimulation. Firing a sense receptor by pressure. Touch and hearing are 'pressure' senses, but mechanical stimulation may also be used to induce visual experience, as when the eyeball is squeezed.

Mechanism. Literally, the interactive structure of a machine; but it may also refer to systematic interaction within the brain and mind.

Mechanistic theory. Any approach to understanding the universe of individual living things in terms of machine-like models.

Mechanoreceptor. A sense organ or cell which principally responds to touch or pressure.

Medea complex. The compulsion of a mother to kill her own children, supposedly motivated by a desire for revenge against the father.

Medial. Towards the middle.

Medial plane. The vertical dividing line from the top of the body or an organ downwards, dividing it into symmetrical halves (left and right).

Median. Common measure of central tendency. When all the individual values in a sample are ranked in order of magnitude, the middle value is the median. (⧫⧫ MEAN; MODE.)

Median grey. The grey that lies just halfway between black and white.

Mediate association. Refers to the situation where a stimulus sets off a chain of ideas or associations and thus achieves its response indirectly.

Mediated generalization. More commonly, SEMANTIC CONDITIONING.

Mediating processes. In psychology any activity, such as thinking or decision-making, which intervenes between the onset of a stimulus and the initiation of its response. When the intervening activity involves the use of words, either spoken or thought, this is known as verbal mediation.

Mediation. The act of linking two structures or processes.

Mediator. A term used in information theory to refer to anything that acts between a transmitter and a receiver.

Medicine. The science and theory of treating disease.

Meditation. Thinking devoted to a particular goal, generally of a mystical or spiritual nature.

Medium. Something acting as a link with something else. Hence, in Spiritualism, a medium is an individual who acts as a mental bridge between the living and the dead.

Medulla. The inner part of any organ.

Medulla oblongata. Often simply referred to as the medulla. Part of the central nervous system, it is the lowest part of the brain lying immediately above the spinal cord, and links the brain and spinal cord. It controls many autonomic functions such as respiration and heart-rate. (⧫ BRAIN.)

Medullary sheath. More commonly, MYELIN sheath.

Medullated. Covered with a protective sheath of myelin.

Megalocephalic. More commonly, macrocephalic. (⧫ MACROCEPHALY.)

Megalomania. Mental disorder in which the individual has a wildly inflated view of his own abilities and importance.

Megalopsia. More commonly, MACROPSIA.

Meiosis. Special type of cell division where the number of CHROMOSOMES is halved prior to fusion with another sex cell. Without meiosis the number of chromosomes would double with each generation. This term should not be confused with MITOSIS.

Meissner corpuscles. Specialized cells in hairless skin, believed to mediate the sense of pressure or touch.

Mel. A unit developed to allow the subjective rating of pitch.

Melancholia. Obsolete term for severe DEPRESSION.

Melancholic type. ➧ TEMPERAMENT.

Melanin. Dark pigment present in the skin, hair, choroid coat of the eye, etc.

Member. Refers to someone who considers himself, and is considered by others, to be a part of a social group of some kind.

Membership character. Gestalt term referring to the subtle change which takes place in a person or thing when it becomes part of a larger unified group.

Membership group. In social psychology, a group of which the individual is an accepted member. These groups may be ascribed (e.g. sex, race, etc.) or attained. Compare REFERENCE GROUP. (➧➧ GROUP.)

Membrane. Thin layer which covers or lines a cell or organ.

Membrane conduction theory. Theory of neural conduction which states that nervous transmission is due to a rapid change in the electrochemical properties of the cell membrane.

Memory. One of the key concepts in psychological theory and experimentation. Memory is essentially that property, shared by a large number of living organisms, of storing information about past experiences so that these can be acted on later to improve the animal's chances of survival. The confusion which often exists between the words learning, memory, remembering, etc., can be ironed out if one looks upon *memory* as the information which is located in store, LEARNING as the process by which the information is put there, and *remembering* as the process of lifting the information from store for inspection.

The nature of memory, even in the simplest of animal forms, is only sketchily understood and there are a number of rival and overlapping theories attempting to explain it. These include *neural theories* in which it is assumed that the anatomy of the brain cells changes somewhat as the result of experience, *electrical theories* which hold that changes in the state of electrical fields in the brain take place, and *biochemical theories* in which it is believed that the stored information constitutes a realignment of the molecular structure of the cells. Theories also exist which embrace all three approaches but the present state of knowledge does not favour any particular point of view. Any successful theory will have to account for the quite remarkable speed with which information can be extracted from store, and also explain how the immense range of human memory can be integrated so successfully. (◆◆ SHORT-TERM MEMORY.)

Memory after-image. A particularly vivid memory of a recent event which endures for seconds or even minutes without losing its intensity. Compare EIDETIC IMAGERY.

Memory colour. The *remembered* colour of an object. This may be vivid enough to affect the perception of a colour seen at a later time.

Memory drum. Device for presenting material to be learned automatically, generally on a rotating drum.

Memory image. A mental reconstruction, generally conscious and voluntary, of a past event.

Memory span. The maximum number of items that an individual can recall after they have been presented to him once.

Memory system. Any aid to learning or remembering things. (◆◆ MNEMONIC.)

Memory trace. When something is learned, a change of some kind must take place within the nervous system. Whether the change is physiological, electrical or biochemical, it is referred to as the memory trace. The word engram is also used occasionally.

Menarche. The first MENSTRUATION in the female.

Mendacity. Compulsive lying.

Mendelism. The theory of inheritance put forward by Gregor Mendel (1822–84) who argued that the cell must contain units (GENES) which may be dominant or recessive in any individual, and which carry the information as to body type from one generation to another. He also argued that within the cell the genetic material must be separated from the other tissue to prevent 'contamination' of information to be transmitted.

Meninges. The three protective membranes covering the brain and spinal cord – dura mater (outer layer), arachnoid (middle) and pia mater (inner layer).

Meningitis. Inflammation of the MENINGES which may cause severe neural damage.

Meniscus. Lens concave on one side and convex on the other.

Menopause. The climacteric or 'change of life', when menstruation and ovulation cease and a woman is no longer able to bear offspring. Accompanied by major biochemical changes in the body, the menopause may induce a period of depression or anxiety.

Menstruation. The monthly release of menstrual fluid and the unfertilized ovum occurring in women of child-bearing age.

Mensuration. Measurement.

Mental age (MA). This is measured by a series of INTELLIGENCE TESTS suitably graded for children of various ages. A child passing the tests suitable for, say, an eight-year-old would be counted as having an MA of eight, irrespective of his or her chronological age (age since birth). From the twin parameters of mental and chronological age is drawn the measure known as IQ (INTELLIGENCE QUOTIENT). This is MA/CA × 100.

Mental chemistry. Obsolete idea that the mind behaves after the fashion of a chemical reaction, fusing ideas and experiences so that they become dramatically transformed from the original state.

Mental deficiency. ➧ MENTAL RETARDATION.

Mental development. The steady evolution of an individual's intellectual powers which take place through the process of MATURATION from birth to adulthood. Compare COGNITIVE DEVELOPMENT. (➧ DEVELOPMENTAL PSYCHOLOGY.)

Mental discipline. ➧ FORMAL DISCIPLINE.

Mental disorder. Any breakdown in the capacity of the brain or mind which hinders its function or disturbs the personality. It is usual to classify these disorders as NEUROTIC or PSYCHOTIC.

Mental element. A psychological process which cannot be subdivided. It was once felt that mental life could be broken down into ideas, images, thoughts, etc., but no further, thus paralleling the doctrines of physical chemistry.

Mental evolution. The pattern of increasing intellectual development as one ascends the biological ladder from simple organisms to man.

Mental function. An activity such as thinking, learning or perceiving.

Mental handicap. A degree of backwardness, not specifically educational, caused by lower than normal intelligence.

Mental healing. The treatment of disorders, physical or psychological, by suggestion, hypnosis, etc.

Mental hygiene. Systematic attempt at the prevention of mental disorders and disease by inquiring into their social and physical origin.

Mental illness. Any disorder of mind or behaviour sufficiently severe to require sustained medical treatment.

Mentalism. The view that psychological phenomena cannot be explained solely in physical terms.

Mental image. Representation 'in the mind's eye' of some past event or fantasy. Mental imagery is predominantly visual but, rather curiously, not everyone seems able to experience it with any degree of clarity. (➧➧ EIDETIC IMAGERY.)

Mental level. Most commonly, one's score or rating on a psychological test; also used by Jung to refer to one of the three levels of the psyche, the persona, the personal unconscious and the collective unconscious.

Mentally subnormal. ➧ MENTAL RETARDATION.

Mental maturity. The maximum level of intellectual development which an adult individual can achieve.

Mental phenomena. All conscious and unconscious processes of the mind.

Mental retardation. Any kind of intellectual subnormality. Strictly speaking it refers to any person whose MENTAL AGE is less than his CHRONOLOGICAL AGE, but this is a rather rigid view.

Confusingly the classification systems vary throughout the world, but the WHO recommended classification, which is becoming widely accepted, is: *borderline* (IQ in the range 70–84); *mild* (55–69); *moderate* (40–54); *severe* (25–39), and *profound* (less than 25). A system introduced in Britain in the 1950s which is still sometimes used grades mentally subnormals as *mild* (IQ in the range 70–85); *moderately mentally subnormal* (50–70), and *severely mentally subnormal* (0–50). The latter group can be further divided by distinguishing patients with IQs of less than 20 as *very severely mentally subnormal*.

Mental retardation is frequently congenital, but may be caused by brain damage in infancy.

Mental science. Obsolete term for PSYCHOLOGY.

Mental set. An attitude of mind which prepares one for a particular event. (➧➧ SET.)

Menticide. ➧ BRAINWASHING.

Meprobamate. A tranquillizing drug.

Merkel corpuscle. Specialized sensory cell located in the tongue and responding to pressure.

Merkel's law. Equal differences between sensations imply equal differences between stimuli. This is a controversial point of view since it seems to conflict with WEBER'S LAW.

Mescaline. Hallucinatory drug derived from the cactus plant peyote; popularized by Aldous Huxley in his book *Doors of Perception*.

Mesencephalon. The midbrain. (➧ BRAIN.)

Mesmer, Franz (1734 – 1815). Austrian physician who believed that he had discovered a biological power capable of influencing other people's behaviour and which he termed animal magnetism. Mesmer became a fashionable figure in eighteenth-century Paris, but after suffering some persecution at the hands of investigating committees had to abandon his practice and experiments. Mesmerism, or HYPNOSIS as it was later called, faded from view until it was revived as a therapeutic aid by James Braid in Manchester and Charcot in Paris. Mesmer was no charlatan in the strictest sense of the word as he believed absolutely in the phenomena he was working with. It was his theoretical explanation that was at fault.

Mesmerism. Early name for HYPNOSIS.

Mesocephalic. Literally, middle-headed i.e. having a cephalic index lying between 76 and 80.9.

Mesoderm. The middle embryonic layer which ultimately forms muscle and bone. The other layers are the endoderm and ectoderm.

Mesokurtic. Having a peak similar to that of the normal distribution curve.

Mesomorph. ➧ SHELDONIAN THEORY; BODY BUILD INDEX.

Message. Information transferred from a transmitter to a receiver.

Metabolism. The changes which take place within a living organism which relate to growth, tissue repair and the elimination of waste. (➧ ANABOLISM; CATABOLISM.)

Metakinesis. Rudimentary conscious processes if and when they occur in simple organisms.

Metalanguage. A special purpose language devised to describe the rules and grammar of another language, e.g. Whorf's 'Standard Average English'.

Metamers. Colour which are normally perceived as different but which may appear identical under certain circumstances, e.g. dim illumination.

Metamorphosis. Any change in shape or structure.

Metaphysics. The study of the meaning and purpose of things.

Metapsychology. Any system which attempts to embrace the whole of psychology and provide a comprehensive theory of all psychological phenomena.

Metazoa. The multi-celled animals.

Metempirical. Speculative beyond the possibility of experimental investigation.

Metempsychosis. Reincarnation.

Methadone. A powerful pain-killer also used to wean addicts off heroin.

Method. Technique for systematic study.

Method of limits. One of the basic techniques of psychophysics used for determining ABSOLUTE THRESHOLDS. The experimenter presents the subject with a series of stimuli in ascending order, beginning way below the expected threshold. The point at which the stimulus can first be detected is noted. The same series is then given in descending order, beginning way *above* threshold, and now the point at which the stimulus can no longer be detected is noted. The threshold is taken as the midpoint of the two values.

Methodology. Literally, the study or philosophy of conducting scientific research, but the meaning of the word has become altered somewhat to imply a particular *approach* to research. Determining the best way to acquire knowledge has been a preoccupation of philosophers and scientists from the time of Aristotle, and the term is sometimes used as a synonym for philosophy of science.

Initially all studies commence with observation of phenomena in their natural state, this being followed by the EXPERIMENT – ideally a controlled replication of one or more aspects of the previously observed phenomena. In many of the physical sciences controlled experiments are relatively easy to specify and perform, as physicalistic phenomena tend to behave in relatively predictable ways. In the biological and, in particular, the psychological sciences, however, it is far less easy to confine the subject matter of the study – animals or humans – to a laboratory setting. When one reaches really diffuse areas of study, such as those involved in sociology, a new problem – the separation of experimenter and his experimental subjects – arises. Thus many sociological studies have to rely on the observer effectively disguising himself as one of the group under study, or falling back on some less direct method of data gathering, such as employing questionnaires or interviews.

Metonymy. Eccentric or bizarre use of language, generally involving the use of words vaguely similar to the intended ones.

Metrazol. A drug used to induce a coma or convulsions. It is an alternative to ELECTROCONVULSIVE THERAPY as a treatment for depression.

Metronoscope. Device which presents printed information at a controlled speed for reading tests.

Meyer, Adolf (1866 – 1950). American psychiatrist who believed that social factors could be exceedingly influential in causing mental illness.

Michotte, Albert (1881–1965). Belgian psychologist best known for his studies of the perception of CAUSALITY. He argued that the brain was so ready to infer causality that it was probably an instinctive process.

Microcephaly. Small-headed. Congenital condition always resulting in mental deficiency.

Microcosm. A small, effectively self-contained aspect of the universe. It sometimes implies 'the self'.

Micron. One thousandth of a millimetre.

Micro-organism. Any living thing requiring a microscope to identify it.

Microphobia. Abnormal fear of tiny objects.

Microphonia. Having an abnormally weak voice.

Micropsia. Disorder of the eye which results in objects being seen as smaller than they should be.

Microsleep. A brief period of sleep, perhaps lasting only seconds and normally undetected by the individual.

Microsplanchnic. Referring to someone with a trunk abnormally small in proportion to the limbs.

Microstructure. Fine detail.

Microtome. Device for sectioning thin slices of tissue.

Micturition. Urination.

Midbrain. Part of the brain, lying above the pons, containing the corpora quadrigemina, the tegumentum and other structures. (➧ BRAIN.)

Middle ear. Part of the EAR between the drum and the inner ear; contains the auditory ossicles.

Midrange value. The average of the highest and lowest in a distribution. It is a rough measure of central tendency.

Midscore. More commonly, the MEDIAN.

Mignon delusion. Belief sometimes found among children that their parents are not their true mother and father and that they are really from a distinguished family.

Migraine. Headache, generally very severe and sometimes preceded by the perception of striking visual patterns known as scotomata. A tendency to migraine is probably hereditary, but the condition may be precipitated by stress, allergy or even diet.

Migration. Seasonal changes of habitat performed by many species of birds, fish and other animals. It poses many problems to ethologists as to the navigation methods employed and the nature of the stimuli triggering the migration.

Mild mental retardation. ➧ MENTAL RETARDATION.

Milieu therapy. Approach to psychotherapy which emphasises the need for readjustments in the individual's environment rather than in his psyche as such. (➧➧ FAMILY-CENTRED THERAPY.)

Mill, John Stuart (1806–73). British philosopher who formulated the laws of inductive thinking. His father, James Mill, was also a philosopher and a leading figure in the Associationist movement. (➧➧ CONCOMITANT VARIATION; RESIDUES METHOD.)

Mimesis. Imitation or copying.

Mimetism. The technique by which one animal copies another's characteristics for protective purposes.

Mind. The sum total of psychological processes, conscious or unconscious. Definitions of this kind unfortunately fail to take into account the significance of the word mind to psychology in general. At one time, for example, the mind was equated with soul or spirit and assumed to be the conscious 'control mechanism' for the body and qualitatively different from it. FREUD's ideas complicated this picture by introducing the disturbing notion of the power of the UNCONSCIOUS which downgraded the status of the mind's conscious component. PAVLOV and the behaviourist school (➧ BEHAVIOURISM) further eroded its significance by eliminating the concept of mind from all experimental and theoretical considerations, and criticizing anyone who dared used the word for being mystical and unscientific. Today the pendulum is swinging back and, while few psychologists think of mind as a spiritual entity separable from the brain and body, most now accept that the richness and reality of mental life cannot be denied and that a place must be found for the word mind in comprehensive theories of human behaviour.

Mind blindness. Obsolete term for VISUAL AGNOSIA.

Mind/body problem. Long-standing philosophical controversy. Are mind and body separate entities? If they are, how and where do they interact?

Mind reading. Refers either to TELEPATHY or a conjuring trick involving muscle reading.

Minimal changes method. ➧ METHOD OF LIMITS.

Minimum audible pressure. The lowest pressure, in the form of sound waves, on the eardrum that can be heard.

Minnesota Multiphasic Personality Inventory (MMPI). Multi-factor personality test containing over 500 statements, such as 'I frequently get bouts of depression', against which the subject ticks 'True' or 'False'.

Miosis. ➧MEIOSIS.

Mirror writing. Back-to-front writing. It may appear in childhood but is also sometimes produced by schizophrenics.

Misanthropy. Hatred of human beings.

Miscegenation. Mixing of the races.

Miso-. As a prefix, refers to hatred or dislike.

Misogyny. Hatred of women.

Mitochondria. Particles within the living cell which break down sugars and fats.

Mitosis. Cell duplication with one cell giving rise to two identical 'daughter cells', the method by which the body grows and replaces cells. This term should not be confused with MEIOSIS.

Mixed cerebral dominance. Condition in which no side of the brain firmly establishes itself as the dominant one.

Mixed reinforcement. Form of CONDITIONING in which the animal is presented with a number of patterns of REINFORCEMENT. The change in the patterns are not signalled to the animal, which has to discover them for itself. Studies of this kind give an indication of its intellectual potential. (➧➧ REINFORCEMENT SCHEDULES.)

Mneme. ➧ MEMORY TRACE.

Mnemonic. A technique used to aid memory.

Mob. Social group acting with a sense of purpose, but over a short period of time.

Mobility. In sociology, the ability of an individual to move from one class or stratum of society to another.

Modality. A major subdivision of something. In psychology it particularly refers to sensory experience – e.g. pressure, cold, pain, etc.

Mode. One of the main measures of central tendency; the most frequently occurring value in a set of data. (⧫⧫ MEAN; MEDIAN.)

Model. A copy of something or a hypothetical representation of how some system might work. The word has a special meaning in social learning where it is something that is copied.

Mode of adjustment. Any strategy adopted by an individual in response to developmental or social demand.

Moderate mental retardation. ⧫ MENTAL RETARDATION.

Modulator. Anything which alters something in a systematic way. The term also refers to a particular type of retinal cell which it has been proposed detects colour by frequency modulation.

Mogilalia. Difficulty in speaking.

Molar. Relating to objects or events as a whole.

Molar behaviour. A major or complete unit of behaviour. Tolman also used the phrase to describe behaviour which is non-random and generally purposive.

Molecular. Relating to objects or events in their elements.

Molecular layer. ⧫ GRANULAR LAYER.

Moment. In statistics, the average of deviations (or some power of them) from the mean of the series or from a particular norm.

Monadism. The theory that the universe is made up of a series of totally independent life units.

Monaural. With one ear.

Mongolism. ⧫ DOWN'S SYNDROME.

Monism. The theory that the universe is made up of essentially only one kind of substance. Contrast with DUALISM.

Monoamine oxidase (MAO) inhibitors. Anti-depressant drugs noted for their long-term action.

Monocular. Relating to one eye.

Monogony. Asexual reproduction.

Monoideism. Excessive preoccupation with a particular thought or idea.

Monoplegia. Paralysis of a single limb.

Monotone. Sound in a single pitch.

Monozygotic twins. Also known as uniovular or IDENTICAL TWINS.

Monster. Technical name for an individual with a grotesque disfigurement at birth.

Montessori method. An approach to education which emphasizes spontaneous action on the part of the child and rejects traditional educational methods. It also emphasizes the value of developing reading and verbal skills at the earliest possible age.

Mood. A transient emotional state; an emotional attitude.

Moon illusion. The moon at the horizon appears to be dramatically larger than when at the zenith. This is probably due to context factors.

Morale. The attitude of an individual to a particular task, particularly when he is part of a group.

Morals. The framework of customs, as opposed to laws, governing human conduct and behaviour.

Morbid. Relating to disease, decay or death. Implies something unwholesome.

Mores. Social customs widespread in a group though not backed by the forces of law.

Morgan, Conway Lloyd (1852 – 1936). Pioneer comparative psychologist, perhaps best remembered for his ruling against anthropomorphism.

Morgan's canon. More commonly, LLOYD MORGAN'S LAW.

Moro response. The startle reflex in infants.

Moron. Obsolete term for a person with a mild degree of mental retardation and with an IQ in the range 50–69. This is now classed as mild mental retardation. (➧ MENTAL RETARDATION.)

Morpheme. The smallest meaningful linguistic unit. Contrast PHONEME.

Morphine. Highly addictive narcotic derived from opium.

Morphogenesis. The development of an organism's structure.

Morphological index. A measure of body proportions.

Morphological inferiority. Adlerian term for a feeling of inferiority engendered by a peculiarity in the size or structure of some part of one's body.

Morphology. The study of the structure of organisms.

Mortido. Roughly equivalent to the death instinct, THANATOS. (⧫⧫ DESTRUDO.)

Mosaic eye. The COMPOUND EYE.

Mother complex. In psychoanalytic theory, the OEDIPUS COMPLEX.

Mother figure. Someone who stands in for the mother and becomes the focus of one's affections and emotions.

Mother surrogate. A substitute mother.

Motile. Mobile, fluid, flexible.

Motion after-effect. A form of APPARENT MOVEMENT. A striking example is the WATERFALL ILLUSION.

Motion parallax. One of the clues in DEPTH PERCEPTION. Objects closer to one in the visual field appear to move more rapidly than those at a greater distance. (⧫⧫ PARALLAX.)

Motion study. ⧫ TIME AND MOTION STUDY.

Motivate. To give an incentive, to move into action.

Motivation. Broadly speaking, why an animal does one thing rather than another. Most theories of motivation bring into play the concept of DRIVES – internal states which push an organism into appropriate courses of action at relevant times, e.g. thirst, hunger, sex, etc. It is also sometimes assumed that motivation plays a part in LEARNING, because a response which follows a reduction in a drive will be more likely to be learned than one which does not.

The most promising area in research into motivation at the present time seems to be the neurophysiology of the brain, particularly since the work of Olds and Milner in the 1950s, who detected an area in the limbic system of the rat which, when electrically stimulated, seemed to give the animal 'pleasure'. (⧫ PLEASURE CENTRE.) The neurophysiological approach, however, is probably limited at the moment to the study of very specific and basic areas of motivation, such as the physiological needs (hunger, thirst, the sex drive, etc.) and, despite the hopes of the behaviourists, it is not really possible to reduce all human and social activity to such basics.

Attempts have been made at developing 'cognitive' theories of motivation – theories which suggest that the individual has a conscious awareness of the needs and goals which involve his personality, his family, his place in society and so on. An early attempt at such a cognitive approach was, of course, the psychodynamic theory of Freud, which stressed that an individual's behaviour could be understood by reference to the perpetual conflict between the unconscious and instinctive wishes of the id and the restrictive forces of society or the 'real world'. Later theories include that of Kurt Lewin, heavily influenced by Gestalt ideas, and, more recently yet, that of Festinger with his notion of cognitive dissonance. In terms of social psychology, motives decidedly more general than such physiologically-based needs as thirst, hunger, etc. need to be considered – e.g. status, power, knowledge, affluence – and much research effort has been put into investigating these areas, largely in the interests of advertising and political persuasion. Compare DRIVE, NEED.

Motivational conflict. ➧ CONFLICT.

Motivational research. The study of the factors which induce consumers to buy one product rather than another. It may rely on Gallup-type polls or 'depth' interviews conducted by psychologists.

Motive. An internal state which leads to behaviour being directed in a particular direction or towards a known goal. Motives differ from drives in that the latter tend to be basic and instinctive whereas motives tend to be acquired, learned and 'higher level'. (➧➧ DRIVE; NEED.)

Motone. A pattern of muscular behaviour.

Motoneurone. A neurone directly connected to a muscle or gland.

Motor. Refers to the activity of any muscle or gland.

Motor aphasia. Loss of speech normally due to lesion in the speech area of the brain.

Motor apraxia. Loss of muscle control due to lesion in the motor areas, and in particular the loss of ability to perform a specific task.

Motor area. Part of the cerebral cortex which controls muscle movement.

Motor end plate. The flattened end of a motoneurone where it interacts with a muscle cell.

Motor equivalence. The principle that one can reach a particular goal by one of a large number of patterns of motor behaviour. This is not easy to understand in simplistic behaviouristic terms.

Motor learning. Learning a pattern of muscular responses.

Motor primacy theory. Theory that motor functions develop before sensory ones.

Motor sense. More commonly, KINAESTHESIS.

Motor set. An adjustment of the muscles in readiness for an anticipated task or situation. (➧ SET.)

Motor skill. ➧ SKILL.

Motor theory of consciousness. Proposal put forward by J. B. Watson, at the height of the behaviourist movement, that consciousness is the end product of muscular activity and glandular action. Tied up with this was the notion that thinking was merely SUBVOCAL SPEECH.

Mouches volantes. Also known as MUSCAE VOLITANTES.

Movement illusion. Illusory feeling of one's body moving when it is not or APPARENT MOVEMENT in objects being viewed.

Movement response. An important response given in RORSCHACH TESTS when the subject reports movement in some part of the inkblot.

Moving average method. Statistical technique for simplifying or reducing data by substituting for each item, the average of the sum of the item and a number of adjacent items.

Müller, Johannes (1801 – 58). Pioneer experimental psychologist who advanced the doctrine of specific nerve energies. (➧ SPECIFIC ENERGY THEORY.)

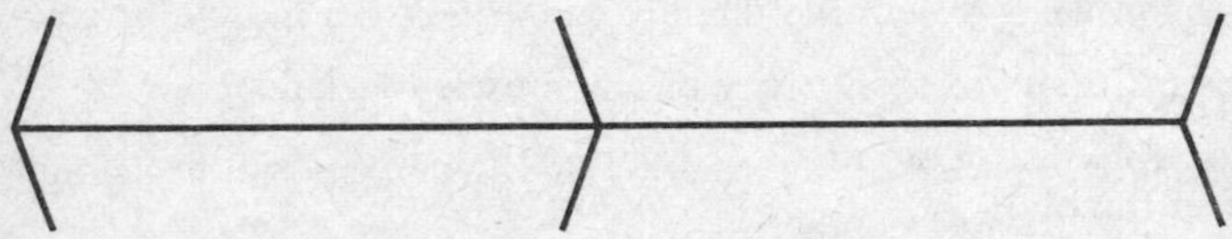

Figure 22. Müller-Lyer illusion.

Müller-Lyer illusion. One of the most striking OPTICAL ILLUSIONS, highly resistant to extinction even after extensive practice.

Müller-Schumann law. When two items have become associated through learning, it is subsequently more difficult to associate either of the items with any other.

Multi-factorial theory. Any theory which can only be understood with reference to a number of interacting factors.

Multimodal. A distribution of data having more than one peak.

Multimodal theory of intelligence. The theory that intelligence is made up of an assembly of different factors, rather than of one general ability. (➧➧ TWO-FACTOR THEORY.)

Multiple-choice test. Any test where an animal or human has to make a decision from a pool of possible situations, each marked by a particular cue. Such tests are used on animals to examine their capacity for sensory discrimination.

Multiple correlation. A coefficient which indicates the degree of relationship between a number of independent variables and one dependent variable.

Multiple personality. Abnormal condition in which the individual's personality seems to change dramatically so that the rival personality emerges almost completely unrelated to the personality it has replaced. In extreme cases the 'personalities' may even deny each other's existence and show distortions or elimination of memories laid down at times when the rival was dominant. A popular account of a well-attested case is *The Three Faces of Eve* by Thigpen and Cleckley. Multiple personality is in fact an hysterical condition and should not be confused with schizophrenia. (➧ DUAL PERSONALITY.)

Multiple reinforcement. A technique in conditioning experiments when the animal is trained by different REINFORCEMENT SCHEDULES, the changes in schedules being signalled to the animal. (➧ MIXED REINFORCEMENT.)

Multiple sclerosis. Progressive disease of brain and spinal cord in which the myelin sheath of the nerves are destroyed and replaced by scar tissue.

Multipolar neurone. Nerve cell with a number of branches or processes leading away from its body.

Multivariate analysis. Any statistical technique, such as factor analysis, which attempts to break down complex data into their various components.

Munsell system. An atlas of colours arranged to allow the comparison of different hues on the basis of brightness, saturation, etc.

Murray, Henry A. (1893 –). American psychologist much influenced by Jung and psychoanalysis, best known for his attempt to explain human personality in terms of a theory of instinctive needs. He developed the THEMATIC APPERCEPTION TEST (TAT).

Muscae volitantes. Fragments of detached cells which float around in the fluid of the eye and can often be seen when gazing at a plain bright surface.

Muscle. Cell, or collection of cells, whose special property is contractile powers. Voluntary muscles are known as striate – because of their striped appearance – while involuntary ones are known as smooth muscles.

Muscle reading. A skill which allows one to guess, by merely touching someone's body, what that individual is about to do. Frequently used by conjurors in 'thought reading' acts, it depends upon the fact that people signal their intentions, quite unconsciously, by minute muscle movements.

Muscle spindle. Nerve cell specialized to detect contractions in muscle fibres.

Muscle tonus. Slight state of tension which all muscles hold, even when inactive or 'relaxed'.

Musculature. The whole of the striate or voluntary muscles.

Mutagen. Anything which increases MUTATION.

Mutation. A permanent change in a GENE which leads to a modification of some characteristic. The vast majority of mutations, being caused by radiation or chemical damage, are lethal in the sense that they do not allow the production of live offspring. The remainder are heritable and form the basis of the slow change in animal form over hundreds of thousands of years.

Mute. Someone unable to speak.

Myasthenia. Muscular weakness due to disease.

Mydriasis. Extreme pupil dilation, sometimes caused by drugs.

Myelin. The white insulating sheath which covers the axon of many nerve fibres (the medullated neurones).

Myelination. The formation of the MYELIN sheath.

Myelitis. Inflammation of the spinal cord.

Myoclonus. Spasmodic contractions of a muscle.

Myograph. A device for measuring muscle strength.

Myopia. Short-sightedness.

Myosis. Contraction of the pupil.

Myotonia. Prolonged relaxation of the muscles after effort.

Mysophobia. Abnormal fear of dirt.

Mysticism. Belief in the power and reality of supernatural forces.

Myth. A widely held belief which has no definable historical background.

Myxoedema. Any disease resulting from an underactive thyroid.

N

Nadir. The lowest point.

Naevus. A birthmark.

Naive. Inexperienced; or a subject who is unfamiliar with an experimental situation.

Nancy school. School of psychotherapy founded by Bernheim in the 1880s which held that hypnosis was a normal phenomenon but involving a high degree of suggestibility. It was in opposition to Charcot's Paris school which took the line that hypnosis was an abnormal condition related to hysteria.

Nanism. Dwarfism.

Nanometer (nm). The preferred SI unit – a metre × 10^{-9}. Once known as one millimicron.

Narcissism. Excessive love for oneself. Psychoanalysts use *primary narcissism* to refer to the uncomprehending selfishness of the child and *secondary narcissism* when this recurs in adult life. FREUD believed that schizophrenia, featuring withdrawal from the world, was exaggerated narcissism.

Narcoanalysis. Psychotherapy in which sleep-promoting drugs are given to weaken ego defence mechanisms and assist FREE ASSOCIATION.

Narcolepsy. Disease featuring uncontrollable sleepiness.

Narcosis. Dozy, withdrawn state induced by narcotic drugs.

Narcosynthesis. The use of the material obtained in NARCOANALYSIS as an aid to psychotherapy.

Narcotherapy. Use of NARCOTICS in psychotherapy.

Narcotic. Any drug which dulls sensibility and induces sleep.

Nares. Nostrils and nasal passages.

Nascent. Beginning; emerging.

Nationalism. In social psychology, an attitude featuring a tendency to hold a relatively low opinion of other nations and a high opinion of one's own. At the heart of nationalism is often the assumption that members of individual nations are genetically endowed with certain favourable or unfavourable characteristics. In fact, despite a long history – dating back to the early nineteenth century – of attempts to identify specific national characteristics, the evidence for the existence in all but the most general sense is weak. Physical differences – in skin pigmentation, stature – obviously occur, but there is no evidence that one national group is on average any more intelligent than another, or more brave, more aggressive, more artistic or whatever. Variations in human behaviour, attitudes, self-expression, etc., tend to be culturally and not genetically determined. (➧ RACE.)

Native trait. An inborn characteristic.

Nativism. The view that most psychological characteristics are innate.

Natural sciences. Those sciences which study nature, including physics, chemistry and biology. Contrast SOCIAL SCIENCES.

Natural selection. Evolution through the Darwinian principle of the 'survival of the fittest'.

Nature-nurture problem. What are the respective roles of heredity and environment in the structuring of human behaviour, intelligence, personality, etc?

Neanderthal man. Extinct species of man who lived approximately 100 000 years ago in Europe and the Middle East.

Near point of convergence. The closest one can bring an object to the eyes without seeing it double.

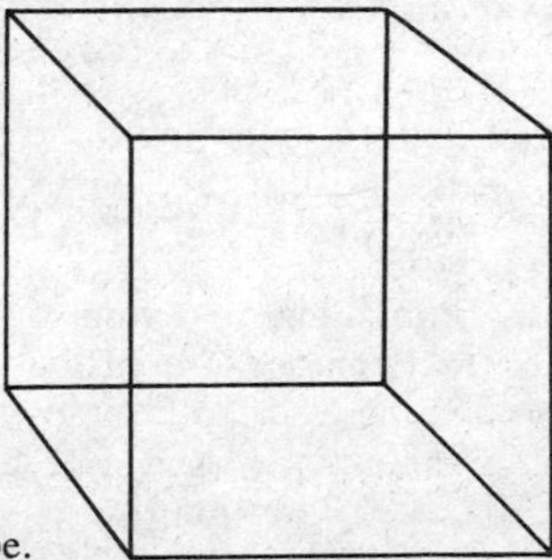

Figure 23. Necker cube.

Necker cube. One of the best examples of an AMBIGUOUS FIGURE; perspective changes are partially under voluntary control.

Necromancy. Magic involving the invocation of the dead.

Necrophilia. Sexual attraction for dead bodies.

Need. A concept of considerable importance to psychology, and in particular to theories of motivation. A need is a state set up within an organism when it is lacking something necessary for its survival or psychological well-being. Needs instigate drives – i.e. they set the animal in motion in search of something to satisfy its need – and some people argue that needs and drives are the same thing. Superficially the idea of explaining all behaviour in terms of need-reduction is a tempting one since so much of what we do is obviously dictated by hunger, thirst, sexual desire, etc. Unfortunately it becomes hard to explain more complex actions – playing chess, sunbathing and gardening, to name but a few – in these terms and most psychologists interested in need-based theories concentrate on animal behaviour to avoid such complications. Compare MOTIVATION, DRIVE.

Need for achievement. ➧ ACHIEVEMENT MOTIVE.

Need-reduction. ➧ NEED.

Negation. Denying or counteracting something.

Negative acceleration. Decrease in rate of growth.

Negative adaptation. Steady reduction in response to a constant or repeated stimulus.

Negative feedback. Occurs when some part of an integrated system generates a signal which keeps the activity of the system within limits. Compare POSITIVE FEEDBACK. (➧ FEEDBACK.)

Negative induction. Term used by PAVLOV to refer to a build-up of inhibition which occurs in an area of the cortex recently subjected to EXCITATION.

Negative practice. Deliberately repeating an error in order to overcome it. This seems to work because the constant repetition becomes identified and labelled in the subject's mind as being 'wrong'.

Negative reinforcement. Punishing or failing to reward a response in order to eliminate it or to decrease the probability of it occurring. (➧ CONDITIONING.) The distinction is sometimes made between negative reinforcement and punishment, the latter being assumed to be cognitive, the other instinctive or automatic.

Negative transfer. ➧ TRANSFER (OF TRAINING).

Negative transference. ➧ TRANSFERENCE.

Negative tropism. Tendency for an organism to move *away* from the source of stimulation.

Negativism. Tendency to resist suggestions or ideas coming from someone else.

Nembutal. The trade name for the narcotic drug pentobarbitone sodium.

Neo-. As a prefix, means new.

Neobehaviourism. A modification of the hard-line position advocated by PAVLOV and WATSON. It holds that while behaviour is still the sole subject matter of psychology, it is unrealistic to ignore verbal behaviour, conscious ideas, thought processes, etc., simply because they cannot be studied with ease in a laboratory.

Neocortex. The isocortex; six layers of cells comprising part of the grey matter of the cerebral hemispheres.

Neo-Freudian. A psychoanalyst who holds to FREUD's main ideas but also accepts important modifications coming from rival theorists, such as Adler, Horney and Fromm.

Neologism. A new word; sometimes used of the bizarre speech of schizophrenics.

Neonate. The newborn infant, up to the age of one month.

Neopallium. The cerebral cortex as a whole but not including the olfactory bulbs.

Neophasia. The peculiar semi-nonsense language often created by schizophrenics.

Neoplasm. A tumour or growth.

Nerve. May mean a single NEURONE, but more generally refers to a bundle of them.

Nerve cell. May refer to a NEURONE, or to the cell body which is its central part.

Nerve ending. The end process of a neurone.

Nerve fibre. An axon or dendrite; the long process running from the cell body.

Nerve plexus. A cluster of integrated neurones.

Nerve root. A collection of neurones joining the brain or spinal cord.

Nervism. PAVLOV's doctrine that all behaviour was under the control of the nervous system.

Nervous breakdown. The popular term for a condition caused by prolonged or severe overload of the nervous system, generally accompanied by anxiety, sleeplessness and extreme emotionalism. More specifically, it means any kind of neurotic illness severe enough to require at least temporary hospitalization.

Nervous debility. ➧ NEURASTHENIA.

Nervous habit. Any repetitive act which reduces psychological tension, e.g. nail biting, smoking, etc.

Nervous impulse. A change in the electrical potential of the surface of a NEURONE which passes from one end of the cell to another at a rate which may exceed 100m a second. The nerve impulse is an all-or-nothing affair – either the cell fires completely or does not fire at all.

Nervous system. The sum total of all the neuronal tissue in the body, and traditionally classified into the central and peripheral nervous systems. The former consists of the brain and spinal cord and the latter of the remainder. From a functional point of view, one can also speak of the somatic and autonomic nervous systems, the former dealing with conscious, deliberate actions, the latter with all automatic behaviour from emotional states to cardiac control. The autonomic system is itself subdivided into the sympathetic and parasympathetic systems whose activities tend to balance each other out.

Nervous tissue. Collections of nerve cells as opposed to any of the other specialized cells in the body.

Nesting. The apparently instinctive home-building activities of birds.

Neural. Relating to nerves or their activities.

Neural arc. A circuit of neurones acting together as a functional system.

Neural discharge. The firing of a single nerve cell.

Neural excitation. The triggering of a nerve cell.

Neural facilitation. Anything which increases the likelihood of a neurone or collection of nerve cells firing. The term also refers to anything increasing the ease with which an impulse crosses a synapse.

Neuralgia. Pain felt along the course of a nerve and often without any clear sign of disease or damage.

Neural groove. The groove in the neural plate of the embryo which turns into the neural tube.

Neural induction. Any positive (enhancing) or negative (damping) effect by one part of the nervous system on another.

Neural irritability. The tendency for a nerve cell to fire when stimulated.

Neural noise. Background activity within the nervous system caused by spontaneous firing of cells.

Neural plate. The tissue in the embryo which develops into the central nervous system in general.

Neural set. A state of readiness to fire (generally to particular stimuli) which may exist in a neural circuit.

Neural tube. The tube in the embryo which develops into the brain and spinal cord.

Neurasthenia. Neurosis marked by chronic tiredness and inability to concentrate.

Neuraxis. Brain and spinal cord.

Neurilemma. The outer covering of nerve cells; may include or be additional to the myelin sheath.

Neurin. Term used for the energy tied up in the nervous impulse; also a protein constituent of neural tissue.

Neuritis. Inflammation of a nerve or nerves, whether of a simple or severe nature.

Neuroanatomy. The study of the structure of the NERVOUS SYSTEM.

Neurobiotaxis. The supposed tendency for neurones to grow or develop towards other neurones with which they regularly communicate.

Neuroblast. A neurone in embryonic form.

Neurocirculatory asthenia. Shortness of breath, palpitations, etc., when neurotic in origin.

Neurocyte. Alternative name for NEURONE.

Neurodermatitis. Skin disorder, neurotic in origin.

Neuroendocrinology. The study of the interaction between HORMONES and the NERVOUS SYSTEM.

Neurofibre. ➧ FIBRE.

Neurofibril. Tiny threads running through nerve fibres and believed to be important in neural conductivity.

Neurogenic. Nervous in origin.

Neuroglia. ➧ GLIAL CELLS.

Neurogram. A permanent change taking place in a part of the nervous system following activity (such as learning). The term is roughly equivalent to ENGRAM.

Neurohumoral. Referring to the activity of chemical substances which are produced by a nerve cell.

Neurology. Study of the anatomy and physiology of the NERVOUS SYSTEM.

Neuromuscular. Relating to the interaction between neurones and muscles.

Neurone. Cell specialized for communication purposes and in particular for the transmission of electrical energy within the body. Neurones consists of a central part (cell body), a long trunk running out from the main body (axon), and a collection of thinner, straggly fibres generally developing out of the opposite side of the cell body (dendrites). The function of the axon and dendrites is to make contact with other cells and thus provide the colossal interwoven network which makes up the NERVOUS SYSTEM.

Neuropathic. Relating to an ORGANIC DISORDER, as opposed to a FUNCTIONAL DISORDER of the nervous system.

Neuropharmacology. The study of the pharmacology of the NERVOUS SYSTEM.

Neurophysiology. The study of the detailed function of the NERVOUS SYSTEM.

Neuropile. Collection of interwoven nerve fibres.

Neuropsychiatry. The study of the treatment of mental illness caused by disorders of the NERVOUS SYSTEM.

Neurosis. Relatively mild behavioural or psychological disorder assumed not to have any organic origin and generally responsive to treatment.

Neurotic. Relating to a NEUROSIS.

Neurotic character. Adlerian term for someone driven to seek power because of his own belief that he is inferior in some way.

Neurotic process factor. Term used by Cattell to refer to the trait, supposedly detectable by certain tests, which most clearly marks out the neurotic from the 'normal' individual.

Neurotic solution. Eliminating a conflict by repressing it or denying its existence.

Neurotic trend. Falling back on childish devices for relieving anxiety. (➧ REGRESSION.)

Neutral. Lying between extremes; uncommitted.

Neutral colour. One of the greys.

Neutralization. Roughly, sublimation; the conversion of strong instinctive drives into 'intellectual' ones.

Neutral stimulus. Stimulus not relevant to a particular sense organ or cell. PAVLOV used the term to refer to the 'to-be-conditioned stimulus' – i.e. the bell which was neutral for the animal until it became conditioned as a signal for food. It is also known as the indifferent stimulus.

Nexus. The point of contact between two forces; any kind of bond or linkage.

Nicotine. Alkaloid with a stimulating effect on the nervous system.

Nietzsche, Friedrich (1844 – 1900). German philosopher who recognized the enormous importance of unconscious forces controlling behaviour and who was the first to use the term ID to describe them.

Night blindness. Weak capacity for dark adaptation; may be due to vitamin A deficiency or deficiency of rods, but the main cause is RETINITIS PIGMENTOSA. Compare HEMERALOPIA.

Nightmare. Violent or extremely unpleasant dream whose content promotes body movement or changes in the autonomic nervous system which lead to wakening.

Night terrors. 'Waking' nightmares or semi-hallucinatory states occurring in childhood. The child sits up in bed, appears to be terrified and cannot be comforted. After a while normal sleep is restored.

Nirvana. A blissful state; in religious terms, the merging of the soul with God.

Nissl granules. Tiny bodies found in the neural cell and believed to have a regenerative function.

Nitrous oxide. Laughing gas; a mild narcotic and anaesthetic.

Nociceptor. A pain receptor.

Noctambulism. More commonly, SOMNAMBULISM.

Nodal points. Important in optical theory, the nodal points are those points in a lens through which a ray of light passes in parallel to itself.

Node. A lump or swelling.

Noesis. Reasoning or conscious judgement.

Noise. In its simplest form, objectionable sound. The term has a special meaning in communication theory where it refers to scattered, unstructured information or anything which interferes with the clarity of a signal.

Nominal aphasia. Inability to name an object.

Nominalism. The philosophy that objects are the only true reality and that concepts, ideas, etc., have no existence in their own right.

Nominal scale. Classification of objects by simply naming them and without any regard to their characteristics.

Nomograph. A chart on which variables can be plotted in such a way that a straight line drawn through two of the known variables will inevitably locate the third. It thus defines a relationship between the three variables.

Nomology. Scientific study of laws and principles.

Nomothetic. Relating to general laws and principles rather than those applying to individuals. Compare IDIOGRAPHIC.

Nonconformity. ➧ CONFORMITY.

Non-continuity theory. ➧ DISCONTINUITY THEORY.

Nondetermination coefficient. In statistics, the amount of variation in the DEPENDENT VARIABLE which is *not* caused by the INDEPENDENT VARIABLE.

Non-directive therapy. An approach to psychotherapy based on the ideas of Carl ROGERS. The therapist acts as a guide and counsellor, directing the course of therapy far less than by the more traditional methods. One of the main aims of the technique is to provide a permissive and non-authoritarian atmosphere in therapeutic sessions, designed to relieve 'clients' (patients) of their guilt and break down the usual doctor-patient barriers. Compare DIRECTIVE THERAPY. (➧➧ CLIENT-CENTRED THERAPY.)

Non-linear. Not following a straight line.

Non-linear regression. A relationship between two variables whose valucs produce a curved line when plotted on a graph.

Non-literate. Anthropological term for a society or culture without a written language.

Nonparametric statistics. Statistical methods applied to data other than normal distributions. (➧➧ PARAMETRIC STATISTICS.)

Non-rational. Outside the bounds of normal reasoning.

Figure 24. Nonsense figures.

Nonsense figure. Form or shape with no meaning or easily describable association. Compare IMPOSSIBLE FIGURE.

Nonsense syllable. A word, such as BIJ or KUG, which can be spoken or written but which has no meaning or obvious associations. Such words were first used by Ebbinghaus in his experiments on the learning of 'fresh' and novel material.

Nonverbal communication. The tremendous power and utility of the spoken language amongst humans leads one to the general assumption that this is the only important method of direct information exchange between people (written language being taken as delayed or indirect). In fact humans use a great variety of nonverbal signs or signals to assist them in communication. At the simplest and perhaps most obvious level, we have grimaces of pleasure, pain or threat, and there is even some suggestion that chemical signals, in the form of PHEROMONES, might give unconscious indicants as to fear or sexual arousal. Recent research, notably by Argyle in England, has studied such relatively specific signals as nods of the head, eye-to-eye contact, hand gestures, body posture and so on. These seem to play a role in maintaining the flow of conversation within a group by indicating such factors as continued attention, comprehension or lack of it, boredom, desire to interrupt and lead conversation, willingness to yield to another speaker, etc.

Nonverbal intelligence. Verbal skills are culturally biased – a normal child from an average home will score higher on verbal tests than a normal child from a culturally-deprived home. For this reason INTELLIGENCE TESTS strive to examine native (e.g. concept formation, psychomotor skills, reasoning powers, etc.) rather than learned abilities, using nonverbal tests wherever reasonably possible. (◆◆ CULTURE-FREE TESTS.) It is this aspect of intelligence that is generally called nonverbal.

Noradrenalin. Also called norepinephrine. It is a hormone secreted by the adrenal glands, believed to assist the transmission of the nervous impulse across some synapses.

Norm. In experimental psychology and statistics, a value which is considered to be representative of a particular group. The term has acquired an important, essentially similar meaning in social psychology where it has come to mean behaviour shared by all members of a group or expected of all members of a group. Within a small group, norms may be enforced and maintained by sanctions such as signs of social approval or disapproval. In larger groups, such as countries, legal sanctions may be invoked. (➧➧ VALUE.)

Normal. Much abused word which has acquired unfortunate connotations of denoting 'rightness' or 'wrongness'. The term actually implies something that does not deviate markedly from the average or standard for a group.

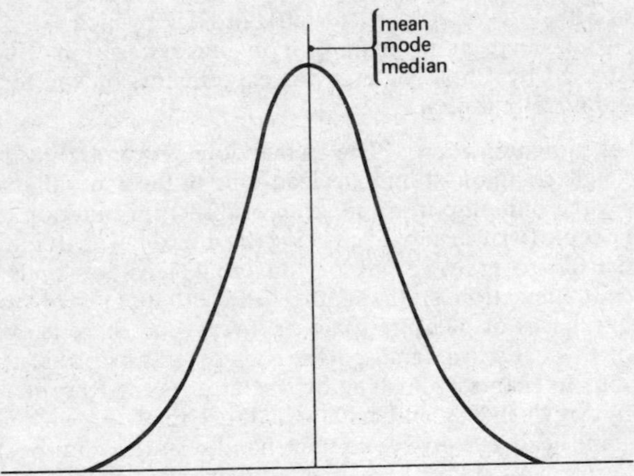

Figure 25. Normal distribution.

Normal distribution. Data which when plotted yield a bell-shaped curve, the largest number of values appearing near the mean with the remainder tailing off more or less evenly to either side of the mean. This is also known as a Gaussian curve.

Normalize. The process of adjusting or correcting data so that they can be measured against a normal distribution curve.

Normative science. The study of correct behaviour, ways of achieving it and means of preventing deviant behaviour.

Nosogenesis. ➧ PATHOGENESIS.

Nosology. The study of the classification of diseases.

Nosophobia. Abnormal fear of disease.

Nostalgia. Poignant feeling associated with a memory.

Notation. A system of symbols.

Notochord. Evolutionary forerunner of the spinal cord present in some fishes and in the human embryo.

Nuclear complex. Psychoanalytic term for the basic and fundamental source of psychological conflict in infancy. Freudians consider it to be the OEDIPUS COMPLEX (or its equivalent, the ELECTRA COMPLEX).

Nuclear family. ➧ FAMILY.

Nucleus. The 'heart' of the living cell, containing the essential mechanisms of reproduction and inheritance.

Null hypothesis. An important concept in experimental design. In a properly conducted psychological study the goal is not to prove that a particular thing is so, but rather to show that the reverse of the hypothesis is *not* so. This peculiar approach actually has advantages from a statistical point of view and leads to a more precise formulation of the problem. A successful experiment therefore is one in which the null hypothesis is overthrown.

Number completion test. Test in which the subject has to complete or fill in a string of numbers which have a definite, logical sequence.

Number factor. The ability to manipulate numbers; assumed to be a significant factor in INTELLIGENCE.

Nurture. The effect of the environment on the growth of an animal.

Nutrient. Substance capable of acting as a food.

Nyctalopia. ➧ NIGHT BLINDNESS.

Nyctophobia. Abnormal fear of the dark.

Nymphomania. Abnormal preoccupation with sex in a woman.

Nystagmus. Involuntary flicking movement of the eyes featuring a slow drift towards a fixation point, a snap back in the opposite direction followed by another slow drift, etc. This is most commonly seen after the individual has been rotated rapidly.

O

O factor. The internal state of an organism which makes predicting its behaviour uncertain even when one has complete control of stimulus variables.

Object. Anything which has sufficient persistence in time for it to be observed or measured.

Object-assembly test. Test in which an object must be assembled out of a collection of parts, e.g. MANIKIN TEST.

Object attitude. ➧ PROCESS ATTITUDE.

Object blindness. Visual agnosia; inability to recognize common objects because of brain damage.

Object cathexis. In psychoanalysis, the focusing of LIBIDO on a normally non-sexual object. (➧ CATHEXIS.)

Object colour. Colour perceived as being present in an object rather than coming from some other source. (➧➧ SURFACE COLOUR; FILM COLOUR.)

Object constancy. Tendency for known objects to appear much the same in shape, size and colour no matter how the environment changes.

Objective. Real to the extent that it is capable of being studied or measured systematically. The term also implies something outside the body and thus capable with being shared by others.

Objective anxiety. Anxiety with an obvious cause (as opposed to neurotic anxiety).

Objective test. Any test whose scoring does not permit experimenter error or bias; also refers to any test which is repeatable and whose results are comparable to those of a previous similar experiment. Contrast SUBJECTIVE TEST.

Oblique muscles. A pair of muscles which rotate the eye.

Oblique solution. Factors not at right angles to each other (in terms of a factor analysis) and therefore shown to be correlated. Contrast ORTHOGONAL SOLUTION.

Obliviscence. Fading of memory due to the passage of time. (⧫⧫ FORGETTING.)

Obscenity. Anything – not necessarily sexual – which offends contemporary taste or values.

Obscurantism. Anything which tends to muddle issues or cloud the truth.

Observation. Systematic inspection of something with the goal of understanding it. This is often the first stage in the scientific method, prior to carrying out an experiment. Ideally an observation should be carried out without influencing the events or phenomena being observed – an ideal less easy to achieve than one might imagine. An experiment, while more specific than an observation, always involves some manipulation of the subject matter under study.

Observer. Someone who inspects something in a systematic way. In psychology, observer (O) is used to denote the subject in an experiment.

Obsession. A thought or idea which preoccupies the mind against the will over a sustained period of time.

Obsessional neurosis. Condition in which an obsession has become so overwhelming that it seriously interferes with the individual's life and well-being. In its common form of obsessive-compulsive neurosis, the individual is not only afflicted by obsessive thoughts but feels compelled to perform ritual, and often seemingly absurd, actions. Psychoanalysts believe that the rituals are a form of 'magical act' which somehow help to ease the unconscious mind of anxiety and guilt.

Obsessive-compulsive neurosis. ⧫ OBSESSIONAL NEUROSIS.

Obsessive personality. Individual with a generally inflexible attitude to life and a tendency to rigidity and intolerance. Compare AUTHORITARIAN PERSONALITY.

Obstacle sense. The ability which many blind people develop to detect objects in their path. It is mainly due to ECHOLOCATION.

Obstipation. Severe, neurotically-induced constipation.

Obstruction method. A technique used mainly in the study of the relative strength of different drives. For example, an animal is taught that food lies at the end of a corridor, but that it must cross, say, an electrified grid to reach it. The time delay before it crosses the grid for food is measured, and this is compared with delays for other drives.

Obtained score. The RAW SCORE.

Occam's razor. An important principle in science and rational argument. In considering rival possible explanations for a phenomenon, the simplest must always be chosen before the more complex, provided that both are in accord with the facts. (⧫⧫ LLOYD MORGAN'S LAW.)

Occipital. Relating to the occiput or back part of the brain and skull.

Occipital lobe. The hind part of the cerebrum which contains the visual cortex. (⧫ CEREBRAL HEMISPHERES.)

Occlusion. A blockage.

Occultism. The quest for hidden (occult) forces in nature.

Occupational norm. The average score for a particular occupation in a specialized test.

Occupational psychology. The study of jobs, their nature and the suitability of various individuals to perform them. (⧫ INDUSTRIAL PSYCHOLOGY.)

Occupational therapy. An approach to psychotherapy in which the patient is given constructive tasks to perform in an effort to build self-confidence.

Ocular. Relating to the eye.

Ocular dominance. Tendency for one eye to be used rather than another. Some degree of ocular dominance is present in everyone, and is related to LATERAL DOMINANCE.

Ocular pursuit movements. Automatic tracking of a moving object by the eye.

Oculogyral illusion. An enhanced form of the AUTOKINETIC EFFECT which occurs following rotation of the body.

Oculomotor. Refers to the control of eye movements.

Oculomotor nerve. The third cranial nerve, controlling most of the extrinsic eye muscles.

Oculomotor nucleus. The point in the midbrain at the level of the superior colliculus, from which the oculomotor nerve emerges.

Odic force. A psychic field supposed to surround all natural things.

Odour. Anything detectable by the sense of smell.

Odourimetry. The measuring of odours, or sensitivity to them.

Odour prism. Three-dimensional diagram which shows how the six primary odours (putrid, fragrant, ethereal, burned, spicy and resinous) are related to each other.

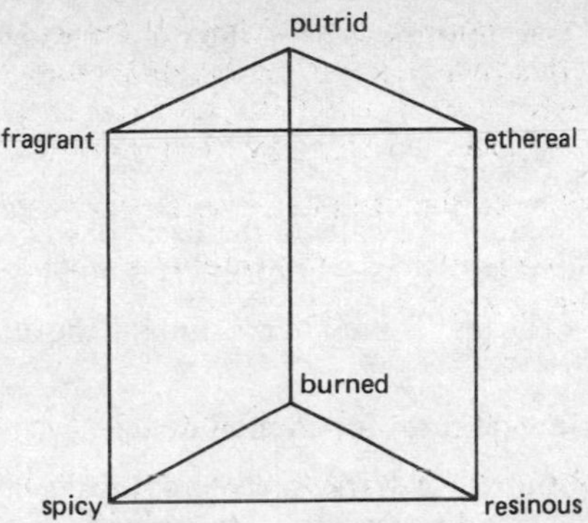

Figure 26. Odour prism.

Oedipus complex. A fundamental concept in the Freudian theory of the personality, and named after the Greek prince Oedipus who killed his father (unwittingly) and married his mother. FREUD first drew attention to the immensely strong ties that exist between mother and son which not only involve maternal tenderness, but also a strong, unconscious, sexual component. The male child, Freud argued, becomes jealous of the place his father holds in his mother's affections and is consumed by feelings of hatred and aggression for him. For obvious reasons these must be thrust down into the unconscious where they smoulder indefinitely – or at least until the boy grows up, marries someone else (often someone physically like his mother) and eradicates the tension between himself and his father. If this is not eradicated, the complex is termed unresolved and leads to tedious complications and conflicts throughout life. (⧫⧫ ELECTRA COMPLEX.)

Oestrogen. Refers to the female hormones which control the oestrus cycle.

Oestrus. Period of 'heat' or heightened sexual receptivity in the female animal.

Ogive. An S-shaped curve, typical of the plot of the progress of learning. (⧫ LEARNING CURVE.)

Ohm. Unit of electrical resistance.

Old age. Refers to the fifth DEVELOPMENT LEVEL lasting from approximately the age of sixty-five to death.

Olfactie. Unit of intensity of smell.

Olfaction. The sense of smell.

Olfactometer. Device for measuring the range and efficiency of one's sense of smell.

Olfactory bulb. One or two small lobes in the cerebral cortex which mediate the sense of smell.

Olfactory cells. Spindle-like cells in the nasal passages which respond to chemical stimulation and are the primary smell detectors.

Olfactory nerve. The first cranial nerve, linking the olfactory cells with the olfactory bulb.

Oligophrenia. General term for mental deficiency.

Omnibus test. Group IQ tests in which items testing the various factors – verbal skills, numerical skills, etc. – are mixed together rather than being presented in separate blocks as in BATTERY TESTS.

Omnipotence feeling. The instinctual belief of the ID that it is omnipotent and that all its wishes must and can be gratified.

Onanism. Withdrawing the penis before orgasm; also loosely used for masturbation.

Oneiromancy. Predicting the future by studying and interpreting dreams.

One-tailed test. In statistics, one of a number of tests which allow one to assess whether the NULL HYPOTHESIS has been rejected or not. A one-tailed test is particularly powerful if the results lie in the predicted direction. (▸▸ TWO-TAILED TEST.)

One-trial learning. Learning something, whether simple or complex, after only a single exposure to it. There is considerable controversy over whether or not such learning can take place and the matter has some theoretical significance for if it could, then any theories of learning or information storage would need to be based on some extremely rapid process such as, say, alterations in an electrical field, rather than some slower process such as a progressive change in the anatomy of nerve cells. The odd fact is that while most learning does seem to proceed rather laboriously and gradually, there are rare occasions when 'one-trial' learning does seem to occur.

Onomatomania. Habit, common among schizophrenics, of creating a new word which suggests, by its sound, the feeling or mood they are trying to convey.

Ontogenesis. The evolution of an individual as opposed to that of a race (phylogenesis).

Ontology. The study of the nature of existence or being.

Oogenesis. Development of the ovum.

Open-cue test. Test in which all cues to the solution of the problem are easy to see and detect, and the test simply measures the subject's ability to make use of the cues in completing the task.

Operant conditioning. CONDITIONING in which the animal performs a particular task, makes a particular movement or emits a particular response and is rewarded for doing so – the emphasis being on the animal manipulating its environment as opposed to its relatively passive role in classical conditioning. The term was introduced by B. F. Skinner and the methodology is the basis of modern behaviourist studies. (◊ SKINNERIAN PSYCHOLOGY.) Operant conditioning experiments involve long series of trials, with cumulative records of the rate and number of responses being plotted on graphs. In this way curves for learning, forgetting, etc., in a variety of different circumstances can be obtained. Compare CLASSICAL CONDITIONING. (◊◊ SUCCESSIVE APPROXIMATING METHOD.)

Operationism. Point of view that one can only understand a phenomenon to the extent that one can describe the techniques or procedures by which one is able to measure and study it.

Operator. In statistics, a symbol which tells one that a particular operation has to be performed on another symbol.

Ophidophobia. Abnormal fear of snakes.

Ophthalmology. Branch of medicine dealing with the structure and functions of the eye.

Ophthalmometer. Device for measuring the curvature of the cornea.

Ophthalmoscope. Device for studying the retina and the interior of the eye.

Opiate. A drug derived from opium; any sleep-inducing drug.

Opinion. What or how one thinks about something. An opinion is close to an attitude but is generally more specific. (◊◊ ATTITUDE; BELIEF.)

Opinion poll. A systematic attempt at assessing public beliefs or attitudes, conducted using a formal questionnaire and, ideally, using unbiased interviewing and classification techniques.

Opium. A narcotic and analgesic drug derived from a poppy; highly addictive.

Opposites test. Test in which the subject is asked to give the opposite to a series of things.

Optical. Relating to vision.

Optical axis. The 'line of vision'.

Optical illusion. Peculiarity of vision in which what is presented to the retinae in physical terms appears systematically distorted in perception. It is a characteristic of most optical illusions that they are seen by all human beings in much the same way, and that they do not diminish significantly with practice at viewing them or with knowledge that they *are* distortions. (➧➧ ILLUSION; GEOMETRICAL ILLUSION.)

Optic chiasma. ➧ CHIASMA.

Optic disc. The point at which the optic nerve leaves the retina. This is insensitive to light and thus known as the blind spot.

Optic lobes. The SUPERIOR COLLICULI.

Optic nerve. The second cranial nerve, the collection of nerve fibres drawn from the retina and carrying visual information to the optic chiasma. From the optic chiasma to the brain the pathway is known as the optic tract.

Optic tract. The upper part of the optic nerve, leading from the chiasma to the thalamus and the superior colliculus.

Optimum. Best or most suitable.

Optogram. ➧ RETINAL IMAGE.

Optokinetic effect. A special case of APPARENT MOVEMENT which may occur when the eyes move in response to visual stimulation. Movement is 'inferred' in the object being fixated.

Optometry. The measurement of the eye and its visual capabilities.

Oral aggressive type. Psychoanalytic term for anyone whose personality is hypercritical, verbally aggressive, jealous and spiteful. These traits are said to be due to a lack of fulfilment during the oral stage of development in infancy.

Oral character. According to psychoanalytic theory, the personality evolves through a number of distinctive phases of which the most important are the oral, anal and genital stages, but for various reasons evolution may be arrested at the oral or anal stages. An oral character carries over into adult life an infantile interest in sucking and related activities, such as cigarette smoking, and is generally self-centred. (➧➧ ANAL CHARACTER; GENITAL CHARACTER.)

Oral dependence. A desire to return to the oral phase of development.

Oral eroticism. Pleasure obtained from oral activities.

Oral-passive type. Psychoanalytic term for an inadequate, over-dependent personality.

Oral stage. Phase of development when an infant gains its maximum pleasure from chewing and sucking.

Orange. The colour perceived when the retina is stimulated with light of approximately 590-640nm wavelength.

Orbital. Relating to the eye sockets.

Order. ➧ TAXONOMY.

Ordinal. Relating to the order of magnitude.

Ordinal scale. Scale with no zero point but which expresses values as first, second, third, etc. (➧➧ RATIO SCALE; INTERVAL SCALE.)

Ordinate. The vertical axis of a graph. (➧ ABSCISSA.)

Orestes complex. Psychoanalytic term for the desire of a son to kill his mother.

Orexis. Emotional rather than intellectual aspects of behaviour.

Organ. Structure in the body with a specific function.

Organ eroticism. Concentration of LIBIDO on a particular organ.

Organ inferiority. According to ADLER, a feeling of inferiority caused by a belief – on real or imaginary grounds – that one is physically deficient in some way, which leads to attempts at compensation.

Organic. Relating to living things.

Organic disorder. Disorder caused by physiological as opposed to psychological factors. Contrast FUNCTIONAL DISORDER.

Organic psychosis. Major disorder of personality caused by some definite physical factor, such as senile psychosis involving degenerative changes in the brain.

Organic variable. ➧ O FACTOR.

Organism (O). Any collection of matter, simple or complex, which acts as a living unit and has the capacity to reproduce itself.

Organismic psychology. An approach to psychology which holds that an animal or person must be studied as a whole if it is to be properly understood.

Organization. In Gestalt psychology, the integration of parts into a unit or whole. The term may also mean a largish group whose members are working together to achieve common goals. In social psychology, the term refers to the patterns of communication within such a group, its structure and the internal cohesive forces which allow it to work towards common goals.

Organizational psychology. ➧ INDUSTRIAL PSYCHOLOGY.

Organ of Corti. Part of the inner ear containing a band of tiny hair-cells which respond to vibrations of the air and convert them into nervous impulses.

Organon. A set of principles concerning the organization and development of a particular branch of knowledge.

Orgasm. An overwhelming peak of excitement – particularly in the climax of the sexual act.

Orgiastic. Frenzied.

Orgone. A vital force supposed to permeate the universe according to the quasi-scientific theories of Wilhelm REICH. Orgone is richly present in the bodies of healthy people and becomes concentrated in the sexual organs during orgasm.

Orientating reflex. Term used by PAVLOV to refer to the way in which an animal responds physiologically (and psychologically) to novel stimuli in its environment.

Orientation. Having an awareness of spatial, temporal or practical circumstances. The term can also mean taking up a position in space with reference to physical stimuli.

Original response. An unusual response made by a subject in a RORSCHACH TEST.

Original score. The RAW SCORE.

Ornithophobia. Abnormal fear of birds.

Orthodox. Normal; according to standard teachings.

Orthogenesis. The theory that evolution is proceeding along a predetermined course.

Orthogenital. Sexually normal.

Orthognathous. Having a non-protruding jaw (a characteristic of modern man). Contrast PROGNATHOUS.

Orthogonal. Forming right angles.

Orthogonal solution. Factors at right angles to each other (in terms of factor analysis) and therefore uncorrelated.

Orthopsychiatry. Approach to psychiatry concentrating on prevention rather than cure.

Orthoptics. Training the eyes to work more effectively together.

Orthosympathetic. The THORACICO-LUMBAR or sympathetic division of the nervous system.

Oscilloscope. Cathode ray tube on which electrical wave forms, such as nervous impulses, can be projected.

Oseretsky test. Test of motor skills in children.

Osmosis. Absorption through a membrane.

Osphresis. More commonly, OLFACTION.

Osseous. Bone-like.

Ossicles. Any small bones, particularly those in the middle ear – the hammer, anvil and stirrup.

Ostwald colours. A set of standard colours with comparison sets of greys matched for brightness.

Otogenic tone. Sound generated within the auditory mechanisms rather than by any external vibration.

Otoliths. Tiny crystals of calcium in the endolymph of the inner ear which stimulate nerve-endings when thc head is moved and which help in maintaining equilibrium.

Otology. The science of the ear and its diseases.

Otosclerosis. Deafness caused by thickening of the auditory ossicles.

Outer-directed. Refers to anyone strongly motivated by social laws and the need for social approval.

Out-group. Any group of which an individual is not a member. Compare IN-GROUP.

Out-of-the-body-experience (OOBE). As the name implies, a vivid sensation of being detached from one's body. OOBEs are considered to be an important field of study in PARAPSYCHOLOGY.

Output. Any signal emitted by a transmitter.

Oval window. The membrane lying between the middle and inner ears against which the auditory ossicles vibrate.

Ovary. The female reproductive organ producing the ova, oestrogen and progesterone.

Overachiever. Any individual, but in particular a child, who exceeds the level of achievement expected from his or her age. Contrast UNDERœ ACHIEVER.

Overcompensation. Overdoing one's response or reaction to something. The term may also refer to attempts at overcoming feelings of inferiority by bombastic behaviour, etc. – an Adlerian concept.

Overdetermination. A term used by Freud to refer to something caused by a number of different factors. Most neuroses are overdetermined, for example; hence the hopelessness of trying to find a simple explanation for them.

Overlapping responses. Occur when a second response begins before the first is completed.

Overlearning. Practice which continues after a habit or task has been learned to a required criterion.

Overt. Open; not concealed in any way. Contrast COVERT.

Ovum. The female sex cell.

Oxycephalic. Having an elongated head.

Oxyopia. Unusually sharp vision.

Oxytocin. A hormone stimulating uterine contraction and the release of milk. It is used to induce labour.

P

P factor. The perseveration factor; tendency to continue with a task once it has been started.

Pacinian corpuscle. Anatomically distinctive nerve ending believed to be sensitive to pressure.

Paedo-. ➧ PEDO-.

Pain. Any unpleasant physical stimulation, rather than that specifically signalled by a particular sense such as a bad smell, taste, etc. Pain remains an outstanding physiological and psychological enigma, though a number of techniques, mainly drugs, have been developed for controlling it. It was once thought to be a definite and distinct sensation triggered off by damage or incipient damage to nervous tissue but this rule turned out to be only partially applicable; later theories suggested that pain occurred when certain deep-seated fibres were stimulated but this also had to be rejected. The most intriguing feature of the problem of pain is perhaps its strong psychological component and the wide variation in the ability of individuals to tolerate it. Experiments on blocking pain by the vigorous stimulation of apparently antagonistic nerve fibres appear to offer the most promising lead in current research. (➧➧ PHANTOM LIMB.)

Pain sense. Refers to the theory (no longer accepted) that pain is a special sense with its own organs, receptors, central nervous system, etc.

Pain spot. Tiny area of the skin highly susceptible to pain.

Paired associates. Pair of words used in studies of learning. After practice the subject is given the first of the pair and asked to recall the second.

Paired-comparison method. Psychophysical technique in which the subject has to compare each stimulus against every other stimulus, pair by pair and in all possible combinations.

Palatable. Literally, tasteable; has come to imply general sensory acceptability.

Paleoencephalon. Those parts of the brain which are oldest in evolutionary terms.

Paleopsychology. The study of behaviour patterns inherited from our evolutionary past.

Pallaesthesia. Sensitivity to vibration, generally through bone conduction.

Pallium. The CEREBRAL CORTEX.

Palmar reflex. ➧ GRASPING REFLEX.

Palmistry. Attempts to infer character and personality by studying the palms of the hands.

Palpable. Touchable; more generally implies detectable.

Palpate. To investigate by touching.

Palpebral. Relating to the eyelid.

Palpitation. Rapid and perceptible action of the heart.

Palsy. Paralysis.

Pancreas. Gland secreting, among other substances, the hormone insulin.

Panic. Extreme fear accompanied by wild and irrational behaviour, rapidly transferred from an individual to a group effect in crowds. Panic is a state characteristic of severe phobic attacks.

Panphobia. Generalized phobia which may extend to any situation.

Panpsychism. The belief that mental or spiritual events are the only true reality.

Pantheism. The belief that God exists in everything.

Panum's areas. ➧ CORRESPONDING POINTS.

Panum's phenomenon. If two parallel lines are presented to one eye, a third to the other and the images are fused in a stereoscope, the one of the two lines in the first eye which becomes fused with the single line in the other eye will be perceived as being 'closer' in the stereo image.

Paper-and-pencil test. Test needing written answers.

Papillae. Small folds occurring in sense receptors, particularly the tongue and skin.

Para-. As a prefix, implies outside or on the periphery.

Paracentral gyrus. Convolution in the middle surface of the cerebral hemispheres.

Paracentral vision. Vision on the edge of the FOVEA.

Parachromatopsia. Partial COLOUR BLINDNESS.

Paracousia. The supposed ability of deaf people to hear better when there is background noise; also refers to relative deafness for deep tones.

Paradigm. A detailed, comprehensive model or theory.

Paradoxical cold. When certain spots on the skin are touched with a stimulus whose temperature is about 42°, a *cold* sensation may be felt.

Paradoxical sleep. Phase of sleep in which muscles are relaxed and the individual appears deeply unconscious, but with vigorous electrical activity occurring in some parts of the brain. The state is often associated with RAPID EYE MOVEMENTS and assumed to be related to dreaming.

Paradoxical warmth. When certain spots on the skin are touched with a stimulus whose temperature is about 30°C, a *warm* sensation may be felt.

Paraesthesia. Inappropriate sensory responses, e.g. when something warm is felt as cold.

Parageusia. A distortion or hallucination of taste perception.

Paragnosia. Alternative name for EXTRA-SENSORY PERCEPTION.

Paragraphia. Inclusion of inappropriate or unusual words into writing; often a symptom of brain damage.

Parakinesis. In parapsychology, movement of objects by supernatural powers.

Paralalia. Loss of the ability to utter certain speech sounds.

Paralexia. Disorder of reading in which words appear nonsensical to the reader.

Parallax. When one moves the head from side to side, near objects appear to move more rapidly than further ones; also, objects further than the fixated point seem to move in the direction of the head movement, while those in front of the fixation point seem to move opposite to it. Parallax is one of the most important cues in DEPTH PERCEPTION.

Parallelism. ➧ PSYCHOPHYSICAL PARALLELISM.

Parallel law. One of Fechner's laws of psychophysics; when two stimuli of different intensity are experienced, their absolute intensity fades as a result of adaptation, but their relative intensity to each other remains constant.

Paralogia. Illogical speech.

Paralogism. Fallacious reasoning of which the perpetrator is unaware.

Paralysis. Any loss of motor function.

Paralysis agitans. ➧ PARKINSONISM.

Paralytic dementia. ➧ PARESIS.

Paramecium. Single-celled organism; one of the simplest forms of life believed capable of rudimentary learning.

Parameter. A constant defining the curve of an equation describing some psychological functions. The term may also be used to describe a variable held constant in one experiment but which may be varied in other experiments.

Parametric statistics. Statistical methods applied to normal distributions. (➧➧ NON-PARAMETRIC STATISTICS.)

Paramnesia. A powerful distortion of memory. (➧➧ DÉJÀ VU.)

Paranoia. A mental disorder which typically features delusions of various kinds, especially of persecution. (➧➧ PARANOID SCHIZOPHRENIA.)

Paranoid. Refers to a personality characterized by suspicion and extreme defensiveness.

Paranoid schizophrenia. A psychosis featuring delusions and hallucinations of a systematic kind, often that the individual is being persecuted by malign forces of whose existence only he is aware. (➧➧ SCHIZOPHRENIA.)

Paranosic. Relates to any gains made by a patient as the direct result of his illness. In psychoanalysis, the term refers to the relief of tension in the unconscious mind that occurs when conflicts are 'discharged' in the form of neurotic symptoms.

Paraphasia. The use of inappropriate words in speech.

Paraphilia. More or less obsolete term for sexual perversion.

Paraphrenia. Obsolete term for a type of schizophrenia.

Paraplegia. Paralysis of the lower limbs.

Parapraxis. Slight errors of speech, thought or writing, e.g. slips of the tongue.

Parapsychology. The scientific study of so-called paranormal phenomena such as telepathy, precognition, psychokinesis, etc., and generally grouped under the heading EXTRA-SENSORY PERCEPTION. Man has an extensive folklore connected with apparent telepathic experience, premonitory dreams and the like but it was not until the foundation of the Society for Psychical Research in London in 1882 that scientists first attempted to investigate this enigmatic material systematically. Even then the main focus of interest was the phenomena of the seance room, which enjoyed a boom with Spiritualism in the nineteenth century.

The foundation of a research laboratory at Duke University in North Carolina in 1927 under McDougall and Rhine marked the birth of parapsychology proper. Here, for almost four decades, Rhine and a team of co-workers laboriously gathered together evidence for ESP, largely by an immense series of carefully controlled tests with cards and mechanically-thrown dice. Despite numerous papers in scientific journals, however, and sustained support from a number of eminent scientists, parapsychology seems to be making slow, if any headway. Its main weakness is the fact that experiments performed in parapsychology laboratories rarely, if ever, seem to be replicable in less sympathetic environments. In 1965 the Parapsychology Laboratory at Duke closed with Rhine's retirement, and no other university in any part of the world is at present carrying on parapsychological research on the scale of the pioneering department at Duke.

Parasympathetic nervous system. Part of the AUTONOMIC NERVOUS SYSTEM controlling what one might describe as the 'resting' functions of the body, including the processes of digestion and elimination, and the maintenance of a steady heart rate. Its functions are integrated with those of the sympathetic nervous system.

Parathyroids. Glands located close to the thyroid and responsible for calcium metabolism.

Paratypic. Relating to environmental influence. Contrast GENOTYPE.

Paresis. Partial paralysis. The term is sometimes used to refer to GENERAL PARALYSIS OF THE INSANE.

Parietal. Relating to the middle part of the top of the cranium. The parietal lobe is a part of the cerebrum lying between the frontal and occipital lobes, and it has an important part to play in sensory functions. (➧ CEREBRAL HEMISPHERES.)

Paris school. The name given to the approach to HYPNOSIS instigated by Charcot in Paris in the late nineteenth century and generally contrasted with the NANCY SCHOOL. Charcot, who taught Freud, believed that hypnosis was essentially an abnormal condition associated with hysteria.

Parkinsonism. Disorder of the nervous system featuring coarse tremor of the limbs and muscular rigidity.

Parosmia. Disturbance of the sense of smell.

Parotid gland. Salivary gland lying just below the ear.

Paroxysm. A convulsion.

Parsimony law. ➧ OCCAM'S RAZOR.

Parthenogenesis. Reproduction of offspring from an unfertilized ovum; occurs in some simple animal forms.

Partial correlation. Statistical term for the correlation that exists between two variables after the effects of other variables on the original correlation have been eliminated or corrected for.

Partial reinforcement. In a learning or conditioning experiment, rewarding an animal intermittently for correct responses. There is some evidence suggesting that partial reinforcement may be more successful at establishing a habit than regular reward.

Participation. A term used by Piaget to describe the way in which children fail to discriminate between externally and internally caused events.

Particular complex. Psychoanalytic term for a COMPLEX induced by some specific event in an individual's life rather than by one of the 'universal' conflicts such as the Oedipus complex.

Partile. Refers to the division of data into a number of equally separated groups or classes, e.g. percentile (100 equal points of separation).

Part method. An approach to learning which stresses the need to break down material-to-be-learned into manageable segments, rather than attempting overall mastery. (➧ WHOLE METHOD.)

Parturition. Childbirth.

Passive. Receptive; not inclined to instigate activity.

Passive vocabulary. The total number of words a person can *understand*, as opposed to the number he can *use* (active vocabulary).

Passivism. Sexual submissiveness.

Pastoral. Counselling: an approach to psychotherapy, common in the USA, in which the therapist is an individual with religious as well as orthodox psychological training.

Patellar reflex. Knee-jerk reflex.

Path. In neurophysiology, a well-established link between one part of the nervous system and another.

Pathogen. Anything which can cause a disease or suffering.

Pathogenesis. The onset of a disease or the conditions associated with its onset.

Pathological. Abnormal, but with an ascribable cause.

Pathology. The study of diseases. It can also refer to any physical disorder of the body including the nervous system.

Pathomimesis. Feigning illness or disease.

Pathoneurosis. Psychoanalytic term for a neurotic condition centred around a genuine physical disability or illness.

Pathos. Suffering; anything arousing sympathy.

Patriarchy. A male-dominated social group. Contrast MATRIARCHY.

Patrilineal. Relating to a society in which lines of descent are traced through the male.

Pattern perception. The detection and recognition of shape and form by the brain or some automatic device.

Pavlov, Ivan Petrovitch (1849 – 1936). Russian physiologist and Nobel prizewinner who had an immense influence on twentieth-century physiology and psychology. In the case of psychology he is best remembered for his work on the conditioned reflex which showed that – contrary to the rather pessimistic mood of the time – animal behaviour could be studied in a systematic way and reduced, if sufficiently rigorous techniques were used, to a sequence of discrete units or building blocks – conditioned reflexes. Out of his ideas sprang the school of behaviourism, which has dominated Western and Soviet psychology in one form or another for fifty years. (➧ CONDITIONING; BEHAVIOURISM.)

Pavlovian conditioning. ➧ CLASSICAL CONDITIONING.

Pavlovianism. An approach to psychology which holds that all behaviour, physical and mental, must ultimately be explicable in terms of conditioned reflexes.

Pavor nocturnus. ➧ NIGHT TERRORS.

Pearson, Karl (1857–1936). British mathematician who pioneered the use of statistical methods in psychology.

Peccatophobia. Abnormal fear of committing a sin.

Pecking order. When animals find themselves living together in a relatively confined space they quickly establish a social hierarchy in which dominant individuals acquire feeding, mating and territorial rights. These are established as the result of ritual 'battles' – pecking contests in the case of birds – which serve to avoid more serious conflict in crowded conditions.

Pectoral. Relating to the chest.

Pedagogy. The scientific study of educational methods.

Pedantry. Excessive desire for orderliness; fussy attention to detail.

Pederasty. Practice of having sexual intercourse with children, particularly boys.

Pediatrics. The study of the diseases and illnesses of childhood.

Pedo-. As a prefix, means relating to children.

Pedophilia. Sexual attraction for young children.

Peer. Someone equal, or of the same age.

Pellagra. A nutritional deficiency which may cause acute nervous disorder.

Penilingus. Another name for FELLATIO.

Penis envy. Freudian concept based on the assumption that little girls envy their brothers because they possess a penis; they also believe that the reason they lack a penis is because they have been castrated as a punishment by a parent. (➧➧ CASTRATION COMPLEX.)

Penology. The study of the prevention of crime and the treatment of criminals.

Pentobarbitone. A barbiturate used to produce sleep.

Pentothal. A drug used as a short-acting general anaesthetic.

Peptic. Relating to the stomach or digestion.

Perceived difference. ➧ SENSED DIFFERENCE.

Percentile. One of the points dividing a population of scores into groups, each of which contains a hundredth of the total number. The fortieth percentile would be that point below which 40 per cent of the group lie and above which 60 per cent lie. The median is, of course, the fiftieth percentile point.

Percentile curve. Cumulative curve, normally ogival (S-shaped), in which scores are plotted on the abscissa and percentiles on the ordinate.

Percentile norm. Norm expressed as the percentile grouping of scores as opposed to their average.

Percept. Whatever it is that is perceived; the final stage in the perceptual process.

Perception. One of the major functions of the brain is to coordinate information coming in through the sense organs and, by relating this to information already stored in the memory, interpret it in such a way that the animal can make accurate, rapid and appropriate responses. The more flexible and complex the brain and the greater the memory store, the more important is this interpretive process. This translation of the raw data from the senses into 'meaning' by the brain is the process known as perception. It needs to be firmly distinguished from SENSATION which is the acquisition of information by the senses and its transmission upwards to the brain. Sensation is essentially a passive activity, perception a dynamic one.

Perceptual defence. A term introduced in the 1950s at the time of the first experimental studies of subliminal perception. Subjects viewing 'taboo' words in a TACHISTOSCOPE would claim not to have recognized the words, but at the same time changes in the electrical conductivity of the skin (GSR) would indicate some level of emotional arousal. The assumption was that some part of the brain was 'defending' consciousness against something perceptually threatening. Part of the effect was probably due to a certain inhibition about speaking the taboo words aloud to the experimenter, and there is still controversy over whether the words were actually recognized at one centre in the brain and then blocked from consciousness by another. (◆◆ SUBLIMINAL PERCEPTION.)

Perceptual distortion. Any mismatch between data provided to the sense organs and the perceptual experience, e.g. illusions.

Perceptual field. All that is consciously perceived in the sensory environment. This need not include all the sensory information present.

Perceptual learning. Learning to interpret, recognize and understand sense data.

Perceptual schema. An internal 'mental map' or framework which allows one to plot behaviour in advance. Compare COGNITIVE MAP.

Perceptual segregation. The division of the perceptual field into separate units or entities – objects, sounds, etc.

Perceptuomotor learning. Acquiring skills which involve the integration of cognitive and motor processes, e.g. ball games, driving, etc.

Percipient. Someone who perceives. The term has a special meaning in parapsychology where it refers to the individual who tries to receive information in an ESP test.

Perfect pitch. ➧ ABSOLUTE PITCH.

Performance. Activity; one's ability (as opposed to one's aptitude) as revealed by a test.

Peri-. As a prefix, implies around.

Perimeter. Device used for mapping the sensitivity of various parts of the retina to colours, shapes, brightness, etc.

Period. The time of one complete cycle when part of a regular series.

Peripheral. On the outer edge or surface.

Peripheralism. Point of view which emphasizes that psychology must concentrate on the observation of peripheral rather than central events – e.g. objective studies of behaviour rather than inferences about mental processes, etc.

Peripheral nerve. Any nerve connecting receptors or effectors with the central nervous system.

Peripheral nervous system. The whole of the nervous system other than the brain and spinal cord. (➧➧ CENTRAL NERVOUS SYSTEM.)

Peripheral vision. Vision involving parts of the retina other than the fovea; the periphery of the retina is largely made up of rods, insensitive to colour but more responsive to low illumination.

Peristalsis. Repetitive contractions of the stomach and intestines which force the contents down the alimentary tract. In antiperistalsis the contents are forced upwards.

Permeability. Penetrability.

Persecution mania. ➧ PARANOIA.

Perseveration. Tendency for an activity to be continued even if it is no longer productive.

Perseverative trace. A term used by HULL to refer to the tendency of a neurone to continue to fire with steadily diminishing activity even after the original stimulus has ceased. This is assumed to be one mechanism by which memories might be established.

Persistence of vision. Tendency for visual experience to persist briefly after the stimulus has been removed. (➧➧ AFTER-IMAGE.)

Persona. Jungian term for that part of the personality which is concerned with conscious experience and interaction with the world. It is roughly equivalent to the Freudian concept of the EGO, but refers more generally to the personality. (▶▶ PERSONAL UNCONSCIOUS.)

Personal construct theory. Theory which says that every individual has a set of ways of construing the world, largely unconscious when being used. These constructs can, however, be elicited by special techniques, e.g. the repertory grid.

Personal equation. When different people perform a task or observe an event, their performance or descriptions of the event vary slightly. This variation is the personal equation.

Personal identity. Awareness of oneself as a separate, distinct being. (▶▶ SELF-CONCEPT.)

Personalism. Approach which holds that individual personality should be the main focus of study in philosophy or psychology.

Personalistic psychology. Approach which holds that behaviour throughout life is determined by personality characteristics rather than the opposite view that personality is moulded by life experiences and behaviour.

Personality. A major field of study – in the view of some theorists *the* major field – in psychology. As a general definition one could say that an individual's personality is an amalgam of all his characteristics and traits including those perceived by himself (conscious personality or self-image), those of which he is not aware but which still partly determine his behaviour (unconscious personality) and all those observable to other people (social or objective personality). Most theories also stress that the concept of personality implies not only a collection of traits and characteristics, but also their interaction in a dynamic, more-or-less harmonious whole.

The study of personality itself can be broken down into three main approaches.

1. Attempts at assessing or measuring it.
2. Attempts at modifying, moulding or controlling it.
3. Attempts at explaining and understanding its mechanisms.

No individual approach can make much headway without taking account of the others and most workers in the field find themselves involved in all three. Despite the enormous complexity of the problem the study of personality has been making steady, if gentle, headway with gradually more reliable tests being developed, methods of treating personality disorders improving and integrative theories – particularly those which take account of unconscious processes – gaining slowly in credibility and usefulness. (▶ ADLER; FREUD; JUNG; CONSTITUTIONAL THEORIES; RATIONAL TYPE; INTROVERSION.)

Personality disorder. Not an illness in the sense of a neurosis or psychosis, but rather a failure on the part of an individual to adjust to society or his fellow men.

Personality inventory. One of a number of personality tests featuring a set of statements such as 'I seldom get depressed' against which the subject selects one of a fixed set of responses, such as 'True', 'False' or 'Doubtful'.

Personality types. Classification of people according to certain dominant, easily-measurable traits. Perhaps the best known are Jung's INTROVERSION EXTRAVERSION traits. (➧ SHELDONIAN THEORY; KRETSCHMER.)

Personal unconscious. Jung's theory held that the personality consisted essentially of three parts – the conscious or PERSONA (roughly equivalent to Freud's ego), the COLLECTIVE UNCONSCIOUS (instincts and memories shared by all mankind) and the personal unconscious. The latter represents all unconscious ideas, memories, etc., which are peculiar to the individual.

Personification. Assigning human-like qualities to inanimate objects or animals. (➧➧ ANTHROPOMORHISM.)

Personnel selection. Attempt at applying objective methods (e.g. the use of standardized tests) in choosing staff.

Personology. Rare term for the study of personality.

Perspective. Refers to the perception of the relationship between things, most commonly their relative position in the visual field.

Perspicacity. Quickness at seeing the root of a problem or its solution.

Perspicuity. Ability of self-expression.

Perturbation. A disturbance of some kind; in information theory, the distortion of a message in the course of transfer from transmitter to receiver.

Perversion. Any change of course away from the real goal; has come to imply sexual deviancy, in particular sexual behaviour which offends the morals of a society. Clearly there are no absolute standards, for what is perversion in one century or society may be treated as normal in another.

Petit mal. Minor form of EPILEPSY in which there is generally no loss of consciousness or convulsions, and in which the major symptoms may be dizziness or a sense of detachment. The condition is seen especially in children.

Peyote. A species of cactus yielding the hallucinatory drug mescaline.

Phaedra complex. Sexual desire by a mother for her son.

Phagocyte. Body cell whose function it is to engulf and destroy bacteria, etc.

Phagophobia. Abnormal fear of eating.

Phallic. Relating to the penis, or phallus.

Phallic phase. In psychoanalytic theory, the first part of the genital stage of development (➧ GENITAL CHARACTER). In the phallic phase the child first becomes aware of the pleasure gained from stimulation of the sex organs, and also begins to attempt to express his or her sexuality (if only unconsciously) on the parent of the opposite sex.

Phallic symbol. Any object which can be taken as representing the penis. Typical phallic symbols include snakes, church steeples, pencils, etc., and according to psychoanalysts are common in art, mythology and in the raw material of dreams. (➧➧ SEXUAL SYMBOLISM.)

Phantasm. A ghost or hallucination.

Phantasmagoria. Conjuring up demons or the spirits of the dead.

Phantasy. ➧ FANTASY.

Phantom limb. After the surgical removal of a limb, the patient may retain an 'image' of the limb as though it were still present. Occasionally PAIN may be felt in the phantom limb and this is not always relieved by local anaesthesia in the stump. The permanence of the image is probably related to the fact that the original limb had built up a good deal of representation in neural terms in the cortex, which of course would not vanish simply because the source of supply of the neurones had been removed.

Pharmacology. The scientific study of drugs and chemicals which affect living things.

Pharmacy. The preparation of drugs in a medical context.

Pharynx. The passageway that leads from the mouth and nose into the oesophagus and larynx.

Phase difference. Differences in the cyclical rhythms of two sounds so that trough and trough and crest and crest fail to correspond.

Phase sequence. A concept used by Hebb in his CELL ASSEMBLY theory of perception. Whereas cell assemblies correspond to the perception of complete patterns, phase sequences are collections of cell assemblies and correspond to continuous rather than momentary perception.

Phenobarbitone. One of the first barbiturates used in medicine; an addictive sedative and anticonvulsant.

Phenomenal field. Everything being consciously experienced at the time.

Phenomenalism. Doctrine advanced by Kant that we can never know true reality but only the representation of it.

Phenomenal regression. Despite rapid changes in the size of its projected image on the retina as an object is moved towards or away from the eye, the object tends not to change its *apparent* size greatly – a phenomenon known as CONSTANCY. However, with repeated observation, the apparent size of the moving object creeps steadily away from 'perfect constancy', and closer to its objective or retinal image size. This shift is known as phenomenal regression.

Phenomenal self. One's perceived self; how one imagines oneself really to be. (⧫⧫ LOOKING-GLASS SELF.)

Phenomenology. The study of consciousness by introspection and subjective inspection of mental events. This approach to psychology is rigorously rejected by behaviourist schools.

Phenomenon. Anything perceivable or observable.

Phenomotive. A motive of which one is consciously aware.

Phenothiazines. A class of modern tranquillizing drugs.

Phenotype. The observable, described characteristics of an animal, or group of animals; assumed to be the result of the interaction of the genetic material (GENOTYPE) with the physical environment.

Phenylketonuria. Mental deficiency caused by an hereditary inability of the body properly to metabolize the amino acid phenylanaline; sometimes known as phenylpyruvic oligophrenia.

Phenylthiocarbamide (PTC). A substance which to most people tastes unpleasantly bitter, to others it is completely tasteless. The ability to taste is known to be genetically determined, and PTC is therefore used in the study of population and race.

Pheromones. Chemical substances given off by animals which trigger courtship, or sometimes aggressive, behaviour in others.

Phi-gamma function. S-shaped curve or ogive obtained when integrated data obtained from a psychophysical experiment employing the constant method are plotted.

Philosopher's stone. Substance sought by alchemists which it was believed would change base metals into gold.

Philosophy. Any systematic approach to the study of the nature of the universe, and also of the methods by which such studies can be conducted.

Phi phenomenon. Form of APPARENT MOVEMENT. Studies of the phi phenomenon gave impetus to the formation of the Gestalt school of psychology.

Phlegmatic. ➧ TEMPERAMENT.

Phobia. An extreme, irrational and more or less uncontrollable fear of an object, living thing or situation. A number of theories have been put forward to explain phobias, one of the most common being the psychoanalytic view that the phobia represents fear displaced from one source to another. The displacement takes place because the original fear is unacceptable – as in the case of Freud's child patient whose phobia of horses was supposed to have been traced to a displaced fear of his father (Little Hans). Other theories take the view that phobias are amplified traces of basic instinctive fears.

Phonation. Producing speech sounds.

Phone. A speech element.

Phoneidoscope. A device which converts sound waves into visual stimuli.

Phoneme. The smallest unit of speech which allows one to distinguish one word from another. For example, the sound of the letter *p* is a phoneme as it discriminates between the two similar words 'gab' and 'gap'.

Phonetics. The study of speech sounds and their classification.

Phono-. As a prefix, relates to sound.

Phonophobia. Abnormal fear of sound, but in particular of hearing one's own voice.

Phonoscope. Any device which converts sound waves into visual stimuli.

Phoria. The movement made by the eyes when they turn to fixate on something.

Phorometry. Measurement of the degree of balance of the eye muscles.

Phosphene. Experience of light when the eyeball is squeezed or knocked; caused by pressure stimulation of the retinal receptors.

Photic driving. Changing the frequency of brain waves by visual stimulation. The alpha rhythm in particular can be brought into phase with a bright, flickering light.

Photism. Any hallucination of light; may also refer to a type of synaesthesia where one vividly associates a particular colour or visual sensation with a sound or touch stimulus.

Photo-. As a prefix, refers to light.

Photochemical. Relates to chemical substances which are affected by light, e.g. the pigments in the retina.

Photochromatic interval. Range of stimulus intensity over which a colour may be seen as light, though not necessarily as a hue.

Photoerythrosity. Heightened sensitivity of the eye to the red end of the spectrum.

Photokinesis. Activity in an animal induced by light.

Photoma. Hallucination of light flashes; 'seeing stars'.

Photometer. A device for measuring light intensity.

Photon. In physics, the smallest unit of electromagnetic energy; in psychology, a measure of low levels of brightness.

Photophobia. Abnormal fear of light.

Photopic vision. Daylight vision; largely involves the fovea and the colour-sensitive cones. Compare SCOTOPIC VISION.

Photoreceptor. A cell whose function it is to react to light. In humans there are basically two types of photoreceptors, the CONES which are colour sensitive and respond most readily to bright light, and the RODS, located in the periphery of the retina and which are most active in low illumination.

Phototropism. Tendency for an organism to orientate itself in response to light. It is synonymous with heliotropism.

Phrenology. The study of mental ability using the shape of the skull as a guide. Bumps and protuberances on the skull are supposed to be associated with particular 'faculties', e.g. 'wisdom', 'mathematical ability', etc. Phrenology now has only pseudoscientific status.

Phylogenesis. The evolution of a race or species as opposed to an individual. Compare ONTOGENESIS.

Phylogenetic principle. The view that each individual, in the course of his development, tends to recapitulate the evolution of his species, particularly in social or behavioural terms – e.g. in childhood he moves through the 'prehistoric' phase of barbarism, etc. This is also known as the recapitulation theory.

Phylogenetic scale. A term used rather vaguely to place animals on an evolutionary ladder, mammals being higher up the scale than reptiles, etc.

Phylogeny. The history of the origin and evolution of species.

Phylum. ➧ TAXONOMY.

Physicalism. ➧ LOGICAL POSITIVISM.

Physiogenic. Relates to disorders which have a definite physical, as opposed to psychological, origin.

Physiognomy. The structure and characteristics of the human face.

Physiological age. One's age in terms of the degree of development or maturation of the body and its organs.

Physiological limit. The limits of performance in a task which are set by the physiology of the system; the point beyond which it is useless to attempt further practice.

Physiological psychology. The study of the physiological processes which underlie mental life and behaviour.

Physiological time. That portion of total reaction time which can be attributed to the time taken for a neural impulse to pass from receptor to the brain, and for the resulting command signal to pass down to the appropriate muscles. The balance of the *total* reaction time is presumably attributable to some central processing activity.

Physiology. The study of the functions of the various parts of a living organism and their interrelationship.

Physique. Body structure.

Pia mater. ➧ MENINGES.

Piaget, Jean (1896–). Swiss psychologist with a pioneering interest in DEVELOPMENTAL PSYCHOLOGY, in particular the evolution of thinking, language and other intellectual processes in the child. (➧ CONCEPT FORMATION.)

Piano theory. ➧ RESONANCE THEORY.

Pica. Eccentric eating habits, such as the craving for peculiar foods common in pregnancy.

Pick's disease. Premature aging of the brain caused by atrophy of the cortex and featuring the symptoms of SENILE DEMENTIA.

Pictogram. Pictorial representation of an idea; believed to be the most primitive form of writing.

Picture completion test. Intelligence test in which the subject has to fill in the gaps in an incomplete picture.

Piderit pictures. Cartoon drawings showing the human face expressing a number of basic emotional states. Parts of the faces – eyes, mouth, etc. – can be interchanged and used as tests of the ability to judge emotions.

Piecemeal activity. A principle put forward by Thorndike to explain the fact that an animal, when taught to respond to a complex set of stimuli, will sometimes later produce the response when only part of the original situation is present.

Pigment layer. The layer of the retina, richly endowed with photosensitive pigments, which lies next to the rods and cones.

Pillars of Corti. More commonly, RODS OF CORTI.

Pilomotor response. Goose pimples; the automatic erection of hair cells on the surface of the body in fright or when cold.

Pilot study. A simplified mini-experiment set up to allow one to decide what form a major experiment should take, or whether one is worth doing at all.

Piltdown man. The name given to what was once thought to be an extinct species of man with distinct ape-like features. The bones – a chimpanzee jaw combined with a human skull – were in fact planted as a hoax.

Pineal gland. Tiny protuberance in the midbrain whose function in man is uncertain, but which in some reptiles functions as a heat-sensitive 'third eye'. Descartes hypothesized that it was the site of the interaction between soul and body.

Pinel, Philippe (1745 – 1826). French physician who pioneered humane treatment for the insane and released lunatics from their chains in Paris hospitals.

Pinna. The external parts of the ear.

Pitch. The frequency of a sound; the human ear is pitch-sensitive in the range 15 to 20,000 Hz.

Pithecanthropus erectus. One of the first extinct species of man to be discovered; also known as Java Man, and more recently as *Homo erectus.*

Pithecoid. Ape-like.

Pituitary. Important gland located deep in the brain below the cerebral hemispheres which secretes a number of important hormones. The anterior lobe of the pituitary secretes growth hormones and others which act as regulators of the endocrine system. The posterior lobe controls water metabolism. (⧫⧫ HYPERPITUITARISM.)

Placebo. A drug or therapy which has its effect because the patient believes in it, rather than because of any direct action.

Place learning. A term used by Tolman to refer to the capacity of an animal to learn the position of a goal in spatial terms. Contrast RESPONSE LEARNING.

Place theory. More commonly, RESONANCE THEORY (of hearing).

Placement test. Vocational guidance or job-selection test.

Placenta. The structure which connects the foetus to the uterus and which transmits food and oxygen from mother to baby.

Planaria. Flatworm with feebly developed nervous system; one of the simplest creatures with which it is possible to demonstrate clear-cut learning.

Planchette. Heart-shaped device with a pencil and roller-bearings used as an aid to spirit communication or 'automatic writing'.

Plantar reflex. Automatic reaction causing the toes to curl downwards when the sole of the foot is touched. It replaces the BABINSKI REFLEX at about the age of two.

Plasma. The liquid component of blood and lymph.

Plasticity. The state of being ready to respond; willingness to change.

Plateau. When performance in a long learning task is plotted on a graph, one sees that progress occurs in surges, interspersed with periods where little headway seems to be being made. These 'flat periods', believed to be in some way related to consolidation of the learned material, are known as plateaux.

Plato (428 – 347 BC). Greek philosopher who was one of the first to introduce the notion of the complete distinction between mind and body – the philosophy now known as dualism.

Platonic love. Deep affection which is devoid of sexuality.

Platycephaly. Having a flattened top to the skull.

Platyhelminthes. ⧫ FLATWORMS.

Platykurtic. Relates to any flattened components of a frequency curve.

Platyrrhines. The 'New World' monkeys; somewhat less close to man than the CATARRHINES.

Play. Any kind of activity apparently indulged in for its own sake and without any obvious goal. Play occurs in animals as well as humans, particularly in the young, and while there is no really satisfactory theory to account for it, it is sometimes viewed as a kind of 'psychic discharge' of emotional energy. It may also allow young animals to get valuable experience practising psychomotor activity, social interaction or testing out 'programs' controlling brain function.

Play therapy. The use of play in child psychotherapy both as an aid to diagnosis (e.g. by observing the areas of social interaction where the child is inhibited) and as a form of therapy (by allowing the cathartic discharge of frustrations and pent-up emotions). (⧫⧫ PSYCHODRAMA.)

Pleasure centre. Part of the septal area in the rat's brain which, when stimulated electrically, appears to give a pleasurable sensation. The discovery of the pleasure centre was made by Olds and Milner in 1954 when they found that animals with electrodes planted in the appropriate area would repeatedly give themselves electrical stimulation if they had the opportunity.

Pleasure principle. An important tenet of psychoanalytic theory which holds that man is fundamentally governed by the desire to seek out pleasure and the need to avoid pain. The unconscious mind is supposed to be particularly motivated by this principle. Compare HEDONISM.

Plethysmograph. Device for recording variations in blood volume in limbs, etc; used as one component of the POLYGRAPH or lie detector.

Plexus. A network – in neuroanatomy, of nerve cells.

Pluralism. The doctrine that reality is made up of a number of discrete and totally different constituents as opposed to merely two (mind and matter) as in DUALISM or only one, as in MONISM.

Pluralistic behaviour. Any behaviour observed in all members of species.

Pneumograph. Device for recording patterns of respiration.

Poetzl phenomenon. Refers to the observation that people may dream about material presented to them subliminally in an experiment, despite the fact that they were not conscious of perceiving it at the time.

Poggendorff illusion. A straight line which passes behind two rectangles seems subjectively not to be straight.

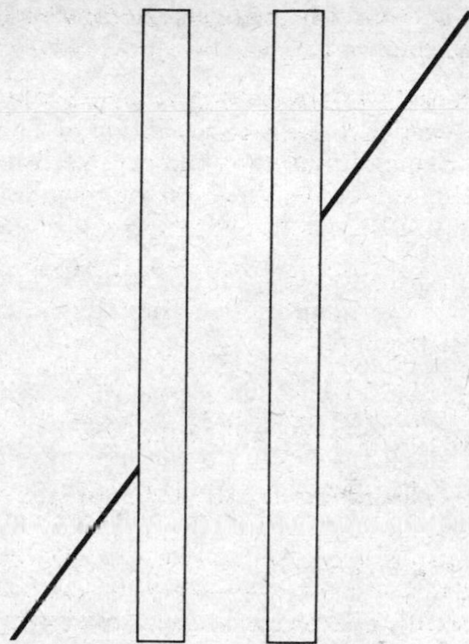

Figure 27. Poggendorff illusion.

Point-biserial correlation. The relationship between two variables, one of which is continuous (e.g. intelligence) and the other dichotomous (e.g. sex).

Point of regard. Fixation point which leads to a particular image being projected on to the fovea.

Point of subjective equality (PSE). In psychophysics, the value of a comparison stimulus which is equally likely to be judged 'higher' as 'lower' than the standard stimulus, and which is therefore effectively equal to it.

Point scale. Any scale which rates an individual's performance in terms of a number of points gained by a series of tests – e.g. IQ tests.

Point-to-point correspondence. A direct relationship between two complex systems so that for each element in one there is a corresponding element in the other. The retina is supposed to have this kind of correspondence with the visual cortex. (⧫⧫ ISOMORPHISM.)

Poisson distribution. An exceedingly asymmetrical distribution obtained when very rare but random events are plotted.

Polar continuum. Series in which the extremes are complete opposites, e.g. introversion/extraversion.

Polarization. State in which energy is concentrated at one point or pole; in optics, the condition in which light rays have been brought into parallel.

Polarity. In physiology, the resting condition of a nerve cell when its electrical state is in equilibrium; in psychology, refers to a mental state or type of personality which features extreme opposites, e.g. manic-depressive psychosis.

Poliomyelitis. A virus disease of the central nervous system causing loss of function in motor neurones and subsequent paralysis. It is also known as infantile paralysis.

Poltergeist. Supposedly mischievous spirit which throws things around, makes mysterious bangs, etc. Parapsychologists tend to believe that poltergeist phenomena are due to some uncontrolled psychic power associated with young children; sceptics believe that they are due to children throwing things around when adults are not looking.

Poly-. As a prefix, means many.

Polyandry. Anthropological term for marriage between one woman and several men. Contrast POLYGYNY.

Polydactylism. Having extra fingers or toes.

Polygamy. Any kind of marriage in which an individual has more than two mates.

Polygraph. Instrument which combines various methods of recording changes in body states not under conscious control – e.g. heart rate, blood volume, the electrical resistance of the skin, brain waves, etc. Polygraphs are employed with arguable success as LIE DETECTORS.

Polygyny. Anthropological term for marriage between one man and several women. Contrast POLYANDRY.

Polymorphism. Passing through a number of different body forms in the course of growth, e.g. from tadpole to frog.

Polymorphous perverse. In psychoanalysis, refers to the sexuality of the young child, who, as he or she passes through the various anal, oral and genital phases, exhibits behaviour which would be 'perverse' in adults.

Polyneuritis. Inflammation in a number of different nerves at the same time.

Polyopia. The formation of multiple images on the retina due to aberrations in the lens or fluids within the eye.

Pons (varolii). Protuberance at the base of the BRAIN largely made up of fibres connecting the cerebrum and cerebellum.

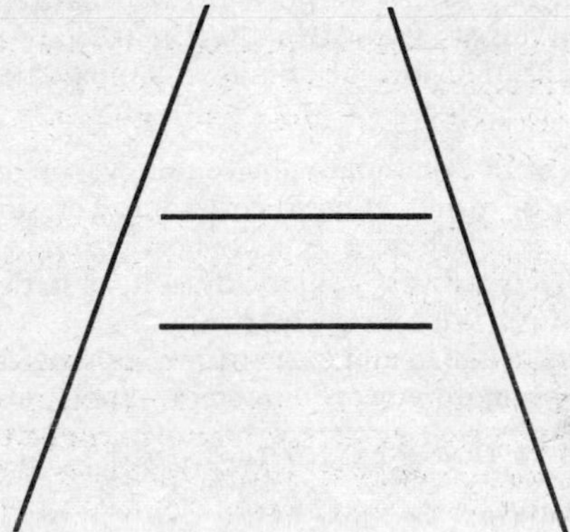

Figure 28. Ponzo illusion.

Ponzo illusion. Illusion probably caused by the assumption of the viewer that the two sloping vertical lines are receding parallels – in which case it would be reasonable to assume that the upper of the two horizontal lines was objectively larger.

Pooling. Combining data from different sources in an attempt to achieve an overall interpretation.

Popular response. In RORSCHACH TESTS, a common response.

Population. In statistics, the complete array from which a representative sample may be drawn.

Poriomania. Desire to wander aimlessly around; often a characteristic of senile dementia.

Pornography. The publication of obscene or offensive material in any of the media.

Porphyria. An hereditary blood disorder causing mental disturbance.

Porter's law. Critical flicker frequency varies according to the log of the brightness of the stimulus.

Porteus test. Test of intelligence which measures ability at solving paper mazes.

Position factor. When forced to make a choice in a learning experiment, an animal will often adopt a particular strategy while solving the problem and stick to it. Jumping or turning in particular directions is a common strategy and this position factor needs to be controlled for in many operant conditioning experiments.

Positive after-image. Brief experience of a visual sensation after the stimulus has been removed. Positive after-images are the same brightness and colour as the original stimuli. Compare NEGATIVE AFTER-IMAGE.

Positive feedback. In experimental psychology, roughly equivalent to giving knowledge of results in an experiment. The term has a special meaning in engineering where it refers to a situation in which increased *input* to a system causes that system to adjust itself to produce increased *output* which in turn leads to greater input. This is observed in the relationship between a man and a car with a slipping clutch – the more the clutch slips, the more power he tends to apply, etc.

Positive transfer. ➧ TRANSFER (OF TRAINING).

Positive transference. ➧ TRANSFERENCE.

Positive tropism. Tendency for an organism to move towards the source of stimulation.

Positivism. ➧ LOGICAL POSITIVSM.

Post-hypnotic suggestion. It is possible to give a hypnotized subject a command that he will, on awakening, behave in a particular way. The instructions may vary from the trivial (e.g. that he will speak a given word aloud) to the more subtle (e.g. that he will be disinclined to smoke). It is alleged that subjects carry out the instructions without being fully aware of their origin, but statements of this kind need to be treated with caution. (➧ HYPNOSIS).

Posterior root. The dorsal root of the spinal cord.

Postpartum psychosis. Severe mental illness which follows the act of giving birth; probably biochemical or hormonal in origin.

Postremity principle. The last act that an animal performs before being rewarded in a learning experiment is the act most likely to be performed when the situation occurs again. (➧➧ LAW OF RECENCY; STATISTICAL LEARNING THEORIES; GUTHRIE.)

Postrotational nystagmus. Rotating a human or animal rapidly will cause jerky movements of the eyes in the opposite direction to rotation. These will persist for some time after the rotation has ceased.

Postulate. An idea or hypothesis which is advanced without experimental support.

Postural set. A posture or adjustment of the muscles which prepares an animal for a particular act or movement.

Potency. Power or potential; also refers to the power of the male to perform the sexual act.

Potential. The latent power to do something; the electrical charge in a nerve cell.

Potlatch. Any extravagant or squandering display of wealth; based on the habits of the Kwakiutl Indians on the American North-West coast who engaged in ritual, lavish destruction of personal property to achieve social status.

Power. In social psychology, refers to the capacity of one individual or group to mould the behaviour of another individual or group according to its wishes. The dominant party is known as the source, the other as the target. In mathematics, power is the superscript to a number which shows how many times it is to be multiplied by itself.

Power test. Test in which individual items become progressively more difficult. The upper limit of achievement rather than speed is measured.

Practical. Workable; measurable.

Practice. Repeating a task in order to learn it.

Practice curve. Plot of performance in a learning task.

Practice limit. ➧ PHYSIOLOGICAL LIMIT.

Practice period. Brief run-up to an experiment to accustom subject and experimenter to the conditions.

Practice theory. The theory that the function of play is to allow young animals to practise psychomotor skills.

Pragmatism. The philosophy that all things should be assessed in terms of their practical value – and that this is the ultimate test of right and wrong.

Prägnanz. One of the laws of GESTALT PSYCHOLOGY which holds that all mental events, in particular perceptual ones, will tend towards the simplest and 'best' possible under the circumstances. For example, if a slightly distorted circle is shown in poor light or for a brief period of time, it will be perceived as a perfect circle. (➧➧ GOODNESS OF FIT.)

Precision law. Gestalt law, effectively identical with PRÄGNANZ.

Precocity. Extremely rapid or early development of mental ability.

Precognition. A term used by parapsychologists to refer to the apparent ability of the mind to acquire information from the future. It has been claimed that scientific evidence for precognition has been gathered in carefully controlled experiments, but these findings are highly controversial. (➧➧ PARAPSYCHOLOGY.)

Preconception. Forming an opinion in advance of the facts.

Preconceptual stage. A subdivision of the pre-operational period in Piaget's theory of cognitive development, covering the years two to four. (➧ DEVELOPMENT PSYCHOLOGY.)

Preconditioning. When two stimuli are presented together in a conditioning experiment, the animal forms some association between them even if they have not been reinforced when presented. This can be demonstrated by the fact that when one of the stimuli is later reinforced, the other also acquires some reward value. Their prior exposure together is called preconditioning. (➧ CONDITIONING.)

Preconscious. Sometimes called the foreconscious, but *not* the same as the unconscious. The preconscious is everything that is not in consciousness at the time, but which can easily be called to memory without special techniques such as dream interpretation, free association, etc. (➧ SUBCONSCIOUS.)

Predication. Association of concepts or ideas.

Prediction. Making a statement about the probability of a particular event occurring.

Predictive efficiency. A measure of the effectiveness of a predictive test.

Predictive validity. The extent to which a test measures what it sets out to measure.

Predisposition. In psychology, refers to an hereditary condition which will cause physical or psychological development to follow particular lines.

Preference method. Refers to any test in which a human or animal has to choose between a number of possible stimuli.

Preformism. The belief that individual characteristics are latent in the genetic mechanism, and will evolve and mature more or less independently of environmental forces. Contrast EPIGENESIS.

Prefrontal area. Part of the frontal lobe lying in front of the motor area.

Prefrontal lobotomy. ➧ FRONTAL LOBOTOMY.

Pregenital phase. According to Freud, sexuality evolves in the normal individual by passing through three main phases – oral, anal and genital. The pregenital phase refers to the oral and anal phases. (➧ ORAL CHARACTER; ANAL CHARACTER.)

Pregnance. ➧ PRÄGNANZ.

Prehensile. Grasping or holding.

Prejudice. A belief strongly held in the absence or in the face of evidence, and in particular which has been arrived at in advance of the evidence. A prejudice is normally emotionally loaded and for this reason highly resistant to logical argument. Prejudice can be both positive and negative. Compare ATTITUDE, BIAS.

Premenstrual tension. Anxiety or changes of mood occurring just prior to menstruation, probably due to hormonal changes in the body.

Premonition. A warning, usually supposed to be supernatural in origin, of some future event.

Premsia. One of Cattell's personality types, associated with sensitivity and TENDERMINDEDNESS.

Prenatal. Before birth.

Prenubile. Before puberty.

Pre-Oedipal phase. Psychoanalytic term for the period when the child is intensely emotionally attached to the mother and before the formation of the OEDIPUS COMPLEX.

Preparation. In physiology, an animal that has been surgically prepared for an experiment.

Preparatory interval. The time between the 'ready' signal and the actual stimulus.

Preparatory response. Response which is not itself rewarded but which is ultimately instrumental in reaching a goal.

Preperception. A state of mind which sets one in readiness to perceive something; may lead to illusions or errors of judgement if the stimulus differs from what has been anticipated. (⧫⧫ SET; EXPECTANCY.)

Prepotency. The characteristics of something which lead it to dominate over others.

Prepsychotic. Relates to a state which gives warning of a developing psychosis.

Prepuberty. The stage of development in the two years before puberty.

Presbyophrenia. Form of SENILE DEMENTIA.

Presbyopia. 'Middle-aged sight': failure of near vision due to hardening of the lens and consequent difficulty with accommodation. Contrast HYPEROPIA.

Presentation. The act of presenting a stimulus to a subject.

Presentiment. Vague feeling of being able to anticipate the future.

Press. A word used by MURRAY in his need theory to describe anything in the environment which has extreme significance for an individual. Compare NEED.

Pressure balance. A device which exerts a controlled amount of pressure on the skin, used in tests of skin sensitivity.

Pressure sense. The sense of touch, but in particular anything more intense than simple contact on the skin.

Pressure spot. Point on the skin particularly sensitive to pressure; tiny cells known as Pacinian corpuscles have been found in pressure spots.

Prestige. The state of being held in high regard and thus more able to influence the behaviour of others.

Prestriate. Refers to parts of the brain which lie in front of the striate areas.

Pretest. A PILOT STUDY.

Preverbal construct. A concept which arose before the individual had learned to speak or before a word or phrase had been developed to describe it.

Priapism. Abnormal sexual desire in the male; persistent abnormal erection of the penis.

Primacy law. Of a series of acts, the first learned is the best remembered. Compare LAW OF RECENCY.

Primal anxiety. In psychoanalytic terms the most basic anxiety of all – the dim memory that all people are supposed to have of their separation from their mother at birth.

Primal scene. Psychoanalytic term for an early sexual memory, generally associated with the infant observing his or her parents in sexual intercourse.

Primary. First in rank or time.

Primary colour. Has two distinct meanings, depending on whether one is talking about pigments or light waves. In the case of the pigments, the primaries are white, black, blue, yellow and red, and they are so called because out of suitable mixtures of them any other colour can be obtained. In the case of light waves the term is used to describe hues which cannot be broken down into others, so the primaries are blue, green, yellow and red.

Primary data. Raw data.

Primary drive. An instinctive or hereditary drive, universal in a species. Contrast ACQUIRED DRIVE.

Primary factor. First order factors obtained from factor analysis.

Primary function. The immediate sensation when a receptor is stimulated; secondary function refers to all after-sensation including memory.

Primary group. A small and intimate group. (➧ GROUP.)

Primary integration. According to psychoanalysis, an important phase in the evolution of the EGO: the moment when the infant realizes he or she has self-identity.

Primary memory image. The image that can be called to mind immediately after the initial stimulus (and any after-images it has caused) has died away.

Primary mental abilities. The basic abilities supposed to make up INTELLIGENCE; according to Thurstone's theory, they include seven traits – verbal fluency, word fluency, numerical ability, space perception, memory, perceptual ability and reasoning.

Primary narcissism. ➧ NARCISSISM.

Primary odour. ➧ ODOUR PRISM.

Primary position. The natural position of the eyes when the person is standing and fixating on a distant object straight in front.

Primary process. Any strategy adopted by the ID to gain immediate gratification of its desires. Contrast SECONDARY PROCESS.

Primary quality. Any aspect or feature of an object without which it would have no perceptual reality or identity. For example, the heat of the sun is not primary but secondary since one can perceive and recognize the sun in its absence; but its round shape is essential to its perception, and thus a primary quality.

Primary reinforcement. Any reward which is intrinsically satisfying to an animal, and whose significance as a reward does not have to be learned. Primary reinforcement normally involves the reduction in a primary drive – food, water and sex are obvious examples. (➧➧ SECONDARY REINFORCEMENT.)

Primary repression. Psychoanalytic term for the mechanism by which the EGO protects itself against unpleasant, instinctive thoughts arising from the UNCONSCIOUS.

Primary zone. Whatever zone of the body gives greatest satisfaction to the LIBIDO.

Primate. A particular order of mammals which includes man, apes and monkeys. (⧫⧫ TAXONOMY.)

Primitive. In anthropological terms, refers to a society which is poorly developed in economic and technological terms. There are few truly primitive societies on earth today.

Primordial. First. Jung used primordial image to refer to any idea drawn from the racial or collective unconscious. (⧫ ARCHETYPE.)

Principal focus. The point at which prevailing parallel rays of light come together after they have passed through an optical system.

Principle. A law of nature; also an idea or hypothesis which can be put forward for testing in an experiment.

Prior entry law. When two stimuli are presented simultaneously, the one that is first attended to also seems to have been the one that appeared first. Experiments designed to demonstrate this law are known as complication experiments.

Prism. A wedge-shaped lens which has the property of dispersing light into its constituent wavelengths and thus generating a band of the seven spectral colours when white light is passed through it.

Prism diopter. Measure of the strength of a PRISM; the tangent of the angle of deflection, multiplied by 100.

Prison psychosis. A general term for a variety of severe mental disturbances induced by long periods in prison; includes 'fake' psychoses (e.g. Ganser's syndrome) but there may also be genuine depressions and delusions of persecution.

Private acceptance. Type of conformity in which an individual accepts group standards and norms in order to belong to that group. These standards and norms are retained by the individual even when he leaves the group's control. Contrast COMPLIANCE.

Privation. State occurring when a need is present and the means to satisfy it are not.

Proactive. Having an effect on something occurring at a later time. Contrast RETROACTIVE.

Proactive inhibition. The negative effect that previous learning may have on a later learning task.

Probabilism. The view that one can, by studying the past and present, make logical and accurate predictions about the future.

Probability (*P*). The likelihood that one event will occur as measured against the likelihood that others will occur. Probability is measured against a sliding scale from 0 to 1, with 0 implying absolute certainty that an event will *not* take place, and 1 absolute certainty that it *will*. A probability of 0.5 denotes maximum *uncertainty* as to whether it will occur or not.

Probability curve. Generally refers to the Gaussian or NORMAL DISTRIBUTION curve.

Probability ratio. The total number of ways in which a *particular* event (P) could occur, divided by the total number of *possible* events (Q).

Probability theory. The mathematical approach to the study of probability; includes theories of chance and randomness and is closely related to statistical methods.

Probable error. Index of the variability of a measure with respect to the degree to which values obtained differ from the mean of the measure. In the normal distribution, about half the values lie in a range of plus or minus the probable error from the mean.

Problem box. ➧ PUZZLE BOX.

Problem solving behaviour. The activity and mental processes involved in overcoming the obstacles, physical or conceptual, which lie between an animal and its goal.

Process. A series of changes or events, but may also refer to the *way* in which the changes are effected. In neurophysiology, a process is anything which grows out from an organ or nerve cell and assists its operation in some way.

Process attitude. In an experiment when the subject is asked to concentrate on his own conscious experience, this is known as process attitude. When he is asked to concentrate on external stimuli this is known as object attitude.

Processing error. Any error occurring while data are being recorded or analysed.

Procreation. Reproducing the species.

Prodigy. An exceptionally gifted person, particularly when signs of the talents appear at an early age.

Prodromal. Refers to anything which gives a warning of a coming illness.

Product moment correlation. Deviations from the mean of two or more variables, raised to a power, multiplied and summated. It is used in correlation techniques and also known as covariance.

Proficiency. The degree to which a skill has been acquired.

Profile. A simplification of data plotted on a graph; e.g. a histogram.

Profound mental retardation. ➧ MENTAL RETARDATION.

Progesterone. A hormone secreted in large amounts during pregnancy and believed to be partly responsible for mood changes, including postnatal depression.

Prognathous. Having a protruding jaw (a characteristic of fossil man and the non-human primates). Contrast ORTHOGNATHOUS.

Prognosis. Prediction of the future course of a disease.

Program. Set of instructions to a computer indicating the way it should tackle a particular task.

Programmed instruction. An approach to learning in which a task is split into a series of clearly defined steps, each with a number of alternatives provided. The trainee has to decide at each step which alternative to select, and if a 'wrong' choice is made an explanation is given and he is obliged to choose again. 'Correct' choices are rewarded by allowing him to continue with the programme. The method is based loosely on behaviouristic theories, particularly those of Skinner, but its main value probably lies in ensuring that the person attends to the task (as opposed to passively reading and perhaps skipping passages of a book). In its simplest form programmed instruction can be carried out using a specially prepared book, but teaching machines or even computers may be employed. (➧ TEACHING MACHINE.)

Programmed learning. ➧ PROGRAMMED INSTRUCTION.

Progression law. A variant of WEBER'S LAW, it states that increments of *sensation* increase at a rate of arithmetical progression, when the corresponding *stimulus* increments increase geometrically.

Progressive matrices test. An intelligence test which concentrates on evaluating clear thinking and the ability to perceive perceptual relationships.

Projection. According to psychoanalytic theory, one of the main mechanisms by which the EGO protects itself against conflicts within the unconscious mind. Projection involves attributing to other people motives, attitudes or problems which in fact are one's own but which cannot be admitted as such because of the threat they pose to the ego. Compare INTROJECTION. (➧ DEFENCE MECHANISM.)

Projection fibres. The nerve fibres which connect the cortex with lower parts of the brain and spinal cord. Compare COMMISSURAL and ASSOCIATION FIBRES.

Projective tests. Any one of a large number of tests which allow the individual to project his own anxieties, unconscious or partly-expressed motives on to an external situation where they may then be studied objectively. Based on the psychoanalytic idea that projection is a mechanism of ego defence, the tests normally consist of unstructured material – the Rorschach inkblot and the ambiguous figures of the TAT are the most common examples – which the individual is invited to describe or free-associate to.

There are fairly well-defined rules for assessing the results of such tests, and a good deal of work has gone into evaluating their effectiveness. There is, however, controversy as to whether the tests offer objective data to the therapist, or whether they are little more than conversational aids which help to loosen up an inhibited patient and thus allow the therapist to use his own experience and insight.

Proliferation. Any rapid expansion in numbers, particularly of cells in living tissue.

Promiscuity. Tendency to engage in a large number of sexual relationships, none of an enduring kind.

Prompting method. Approach to verbal learning which measures progress by the number of prompts necessary in the course of learning the task.

Proof. Evidence which convincingly supports belief.

Proofreader's illusion. Failing to notice typographical errors, etc., because of the words' familiarity.

Propaedeutic. Relates to learning which allows further, more complex learning to take place.

Propaganda. Attempting to influence public attitudes by sustained, systematic methods. Technically this includes advertising, but generally refers to political influence.

Propagation. In physiology, the transmission of the neural impulse; in biology, reproduction.

Propensity. A strong tendency, short of a compulsion, to do something.

Prophylaxis. Prevention of disease.

Proportion. The relative magnitude of two values.

Proposition. A statement put forward for examination and testing.

Proprioception. The senses involved in determining the position and movement of the body and limbs.

Proprioceptor. A sensory cell or organ which assists PROPRIOCEPTION. This includes the vestibular system in the inner ear, specialized cells in muscles and joints, and pressure-responsive cells in the skin.

Proprium. Word used by Allport to refer to those aspects of personality which make up the conscious self; rather similar to the Freudian concept of the EGO.

Prosencephalon. The forebrain. (➧ BRAIN.)

Prosthesis. An artificial organ or limb.

Protanomalous. Relative insensitivity to the colour red.

Protanopia. Partial COLOUR BLINDNESS characterized by confusion between reds and greens and insensitivity to red.

Protein. Molecule made up of amino-acids which are an important constituent of animals and plants.

Protensity. A term introduced to refer to the temporal qualities of a sensation.

Proto-. As a prefix, means first.

Protocol. The original records or notes of an experiment.

Protopathic. Relating to major or gross sensations (e.g. *intense* cold or pain) or general rather than specific sensations. Contrast EPICRITIC.

Protoplasm. The main substance of living cells.

Protozoa. Single-celled organisms.

Proverbs test. An intelligence test in which the subject is asked to explain the meaning of a simple proverb.

Proximal. Near; close to the central axis of the body. Contrast DISTAL.

Proximal stimulus. The stimulus when it excites a sensory receptor. The distal stimulus is the stimulus at its *source*.

Proximity principle. ➧ CONTIGUITY LAW.

Proximodistal. Refers to the developmental trend by which functions near the central axis of the body develop sooner than those in the periphery.

Pruritis. Itching not caused by any obvious physical stimulus.

Pseudaesthesia. Any illusion or false sensation.

Pseudo-. As a prefix, means false.

Pseudochromaesthesia. ➧ CHROMAESTHESIA.

Pseudo-conditioning. For a short period after a conditioning experiment, the conditioned response can sometimes be elicited by a totally neutral stimulus which has not previously featured in the experiment. Pseudo-conditioning is believed to be a 'raised sensitivity' of the kind which leads to false starts in races, etc.

Pseudodementia. State of apparent indifference to one's surroundings, but not accompanied by mental impairment.

Pseudoisochromatic. Relates to charts used for testing COLOUR BLINDNESS. (➧ ISHIHARA TEST; STILLING TEST.)

Pseudologia fantastica. A clinical syndrome featuring fantastic and extravagant claims about oneself.

Pseudomnesia. A false memory containing much elaborate detail, but unrelated to fact or reality.

Pseudophone. Device for testing ability to localize sounds.

Pseudopsychology. Any non-scientific system or philosophy which nevertheless claims to concern itself with human behaviour, e.g. palmistry, phrenology.

Pseudoscope. Device – generally spectacles with special prisms – which distorts perception in a systematic way. The most famous examples are the spectacles with inverting lens worn in STRATTON'S EXPERIMENT.

Psi. Parapsychological term for any form of EXTRASENSORY PERCEPTION – or, more exactly, the processes which lie behind it.

Psilocybin. An hallucinogenic drug derived from a mushroom, with effects similar to those of mescaline and LSD.

Psi-missing. In their studies of so-called telepathic phenomena, parapsychologists claim that on occasions subjects score significantly *below* what is expected by chance – above-chance scores being attributed to one individual extracting information from the mind of another and thus implying TELEPATHY. Below-chance results are extremely peculiar, however, for they also imply some exchange of information – you need to know what is in the other person's mind in order to be sure of getting it wrong! Parapsychologists suggest that psi-missing may occur in people who are opposed to the concept of telepathy and thus reject any telepathic information when it comes. Sceptics argue that in any long run of random guesses, one will get streaks of 'plus' scores, which will be attributed to telepathy, and streaks of 'minus' (psi-missing). This problem indicates the theoretical and practical difficulties which make PARAPSYCHOLOGY such an uncertain area in modern science.

Psychalgia. Pain without any obvious physical basis.

Psychasthenia. Obsolete term for neurotic states featuring phobias, obsessions and general anxiety.

Psyche. The Greek word for life or soul; today used for mind or 'self'.

Psychedelic. Relating to anything causing major changes in mental processes, particularly where these cause apparent expansion in awareness or heightened perceptual sensitivity.

Psychergograph. A device used in studies of stamina and fatigue which automatically presents a new task or problem immediately the previous one has been dealt with.

Psychiatric social worker. Person, normally trained in psychology and sociology, who assists psychiatrists by helping patients and their families to deal with social and personal problems caused by mental illness.

Psychiatrist. Individual qualified as a physician and also specially trained in abnormal psychology, its diagnosis and treatment. (➧➧ PSYCHOTHERAPIST.)

Psychiatry. The branch of medicine which deals with mental disorders, their origins, diagnosis, treatment and prevention. Lay people often muddle, or use synonymously, the terms psychiatry, psychology and psychoanalysis, though the first is the study of medicine as applied to psychological problems, the second the study of the mind and behaviour, and the third a special approach to understanding the mind and treating mental disorders. Psychiatry has a long and controversial history, but probably dates back to the pioneering efforts of the French physician Pinel who, by releasing the mentally sick inmates of the Salpétrière from their chains in 1794, ushered in a new approach to the treatment of mental illnesses.

In the early part of the twentieth century, psychiatry was dominated by psychological, and in particular psychoanalytic, concepts – in other words mental disorders, from mild hysteria to full-blown psychoses, were assumed to be fundamentally a failure of the individual to adjust to the world which resulted in disruption of the normal processes of personality. As research advanced, however, the biochemical nature of many mental illnesses became obvious, and the psychological approach gave way to physicalistic theories and treatments. This approach peaked some time in the 1960s, at about the time that the radical theories of psychiatrists such as R. D. Laing began to emerge, and crudely physical approaches to treatment, such as those employing ECT and psychosurgery, began to fall out of favour.

The trouble with psychiatry today is that it is still without a working theory, not just of the mind but also the disturbed mind. Even a definition of mental illness is not easy to come by, so perhaps it is not surprising that to this date psychiatric methods have inevitably been of a hit or miss variety.

Psychic. In its most general sense, relating to the mind; in a more specialized sense, relating to unusual or paranormal powers of the mind, such as those investigated by PARAPSYCHOLOGY.

Psychical research. The investigation of paranormal phenomena such as telepathy, poltergeist activity, etc. The term PARAPSYCHOLOGY is used for the specifically scientific approach to the topic. (➧ EXTRA-SENSORY PERCEPTION.)

Psychic blindness. Inability to recognize common objects as a result of brain damage.

Psychic determinism. The theory, first explicitly advanced by Freud, which states that all mental and behavioural events have a definite cause, even if this is unconscious. This extends to dreams, slips of the tongue, lapses of memory, etc.

Psychic energy. Refers to the somewhat elusive concept of mental or emotional dynamism; also, in Freudian terms, the LIBIDO.

Psychic isolation. Jungian term for withdrawal from all social contacts as a form of DEFENCE MECHANISM. It was once believed that the severest forms of catatonic schizophrenia were extreme cases of psychic isolation.

Psychoacoustics. The study of the perception of sounds.

Psychoactive. ➧ PSYCHOTROPIC.

Psychoanalysis. A system of psychology largely developed by Sigmund FREUD and which has continued to evolve, with minor modifications, since his death. Psychoanalysis is both an attempt at providing a fairly comprehensive theory of the mind and its functions, and also a system devoted to correcting disorders arising from conflicts within the mind.

As far as the theory goes, a brief summary can only do partial justice, but central to it is the notion of the libido, a driving force present at birth which expresses itself mainly as sexual energy but which is also manifested in other forms of energy including the will to live. In the course of childhood the libido seeks to express itself in whatever way it can, and blocking or misdirecting its energy can lead to conflicts which appear later in life. Another concept of fundamental significance to psychoanalysis is that of the differentiation of the mind into three partially independent units – id, ego and superego – each with its own wishes or desires, conscious and unconscious, which are seldom in complete harmony. The id is mainly instinctive, blindly interested in self-gratification and is the only part of the mind really developed at birth. Immediately after birth the id forces find themselves in increasing conflict with external forces – the 'dos and don'ts' imposed by parents and the other realities of society. These become built into the mind and continue to develop steadily into the superego. With increasing maturity a third subsystem emerges – the ego, largely conscious and essentially what most people think of as the 'self'. The part of the ego which is conscious is largely unaware of the existence of the id, but the part which is unconscious is not so blissfully ignorant, and devotes much of its time to maintaining peace between the conflicting forces of id and superego. These conflicts, which are exceedingly painful and tedious, tend to be rammed down into the unconscious by the ego whenever they show signs of emerging – the technique known as repression. This technique works satisfactorily unless the conflict is a major one, when neurotic (or even, according to doctrinaire psychoanalysts, psychotic) symptoms may occur.

The technique of psychoanalysis consists of a systematic attempt to identify the areas and sources of the unconscious conflicts which may cripple the neurotic patient, and use up valuable psychic energy in even the most 'normal' human. The approach involves seeking out clues as to the nature of the conflicts – clues which Freud believed revealed themselves in the thematic material of dreams, in the raw material of free association, in the nature of the symptoms themselves, and in such odd phenomena as slips of the tongue and brief lapses of memory.

The assessment of the value of psychoanalysis, both in theory and therapy, is very difficult. Tens of thousands of patients have claimed that their lives have been rebuilt through Freudian analysis and some of its offspring (Jungian, Adlerian, etc.) but objective evidence of the success of such treatment is hard to come by, as H. J. Eysenck has poinfed out. The theory is even harder to evaluate though it has many exciting and logical components to it. Perhaps the firmest thing one can say is that it is unique – and no other theory of mental life has been put forward to this date which has the scope, the power and at least the superficial credibility of the Freudian system. (♦ DREAMS; DEFENCE MECHANISMS; TRANSFERENCE; FREUD; *et al. passim*.)

Psychoanalyst. Someone trained in psychoanalytic theory and methods – generally through a training analysis – who practises one or other variant of the Freudian system. It is not essential, though it may be advisable, to undergo medical training in order to practise psychoanalysis. (♦♦ PSYCHOTHERAPIST.)

Psychobiology. The use of biological knowledge to advance the understanding of psychology: also the name of a school of psychiatry which emphasizes understanding the patient as a human being.

Psychodiagnostics. Originally referred to assessing personality through the study of external features, such as facial expression, by graphology, etc. More recently the term has been used to imply any type of psychological assessment using objective tests and experiments.

Psychodrama. An approach to both diagnosis and therapy, based on the theories of Morena, in which patients act out, before a group of other patients and therapists, what they believe to be at the heart of their internal or social conflicts. Psychodrama may be successful in helping inhibited patients to 'loosen up', but it may also serve to bring to the surface unconscious problems which reveal themselves in the structure of the patient's personally composed drama. The method has something in common with PLAY THERAPY for children. (⧫⧫ ROLE PLAYING.)

Psychodynamics. The study of emotion and motivation.

Psychogalvanic reflex (PGR). ⧫ GALVANIC SKIN RESPONSE.

Psychogenesis. The origin and development of mental phenomena; alternatively, the origin and development of the mind.

Psychogenic. Relating to an illness which has no obvious organic basis.

Psychognosis. ⧫ PSYCHODIAGNOSTIC.

Psychograph. A chart which shows a more or less comprehensive profile of an individual's personality by plotting his performance on various tests alongside each other.

Psychoid. Relating to the mental or psychic.

Psychokinesis (PK). The term used by parapsychologists to refer to the supposed ability of the mind to move material objects at a distance and without physical contact. The evidence for PK is highly controversial, not all parapsychologists accepting its existence. (⧫ PARAPSYCHOLOGY.)

Psycholagnia. The process of forming and indulging sexual fantasies.

Psycholinguistics. The scientific study of the nature of language, and in particular its relationship to psychology. A largely post-war development, it gained impetus in the early 1960s following the work of the philosopher Noam Chomsky, and is associated with the current anti-behaviourist movement. The field is theoretically abstruse, but not totally removed from experimental investigation. It draws not only upon traditional linguistics, but also information theory, statistical methods and even the study of computer programming. (⧫ CHOMSKY; TRANSFORMATIONAL GRAMMAR.)

Psychological field. A term used by Lewin to refer to the LIFE SPACE of the individual, both physical and psychological.

Psychologism. The view that psychology is, or should become, the most basic and important science.

Psychologist. Someone trained in the study of psychology; technically the word should include psychiatrists, but it is usually reserved for a person qualified to investigate psychological matters through science, rather than someone seeking to understand and treat mental illness through medical techniques. (⧫⧫ PSYCHOTHERAPIST.)

Psychology. Literally, the study of the mind or spirit, but defined in various ways which depend rather upon the personal interests of the individual. Until the middle of the nineteenth century the subject matter of psychology (in which one would include the nature of consciousness and mental life and the causes of human behaviour) was largely identified with philosophy.

The work of Wundt and other European pioneers who set up the first laboratories to study human thought processes, perception and learning led to the realization that this largely unexplored territory could be treated as a field of science. Early work concentrated on introspection, but in the early twentieth century the Russian Pavlov, through his studies of CONDITIONING, introduced the essentially physiological approach which has remained one of the major strands of the subject until the present day. In parallel, there also arose the medically-orientated work of FREUD and the psychoanalytic schools, though this diminished in importance (from a scientific as opposed to a theoretical point of view) in the face of the rise of modern BEHAVIOURISM – a sophisticated expansion of Pavlov's original ideas and technique.

Psychology then became exclusively the study of behaviour to the extent that for a period peaking in the late 1950s references to mental and even conscious processes were treated as being irrelevant or misleading to the advancement of the topic. Today the inevitable counterswing of the pendulum is occurring, with a growing interest in consciousness and other states difficult to examine by behaviourist techniques. But it would be a mistake to assume that this swing implies a rejection of traditional scientific methodology – it simply rejects the notion that the strategies of behaviourism are the *only* way to reach an understanding of man's nature, which is after all the real raw material of psychology.

Psychometric. Relating to the measurement of psychological factors – e.g. performance tests, IQ tests, etc.

Psychometric function. A formula expressing the relationship between the variation in a set of quantitatively different stimuli and the judgements made by the subject examining the stimuli. Used in psychophysical studies.

Psychometry. Literally, measuring the mind: mental testing. The term is also used to describe a spiritualistic practice by which a medium touches an object and tries to get 'extra-sensory' impressions about its owner.

Psychomotor. Relating to the control of muscles by the brain.

Psychomotor attack. A type of EPILEPSY associated with temporal lobe activity.

Psychoneural parallelism. The principle that for every mental event there must exist a corresponding neural event.

Psychoneurosis. ◆ NEUROSIS.

Psychonomics. The study of the development of mental faculties, and their relationship to the individual's environment.

Psychopath. A term once used for anyone with a personality or behavioural disorder severe enough to produce personal and social complications but not to warrant hospitalization. Today the term is used, more specifically, to refer to an individual dominated totally by present needs and indifferent to the future consequences of his actions.

Psychopathology. The study of mental functions with particular reference to the origins of mental illness.

Psychopathy. Any mental disorder or abnormality featuring anti-social behaviour.

Psychopharmacology. The study of the effect of drugs on mind and behaviour.

Psychophysical. Relating to events or processes which have both physical and mental characteristics.

Psychophysical parallelism. The view that mind and body (matter) are separate and distinct in their nature, and yet exist side by side, somehow capable of working in harmony. This is close to the dualistic position.

Psychophysics. The basic subject matter of experimental psychology – the study of the relationship between physical events in the external world (stimuli) and the corresponding processes of perception, observation and judgement occurring in the brain. The first experimental research laboratories were devoted to fundamental psychophysics, and a number of traditional methods for investigation were developed, in particular the METHOD OF LIMITS. (◆◆ SIGNAL-DETECTION THEORY.)

Psychophysiology. ◆ PHYSIOLOGICAL PSYCHOLOGY.

Psychosexual. Relating to sexuality, in particular the link between one's mental state and the characteristics of one's sex life.

Psychosis. A mental or personality disorder sufficiently severe to disrupt the individual's personal and social life, and normally demanding special treatment and hospitalization. It has been usual to describe psychoses as being either organic – when they can be shown to stem from some definite pathology such as a brain tumour or disease – or functional, when no organic basis can be determined.

Fifty years ago a functional basis was assumed in all but the most obviously organic cases (senile dementia or brain damage due to syphilis, for example), and most schools of psychoanalysis still view them as being severe personality disorders caused by mental conflict. But with increasing evidence of the immense role played by biochemical processes in mood changes, and the dramatic effects of 'antipsychotic' drugs, the tendency nowadays is for an organic cause to be assumed in the majority of cases. The most common psychoses include schizophrenia (itself rather a general term), manic-depressive psychosis and paranoid states. Contrast NEUROSIS.

Psychosocial. Relates to anything involving interplay between psychological and social factors.

Psychosomatic. Relating to phenomena which are part physiological and part psychological. A psychosomatic disorder is one in which physical symptoms are being produced by an essentially mental or psychological problem. Compare SOMATIC DISORDER.

Psychosurgery. The use of surgery to alleviate or cure psychological disorders. (⧫⧫ FRONTAL LOBOTOMY.)

Psychotechnology. The application of psychological knowledge to solving practical problems. (⧫⧫ APPLIED PSYCHOLOGY.)

Psychotherapeutic. Relating to psychotherapy.

Psychotherapist. Someone with specialist training who practises PSYCHOTHERAPY. Psychotherapists may be psychiatrists (in which case they will be trained as medical doctors), psychoanalysts (in which case they will have been trained in one or other of the schools of psychoanalysis) or clinical psychologists (in which case they need not be *medically* trained, but will have a university training in the principles of abnormal psychology).

Psychotherapy. The treatment of mental or behavioural disorders by one of a large variety of techniques. Strictly speaking it includes therapy involving drugs, etc., but in practice the term is used for therapy involving psychological techniques, such as counselling, psychodrama, psychoanalysis, behaviour therapy.

Psychotic. Relating to a psychosis; someone suffering from a psychosis.

Psychotomimetic. Referring to anything, but in particular a drug, which produces symptoms similar to those of a psychosis.

Psychotropic drugs. Drugs which have a generally short-term effect on the nervous system, particularly involving changes in levels of consciousness or variations in mood. They include the hypnotics, stimulants, anti-depressants, psychotomimetics and tranquillizers.

Ptosis. Involuntary drooping of the eyelids.

Pubertas praecox. Unusually early onset of PUBERTY.

Puberty. The stage, lasting two to three years, of development at the end of which the reproductive organs become fully functional and secondary sex characteristics (pubic hair, changes in the pitch of voice, etc.) appear. The age at which it is reached is normally fourteen in boys and thirteen in girls. (⧫⧫ ADOLESCENCE.)

Puberty rite. *Rites de passage*. (⧫ INITIATION RITE.)

Pubes. The hairy region surrounding the genitals.

Pubescence. The time of reaching PUBERTY.

Public opinion. The overall trend of opinion in a society.

Pudenda. The external genitals.

Puerilism. Behaviour or characteristics present in an adult which would be more appropriate to a much younger age.

Puerperal. Following childbirth.

Pulfrich effect. If one views, with one eye covered by a filter, a pendulum swinging to and fro across one's visual field, it seems to be moving in an elliptical path.

Pulse. The rhythmic surge of blood through the arteries caused by the action of the heart.

Punctate. Relating to a point on the surface of the skin.

Punctiform. Point-like.

Punishment. In experimental psychology refers to anything administered to an individual after an act or task has been performed which is designed to prevent the individual repeating the act; the opposite of REWARD. (⧫⧫ NEGATIVE REINFORCEMENT.)

Pupil. The opening in the iris which can control the amount of light let in to the interior of the eye.

Pupillary reflex. The automatic constriction of the pupil when light levels are raised, and expansion when they are lowered.

Pure. Not mixed with anything else, e.g. colours or tones.

Pure-stimulus act. A term used by HULL to refer to any act which does not itself bring the animal nearer to its goal, but which changes the environment in such a way that a more goal-directed act can occur.

Purkinje after-image. After fixating on a bright light and then closing the eyes, one sees a fleeting after-image in the same colour as the original stimulus (Hering after-image), followed by another brief after-image in the complementary colour. This second image is the Purkinje after-image, also known as Bidwell's ghost.

Purkinje cell. A rather large cell with numerous branches, found in the middle layer of the cerebral cortex. (⧫⧫ GRANULAR LAYER.)

Purkinje effect. The decline in the visibility of the long-wave end of the spectrum with decreasing illumination – the reason why blues and greens seem more vivid than reds and oranges at dusk. The reverse effect – the increased responsiveness of the retina to reds with increased illumination – is known as the Betzold-Brücke effect.

Purkinje figures. A vivid illusion caused by shadows of cells on the front layer of the retina, thrown on the back of the retina when the eye is very brightly illuminated.

Purkinje-Sanson images. If one looks closely at a person's eye when they are fixating on something one may see three separate images of the object reflected in their eye. These are respectively reflections from the corneal surface and the front and back of the lens.

Purple. The colour seen when the two ends of the spectrum (i.e. red and violet) are mixed.

Purpose. An awareness on the part of an animal, no matter how limited, and whether conscious or unconscious, that a goal exists.

Purposive behaviourism. ⧫ TOLMAN'S LEARNING THEORY.

Purposivism. The point of view that all behaviour is related to purposes of some kind, and is not merely a completely automatic response to stimuli – the latter being the extreme position of behaviourism.

Pursuit meter. A device for testing psychomotor skills and coordination in which one has to cause a pointer or similar instrument to follow a randomly moving target.

Putrid. One of the 'primary' smell sensations – associated with decaying matter. (⧫ ODOUR PRISM.)

Puzzle box. A device used in studies of animal learning, perception and intelligence and first used by Thorndike in his famous TRIAL-AND-ERROR experiments. The animal is placed in a box and must learn the trick of releasing itself – pressing a lever, pushing a button, standing in a certain corner, etc. It was the forerunner to the SKINNER BOX.

Pyknic type. ➧ KRETSCHMER.

Pyramidal tract. A collection of motor neurones which commence in the motor cortex and pass down, through the medulla, to the motor neurones in the spinal cord.

Pyramids. The raised areas on the front of the medulla.

Pyromania. Obsessive interest in fire and in creating fires.

Pyrophobia. Abnormal fear of fire.

Pyrosis. Heartburn.

Q

Q data. Material gained through a questionnaire.

Q sort. Form of personality rating technique in which a number of statements about an individual's personality are sorted by him into piles according to the degree to which he believes they apply to him.

Q technique. Factor analysis allowing the correlation of the scores of a number of people on a variety of tests.

Quadrigemina. ➧ CORPORA QUADRIGEMINA.

Quadriplegia. Paralysis in all four limbs.

Quale. The simple description of an experience without any reference to its meaning.

Qualitative. Relating to a difference in kind rather than degree.

Quality. That thing or assembly of things which allows one to discriminate one *type* of sensation from another.

Quantal. Relating to a variable which changes by discrete steps, or 'quanta'.

Quantification. The process of subjecting experimental data to numerical assessment and analysis.

Quantitative. Referring to a difference in degree rather than kind.

Quartile. One of the three marker points dividing a frequency distribution into equal quarters. (➧➧ INTERQUARTILE RANGE.)

Quartile deviation. ➧ PROBABLE ERROR.

Quasi-. As a prefix, means resembling or simulating.

Quasi need. Needs are particular states of deficiency in an organism; quasi needs represent the *purpose* which sets the animal to satisfy its need.

Quota sampling. Selecting from a great mass of data a set of samples equivalent to the sub-groups within the population. (➧➧ STRATIFIED SAMPLE.)

Quotidian. Occurring on a daily basis.

R

Race. One of the biological subdivisions of the species *Homo sapiens* (➧ TAXONOMY). Humans differ fairly markedly in their physical appearance (colour of skin and hair, stature, facial structure and expression, etc.), and these variations are partly related to geographical location – e.g. heavily pigmented people tend to live in tropical areas where paler skins would suffer from severe sunburn. When these characteristics are genetically determined and reappear frequently and consistently within particular populations anthropologists find it useful to classify all individuals having these characteristics as belonging to the same race.

Fairly recently a contentious dispute has arisen as to whether non-physiological factors, such as INTELLIGENCE, differ from race to race. The problem is complicated by the fact that it is frequently difficult, if not impossible, to separate out low intelligence *per se* from the effects of cultural and educational deprivation, and it is undeniably true that many racial groups – particularly the North American Negroes – have traditionally suffered such deprivation. At the moment easily the majority view, among those qualified to judge, is that there is no evidence of innate differences in intelligence between races, and that any differences which do appear to exist are artificial and would be expected to disappear as educational and cultural factors are balanced out.

Racial memory. ➧ COLLECTIVE UNCONSCIOUS.

Radiance. Rate of emission of RADIANT ENERGY from a given source area.

Radiant energy. Electromagnetic energy which travels at the speed of 186 000 miles per second – principally light and radio waves.

Radical. The mathematical sign for square root; also refers to any person interested in bringing about rapid social change.

Radionics. Pseudoscience concerning itself with the investigation of quasi-electrical energies not detectable by normal equipment, and in particular their utilization as diagnostic and therapeutic aids.

Radix. A major nerve root at the point where it joins the central nervous system.

Rami communicantes. The neural bundles which connect the sympathetic ganglia with the spinal nerves and their ventral roots.

Ramus. A branch of a nerve or blood vessel.

Random. Totally unpredictable; occurring by chance. (➧ CHANCE.)

Random error. That part of any variability which is due to CHANCE. Random errors are found to be normally distributed about the mean.

Random sample. Selection from a population chosen at random and assumed to be representative of the total population.

Range. The interval between two extremes on a scale.

Range effect. In any tracking task, the tendency to make movements too small when the target movement is large (and *vice versa*).

Rank. Position in a series.

Rank order. A set of values arranged in a series according to their order of magnitude.

Rank-order correlation. Technique for finding the correlation between two sets of ranked data.

Rapid eye movements (REMs). Jerky movements of the eyes occurring in periodic sessions throughout the sleep period. Although the movements occur in all humans, for up to one fifth of the total sleep time, their universality was not discovered until the work of Dement and Kleitman in the 1950s. People awakened during REM periods frequently report a dream. (➧➧ DREAM; SLEEP.)

Rapport. A close mental or intellectual bond between people. Compare EMPATHY.

Rate. Measurement of change per unit time.

Rating. Assigning a rank or score.

Ratio. The quantitative relationship that two things bear to each other.

Ratiocination. Reasoning; clear thinking.

Rational. Related to reasoning and logical behaviour.

Rationale. The reasoning behind an hypothesis.

Rationalism. The philosophical point of view that only by reasoning and logical thinking can one hope to reach the truth.

Rationalization. Literally, explaining or 'getting to the bottom' of something; has come to mean explaining or finding justification for behaviour *after* it has taken place. According to psychoanalytic theory, rationalization is one of the main mechanisms by which the EGO defends itself against feelings of guilt caused by previous wrong-doings or failures.

Rational type. In Jungian personality theory all individuals could be classified as one of two basic character types, rational and irrational, these being further subdivided into thinking and feeling types and intuitive and sensation types respectively. The categories are in fact more or less self-explanatory but the system, unlike Jung's extraversion/introversion continuum, has not turned out to be particularly valuable.

Ratio scale. Scale in which all the intervals are equal in magnitude and thus can be added, divided, etc. Ratio scales, unlike interval scales, have a zero point. (⧫⧫ ORDINAL SCALES; INTERVAL SCALES.)

Rat Man. A patient cured of obsessive-compulsive neurosis by Freud and cited as a classic example of successful psychoanalysis.

Rauwolfia. Plant whose root contains substances with a powerful anti-psychotic effect and from which the drug reserpine is derived.

Raw score. Test score before it has been analysed or treated statistically.

Reaction. Response to a stimulus.

Reaction formation. One of the major mechanisms of ego defence according to Freudian theory. In reaction formation the EGO responds to threatening drives from the ID *not* by blocking or controlling them (the 'healthier' attitude) but by setting up particular attitudes which actively oppose them in consciousness. For example, someone aware of latent homosexuality in himself will be loud in his denunciation of homosexuality in others. (⧫ DEFENCE MECHANISM.)

Reaction time. The delay between the onset of a stimulus and the appearance of a response.

Reaction type. In a reaction time experiment people tend to adopt one or other of a number of attitudes or sets to the expected stimulus, these being classed as stimulus, motor or mixed. The particular attitude adopted is the reaction type. (⧫⧫ SET.)

Reactive depression. A depressive illness which can be attributed to an external event, e.g. the death of a near relative.

Reactive inhibition. A term used by HULL to refer to the steady weakening in the strength of a response which takes place over time and with (or despite) continued practice.

Readiness law. One of THORNDIKE'S principles of behaviour; broadly speaking, when a stimulus-response unit is ready to respond, activation of the unit is 'satisfying' and failure to activate it is 'unsatisfying'.

Reading quotient. Measure of a child's relative reading ability; one takes the reading age (as measured by a standard test), divides this by the chronological age and (as with IQ) multiplies by 100.

Reading span. The number of words that can be perceived with a single fixation.

Real. Existing in the sense that it can be measured or demonstrated by experiment.

Real anxiety. ➧ OBJECTIVE ANXIETY.

Realism. The view that the world exists quite independently of human experience.

Reality principle. According to Freud, while the id is concerned with blind gratification of its desires (the pleasure principle), the ego attempts to strike a balance between these demands and the hard facts of the external world which make such gratification impractical. In maintaining this compromise the ego is guided by the reality principle.

Reality testing. The judgements and assessment of the world which the ego makes in attempting to follow the REALITY PRINCIPLE.

Reason. The capacity for logical thought; also refers to the 'higher' intellectual processes, particularly those untainted by emotion.

Reasoning. Logical thinking and problem solving.

Rebirth fantasy. Psychoanalytic term for fantasies involving birth or being born again, symbolized in dreams of swimming or emerging from water.

Recall. The process of extracting information from the MEMORY. Compare RECOGNITION and REMEMBERING.

Recall method. Measurement of the progress of learning by noting the number of items on a test that can be recalled. (➧ RETENTION.)

Recapitulation theory. ➧ PHYLOGENETIC PRINCIPLE.

Receiver. Something which translates a signal into a message.

Receiver operating characteristic (ROC). ➧ SIGNAL-DETECTION THEORY.

Recency law. ➧ LAW OF RECENCY.

Receptive character. Someone heavily reliant on psychological and emotional support from others. (➧➧ DEPENDENCY.)

Receptivity. Willingness to receive suggestions; open-mindedness. In physiology refers to a state of readiness to respond.

Receptor. Structure, normally a physiologically distinctive cell, which is sensitive to a particular kind of stimulus. The sense organs and skin surface are richly endowed with receptors and these are usually classed as:

1. Photopic, i.e. reacting to light.
2. Mechanical, i.e. reacting to pressure (thus including the hearing receptors).
3. Chemical, i.e. reacting to taste and smell.
4. Thermal, i.e. reacting to heat and cold.

Recessive. Disinclined to show itself; in the case of genetics refers to a GENE whose effects are masked or suppressed by another (dominant) gene.

Recidivism. Repetitive criminal behaviour; more rarely, recurring mental illness.

Reciprocal altruism. Activity, rare in the animal kingdom but exhibited by man and ants, in which 'helpful behaviour' is extended by an individual to members of the species other than those in his immediate family.

Reciprocal inhibition. Inhibition of one reflex by the activation of another. Recently the term has been applied to BEHAVIOUR THERAPY when the undesirable response (say a phobic reaction) is paired with a stronger and incompatible response.

Reciprocal innervation. In physiology, systems which work in harmony and yet have opposing effects – e.g. the contraction of one muscle leading to the relaxation of another.

Reciprocity. The law which states that responses are a function of the duration and the intensity of a stimulus. A good example is the Bunsen-Roscoe law.

Recognition. Judgement of the degree to which a present or occurring stimulus corresponds to a previous one. Compare RECALL and REMEMBERING. (➧ RETENTION.)

Recognition method. Measurements of the progress of learning by noting the accuracy with which a subject is able to recognize whether items presented to him in a test have in fact been shown to him earlier in the test. (➧ RETENTION.)

Recollection. The process of recall.

Reconditioning. Re-establishing a conditioned response after it has been extinguished.

Reconstruction method. Measurement of learning which requires the subject to rearrange jumbled test items in the order they were originally presented.

Recovery. A return to normal, or in the case of a neurone, to its resting state.

Recovery time. Time taken for a neurone to return to its resting state after having fired.

Recruitment. The hypothesis that repeated firing of cells in a neural system will in due course lead to cells in the neighbourhood being activated and later drawn into the system. (⧫⧫ FRACTIONATION.)

Rectilinear. Linear; characteristic of a straightline function.

Rectilinear distribution. Distribution in which there are more or less an equal number of cases in all categories. This contrasts with a normal distribution where the largest number of cases tend to be clustered around the mean.

Red. The colour perceived when the retina is stimulated with light of approximately 650–750 nm wavelength.

Red-green blindness. The most common form of COLOUR BLINDNESS and far more frequently observed in males than in females. (⧫ PROTANOPIA; DEUTERANOPIA.)

Redintegration. The perception of a complete unit after only a part has been presented – a few notes of music may allow one to recall the whole tune.

Reduced cue principle. The more completely one has learned something, the smaller the portion of the original stimulus complex is needed to bring about a response.

Reduced eye. A simplified drawing or model of the eye showing its basic principles.

Reduced score. Score which has been simplified for analysis by removing a constant.

Reductionism. The philosophy which argues that the best method of understanding a phenomenon is to break it up into its basic components, e.g. any explanation of mental phenomena which considers them as being ultimately reducible to conditioned reflexes. Contrast GESTALT PSYCHOLOGY.

Redundancy. An important concept in information theory; broadly speaking it refers to the repetition of elements within a message. This increases the length of the message but also means that it is less at risk, overall, from noise or signal interruption.

Reference group. Sociological term to refer to any group with which an individual identifies, whether or not he is accepted as a member of it. Such a group provides norms of behaviour for the individual who 'refers' to it. (⧫⧫ MEMBERSHIP GROUP; GROUP.)

Referral. Passing a patient on to another doctor or hospital.

Referred sensation. Locating a sensation in some part of the body other than the 'real' site of the sensation. Perhaps the most common example is referred pain – toothache is frequently located by the patient in the wrong jaw, and the pain of a heart attack may be referred to the arms.

Reflection. The turning back of radiation or waves from a surface; also implies mulling over past events or scanning the memory – directing one's thoughts 'into the mind' and reflecting them back.

Reflection response. In Rorschach testing, refers to any response which treats one half of the blot as simply a mirror image of the other.

Reflex. In its simplest form an unlearned or instinctive response which always occurs when a particular stimulus is present. It assumes an apparently direct connection between a receptor or sense organ and a motor unit in the brain which can produce a response appropriate to whatever it is that has activated the receptor. Good examples of instinctive reflexes are the corneal reflex (eye closes when cornea is touched) or the patellar (kneejerk) reflex. Pavlov widened the scope of the concept by introducing the notion of the conditioned, and therefore learned, reflex. (➧ CONDITIONING.)

Reflex arc. The physiological link between stimulus and motor response unit which is presumed to underlie a reflex.

Reflex circle. Tendency for muscular contractions to activate reflex loops which lead, by positive feedback, to even stronger contractions.

Reflex inhibition. Blocking one reflex by activating a stronger, incompatible one.

Reflex latency. The delay between onset of stimulus and onset of reflex response.

Reflexogenous zones. Parts of the body which when stimulated are particularly likely to induce reflex behaviour.

Reflexology. The view that in the long run all behaviour and mental life will be describable in terms of conditioned and unconditioned reflexes. This is the extreme behaviourist position.

Reflex reserve. Skinnerian term for the number of occasions a conditioned response will continue after reinforcement has ceased.

Refraction. A change in the direction of a wave (particularly light).

Refraction errors. Distortions of the retinal image caused by defects in the refracting media of the eye.

Refractory period. Period following the stimulation of a nerve during which no second stimulus will produce a response. This period is known as the absolute refractory period, and it is followed by a phase when an extremely strong stimulus will *just* elicit a response (the relative refractory period).

Regeneration. Rebuilding or recreating something.

Register. The range of frequencies the human voice can produce.

Regression. Any movement backwards or a return to an earlier phase of existence. In psychoanalysis, one of the mechanisms by which the EGO protects itself against conflict or anxiety. In this case the tactic is for the individual to look back to some time in the past when a similar problem was satisfactorily solved or avoided – generally by adopting an infantile attitude to it. (➧ DEFENCE MECHANISM.) For other meanings of the word ➧ FILIAL REGRESSION, PHENOMENAL REGRESSION.

Regression curve. Curve fitted to the means of a group of variables on a correlation table.

Regression line. Line showing the relationship between two variables.

Regression time. In reading, either the time taken to move from the end of one line to another, or the time spent rescanning misread words.

Regression to the mean. ➧ FILIAL REGRESSION.

Rehabilitation. Restoring an individual to normal, or as satisfactory a state as possible, following an illness, criminal episode, etc.

Reich, Wilhelm (1892–1957). One-time disciple of FREUD who broke away to form his own approach to therapy – character analysis. He later founded the pseudoscience of orgonomy. (➧ SEXUAL ECONOMY; ORGONE.)

Reification. Behaving as if a fantasy or concept was a real thing.

Reinforcement. Literally, strengthening something. In psychology, it refers to the strengthening of a behavioural response by one means or another – normally a reward. This may seem straightforward enough, until one attempts to pin down the precise meaning of the word reward. Pavlov stated that reinforcement occurred when the unconditioned stimulus (food) was presented at the same time as the conditioned stimulus (buzzer), thus implying that reinforcement was the actual association in time of a 'new' behaviour pattern with a deeply-established or instinctive one (➧ CONDITIONING). Hull, a later theorist, argued that reinforcement took place when a particular behaviour pattern was accompanied by DRIVE REDUCTION, and there have been a large number of changes rung on this theme. In the long run, since one has more or less no idea as to how learning itself is laid down, and therefore no physiological model for how reinforcement might occur, one is forced to fall back on the definition originally put forward – that reinforcement is simply the strengthening of a pattern of behaviour so that it is more likely to occur on a future occasion.

Reinforcement schedule. In studies of CONDITIONING, many of which are carried out with complete automation of the experiment, animals may be reinforced according to a number of different schedules. For example, reward may be given with *every* successful response, or randomly, or again at fixed intervals, etc. The particular programme adopted is called the reinforcement schedule.

Reinforcing stimulus. The stimulus which acts as or signals the reward after the initial appropriate response has been made.

Reintegration. ◆ REDINTEGRATION.

Rejection. In psychoanalysis, a mechanism of EGO adjustment. Unacceptable desires from the ID are rejected, but still admitted in consciousness – i.e. they are not repressed.

Relationship. A link between two variables so that a change in one produces some kind of change in the other.

Relative. Requiring comparison with something else.

Relativism. The view that there are no absolute standards of right and wrong, good and bad, etc., but that these are dependent upon their context in space and time. (◆ CULTURAL RELATIVISM.)

Relaxation. Return of a muscle to its resting state.

Relaxation therapy. An approach to PSYCHOTHERAPY in which the emphasis is placed on getting the patient to relax, by hypnosis, sedation, special exercises, etc.

Relearning method. Studying the depth of retention by having the subject learn something, and then after a period of time, relearn it. RETENTION is a function of the time saved on the second learning session.

Releaser. Any stimulus which automatically evokes a very specific pattern of behaviour. (◆◆ INNATE RELEASING MECHANISM.)

Release therapy. PSYCHOTHERAPY which guides the patient towards the expression of pent-up emotions and thus the release of tension. (◆ CATHARSIS.)

Reliability. In statistical terms, the extent to which a test or experiment has INTERNAL CONSISTENCY. This is normally measured by repeating it under highly similar conditions, with the results on the two occasions being compared. The higher the correlation, the greater the reliability.

Religion. A system of beliefs which allow man to relate himself to and understand the universe, particularly those aspects which, for one reason or another, seem to be outside the province of science. This definition perhaps best expresses the anthropological view of religion, where it is seen as performing a specific function within a society, providing a coherent set of beliefs for the society as a whole and allowing the individual some explanation of various mysteries and enigmas.

To the psychologist, religions are intriguing and suitable subject matter for study on a number of counts, but with three questions perhaps being foremost. First, does the holding of a set of religious beliefs have a really positive value to the individual, both in the routine course of his life and also in time of crisis, and if it *does* have a positive value, why? Secondly, what is the relationship between personality and tendencies to hold religious beliefs (or be violently opposed to them)? Thirdly, do any aspects of religious belief or practice have validity as psychological phenomena (e.g., do religious or mystical experiences *really* induce changes in levels of consciousness, and if so, do these provide any special insights, reduce tension or aid perception in any way)?

These three rather broad areas have attracted the interest of a number of psychologists, more or less from the time of William James, whose *Varieties of Religious Experience* is still a classic. James was interested not only in specific experiences such as dreams, fantasies, drug-induced reveries, etc., but also in the phenomenon of religious conversion – which he took to denote an invasion from the unconscious mind. Freud, on the other hand, took a predominantly atheistic view, holding that religious beliefs were simply manifestations of infantile behaviour – a rejection of the harsh world of reality with God standing in as a kind of father image. Jung's approach was characteristically different, being very much more sympathetic to religion, or at least to religious symbolism and ritual. He believed religion reflected the architecture of the collective unconscious, and offered guidelines to creativity and self-understanding.

These approaches are, of course, theoretical – not surprisingly, since it is difficult to see how religion could be considered as an experimental topic. Stretching things a bit, however, one might consider some aspects of parapsychology – in particular investigations of telepathy, out-of-the-body experiences and even life after death – to be in this category. The fact that James's *Varieties of Religious Experience* is still enormously readable and rich in insights suggests, however, that the psychology of religion has not really made much headway in the past century.

Religious mania. ➧ ECCENTRIC PARANOIA.

Remedial. Refers to an individual whose performance in one particular area is not matched by his intellectual ability. It is important to realize that with additional education or training he or she can make up the deficit. Compare SLOW LEARNING, BACKWARDNESS, RETARDATION.

Remedial training. Teaching methods designed for use with the handicapped, including the socially maladjusted.

Remembering. The process of bringing learned information out of the memory store. The term is close in meaning to recall, but generally implies something a little more definite and concrete than recollection. (⧫⧫ LEARNING; MEMORY.)

Reminiscence. Running over a previous memory or sequence of memories, often in an aimless way.

Remission. A period in which the symptoms of an illness or its progress are temporarily arrested.

Remote association. In learning a series of items, making connections between items which are not next to each other on the list.

Renal. Relating to the kidneys.

Renifleur. Someone who gets sexual excitement from odours.

Repertory grid. A technique featuring the eliciting from an individual of a series of judgements about objects or individuals important to some aspect of his life. It is used in a wide range of fields from personality assessment and psychotherapy to management studies.

Repetition-compulsion. Overwhelming need – common in obsessive neuroses – for a particular behaviour pattern to be repeated over and over again.

Replication. Repetition of an experiment.

Representation. Standing for, or symbolizing something.

Representative sample. A sample whose composition is similar to that of the population from which it is drawn. (⧫⧫ STRATIFIED SAMPLE.)

Repression. A key concept in the Freudian theory of personality. The EGO, when faced with threatening or unacceptable ideas welling up from the ID, and aware of the conflict which these will inevitably bring about with the SUPEREGO, banishes them into the unconscious where their threat at least *seems* to be less. Unfortunately, repressed material tends to smoulder away in the unconscious, ultimately expressing itself in neurotic symptoms of one kind or another – the origin of which is, of course, unclear to the ego. Evidence of the existence of repressed material, Freud argued, arises through slips of the tongue, eccentric behaviour and especially through dreams. Because repression fails to eradicate the root of the problem and merely removes it from consciousness, the mechanism is technically an unsuccessful one.

Incidentally, Freud stressed that repression is an involuntary and totally automatic act, and was not the same phenomenon as *suppression*, which was the deliberate, completely *voluntary* elimination of material from consciousness – e.g. as when one makes an effort not to brood on tomorrow's dental appointment. Suppressed material can be recalled from consciousness at any time; *re*pressed material is far less accessible and in fact actively resists being pulled into the open. (➧ DEFENCE-MECHANISM.)

Reproduction. Any of the processes involved in the propagation of the species.

Reproduction method. A measurement of learning which requires a subject to reproduce material previously learned without having cues or memory aids. (➧ RETENTION.)

Research. ➧ METHODOLOGY; EXPERIMENT.

Reserpine. ➧ RAUWOLFIA.

Residual. Whatever it is that remains after damage has occurred; in factor analysis, refers to the variance remaining after all factors have been extracted.

Residues method. A principle of induction first put forward by J. S. Mill: in examining a phenomenon, if we extract from it all aspects known to be caused by particular previous events, then the remaining or residual aspects have been caused by all the other events.

Residum. Anything remaining; sometimes used as an alternative to an ENGRAM.

Resinous. One of the 'basic smells' – characteristic of pine or tar. (➧ ODOUR PRISM.)

Resistance. In psychology, principally a term used in a psychoanalytic context. Material forced into the unconscious by the mechanism of REPRESSION now resists any attempts at dragging it back into consciousness. Similarly, on a broader scale, patients in psychoanalysis – particularly its early stages – put up a resistance to the probing of the analyst when he seems near to uncovering the cause of their unconscious conflicts. Success in psychoanalysis is supposed to be largely a matter of overcoming the mechanisms of resistance.

Resolving power. The capacity of the eye to detect the difference between two separate objects whose retinal images are close together. (➧ VISUAL ACUITY.)

Resonance. Vibratory or oscillatory response of an object to some periodic external stimulation.

Resonance theory. Refers to Helmholtz's theory of audition which proposed that the basilar membrane is the site of pitch detection, the short fibres being responsive to high-pitched sounds, the long fibres to low pitch, and the middle-length fibres to medium pitch. Because the fibres are arranged along the membrane in order of increasing length, the resonance theory is also sometimes known as the place theory. It is also known as the piano or harp theory. (♦♦ HEARING THEORIES.)

Resonant. Particular sound form in which the mouth is used as a resonating cavity; all vowels, the *l* and *r* sounds, the nasals (*n, m,* etc.) and the semi-vowels (*y* and *w*) are resonants.

Resonator. Any device which uses the principle of resonance to intensify a sound.

Respiration. Whatever system an animal uses to take in oxygen and expel CO_2.

Respondent. Relates to behaviour which is the direct result of a stimulus; contrasts with operant behaviour, which instigates an event in the external world.

Response (R). In its broadest terms, anything elicited by a stimulus. In psychology, the word is taken to imply something which takes place in an organism, not *directly* as the result of a STIMULUS, but after some intervening event has taken place. For example, in the case of something as basic as the eyeblink reflex, the stimulus would be, say, a bright light, and the response the closing of the eye. The intervening event or variable would be the firing of some appropriate neural circuit in the brain. A response therefore involves some measure of selectivity on the part of the organism, even if this is only minimal as is the case with reflex behaviour.

Response amplitude. ♦ RESPONSE STRENGTH.

Response bias. Tendency to respond in a particular way to a given set of circumstances – particularly a questionnaire, interview, etc. (♦♦ RESPONSE SET; BIAS.)

Response detail. In Rorschach testing, any response which involves only some part of the total figure.

Response generalization. Tendency for a stimulus which has been conditioned to evoke a particular response also to evoke on occasions one or more of a set of rather similar responses.

Response hierarchy. A set of possible responses to a particular stimulus, arranged in order of the probability of their occurrence. The concept is used in some models of animal learning.

Response latency. The time lag between the onset of a stimulus and the onset of a response.

Response learning. Learning which involves acquiring a sequence of responses to achieve a goal, rather than the acquisition of any cognitive overall map of the path to the goal. It is assumed that this is a simple and largely 'automatic' form of learning with the animal ending up totally confused if it is prevented from making even one of the linked chain of response sequences. Contrast PLACE LEARNING.

Response set. In preparing to make the most rapid response to a particular stimulus, a person (or animal) will often focus attention on setting up the necessary muscular activity – the response set. When the individual concentrates instead largely on *receiving the stimulus*, this is known as a stimulus set. (⧫⧫ SET.)

Response strength. Some measure of the magnitude or intensity of a particular response. It may be measured in a number of ways – e.g. how *strongly* an animal presses a bar in an experimental situation, how *frequently* he presses it, how *rapid* is his response to the initial stimulus, etc.

Restructuring. The term used by Lewin to refer to any changes in perception which occur as the result of changes taking place within the brain, rather than in the stimulus which first induced the perception. The most likely changes of this kind would be those induced by conscious attention.

Retardation. The condition of being slowed down or restricted in development. MENTAL RETARDATION is measured in terms of the difference between what an individual scores on a test and the score that would have been appropriate for his age. Compare BACKWARD and REMEDIAL.

Retention. Whatever it is that remains in the brain's memory store after the passage of time and which is available for the individual to use in one form or another; alternatively, whatever it is that is *not forgotten* (⧫ FORGETTING). The degree of retention is normally measured by one of four methods: recognition, relearning, reproduction and recall. (⧫ MEMORY.)

Retention curve. Plot of the amount of learned material which is retained with the passage of time.

Reticular activating system (RAS). Also known as the reticular formation. It comprises a network of nerve fibres lying within the brain stem and the upper part of the spinal cord whose function appear to be to despatch arousing or excitatory signals into various other parts of the brain and cortex. The discovery of the role of the RAS by Moruzzi and Magoun in 1958 led to a major shift in physiological theories of sleep and wakefulness, motivation, attention and also of mental illness.

Reticular formation. ➧ RETICULAR ACTIVATING SYSTEM.

Retifism. Shoe or glove FETISHISM.

Retina. The light-sensitive layers of cells on the back surface of the eye, which act as a kind of projection screen for light images projected through the cornea and lens. The principal constituents of the retinal cells are photosensitive pigments which convert light, by a chemical reaction, into nervous impulses transmitted along the optic nerve to the brain. The retina is equipped with two main types of sensory cell, the rods and the cones. The former lie in the periphery and are mainly responsive in dim illumination, while the latter lie in the central portion (the fovea) and respond to bright light. The retina is a highly complex structure, with many layers of cells, and featuring a very elaborate network of interconnections. (➧ EYE.)

Retinal disparity. The fact that when the eyes focus on an object they view it from slightly different positions means that slightly different 'images' are transmitted upwards to the brain. The difference between these two images is the retinal disparity. Disparity, of course, decreases the further away the fixated object is from the observer, and therefore acts as an important clue in DEPTH PERCEPTION.

Retinal elements. The cells – rods and cones – which are the active constituents of the RETINA.

Retinal field. The sum total of retinal cells excited by a particular stimulus.

Retinal image. The image of external visual stimuli projected on to the RETINA by the focusing system of the eye.

Retinal light. Vague sensations of light perceived even in complete darkness and presumably due to spontaneous firing of retinal cells.

Retinal rivalry. In normal circumstances when the two eyes focus on an object the slightly dissimilar patterns of stimuli presented to the two retinae are fused by the brain into a single perceptual image. Occasionally, however, because the two images are incompatible (as when one vivid colour is presented to one eye and a different colour to the other), fusion may prove to be too big a problem for the brain, in which case a series of alternating images from the two eyes are seen. This is also known as binocular rivalry.

Retinene. Retinal pigment from which rhodopsin (visual purple) is formed.

Retinitis. Inflammation of the retina.

Retinitis pigmentosa. Pathological weakness in retinal pigments, resulting in reduced colour sensitivity, particularly to blue. (⧫⧫ NIGHT BLINDNESS.)

Retinoscope. Device for examining the interior of the eye and retina.

Retroactive. Acting backwards in time; specifically refers to the influence of currently learned material on the retention of earlier items. In retroactive inhibition, new material *adversely* affects the old, while in retroactive facilitation, it *assists* the retention of previous material. Contrast PROACTIVE.

Retrobulbar. May refer either to the back of the eye, or to the back of the medulla.

Retrocognition. In an ESP experiment, attempting to guess not the item presently being offered in the test, but one which has occurred earlier in the sequence. Contrast PRECOGNITION.

Retrograde. Moving backwards; degenerating.

Retrograde amnesia. When amnesia occurs for events prior to the trauma. Contrast ANTEROGRADE AMNESIA.

Retrospection. A deliberate attempt at recreating the mental processes involved in a past experience.

Reverberation. Repetition of a stimulus caused by its interaction with something else – e.g. an echo.

Reverberatory circuit. A group of cluster of cells which continue to fire as a unit for a measurable period after the original activating stimulus has ceased. Such circuits may be involved in some aspects of the learning process, for example by allowing the MEMORY TRACE to become established.

Reverie. Daydream.

Reverse halo effect. ⧫ HALO EFFECT.

Reversible perspective. Condition occurring with AMBIGUOUS FIGURES. (⧫⧫ FIGURE-GROUND PHENOMENON.)

Reversion. ⧫ ATAVISM.

Reward. Anything which is pleasant or satisfying to an organism, but in particular anything which, when presented after a particular pattern of behaviour has been performed, increases the likelihood that that behaviour will be performed again. The concept of reward is an important, but elusive one (⧫ REINFORCEMENT).

Rh factor. About 84 per cent of the population have the Rh factor in their blood and are known as Rh positive. In people with Rh negative blood group introduction of Rh+ blood into the body produces antibodies. These antibodies may cause brain damage, still birth or jaundice in a Rh+ foetus.

Rhabdomancy. ➧ DOWSING.

Rheobase. Any electrical current strength sufficiently strong to activate a nerve.

Rhine, Joseph Banks (1895 –). Psychologist who pioneered laboratory studies of ESP and who headed the world-famous department of parapsychology at Duke University, North Carolina. (➧ PARAPSYCHOLOGY; EXTRA-SENSORY PERCEPTION.)

Rhinencephalon. Part of the brain including the olfactory nerves, bulbs and tracts, and the limbic system. It is known to be involved in the perception of smell and also in some aspects of emotional behaviour.

Rhodopsin. A pigment, also known as visual purple, which is present in large quantities in the RODS in the retina. Rhodopsin is highly responsive to light, becoming bleached out in daylight, but reacting less strongly in dim light.

Rhombencephalon. The cerebellum, pons and medulla; the hindbrain.

Rhythm. A regular sequence of stimuli.

Ribonucleic acid (RNA). A biochemical substance which exists in all living cells and which is believed to be the main carrier of the genetic message. (➧➧ DEOXYRIBONUCLEIC ACID.)

Ribosomes. Granules in the cytoplasm of the cell within which proteins are synthesized.

Right-and-wrong cases method. ➧ CONSTANT METHOD.

Right associates method. ➧ PAIRED-ASSOCIATES METHOD.

Righting reflex. Reflex which causes an animal to resume its correct posture when thrown off balance or placed on its back.

Rigidity. Refers to a personality type characterized by general inflexibility and unwillingness to accept the opinions and advice of others. It also refers to an extreme case of muscle contraction.

Risk level. In any statistical sampling, the risk level is the percentage of measures which will, by chance, fall outside the 'normal' range.

Risky shift. Sociological term referring to the tendency for groups on some occasions to take greater chances than individuals.

Rites de passage. ➧ INITIATION RITE.

Ritual. A sequence of stereotyped behaviour generally with a particular purpose or having symbolic value.

Robot. Any automatic device which copies some aspect of human behaviour; more specifically a mechanical or artificial man. (➧➧ ANDROID.)

Rods. Elongated cells embedded in the retina which contain a pigment, rhodopsin, extremely sensitive to light. The rods, which number about 120 million in humans, tend to be distributed in the peripheral regions of the RETINA and achieve their maximum effectiveness in dim illumination. They do not respond selectively to colours, this function being reserved for the CONES which fill the central portion of the retina.

Rod vision. Vision in poor illumination which, because of the geographical distribution of the rods, is most effective in the periphery of vision ('out of the corner of the eye'). It is also known as scotopic vision.

Rods of Corti. Part of the organ of Corti which contains the hair cells involved in the perception of sound.

Rogers, Carl (1902–). American psychologist who introduced CLIENT-CENTRED THERAPY as a novel approach to psychotherapy and who was responsible for the development of counselling techniques in clinical psychology. (➧ HUMANISTIC PSYCHOLOGY.)

Rolandic fissure. ➧ CENTRAL FISSURE.

Role. An important concept in social psychology which refers to the behaviour expected of an individual in accordance with the position he holds in a particular society. If the word seems to have theatrical connotations then this is perfectly apt, for a 'role' is more or less exactly the part played by an individual in the drama of life. Teachers, for example, are expected to behave in certain ways – their roles as teachers – and if they deviate too drastically they meet society's disapproval. But a student or pupil is also taking a role, and he too is expected to adopt certain conventions. Other common key roles include those of being a mother, father, brother, sister, etc., and it should be clear from this that in the course of life the average individual will be called upon to play numerous roles, most interlocking but some, inevitably, at odds with each other. When this happens – as when a mother has to sacrifice some of her mother role in order to become a breadwinner – role-conflict is said to occur.

Other concepts in this area include that of role-taking – the extent to which an individual can see himself in the role that others have to play and, by doing so, show understanding, social awareness and tolerance.

With the adolescent or developing individual, the role they are to take is not always obvious to them and society sometimes has to dramatize and impose the role on them – a particularly interesting example of this being the initiation ceremonies adopted at puberty in many societies where the transfer from the rôle of childhood to that of adulthood is symbolically spelled out. Roles can be of two types, those which are ascribed (e.g. sex, age) and those which are attained (e.g. status, occupational).

Role playing. The adoption by one individual of another's role, or the acting out of one's own role. This is used as an adjunct to psychotherapy, particularly group therapy, where patients help each other identify the essence of their problems by defining and adopting each other's roles.

Romberg sign. Uncontrolled swaying of the body when the eyes are closed; a symptom of *tabes dorsalis*.

Root conflict. A fundamental neurotic conflict assumed to have its roots in infancy or childhood.

Rorschach test. One of the most famous PROJECTIVE TESTS and used widely in clinical diagnosis. The test consists of one of a standard set of ten inkblots on a sheet of paper, the sheet being folded once and the resultant bisymmetrical splurge being shown to the patient. The clinician invites the patient to free-associate on the basis of its shape, listens to his responses and notes any bizarre imagery reported, particularly stereotyped responses, signs of inhibition or repression, etc. There is controversy over the degree of objectivity of the Rorschach scoring methods and some critics argue that the test merely serves to 'get patients talking' and allow the clinician to use his intuition in diagnosis.

Rosenzweig test. A PROJECTIVE TEST in which the patient is shown a number of pictures featuring people in slightly frustrating circumstances, and is invited to state how they would behave or what they would say.

Rostral. At the head of something.

Rotary pursuit meter. ➧ PURSUIT METER.

Rotation. A term used in FACTOR ANALYSIS to denote the state when factor axes are shifted from the positions occurring after factor extraction.

Rotation perception. The sense of movement perception which occurs when the fluids in the semicircular canals move as the result of acceleration, deceleration, or rotation of the head.

Rote learning. Learning featuring little conscious comprehension of the topic and normally involving repeated presentation of the items to be learned; contrast IDEATIONAL LEARNING.

Rubin's figure. Ambiguous or reversible figure which illustrates the FIGURE-GROUND PHENOMENON.

Rubric. A heading.

Ruffini corpuscle. A specialized nerve-ending found in the skin which is believed to mediate the sense of warmth and/or pressure.

Run. A single trial in an experimental series.

Runway. Pathway in a maze or other device for testing animal behaviour.

S

S factor. Specific ability factor. (➧ SPECIFIC ABILITY.)

Saccade. The movement made by the eye when it jumps from one fixation point to another.

Saccule. One of the two sac-like bulges in the vestibular system of the inner ear. (➧➧ UTRICLE.)

Sacral division. The lower division of the CRANIO-SACRAL DIVISION of the autonomic nervous system.

Sadism. Pleasure, generally sexual, obtained through the inflicting of pain or suffering on others; named after the Marquis de Sade, a noted eighteenth-century sexual eccentric. Freud argued that sadism was a highly exaggerated version of the normal pattern of male aggression in sexual life. Contrast MASOCHISM.

Sadomasochism. Tendency towards SADISM *and* MASOCHISM.

Sagittal fissure. The longitudinal fissure dividing the two cerebral hemispheres. It is also known as the hemispherical fissure.

Sagittal plane. A vertical plane passing through the body from front to back.

St Vitus's dance. A form of chorea (a disease of the nervous system) involving emotional disturbance and featuring uncontrolled movements of the limbs, facial muscles, etc. It is also called acute chorea and Sydenham's chorea.

Salivary reflex. Automatic secretion from the salivary glands when food is presented to a hungry animal. Pavlov used this reflex as the basis for his early studies of CONDITIONING.

Salpêtrière school. A school of psychotherapy founded by Charcot which employed HYPNOSIS extensively in the treatment of mental illness.

Salt. One of the four dimensions of TASTE.

Saltatory. Relating to leaping movements as in chorea.

Sample. A relatively small group which is assumed to be representative of the larger group from which it is drawn. (⧫⧫ STRATIFIED SAMPLE.)

Sampling error. Predictive error brought about because a SAMPLE was not truly representative of its parent population.

Sampling procedures. Techniques for ensuring that a SAMPLE is truly representative of the population from which is has been drawn.

Sampling variability. The degree to which samples vary from an ideal 'random' selection.

Sanction. A response, either positive or negative, by members of a social group to activity or behaviour on the part of one or more of its members. It may vary from a rule with the force of law to simple signs of social approval or disapproval. (⧫⧫ NORM.)

Sanguine. ⧫ TEMPERAMENT.

Sanity. Mental condition in which the individual is free from any prolonged disturbances or disorders and is capable of normal integration with his social environment.

Sanson images. ⧫ PURKINJE-SANSON IMAGES.

Sapphism. Lesbianism; female homosexuality.

Satiation. Total satisfaction; more specifically, the state following the reduction of a particular drive.

Satisfaction. Subjective sense of pleasure after a goal has been achieved – whether the goal has been physical or psychological.

Satisfier. Term used by Thorndike as synonymous with REWARD. Contrast ANNOYER.

Saturated test. In FACTOR ANALYSIS a test correlating highly with a particular factor.

Saturation. In FACTOR ANALYSIS, the extent to which a particular test and a factor are correlated; also refers to the purity or 'depth' of a colour.

Satyriasis. Obsessive and dominating interest in sexual behaviour on the part of the male; male equivalent to nymphomania.

Savings method. ⧫ RELEARNING METHOD.

Scala media. The COCHLEAR CANAL.

Scalar analysis. The determination of where an item should lie on a scale.

Scala tympani. The lower passage of the bony canal of the cochlea.

Scala vestibuli. The upper passage of the bony canal of the cochlea, connecting the oval window to the apex.

Scale. Items arranged in a series according to value or magnitude, against which another item can be measured or placed.

Scale value. The number given to an item according to its position on a particular scale.

Scaling. Broadly speaking, the assigning of numbers or values to objects; more specifically, the theory and practice of devising measurement scales.

Scalogram. A cumulative SCALE.

Scanning. The process of examining a number of items briefly and often repetitively in order to get an overview.

Scapegoating. In sociological terms, the transferring of aggression or blame from an individual or group as a whole on to another individual or group. The concept is important in trying to explain the mechanisms and origins of stereotyping.

Scatology. Abnormal interest in excrement.

Scatter. The spread of items around or about the mean. One of the most common measures of scatter is the STANDARD DEVIATION.

Scatter diagram. Diagram which allows two variables to be plotted so that their relationship can be measured.

Schafer-Murphy effect. Relates to the fact that the perception of an ambiguous figure can be affected by systematically rewarding the presence of one of its phases (i.e. the phase that is rewarded becomes more likely to be perceived on future occasions).

Schedule. A plan, proposal or format.

Schedule of reinforcement. ➧ REINFORCEMENT SCHEDULE.

Schema. A mental model, framework or overall strategy. The term is also used by Piaget as a fundamental concept suggesting that children build up 'schemas' of the world around them.

Schizoid. Relating to SCHIZOPHRENIA.

Schizophrenia. One of the major forms of PSYCHOSIS – actually a group name for a variety of psychotic reactions, all of which involve major personality disturbances. The term was first used in the early part of the century to describe disorders in which the individual's personality seemed, in one way or another, to be at odds with itself – the so-called split mind. The term dementia praecox (early or youthful insanity) was also used to describe schizophrenic conditions, though this is now obsolete.

Today schizophrenia is often grouped into four classes: simple (featuring a progressive loss of interest in the external world), hebephrenic (featuring peculiar emotional responses, hallucinations and delusions), catatonic (featuring long periods of immobility, sometimes punctuated by wild or agitated behaviour) and paranoid (where unrealistic thinking, hallucinations and delusions of persecution are common). The boundary between the four 'types' is tenuous, however, and there is a good deal of argument as to whether this common classification is helpful from the point of view of therapy.

Perhaps the most controversial aspect of the problem lies in attempts at establishing the aetiology – origins – of this psychosis, with the main battle taking place between those who hold that it is physiological or biochemical in origin, and those, like many psychoanalysts, who follow Freud's view that it is psychological, being an extreme case of conflict between the different aspects of the personality. It is certainly true that there is only slender evidence that schizophrenia responds to psychoanalytic therapy, but it is equally true that biochemical treatment seems at present able only to alleviate the symptoms of the disorder. Schizophrenia is common in all societies, particularly in the age group twenty-five to thirty-five, and is the major cause of hospitalization amongst the mental illnesses.

Schizothymic. ➧ KRETSCHMER.

School. Any place where systematic teaching or training is carried out. The word is also used to refer to a group of psychologists who follow a particular line of theory or a particular approach to experimental research.

Schopenhauer, Arthur (1788 – 1860). German philosopher who advanced a metaphysical doctrine on the nature of the human will and mind; he also seems to have been one of the first people to put forward the idea that the roots of madness lay in the unconscious mind.

Schroeder staircase. Well-known and effective alternating or ambiguous figure, also known as the staircase illusion. (➧ Fig. 29 on p. 321.)

Science. The acquisition of knowledge through the systematic study of the universe.

Scientology. ➧ DIANETICS.

Scintillating scotomata. Bright flashes of light seen even when the eyes are closed.

Sciosophy. Any pseudoscientific system of belief.

Sclerosis. Hardening of biological tissue.

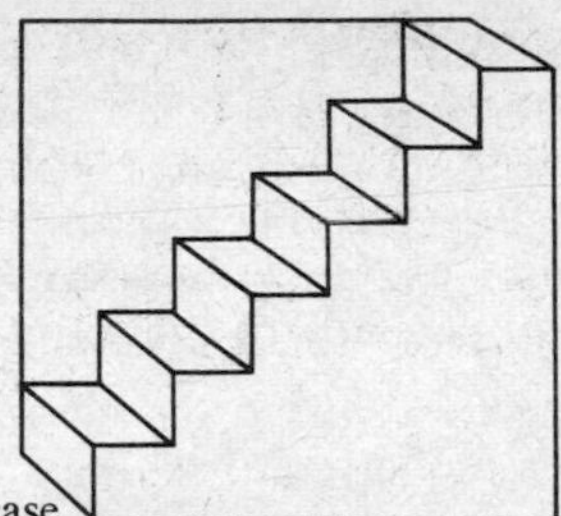

Figure 29. Schroeder staircase.

Sclerotic. The tough outer coating of the eyeball.

Scopic method. Gathering data by direct observation of the phenomena rather than by instruments or other recording devices (graphic method).

Scopolamine. A sedative drug which weakens concentration and was at one time used as a TRUTH DRUG.

Scopophilia. Voyeurism; gaining pleasure principally by watching others perform sex acts.

Score. A quantitative value which can be assigned to a particular event, activity, response or sequence of these.

Scoterythrism. Type of COLOUR BLINDNESS in which reds tend to be seen as darker than they are.

Scotoma. An area or part of the visual field which is insensitive to light. In addition to that part of the retina where the optic nerve leaves the eye (blind spot), a scotoma may occur because of retinal damage or injury to the visual cortex.

Scotomata. Plural of SCOTOMA, but with a special meaning inasmuch as it refers to the peculiar visual hallucinations – zigzag patterns of light, etc. – which often precede an attack of migraine.

Scotomization. Having a mental 'blind spot'; failing to recognize faults in oneself. In psychoanalytic terms, anything which will lead to conflicts with the EGO.

Scotopic adaptation. Dark adaptation.

Scotopic vision. Vision in dim or poor illumination when the colour-sensitive CONES in the fovea have ceased to function and the colour-blind RODS in the periphery have become fully active. Compare PHOTOPIC VISION.

Scratch reflex. Scratching movements which may be elicited by rubbing the neck or side of an animal.

Screening. A process of preselection prior to a major study or test.

Screen memory. A term used in psychoanalysis to refer to any memory – perhaps of a quite insignificant event – which rises into consciousness, either in dreams or in the course of free association, and whose function is to cover or divert attention from a more significant repressed memory. Screen memories are frequently of childhood events.

Scrying. Attempting to 'see into the future' by gazing at a highly polished surface, such as a crystal ball.

Seance. Literally, a sitting or meeting, but generally used to refer to a ritual featuring an attempt by a Spiritualist medium to communicate with the dead.

Seashore test. Set of tests of pitch discrimination, rhythm sense, tonal memory, etc., used as a basic measure of musical aptitude.

Secondary. Drawn or elaborated from something else.

Secondary drive. More commonly, ACQUIRED DRIVE.

Secondary elaboration. Psychoanalytic term for filling in detail in a dream or anecdote in order to make a 'better' or more convincing story.

Secondary extinction. As one particular conditioned response becomes weakened, other responses of a similar kind also become weakened.

Secondary function. ➧ PRIMARY FUNCTION.

Secondary gain. The advantage, whatever form it takes, which a person gets from being ill.

Secondary group. ➧ GROUP.

Secondary integration. According to psychoanalysis, the second major stage in the evolution of the personality which features the unification of the various pregenital components. Contrast PRIMARY INTEGRATION. (➧➧ ANAL CHARACTER; ORAL CHARACTER.)

Secondary narcissism. ➧ NARCISSISM.

Secondary process. Psychoanalytic term for conscious activity aimed at satisfying needs. Primary processes are purely instinctive strivings, though with the same goals.

Secondary quality. ➧ PRIMARY QUALITY.

Secondary reinforcement. In conditioning experiments, whatever it is that satisfies a need-state – e.g. food to a hungry dog – acts as a *primary* reinforcer or reward. In due course objects or events associated with the primary reinforcer can themselves become rewarding, and may come to act as goals. For example, monkeys will work in order to receive coloured tokens which they can *subsequently* exchange for food. Furthermore, they will also learn new tasks (or acquire conditioned reflexes) when only rewarded by the token. The tokens are now secondary reinforcers.

Secondary repression. The repression into the unconscious of unpleasant or threatening thoughts which, while not necessarily instinctive (➧ PRIMARY REPRESSION) are associated with instincts.

Secondary sex characteristics. Psychological and physiological features which discriminate the sexes but which do not themselves play a part in reproduction (voice quality, hairiness, physical strength, etc.).

Second sight. Popular term for alleged extra-sensory abilities.

Second signal system. A term introduced by PAVLOV to refer to the ability of an animal *to signal to or instruct itself*; as opposed to first order signals which come from the environment. For example, the smell of food which elicits salivation is a first order signal; the decision or 'command' that the animal gives itself to go to a particular place is a second order signal. Luria has elaborated this notion to help explain some aspects of linguistic learning and behaviour.

Sect. A group, generally religious, united by holding a set of beliefs in common.

Section. In physiology, a slice of tissue.

Secular. Enduring or changing only slowly; relating to non-religious things.

Sedative. Drug which lowers central nervous system activity and produces sleep in higher doses.

Segregation. In sociology, the splitting up of individuals into groups and isolating them from the rest of society. In GESTALT PSYCHOLOGY, the tendency for a segment of a whole pattern to assume its own identity in the perceptual field when separated from other elements.

Seizure. A convulsion or other sudden attack of a disease.

Selection. Choosing with a particular purpose and according to some special criteria; in genetics, the favouring of certain groups of genes because of their survival value. (➧ EVOLUTION.)

Selective answer test. Test in which the individual chooses between a number of given possible answers – e.g. a multiple-choice test.

Selective attention. Focusing attention, at will, on some aspect of the environment.

Selective reinforcement. ➧ DIFFERENTIAL REINFORCEMENT.

Self. May be defined in a number of ways, none of them entirely satisfactory. Probably the most commonly accepted definition within the context of psychology equates 'self' with 'ego' – the Freudian concept of that aspect of the personality which is conscious of its own identity and is aware that it has a persistence in time. Self also seems to imply an awareness of the existence of other 'selfs' in the environment and also a realization that whatever constitutes the self is in some way distinct and separate from all other aspects of the environment.

The question of how this aspect of mental life gives rise to the feeling of 'selfishness' must be one of the great riddles of psychology, physiology and philosophy. From a naive and traditional point of view the self is a spiritual, non-material being which controls the body and possibly survives death. At the other extreme, to the behaviourist the self is a state of consciousness arising out of the vast complexity of the brain and a natural consequence of evolutionary development – but in no way separate from the physical body and brain.

Self-abuse. Obsolete term for masturbation, heavy with the Victorian attitudes to the practice.

Self-actualization. A constant striving towards fulfilling one's potential. According to both Rogers and Maslow, a healthy personality is one which fully attains self-actualization.

Self-analysis. Any systematic attempt to understand one's own motivation, goals and achievements. FREUD believed that a trained individual, given enough courage and insight, could undertake the equivalent of a depth analysis on himself. In fact he claimed that he had himself been at least partially successful in a self-analysis, but at the same time realized that many of the subtleties of the unconscious mind would be too devious to reveal their secrets to the conscious mind of the same individual.

Self-awareness. Insight into one's own motives, potential and limitations.

Self-concept. The sum total of an individual's attitudes towards himself and evaluation of his achievements.

Self-consciousness. Any degree of introspection about one's behaviour or mental activity which is sufficiently intense to hamper the performance of a task. Compare SELF-AWARENESS.

Self-consistency. Reliability of behaviour, performance or of a test, over a substantial period of time.

Self-correlation. The relationship of a test or measure with itself – e.g.

how well do different parts of a test compare with each other in accuracy and measuring power?

Self-demand schedule. Allowing an infant to decide when and what it should be fed.

Self-distribution. Gestalt term for whatever it is in a perceptual field that leads to its organization into units, patterns or wholes. (➧ GESTALT PSYCHOLOGY.)

Self-expression. Any activity or behaviour which reveals aspects of one's nature to others or to oneself.

Self-image. View of oneself as one believes others see one. Compare LOOKING-GLASS SELF, SELF-CONCEPT.

Self-inventory. Personality test in which the individual attempts to assess his own characteristics against a checklist.

Self-observation. ➧ INTROSPECTION.

Self-stimulation. Generally reserved for self-stimulation by an animal of PLEASURE CENTRES in its own brain.

Selye, Hans (1907 –). Austrian psychologist best known for his theory of stress and for introducing the concept of the general adaptation syndrome (GAS). (➧ STRESS.)

Semantic conditioning. Simply, learning the name of an object.

Semantic differential. A technique developed by Charles Osgood to assess the relative meanings of words, ideas or concepts – or more properly, how they are understood by different individuals. Subjects 'rate' words along a series of scales – good/bad, strong/weak, active/passive, etc. – and the ratings made by different individuals are later compared. The three basic dimensions arising from the technique are potency, activity and evaluation.

Semantics. The study of meaning.

Semantic therapy. An approach to psychotherapy which holds that many minor mental illnesses are due to confusion about the meaning of words, and seeks to track down the sources of these confusions and correct them.

Semen. The fluid containing male spermatozoa.

Semicircular canals. Three bony canals or tubes set deep in the inner ear and located at right angles to each other. The semicircular canals contain ducts which are filled with fluid and lined with tiny hair-like sensory cells. Movement of the head in any one plane will cause minute tides in the canals, thus stimulating the cells which pass appropriate information to the brain. The semicircular canals are vital to the sense of balance and movement perception.

Semiology. The study of signs and language; includes semantics.

Senescence. The process of aging and the physiological changes which accompany it.

Senile. Relating to old age.

Senile dementia. Disruption of normal mental processes as the result of the aging of the brain.

Senile psychosis. Relatively severe mental disorder caused by the degeneration of brain tissue with age. Memory disorders and mental confusion are the most common symptoms, and these may be accompanied by great anxiety.

Senility. Old age.

Sensation. Literally, any response within the nervous system caused by the stimulation of a receptor or sense organ. By this definition it would seem that a sensation need not be *consciously* experienced by the individual, which may sound like a contradiction in terms. The problem here can best be understood when one realizes that psychologists make an important distinction between sensation and PERCEPTION – the first being the acquisition of data by the nervous system, the second being the interpretation of those data by the brain and their relationship to other sensations or to memory systems.

Sensationalism. An early approach to philosophical psychology; better known as EMPIRICISM.

Sensation increment. A term used in psychophysics to refer to any increase in the intensity of sensory experience.

Sensation level. The level of intensity of a sensation; most commonly used in audition where the measure is given in decibels.

Sensation threshold. ➧ ABSOLUTE THRESHOLD.

Sensation type. ➧ RATIONAL TYPE.

Sensation unit (SU). Any measurable change in sensory experience. In audition it is the unit of loudness corresponding to the decibel.

Sense. A word with different shades of meaning in psychology, but generally referring to the body's mechanisms for gathering data from the external world. Traditionally there are five senses – sight, sound, taste, smell and touch – but from a physiological and even a subjective point of view this is not a complete or satisfactory list. To it should be added at least kinaesthesis (movement sense), temperature, balance and possibly pain. Establishing whether something is a sense or not depends upon whether there are special sets of organs serving it, and whether these respond to a particular set of stimuli only. The outsider here is evidently pain for which no specific organs or receptors have as yet been detected.

Sense datum. Information passed on to the brain by a sense organ.

Sensed difference. Any noticeable difference between two stimuli.

Sense-feeling. The pleasantness or unpleasantness of a sensation.

Sense limen. ➧ ABSOLUTE THRESHOLD.

Sense modality. Particular type of sensation – touch, vision, hearing, etc. It is a characteristic of some people that one sense modality takes preference over the others – e.g. visile, audile.

Sense organ. A receptor, or more commonly a collection of receptors, which respond selectively to particular types of stimulation.

Sense perception. A judgement or conscious awareness of some aspect of the environment made on the basis of information flowing in from the senses.

Sense quality. The characteristics of a sensation which allow the brain to distinguish it from other types of sensation.

Sensibility. The ability to respond to sensory stimulation; it is important not to confuse this with SENSITIVITY.

Sensitive. Highly responsive to stimulation; in psychical research, refers to someone capable of receiving information paranormally, e.g. a Spiritualist medium.

Sensitive zone. Part of the body highly responsive to stimulation.

Sensitivity. Tendency to respond to very low levels of physical stimulation.

Sensitivity training. An approach to the study and improvement of human relationships using group discussions and interaction. Based loosely on group psychotherapy techniques, it involves the formation of small groups united by specific goals, and meeting regularly to discuss the best methods of attaining them. The technique is supposed to train individuals in more effective methods of communication and in achieving greater understanding of their own strengths and weaknesses. Such groups are also known as encounter groups or T groups.

Sensitization. The process of becoming more receptive to sensory stimuli.

Sensor. Something capable of detecting stimuli; a receptor or sense organ.

Sensorial. Relating to the sensory areas of the brain.

Sensorimotor. Relating to activity which involves input from the senses and a corresponding response in musculature or motor activity.

Sensorimotor arc. A neural link, either instinctive or learned, between a particular set of stimulus receptors and a particular set of effectors or motor neurones; a reflex arc.

Sensorium. Obsolete term for the sensory areas of the brain.

Sensory. Relating to all physiological and psychological aspects of sensation.

Sensory acuity. The ability of the senses to discriminate between small differences in stimulation.

Sensory adaptation. The tendency for a sensory receptor or a sense organ to change the rate of intensity of firing as the result of prolonged exposure to a particular stimulus. Generally the change involves a reduced response, but in certain circumstances (e.g. dark adaptation) sensitivity may be raised.

Sensory areas. Areas of the cortex which receive information from the various sense organs, e.g. occipital or visual cortex.

Sensory deprivation. Condition in which the nervous system is subjected to markedly reduced sensory input. The most famous experiments of this kind involved isolating humans in totally dark, soundproofed cubicles for periods of hours or days. Most subjects found the deprivation to be unpleasant and occasionally frightening; hallucinations and panic were common, lending some support to the theory that creatures with complex nervous systems 'need' a constant supply of sensory input to operate effectively.

Sensory organization. Whatever it is that leads the brain to perceive groups, clusters or patterns. According to Gestalt psychologists the perception of patterns was dependent upon, first, basic structures existing in the environment, and, secondly, the presence of built-in organizing forces within the brain. (⧫⧫ GESTALT PSYCHOLOGY.)

Sensory process. All the activities involved in sensation.

Sensory root. A dorsal root in the spinal cord which has a role in sensation.

Sensual. Relating to those sensations which give positive pleasure.

Sensuality. The pursuit of sensation because of the pleasure it gives.

Sensum. ➧ SENSE DATUM.

Sensuous. Relating to the senses, but in particular to the pleasant indulgence of sensory experience.

Sentence completion test. Test in which the subject has to fill in the missing words or phrases in a sentence. It may be used, with appropriate modifications, either as an intelligence or a personality test.

Sentience. The ability of an organized system to receive information and have some degree of awareness of it.

Sentiment. A tendency to feel or respond in a particular way to something; an emotional attitude.

Sentimentality. Tendency to allow emotional feelings and attitudes to override objective judgements.

Separation anxiety. A child's fear of being parted from his or her mother; an important concept in psychoanalytic theory. (➧➧ ATTACHMENT.)

Septal area. Area of the brain close to the hypothalamus; it is here that the PLEASURE CENTRE of the rat brain lies.

Septum. A division or partition.

Sequelae. The aftermath of an illness or operation.

Sequence. A series of events linked by some common thread or cause.

Sequential analysis. Statistical test which, broadly speaking, tells one whether an experiment is complete or whether further data are needed.

Serial anticipation method. An approach to learning in which the subject is presented with a list of paired associates and required to memorize them. The list is taken as being learned when he can correctly call out the second word of each pair as soon as the first is presented provided that the original word sequence is retained. In the serial probe method a slightly more difficult task is involved, with the experimenter calling out any item from the list and requesting its pair.

Serial learning. Learning items in a pre-arranged sequence.

Serial-position effect. The effect of the position of an item within a list on the ease with which it is learned (e.g. items at the beginning and end of a list tend to be learned more readily than those in the middle).

Serial probe method. ➧ SERIAL ANTICIPATION METHOD.

Serial reinforcement. In a task featuring a series of choice points, whenever a correct choice is made this in itself rewards or reinforces the particular piece of behaviour that led up to it. The learning of a complex task therefore involves reaching a series of sub-goals and rewards, leading up to a final reward which comes on the completion of the task – e.g. finding food at the end of a maze.

Seriation. Arranging data into a series.

Serotonin. The popular name for the drug 5-hydroxytryptamine which is assumed to play a significant role in the sleep-wakefulness cycle; it was once believed that serotonin was present in unusually low quantities in the brains of schizophrenics, but this hypothesis is now generally rejected.

Servomechanism. A system which has the capacity to alter and control the activity of another system. (➧ FEEDBACK.)

Sessile. Relating to organisms which are unable to move themselves around.

Set. A temporary state of an organism which prepares it for a particular course of action – 'stimulus set' if it is to prepare it to receive information, 'motor set' if to make a response. Set, or *Einstellung* as it was known to the early German experimentalists, has long been realized to be a highly significant factor in experimental psychology; whether an animal or person has a set for something can greatly influence the results of an experiment and fairly elaborate controls are needed to allow for the effect of set or minimize it. (➧➧ EXPECTANCY; PREPERCEPTION.)

Set-theory. In mathematics, the theory of data in series or groups.

Severe mental retardation. ➧ MENTAL RETARDATION.

Sex. The division of species into two distinct types of organisms, the differences being in one way or another essential to the reproduction of the species. The word is also commonly used to denote sexual behaviour – the patterns of activity which precede and include mating, or which in the case of homosexuality and other deviations are based on or related to mating. Sex is one of the primary drives, taking its place alongside hunger and thirst as being a powerful motivator of behaviour. Unlike hunger and thirst, however, it is not vital to the individual (to the extent that he or she will not die if deprived of it), but it is of course vital to the *species*.

The study of sex can be looked at from three points of view, all overlapping to some degree – as a physiological, as a psychological and as a sociological phenomenon. The physiology of sex is somewhat outside the scope of this dictionary and concerns itself with genetic and hormonal factors, and with the rather elaborate patterns of autonomic behaviour which control sexual arousal, coitus and the poorly understood phenomenon of orgasm. The changes in the reproductive system which take place with age are, however, relevant where they impinge directly on psychology, in particular those occurring in puberty which signal the transition of the child into adult, those occurring at or around the menopause when the woman ceases to be capable of bearing offspring, and in old age when physical deterioration leads to a steady reduction in sexual activity. These three transitional zones bring with them considerable psychological stresses, mainly related to the individual's need to acquire, understand and adjust to the new role which these changes demand he or she plays.

Superficially it may seem surprising that the psychology of sex should be so important in view of the fact that many aspects of sexual behaviour are instinctive, or very readily learned. So far as one can tell, psychosexual problems – other than those of frustration due to deprivation – do not occur in animals, so why should they exist in humans? The main reason, as Freud powerfully argued, is because the demands of one's physical self (the need to get immediate gratification of the sexual drive by mating) inevitably conflict with the reality of society. To avoid social conflicts, most societies exercise control of human behaviour in three fundamental ways. First, systems of marriage are introduced with the goal of giving male and female exclusive sexual rights to each other, thus reducing constant competition and allowing energy to be diverted elsewhere. Secondly, society prohibits rape and other forms of 'sex by force', again with the aim of prohibiting sexual strife. Thirdly, society prohibits sexual liaisons between particular individuals – father and daughter, with minors, etc. These constraints generally have the desired effect of reducing conflict within the society, but at the same time promote conflict within the individual as his instinctive desires are repressed. When this repression is extremely severe or applied in a non-explanatory way – as when young children are punished for masturbation or lectured on the 'wrongness' of sexual feelings – the conflicts which ensue may linger and inhibit subsequent sexual evolution.

From a societal point of view, the dangers of over-rigorous application of the mechanism of sexual control seem to be at least unconsciously recognized. For example, most societies sanction divorce under appropriate circumstances, at least turn a blind eye to adultery and various forms of sexual deviation such as homosexuality, and even permit, to varying degrees, the expression of unusual or 'abnormal' practices through 'pornographic' literature, stage plays and cinema films.

These examples should indicate how a study of human sexual behaviour involves the physiological, the psychological and the sociological viewpoints and how the three are interrelated. A good illustration of this can be seen in the sweeping changes in the psychological and sociological aspects of sexual behaviour which have followed the essentially physiological fact of the development of a reliable birth control pill. Not only are women free for the first time in history of the physical burden of pregnancy, but their own mental attitudes to sex have been transformed – as have the attitudes of society itself to women's sexuality, and indeed much of the role of women in society.

Sex characteristic. Feature present in one sex and not in another. Primary sex characteristics are those directly involved in reproduction, while secondary characteristics are those playing no direct role.

Sexism. Social or political attitudes which argue that an individual's role in society should be determined largely by his or her sex.

Sexology. The scientific study of sexual behaviour.

Sex role. The patterns of behaviour and psychological attitudes expected of an individual which are dependent on his or her sex. (➧➧ SEX-ROLE STEREOTYPING.)

Sex-role stereotyping. The tendency to ascribe to an individual those patterns of behaviour expected of him or her because of his or her sex, whether or not these are necessary or appropriate.

Sexual. Relating to sex and reproduction; also relating to the pleasure associated with the act of reproduction.

Sexual anomaly. A deviation in sexual behaviour from whatever is accepted as 'normal' in the society.

Sexual economy. The theory of sexuality developed by Wilhelm REICH, a former associate of Freud, who held that the orgasm is important because it balances energy forces within the body. His theory later developed into the pseudoscience of orgonomy.

Sexual infantilism. Lack of development of the sex organs or primary sexual characteristics; also refers to a failure to evolve sexually from the psychological point of view – e.g. remaining basically narcissistic rather than engaging in heterosexual behaviour.

Sexuality. The aspects of an individual that make him capable of sexual behaviour, and also those which make him or her attractive to the opposite sex.

Sexual latency. ➧ LATENCY PERIOD.

Sexual perversion. A somewhat loaded term for any major deviation in sexual practice from what is assumed to be the norm for a particular society. With the shifting attitudes of our present society, practices which were considered to be perverted two decades ago are now considered to be merely deviations – homosexuality, both male and female, being a good example. Nevertheless sadism, masochism, exhibitionism and pedophilia (sexual intercourse with children) are still classed as perversions, at least in a legal sense. Clearly there can be no *absolute* assessment of whether a practice is perverted or not. Perhaps the most satisfactory guide is whether or not the behaviour involves other people against their will and at the same time offends them or society as a whole.

Sexual reproduction. The creation of a new individual through the genetic mixture achieved by the union of the male and female sex cells.

Sexual selection. The choice of a mate according to preferred (normally secondary) sexual characteristics. Such choices – e.g. for blond women or tall men – lead to significant changes in the long-term characteristics of a species.

Sexual symbolism. Representing some aspect of sexual life by something else, in particular by a symbol, phrase or picture. Sexuality has always been an emotionally ambiguous facet of man's existence with elaborate rules governing and controlling sexual behaviour – often running counter to his instinctive desires. It is not surprising, therefore, to find taboo areas of sexuality treated in symbolic form in all aspects of the arts, and in the last century the intrusion of symbolism into dream imagery was recognized by FREUD. The Freudian argument – that symbolism made a potentially dangerous dream more 'safe' – had a good deal of force in Victorian times, but it is not clear how it stands up in the face of the new sexual freedoms of our more permissive society.

Sexual trauma. An unpleasant or emotionally shocking experience connected in some way with sexual behaviour and supposed, according to psychoanalytic theory, to lead to neuroses or personality disorders in later life.

Shading shock. An emotional response to the shaded parts of an inkblot in a RORSCHACH TEST.

Shadow. Jungian term for all aspects of the PERSONAL UNCONSCIOUS and COLLECTIVE UNCONSCIOUS which oppose the wishes of the conscious and resist integration with the ego. The shadow forms a kind of sub-personality which needs to be contacted in successful Jungian analysis.

Shaman. A medicine man.

Sham feeding. Feeding in experimental animals in which all food passes out through a hole in the oesophagus and therefore never reaches the stomach.

Sham rage. Wild activity, suggestive of rage, which can be elicited in decorticate animals by stimulation of a particular part of the brain.

Shannon, Claude (1916 –). Pioneer of information theory who showed, with Norbert Wiener, that a concept as elusive as information could be expressed precisely in mathematical terms.

Shape constancy. ➧ CONSTANCY.

Shaping. ➧ SUCCESSIVE APPROXIMATION METHOD.

Sharp. Describes a tone whose pitch has been raised by a semitone.

Sharpeners. Refers to individuals who are well able to tolerate ambiguities, inconsistencies or uncertainties. Contrast LEVELLERS.

Sheldon, William H. (1899 –). One of a number of psychologists who have attempted to link personality to body shape and size. (➧ SHELDONIAN THEORY.)

Sheldonian theory. A theory of personality put forward by W. H. Sheldon which hypothesizes three basic temperaments, some aspects of all three being present in all individuals, though with one generally dominating in each person. The three types, viscerotonia (featuring a love of physical comfort and a generally relaxed way of living), somatotonia (featuring a more aggressive, physically active type) and cerebrotonia (highly sensitive, shy and somewhat restricted personality), are themselves supposed to be related to three distinct body builds. These are, in the order relating to the personality types above, endomorphy (a rounded, heavy frame), mesomorphy (stocky, muscular) and ectomorphy (tall and skinny). Sheldon's ideas are intriguing, but have not stood up particularly well to independent investigation. (➧➧ CONSTITUTIONAL THEORIES.)

Shell shock. ➧ BATTLE FATIGUE.

Sherrington, Charles Scott (1857–1952). British neurophysiologist whose ideas on reflex arcs, the neural impulse and function of the synapse have dominated Western physiology in the twentieth century.

Shock. Major interruption of the integrated action of the nervous system which may be caused by surgery or injury. Shock can also occur when there is no injury but when psychological stresses have been great – e.g. the death of a relative.

Shock therapy. Form of treatment for some mental disorders by which the patient is rendered unconscious by a brief electric current being passed through the brain or by a convulsive drug. (➧ ELECTROCONVULSIVE THERAPY.)

Short-term memory. The capacity of the brain to hold information in a kind of immediate-access store for a short period after it has been presented. Current theories of MEMORY propose the existence of two memory systems, a short-term and a long-term – material for the latter presumably being acquired as the result of some kind of selection procedure or 'sort' of the former. The extent of the short-term store is defined by, first, the number of items that can be recalled following a single presentation, and secondly, the length of time for which the items can be held without further rehearsal or representation.

Sibling (sib). Children born of the same parent.

Sibling rivalry. Competition, often for the affection of the parents, between sibs.

Sigma. Greek letter σ, employed as an abbreviation for STANDARD DEVIATION.

Sigma score. A score which uses as its unit the STANDARD DEVIATION of the population under study.

Sign. Anything which acts as a signal initiating some activity, or which indicates the presence of something else.

Signal. Anything that can be used to initiate a message, or convey information from one place to another.

Signal-detection theory. A relatively new approach to PSYCHOPHYSICS which takes account of the fact that a reaction to a stimulus is not just a matter of the strength of the stimulus, but also of factors such as the motivation, past experience and set of the observer. An important feature of the approach is the abandonment of the old concept of THRESHOLD, which in classical psychophysics is assumed to have a real value dependent upon the physiological capacity of the receptors or detecting mechanism. In its place has been introduced the concept of the receiver operating characteristic, acknowledging the very considerable pyschological component of any psychophysical experiment.

Sign-Gestalt. A term used by Tolman to describe the specific goals set up in the mind of an individual in the course of cognitive learning.

Significance. The relevance or meaning of something. In statistics, one uses the word in the context of what one can deduce from experimental data (➧ STATISTICAL SIGNIFICANCE).

Significance level. ➧ STATISTICAL SIGNIFICANCE.

Significant difference. A difference between two sets of data which, mathematically speaking, is assumed to be unlikely to have occurred as the result of chance. (➧ STATISTICAL SIGNIFICANCE.)

Sign learning. A term used by Tolman to denote the process by which an animal learns that particular signs or cues indicate other things – e.g. the presence or absence of food – in a learning task. (➧ TOLMAN'S LEARNING THEORY.)

Sign stimulus. Refers to those aspects of the environment which are learned by an animal as denoting cues to other things. (➧ SIGN LEARNING.)

Similarity law. One of the first laws of association which were assumed to underlie memory: things which are similar to each other tend to be linked in memory. (➧ ASSOCIATION LAWS.)

Similarity paradox. ➧ SKAGGS-ROBINSON HYPOTHESIS.

Simple schizophrenia. A type of SCHIZOPHRENIA in which the principal features are a dramatic loss of motivation and interest in contact with others.

Simulation. Any attempt at producing, under test or demonstration conditions, phenomena which would occur in real life. Simulation may range from acting (as in group psychotherapy) to complex mathematical modelling.

Simultaneous contrast. When two things are presented next to each other, in space or in time, they tend to affect each other's perception (➧ CONTRAST). In *simultaneous* contrast the proximity is in space, in *successive* contrast it is in time. A striking example of the former is when a colour placed against a grey background induces the perception of its complementary in the surrounding field.

Sine wave. A rhythmic wave in which rise to crest and fall to trough are symmetrical.

Single-blind experiment. ➧ DOUBLE-BLIND EXPERIMENT.

Single variable law. In an experiment, only one factor at a time should be taken as the independent variable.

Sinistrad writing. Writing from right to left. This is also known as mirror writing.

Sinistral. Pertaining to the left – e.g. sinistrality is left-handedness.

Sinus. Any kind of cavity or pocket within the body.

Sinusoid. Relating to a sine wave.

Sitophobia. Abnormal fear of eating.

Sitter. In psychical research someone, other than the medium, who takes part in a SEANCE.

Situation neurosis. A term used by Karen Horney for a neurosis induced by a specific event or trauma, rather than by a build-up of problems over an extended period. Contrast CHARACTER NEUROSIS.

Situation test. Test which requires an individual or group to solve a real-life problem in a realistic setting.

Sixteen factor test (16PF). Test devised by Cattell which explores personality along a sixteen-point continuum – e.g. intelligence, emotional stability, dominance, trust, etc.

Size-age confusion. The tendency to expect too much emotionally and intellectually from children who are large for their age.

Size constancy. Tendency for an object to appear to remain relatively constant in size even though it is moved towards or away from the viewer. (➧ CONSTANCY.)

Size-weight illusion. Large objects are instinctively judged to be heavy, and therefore when handled for the first time they sometimes appear surprisingly light. The reverse conditions of course apply for small objects, which often feel heavier than they look.

Skaggs-Robinson hypothesis. Sometimes known as the similarity paradox. If two sets of material are to be learned successively, the degree of similarity of the material significantly affects the ease of retention. Perhaps a little surprisingly, the inhibiting effects are least when the sets of material are either extremely similar or extremely dissimilar, and greatest when the material is of 'average similarity'.

Skeletal muscles. The STRIATE MUSCLES.

Skewed regression. ➧ NON-LINEAR REGRESSION.

Skewness. A property of any frequency curve which is not bilaterally symmetrical.

Skiascope. Device for measuring the refraction of the eye.

Skill. Any ability, generally assumed to have been learned, to perform a complex task involving psychomotor coordination with ease, speed and accuracy. The term social skill is used to refer to the mastery of one or more aspects of social interaction.

Skin. Outer layer of the body of animals – generally consisting of two levels, the dermis (lower) and epidermis (outer).

Skinner box. The name given to more or less any container in which an animal can be confined in studies of OPERANT CONDITIONING. Basically the 'box' must have some apparatus, such as a lever, which when operated allows the animal to control or manipulate its environment. This could be switching on a light, delivering an electrical stimulus to its own brain or, as in the most common case, providing itself with food. The Skinner box actually has its origins in Thorndike's PUZZLE BOX.

Skinner, Burrhus Frederick (1904 –). Professor of psychology at Harvard University since 1948, and one of the most influential figures in twentieth-century psychology; noted in particular for his experimental and theoretical approaches to the study of behaviour. (➧ SKINNERIAN PSYCHOLOGY.)

Skinnerian psychology. A general term for the approach to theory and experimental method in psychology championed most vigorously by B. F. Skinner since the mid-1930s and which probably reached the peak of its influence in the early 1960s. Skinner's outlook is essentially an evolution of the behaviourist views of J. B. WATSON, which in turn grew out of the theories of the great Russian physiologist Pavlov, originator of the concept of the conditioned reflex (➧ BEHAVIOURISM; CONDITIONING). At heart, Skinner's philosophy can be summed up in the following way: man shares essentially the same kind of nervous system as most of the higher animals, though his may be of a greater complexity than theirs. This similarity suggests that the mechanisms of learning, perception, memory, and so on are shared, and as these can more easily be studied in animals, in particular by using conditioning techniques, the bulk of effort in experimental psychology should concentrate on animal experimental studies.

Skinner is often (wrongly) attacked on the grounds that he denies the reality of consciousness, cognitive and mental processes, etc. In fact his view is that with existing knowledge and techniques these 'internal variables' simply do not lend themselves to objective investigation and are therefore not productive subject matter for the psychologist. In the 1950s most schools of experimental psychology were strongly Skinnerian in their outlook, and at one stage behaviour of the pigeon appeared to be the most important focus of research. A decade later, however, partly because of the rise of the study of PSYCHOLINGUISTICS, the strictly behaviourist bias has been counterbalanced. (➧➧ OPERANT CONDITIONING.)

Skin potential. ➧ GALVANIC SKIN RESPONSE.

Skin resistance. ➧ GALVANIC SKIN RESPONSE.

Skin senses. ➧ DERMAL SENSITIVITY.

Sleep. Normal state appearing on a rhythmic basis in all the higher animals and in many simpler animals, including fish, amphibia and (possibly) in some insects. The main characteristics of the sleep state, as contrasted with wakefulness, are a dramatic reduction in responsiveness to sensory stimuli, coordinated muscle activity and consciousness. At one time it was assumed that the principal function of sleep must be to rest the body and to allow metabolic, and possibly cerebral, functions to recuperate. Research, however, has failed to show that physiological rest is dependent upon loss of consciousness, and the evidence yielded by taking records of the electrical activity of the brain (EEG) shows a change in the *nature* of this activity, but no significant change in the *amount*. In fact the latest studies suggest that the human and animal brain is in a highly active state during at least some periods of sleep, even though consciousness is absent.

Theories of the nature of sleep vary from the traditional – that it is an enforced period of rest for body and brain – to a series of not necessarily exclusive hypothosis – e.g. that it allows toxins to be eliminated from nervous tissue, protein synthesis to take place in the brain, memory traces to be established, etc. The discovery of the important phase known as REM sleep, and its apparent relationship to dream activity, has introduced an extra possibility – that one of the functions of sleep is to allow dreaming to take place. (➧➧ DREAM.) At the moment, however, most of the rival theories are primarily speculative and await support or rejection from the physiological studies of the future.

Sleep centre. Portion of the hypothalamus which, when stimulated, induces sleep.

Sleep deprivation. State in which a person or animal is prevented from sleeping for an extended period. The effects of sleep deprivation get more severe with time and vary from muddled thinking or lack of motor coordination, to hallucinations, extreme irritability and, ultimately – in the case of some animals – death. (➧➧ DREAM OF DEPRIVATION.)

Sleeping sickness. Form of encephalitis which leads to long periods of sleep and drowsiness.

Sleep learning. ➧ HYPNOPAEDIA.

Sleep-walking. ➧ SOMNAMBULISM.

Slow learner. The term used of a child who may be slightly mentally retarded or for some other reason fails to keep up with his peers, but whose rate of learning is in accord with his IQ. Compare REMEDIAL.

Small groups. ➧ GROUP.

Small-sample theory. Statistical approach which allows one to infer something from studying just a few cases or examples.

Smell. The olfactory sense; of less significance to man than to most other animals but still a highly developed sense. The mechanism for detecting odours consists of an array of chemically sensitive receptors lining the internal cavity of the nose. As taste is almost entirely dependent upon the smell receptors being functional (food becomes almost tasteless if the nasal passages are blocked) some people propose that gustation and olfaction should be classed, in man, as a single sense. (➧➧ ODOUR PRISM.)

Smooth curve. Curve without any abrupt change in its form.

Smoothed curve. Curve in which minor irregularities have been 'ironed out' by applying a statistical formula.

Smooth muscle. Muscle not under voluntary control, so called because it has a generally smooth appearance unlike the striped or striate muscles which *are* under voluntary control. Most autonomic functions – peristalsis, blood flow, etc. – are operated by smooth muscles.

Snellen chart. The standard optician's eye test featuring words and letters of varying size. (⧫⧫ VISUAL ACUITY.)

Sociability. An individual's ability to adapt himself to his social environment; can also mean a desire for forming social relationships.

Sociability rating. Comparison of how one individual compares with others in the ease with which he accepts social interaction.

Social. Concerning the relationship between people, or members of any species.

Social adaptation. The process of changing behaviour or attitudes in response to the requirements of society. (⧫⧫ CONFORMITY.)

Social anthropology. The study of man as a social animal, in particular the cultural, economic, political and religious systems he has adopted in various societies in different parts of the world. It is close to sociology in its subject matter – possibly sociology could be said to be more concerned with contemporary society. (⧫ SOCIAL PSYCHOLOGY.)

Social atom. Term used to refer to the relationship between an individual and the smallest unit of society – generally a man and his nuclear family.

Social attitude. May either mean a tendency to behave in a particular way to other people, or an attitude held by a group of people.

Social behaviour. Group behaviour; also behaviour which is influenced because of the presence or activity of others. Compare APOPATHETIC BEHAVIOUR. (⧫⧫ SOCIAL FACILITATION.)

Social change. The origins and mechanisms of social change are one of the main problems investigated by sociologists and can be traced back to the pioneering work of Auguste Comte – himself often known as the 'father of sociology'. Until the end of the eighteenth century and the onset of the French Revolution, changes in society tended to be so gradual as to be almost undetectable in an individual's lifetime, or if rapid could be attributed to a change of ruler, invasion by some foreign power, etc. The rapidity and radical nature of the social change occurring in less than a decade with the French Revolution, however, led to a surge of interest in the topic and an attempt to formulate theories of change. Amongst the most famous and enduring of these was that of Karl Marx who argued that industrial and agricultural productivity were the fundamental features of any society, and that any change in this productivity – such as might be achieved by industrialization, for example – would be bound to have tremendous effects on the structure of the society. Attempts to formulate all-embracing theories of social change to rival or replace Marxist ideas are not particularly fashionable in modern sociology; most workers tend to concentrate on mechanisms of change within small groups.

Social class. One stratum of society, defined on the basis of such criteria as religious belief, economic status, educational background, etc. Social class is quite arbitrary and depends entirely upon what parameters of society the classifier is interested in measuring. Nevertheless, people do tend to cluster themselves together in classes, not simply determined by kinship ties or geographical location, and these groups tend towards particular patterns of behaviour. One formal attempt at defining social class has been the Registrar General's classification of occupation – a system which is also generally applied in market research.

Social climate. Generally speaking, the 'mood' of a group or society which in turn reflects its attitudes to other individuals, groups and their behaviour.

Social consciousness. Awareness that one is a member of a social group and has certain responsibilities towards it and other individuals.

Social control. Methods by which a group ensures that its members accept the goals and wishes of the group. These are also known as social sanctions.

Social distance. The extent to which an individual has adjusted to the attitudes and behaviour of others, or has been able to identify and associate with a group.

Social dyad (diad). A group of two when viewed or studied as a social unit.

Social dynamics. The processes occurring as a society evolves and changes. Compare GROUP DYNAMICS.

Social facilitation. Any improvement in behaviour, increase in output or whatever in a group which takes place as the result of the presence of other individuals. A classic example is the HAWTHORNE EFFECT.

Social factors. Any of the influences and pressures, positive or negative, which a society exerts on its members.

Social group. Collection of individuals united by at least one common goal.

Social immobility. Tendency for an individual to be constrained in his mode of life by the stratum of society in which he exists.

Social instinct. An obsolete term for GREGARIOUSNESS.

Social intelligence. The capacity to be aware of other individuals and sensitive to their feelings. Compare EMPATHY, SYMPATHY.

Socialization. The process by which an individual learns the rules of society. More specifically, it refers to the learning of the patterns of behaviour expected of one by society as a whole, and by the segment of society – sex, race, religion, social background, etc. – of which one is a part. The process begins in infancy and, while it is in its most critical period in childhood when parental influences are at their most powerful, it continues more or less throughout the whole of life. The more mobile (in social terms) an individual is, the longer and more important is the process of socialization as he needs to acquire new values and to understand the new roles he will be called upon to play. Freud had a specific definition of socialization, which he believed was the mechanism by which the child acquires the norms and values of his parents and those in immediate authority over him – in fact the formation of the SUPEREGO. Until the 1920s the term education was used also for the process of socialization. (➧ Fig. 30 on p. 343; ➧➧ SOCIAL LEARNING.)

Social learning. The process of acquiring, by observation or imitation, various behaviour patterns relevant to an individual's interaction with his group or society. (➧➧ SOCIALIZATION.)

Social maturity. The state of having achieved whatever social skills and understanding are appropriate for one's age. It is measured by such tests as the Bristol Social Adjustment Scale or the Vineland Social Maturity Scale.

Social medicine. The study of the health (used in the broadest sense) or well-being of a society.

Social mobility. The capacity of an individual to move around in a society and be relatively independent of the class or stratum in which he exists or into which he was born.

Social motive. A learned motive, culturally determined and related to the individual's interaction with other members of his society. (➧➧ ACQUIRED DRIVE.)

Social norm. Whatever is recognized by a society as being a correct or appropriate standard or pattern of behaviour. (➧➧ NORM.)

Social perception. The ability to recognize and be aware of the attitudes and motives of others.

Social power. ➧ POWER.

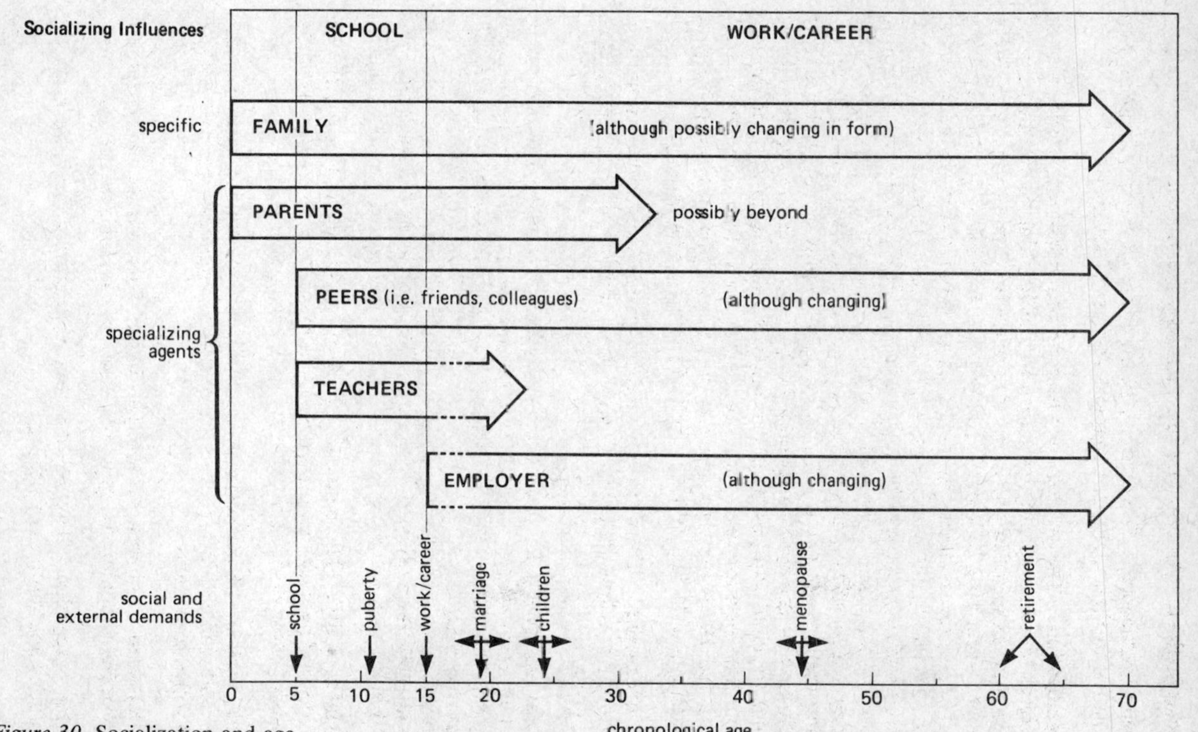

Figure 30. Socialization and age.

Social process. Change taking place within a society or group. Interaction between individuals in a group is known as a social interactional process.

Social psychology. That aspect of the field of psychology which concerns the behaviour of people in groups, the various means of communication within groups and the effects of an individual's behaviour on the group and vice versa. The boundaries between social psychology, sociology and, to some extent, social anthropology tend to be blurred. If one had to separate the three, one might say that:

1. Social anthropology concerns itself with the study of all human societies, and in particular the origins of their social structure.
2. Sociology is concerned with the specific study of contemporary society, its interrelationships and their theoretical background.
3. Social psychology is concerned with the experimental investigation of these interrelationships and the application of findings arising from them.

The origins of social psychology lie in the work of the French philosopher, Auguste Comte, also known as the 'father of sociology'. Comte, who had watched with much gloom the unrest and social uncertainty that followed the French Revolution, was convinced that the behaviour of human beings in groups or societies must obey certain rules or principles, and that once these could be determined, society could be modified for the better.

The first psychologist to attempt a formulation of these principles was McDougall, who leaned heavily on instincts in his *Introduction to Social Psychology*, first published in 1908. The subject really only began to evolve when experiments moved out of the laboratory and into the 'real world'. Here the work of Allport and Lewin, concentrating on dynamic interactions with established groups, was the most influential and still permeates current research. From their work came the realization that the personality of an individual can have a profound effect on the behaviour of a group and, as the result, dimensions of personality such as 'authoritarianism', 'submissiveness', 'conformity', 'prejudice', etc., were explored and some attempt made to quantify them.

Social psychology, which is the bridge between sociology and psychology, has been making slow but measurable progress in the past few decades, but has been inhibited largely because it has no generally acceptable model to build on – at least none comparable in power with, say, the Freudian model of personality or the Pavlovian model of conditioning and learning. But, despite this slow progress, it is clearly an enormously important aspect of psychology if only for its potential. If clear-cut rules of social behaviour could be established, as Comte and the pioneers had hoped, then the causes of breakdowns in social organizations leading to civil unrest and war might be understood and their consequences prevented.

Social sanctions. ➧ SOCIAL CONTROL.

Social science. Any branch of science which deals with man and his interaction with society at large; these include psychology, anthropology, sociology, politics, economics and the study of religion.

Social self. Those parts of the SELF or personality which are specifically concerned with or affected by relationships with others; one's self as perceived by others in social relationships. (➧➧ LOOKING-GLASS SELF.)

Social skill. ➧ SKILL.

Social status. An individual's position within society relative to other individuals. Status determines not only the rights of that individual, his duties towards society, and his behaviour to others, but also society's duties towards him. (➧➧ ROLE; POWER.)

Social stratification. The segmenting of society into a number of different strata or classes.

Social transmission. The various mechanisms by which goals, attitudes and various cultural factors are propagated within a group and which help preserve its distinctiveness. (➧➧ IMITATION; IDENTIFICATION.)

Societal. Relating to SOCIETY.

Society. In the broadest sense the term refers to the human species, but this is idealistic rather than practical as the concept of a society implies that all its members share a formal organization, and also a substantial number of goals in common. In particular, a society has a set of rules or laws which are binding on all its members, and sanctions (both formal and informal) which allow these rules to be enforced. Societies therefore may consist of quite small groups – themselves part of larger societies. The largest units that may be truthfully called societies on earth are probably the big national or political blocks – the USA, China, the USSR, etc.

Sociobiology. The study of possible genetic bases of social behaviour.

Sociocentrism. The view that individual behaviour should be largely determined by the needs of SOCIETY.

Sociodrama. ➧ PSYCHODRAMA.

Sociogenesis. The origins of a particular pattern of social behaviour.

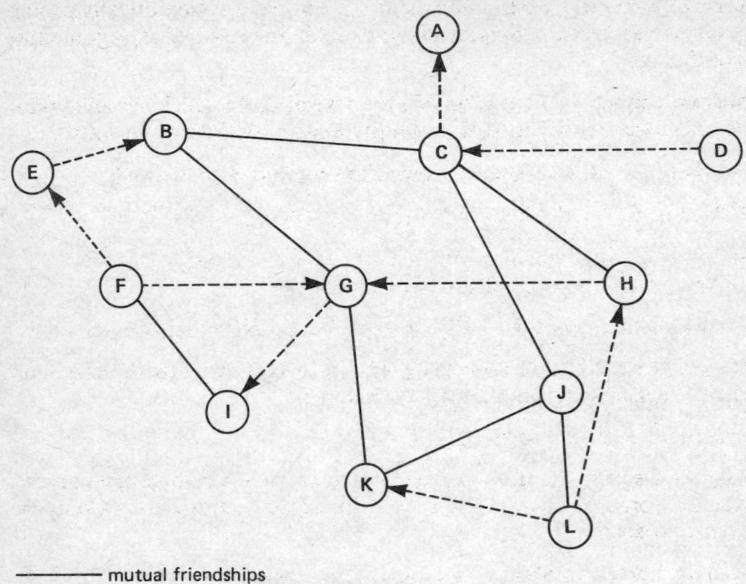

Figure 31. Sociogram.

Sociogram. A form of diagram, used extensively in sociology and social psychology, which expresses the relationship between people in the form of a series of cells, representing the individuals, and lines linking them, which express their thread of interactions.

Sociology. Literally, the study of SOCIETY, and generally assumed to be almost synonymous with social psychology. (*But* ➧ SOCIAL PSYCHOLOGY.)

Sociometry. The study of the interrelationships within a group, and in particular attempts at measuring or describing these relationships. A pioneer of the topic is the American psychiatrist, J. L. Moreno, and one of its most common devices is the SOCIOGRAM.

Socionomics. The study of the effect of natural phenomena – i.e. those not under human control – on society.

Sociopathic personality. A disturbed individual whose problem is largely a matter of social failure or antisocial behaviour. The term is roughly equivalent to PSYCHOPATH.

Sociotype. STEREOTYPE applied to a group rather than an individual.

Socratic method. Instruction using the device of systematically posing questions and then providing the answers in the form of an argumentative dialogue.

Sodium amytal. The trade name for a barbiturate which has an hypnotic and sedative effect. It is popularly known as the TRUTH DRUG.

Sodomy. Anal intercourse; sexual intercourse with animals.

Soft colours. The blues and greens. (➧ HARD COLOURS.)

Solipsism. The philosophy which argues that the only certainty in the universe is one's own existence and identity.

Soma. The sum total of all cells in the body other than the sex cells.

Somaesthesia. Those aspects of sensations concerned with body feeling – touch, temperature, sense of balance.

Somatic. Relating to the body.

Somatic disorders. Bodily disorders which do not involve the nervous system; organic as opposed to functional disorders. Compare PSYCHOSOMATIC.

Somatic nervous system. ➧ NERVOUS SYSTEM.

Somatogenesis. The originating of something within the body tissues.

Somatology. The study of the physical characteristics of the body.

Somatoplasm. The SOMA; also used in some cases to denote those parts of a living cell other than the genetic material.

Somatopsychic. Relating to the influence of physical or bodily factors on mental processes. Compare PSYCHOSOMATIC.

Somatotonia. ➧ SHELDONIAN THEORY.

Somatotype. ➧ BODY TYPE.

Somatotypology. Any approach which tries to establish a classification of people according to their body build. (➧ SHELDONIAN THEORY; CONSTITUTIONAL THEORIES.)

Somnambulism. Sleep-walking. In the somnambulistic state individuals may perform relatively complex acts and yet show no conscious awareness of what they are doing – as though one portion of the brain was active and functioning normally while the rest was still in sleep. The practice seems to be more common amongst children than adults, though it is easily simulated and may be a device for attention-getting.

Somniferous. Hypnotic, sleep-inducing.

Somnolence. Drowsiness; the state of being on the verge of sleep: unnatural sleepiness.

Sonant. A voiced speech sound. Compare PHONEME.

Sone. Unit of loudness; a sone corresponds to a 1000 Hz sound, 40 dB above threshold.

Sonometer. A device fitted with strings over a resonating box and used in experiments on audition.

Sophism. A fallacious argument cleverly disguised to conceal its fallacy.

Soporofic. Something which induces sleep.

Sorting test. Test of the ability to generalize, conceptualize and abstract, in which a collection of objects have to be sorted into a set of sub-groups or classes, e.g. size, colour, usefulness.

Soul. The theological concept of the immortal component of man.

Sound. Any vibration or disturbance of the air which can be detected by the body – in particular the auditory system. (➧ EAR.)

Sound cage. Experimental cubicle used for the study of an individual's ability to localize sound.

Sound-pressure. The intensity or loudness of a sound, measured in decibels.

Sound spectograph. Device which plots the intensity and duration of sounds.

Sour. One of the four main dimensions of TASTE (the others are sweet, salt and bitter).

Source trait. A major as opposed to a minor attribute of personality. Source traits (e.g. extraversion, introversion) are supposed to be sufficiently strong to give rise to a set of other lesser 'surface' traits; surface traits tend to be easy to measure but are less indicative of the individual's basic personality, and less useful from the point of view of predicting his behaviour.

Space error. A common constant error of judgement met in psychophysical experiments, generally induced when stimuli are presented for comparison but in different spatial positions relative to the observer.

Space orientation. The ability to locate oneself in space and in relationship to other items in the environment; adjustment of body position in space.

Space perception. The ability of the brain to identify objects in the environment, assess their distances and integrate their presence with that of other objects. The term refers to all sense modalities. (➧ PERCEPTION.)

Space psychology. The application of psychological knowledge to the space sciences, in particular any changes in human perception and psychomotor skills occurring in the alien environments of space.

Space repetition. The presentation of material in a learning task in a sequence with regular spacing between the presentations. Consistent spacing may assist retention.

Span of apprehension. ➧ APPREHENSION SPAN.

Spasm. A vigorous, involuntary muscle contraction.

Spasticity. A condition of stiff, poorly-controlled muscles.

Spatial threshold. ➧ TWO-POINT DISCRIMINATION.

Speaking in tongues. ➧ GLOSSOLALIA.

Spearman, Charles Edward (1863 – 1945). British psychologist who made pioneering use of statistics in psychology and who developed the TWO-FACTOR THEORY of intelligence.

Spearman footrule. Short and simpler version of Spearman's correlation coefficient.

Species. A subdivision of animal life lying, on the taxonomic system, between genus and variety. (➧ TAXONOMY.) All animals in the same species mate freely together and can produce fertile offspring. Extra-species breeding leads to infertile offspring.

Specific ability. Spearman hypothesized that intelligence consisted of a 'general' factor which partly determined one's performance on almost any IQ test, and also a series of 'specific factors', which were relevant only to particular skills or areas of ability. Thus all tests measured both the general and special ability – the so-called TWO-FACTOR THEORY of intelligence.

Specific energy theory. An early view of neural operation which suggested that each nerve sent up a distinct *type* of energy to the brain (as contrasted with the contemporary view that all neural impulses are electrical).

Specificity. Related to a particular thing only; in the case of receptors or sense organs, implies that they have only one function.

Specious present. The subjective experience of 'now'; impossible to measure objectively, but often taken as lasting about two or three seconds.

Spectral. Relating to the SPECTRUM.

Spectrometer. Device for measuring wavelengths in a SPECTRUM.

Spectroscope. Device for observing a SPECTRUM.

Spectrum. The array of colours – violet, indigo, blue, green, yellow, orange, red – obtained when white light is passed through a prism.

Speculation. Reasoning which is not based on adequate evidence.

Speech centre. Segment of the left cerebral hemisphere (in right-handed pèople) known as Broca's area, which when damaged causes a loss of ability to utter words correctly (➧➧ APHASIA).

Speed test. Test in which success is measured by the number of items correctly completed in a given time. Contrast POWER TEST.

Spherical aberration. In an 'ideal' lens light rays passing through should converge on a single point. However, the different refractive powers of the outer and inner parts of the lens lead to a slight spread of focus – spherical aberration. (➧➧ CHROMATIC ABERRATION.)

Sperm. The fluid in which the male sex cells live; the male sex cells themselves.

Sphincter. A ring muscle.

Sphincter morality. A psychoanalytic concept referring to excessive prudishness, fussiness and pedantry assumed to have been induced in the individual by over-zealous toilet training when a child. Compare ANAL CHARACTER.

Sphygmograph. Device which records the pulse.

Sphygmometer. Device for measuring blood pressure.

Spicy. One of the primary classifications of odours – e.g. the smell of nutmeg. (➧ ODOUR PRISM.)

Spike. The peak change of potential which occurs just as the nervous impulse is triggered.

Spina bifida. A congenital condition in which there is defective closure of the bones round the spinal cord.

Spinal animal. Refers to an animal prepared surgically for an experiment with the brain completely severed from the spinal cord.

Spinal cord. The long trunk of nerves which runs from the brain down the back and is encased in the vertebral column.

Spinal ganglia. Clusters of cells bodies of sensory neurones which form nodules on the dorsal roots of the spinal cord.

Spinal nerves. At each of the thirty-one vertebral levels a pair of nerves leaves the spinal cord; the spinal nerves are made up of eight cervical, twelve thoracic, five lumbar, five sacral and one coccygeal.

Spinal reflex. A basic and essentially simple reflex in which the complete nervous pathway, featuring at least a sensory nerve and a motor nerve, is located in the spinal cord – e.g. the patellar reflex. Since the brain is not involved, spinal reflexes are unlearned and apparently immune to conditioning.

Spinal root. That part of a spinal nerve that joins the spinal cord. Dorsal spinal roots involve sensory nerves, the ventral involve motor nerves.

Spindle. Spindle-shaped nerve cell, generally found in muscles and tendons.

Spiritualism. Minority religion in which the principal tenet of belief is that it is possible to prove the survival of the human personality after death by direct communication with the spirits of the dead.

Spirograph. Instrument for measuring depth and rate of breathing.

Spirometer. Instrument for measuring the amount of air that can be expelled following a single breath.

Splanchnic. Relating to visceral organs.

Split-brain technique. The bilateral symmetry of the brain poses interesting problems as to the role of the respective hemispheres, and their relative dependence or independence of each other. By making an incision in the corpus callosum – a structure which joins the two hemispheres – their independent action can be studied, in particular such matters as how handicapped an animal is if information fed into one hemisphere may no longer be transferred to the other.

Split-half method. A way of assessing the RELIABILITY of a test, by splitting it into two equal parts, administering the test as though it were two and then comparing the results of one test with the other. A high correlation suggests that the test is reliable.

Split personality. Obsolete popular term for SCHIZOPHRENIA. Not to be confused with MULTIPLE PERSONALITY.

Spontaneity therapy. An aspect of PSYCHODRAMA in which the individual freely and without rehearsing acts out his or her problems before a group. The dramatization of the problems is supposed to have some cathartic effect.

Spontaneous firing. The triggering or activation of a neurone without any apparent stimulus to set it off. It is sometimes assumed that much of the background activity of the ELECTROENCEPHALOGRAPH reflects the spontaneous firing of cortical neurones.

Spontaneous phenomena. In psychical research, paranormal phenomena which occur outside a laboratory setting – e.g. poltergeists, ghosts, precognitive dreams, etc.

Spontaneous recovery. Recovery from an illness without any medical treatment. The term also refers to the reappearance of an extinguished conditioned reflex after a period of rest.

Spread of effect. A principle advanced by Thorndike saying that the satisfaction (or dissatisfaction) linked to a particular response will spread to other responses which are close in time, or similar in kind to the first.

Spurt. A sudden increase in performance occurring in the middle of a task.

Squint. ➧ STRABISMUS.

Stabilimeter. Instrument for measuring the degree of sway in an individual's body when he is attempting to remain immobile.

Stabilized retinal image. If a pattern is projected on to the retina in such a way that the effects of eye movements are eliminated (generally achieved by attaching the pattern to a contact lens so that wherever the eye moves, the pattern moves with it) the perceived 'stabilized' image vanishes, fragmenting into neat, 'meaningful' segments in a fashion reminiscent of Gestalt perceptual phenomena. These experiments suggest that pattern perception requires a series of eye movements to be made, presumably to scan the features present.

Staircase illusion. ➧ SCHROEDER'S STAIRCASE.

Staircase phenomena. ➧ TREPPE.

Stammering. ➧ STUTTERING.

Standard. A model, guide or criterion against which something can be measured and assessed.

Standard deviation (SD). One of the most useful measures in basic statistics. In examining a set of scores or values in order to compare them with some other set – as in the comparison between experimental and control groups in a laboratory study – it is generally more useful to look at the MEAN or average of the two sets of values than to attempt to compare single items with each other. The means can, however, be misleading, mainly because they give one no idea as to how widely the individual values are scattered. For example, in measuring the IQ of a group of children, one might end up with a mean of 100, yet this could have been found in a group whose individual IQs varied from 60 up to 140, or in another quite different group whose IQs were more closely clustered, between say 90 and 110. The two samples would clearly be extremely different, and yet the means would be identical. The standard deviation is a measure of to what degree items are clustered (or scattered) around the mean, and it is reached by applying the formula:

$$SD = \frac{\Sigma(X-\bar{X})^2}{N-1}$$

where Σ is 'the sum of ', X is each individual value, $\bar{X}$ the mean, and N the total number of values. The standard deviation is at the heart of many other useful psychological statistics. In a normal distribution, just about 70 per cent of the values fall within 1SD plus or minus the mean.

Standard error. A measure of the degree to which a statistic will differ from its true value by chance. It is most usefully applied in psychology in deciding whether two means are significantly different – a technique which yields a value known as the critical ratio.

Standard error of mean. An estimate of the degree to which an obtained mean may differ by chance from the true mean.

Standardization. A method important in developing an effective test. The proposed test is applied to a large number of individuals and examined for reliability, repeatability, procedural problems, etc. Standardization is also helpful in establishing norms and standards for the test.

Standardization group. A group believed to be representative of the population at large which can be used for evaluating new tests.

Standardized tests. Tests which have been subjected to proper evaluation, and examined for reliability, etc. (⧫⧫ STANDARDIZATION.)

Standard measure. ⧫ STANDARD SCORE.

Standard ratio. The difference between two means divided by the STANDARD ERROR of that difference.

Standard score. An individual's score as it relates to the STANDARD DEVIATION. Known as the Z-score, it is obtained by taking the difference between the obtained score (X) and the mean ($\bar{X}$) and then dividing by the standard deviation (σ):

$$Z = \frac{X-\bar{X}}{\sigma}$$

Standard stimulus. In psychophysics, the stimulus against which others are compared.

Stanford Achievement Test. Test designed particularly to assess linguistic skills, word meaning, grammar, etc.

Stanford-Binet Test. One of the earliest and most durable INTELLIGENCE tests designed for the English language. The original IQ test, the Binet-Simon, was in French and the Stanford revision for American usage first appeared in 1916. After numerous updates and revisions it is still in use, though it is still not considered to be a completely CULTURE-FREE TEST.

Stapes. ➧ STIRRUP.

Startle pattern. Stereotyped posture adopted, quite automatically, by all human beings when they are badly frightened by a sudden stimulus, such as a loud bang. High-speed photographs show the face to be distorted, the hands raised towards the head, the shoulders hunched and the body moving into a crouch position.

Stasis. An immobile state; the state of rest.

Static reflex. Automatic 'righting' posture when the body is put off balance.

Static sense. Broadly speaking, the sense of balance, mediated by mechanisms in the labyrinth of the inner ear.

Statistic. Any value achieved as the end product of a counting or sampling procedure.

Statistical constant. Any quantity which, in a repeated computation, is kept constant.

Statistical learning theory. Any approach to the study of learning or predicting the outcome of learning experiments which uses mathematical models of a probabilistic kind. Statistical theories began to appear in the mid-1950s, but they were anticipated in spirit by the work of E. R. Guthrie. Guthrie rejected the classical view that something is only learned when the final stage in the act is reinforced or rewarded, and instead argued that *every* behaviour pattern is learned immediately it is performed.

The reason that it took so long apparently to establish a particular behaviour pattern was that the animal had to establish a large set of responses to a large set of slightly different stimulus configurations. To give an example, one might present a rat with a light on one occasion, this being followed by a particular response, and therefore expect that the next presentation will induce the response. The point here is that while the *experimenter* might count the two light presentations as being identical, to the rat they might be perceptually quite distinct – its head might be turned in a different way when the light flashed, for example. Learning to such a level that the experimenter can predict what the rat will do depends, therefore, upon the animal experiencing a wide range of rather similar stimulus 'scenes' and thus the more restricted the perceptual world, the quicker all the possible permutations of input will occur.

Guthrie did not himself attempt to produce statistical models, but later workers – notably Estes – used his simple, if controversial, idea to produce theories explaining learning as being dependent upon more or less random sampling of the environment by the animal, repeated sampling leading to a reliable pattern of behaviour appearing according to fairly straightforward probability laws. Not all psychologists are happy with this approach, but statistical models do have the tempting advantage that the elusive concept of reward or reinforcement is in principle made redundant.

Statistical significance. In any experiment one normally ends up with at least two sets of data – the experimental and the control – which, depending upon one's initial hypothesis, should either be measurably different or more or less identical. If one expects that a drug will improve learning, for example, one anticipates finding differences between the experimental (drugged) group and the control (non-drugged) group, with the experimental scoring higher on later tests. But how much higher is 'higher'? If the average score of the experimental group is 102 correct and that of the control group 100 correct, can one say that the drug has worked? Might not these averages represent 'chance' differences anyway? In the long run the whole weight of statistical methods in psychology is directed to attempting to assess whether such differences are simply part of the random noise or chance effect in any experimental set-up or whether the experimental factor has caused them.

Experimental problems are rarely as straightforward as the one given above, and statistical methods today often need to be sophisticated and ingenious. When a test *does* suggest that it is exceedingly unlikely that the given results could have been achieved by chance – 100-1 against is considered to be a pretty safe bet – then the test is stated to have achieved statistical significance. It is important to realize, however, that such significance does not imply certainty – the results *could* have fallen that way by chance, even if only once in every 100, or even once in 1000 times. Technically where the significance level is set is up to the experimenter, and depends upon how cautious he is, how important are the data he is working on, and how much time he has on his hands to repeat the experiment as a double check. In fact the repeat experiment is really the key to the matter, and some theoreticians argue that all that a statistical test shows, *whatever* level of 'significance' has been achieved, is just how likely it is that you will get the same result if and when the experiment *is* repeated.

Statistics. That aspect of mathematics which deals with gathering and evaluating numerical data. (➧ STATISTICAL SIGNIFICANCE; STANDARD DEVIATION.)

Statokinetic reflexes. Postural reflexes which adjust the body appropriately in response to movement, acceleration, etc.

Status. Position; the place of an individual in a group which partly defines his relationship to them – and their's to him.

Status need. Deep-seated desire supposed to be present in all people to improve their status in a group or society. Compare ACHIEVEMENT MOTIVE.

Steady state. ➧ HOMEOSTASIS.

Stekel, Wilhelm (1868 – 1940). Early associate of Freud, and a pioneer sexologist. He argued that psychoanalysis of an individual should achieve its effects relatively rapidly, or be abandoned.

Stens. Units proposed by R. B. Cattell to allow individual scores on tests and questionnaires to be compared with standardized scores or values obtained from a wider population. The standard sten scale consists of ten units or scores, with each step being one half of a standard deviation.

Step interval. The range of values of a particular class or step in a frequency distribution.

Stereognosis. Perception of depth or three-dimensionality by any of the senses.

Stereogram. Pair of pictures, each representing slightly different views of the same scene, which when placed in a stereoscope give a vivid three-dimensional image.

Stereopsis. The perception in vision of objects in depth by the brain. True stereopsis depends upon two major factors – the existence in the animal of a pair of eyes capable of resolving reasonably fine detail, and the fact that the eyes are so positioned as to provide rather similar views of some part of the animal's environment. In this way the left eye views an object from one angle, the right eye views the same object from a slightly different angle. The differences, however, must not be so great that when the 'scenes' from the two separate retinae are dispatched to the visual cortex, the brain is unable to integrate them. The fusion or integration of the two 'scenes' yields the perception of three-dimensionality which so vividly enriches our own perceptual world, and also greatly improves hand and eye coordination, the judgement of distance, etc. Though stereopsis is one of the most powerful factors in DEPTH PERCEPTION, the two terms are not identical.

Stereoscope. Device featuring a pair of lens, prisms or mirrors which provide a three-dimensional image when a pair of slightly dissimilar pictures are presented to the eyes. For effective stereoscopy, the scene must be photographed by a camera with twin lens, set apart at approximately the same distance as the human eyes.

Stereotaxic map. Map of the brain used as an aid in experimental brain surgery.

Stereotype. A belief which tends to be (a) prejudicial, in the sense that it persists in the face of evidence to the contrary, and (b) vastly over-simplified. A typical stereotype is expressed in the statement 'Jewish people are wealthy and mean' or 'Highly intelligent people tend to be mentally unstable'.

Stereotypy. Abnormal state, often associated with psychoses, where behaviour patterns are repeated endlessly and inappropriately; may also refer to ceaseless rumination over particular ideas or chains of thought. A third meaning comes from social psychology where it refers to excessive use of social STEREOTYPES.

Sterility. Inability to produce offspring.

Stern, Wilhelm (1871 – 1938). German psychologist who introduced the concept of the IQ (mental age divided by chronological age, multiplied by 100).

Sthenia. Strength.

Stigmata. Plural of stigma – a mark or blemish. Stigmata is the name given specifically to marks or wounds supposed to emulate those of Christ at the crucifixion, and which sometimes appear on the hands and feet of certain deeply religious people. It has never been indicated that these are anything other than psychosomatic in origin.

Stiles-Crawford effect. The name given to the discovery that light passing through the edge of the pupil is less potent in its effects on retinal cells than light passing through the centre.

Stilling test. Test for COLOUR BLINDNESS which uses numbers set against multicoloured backgrounds. The colour-weak eye fails to discriminate between figure and ground, and the numbers cannot be recognized. It is rather similar to the more common ISHIHARA TEST.

Stimulant. Any drug or process which increases physiological activity.

Stimulation. Causing a receptor to fire; may also refer to anything raising general activity in an organism.

Stimulus (S). Something that triggers activity of some kind, whether it be the firing of a single receptor or the setting in motion of a more general pattern of behaviour. The stimulus is an important concept in experimental psychology which, seeking to set out the simplest model of behaviour around which meaningful experiments can be conducted, uses the basic formula S–R (Stimulus–Response), or more realistically S–O–R (Stimulus–Organism–Response). Both stimulus and RESPONSE are (sometimes) relatively easy to describe precisely. Modern psychology is having considerable trouble with the O in the middle, however.

Stimulus attitude. In an experiment, the focusing of attention on a particular aspect of the environment where the stimulus is occurring or is about to occur.

Stimulus continuum. An unbroken series of stimuli with little, if any difference between discrete stimuli.

Stimulus differentiation. The term used in GESTALT PSYCHOLOGY for the process of learning to discriminate a series of parts or patterns out of a relatively even field.

Stimulus equivalence. The eliciting of similar responses by different stimuli.

Stimulus error. Common error, discovered in the early studies of psychophysics, to the effect that a subject asked to report on a stimulus will frequently report on its *meaning* or previous associations rather than its particular physical qualities.

Stimulus generalization. Eliciting a response originally learned to a particular stimulus, by rather similar stimuli. (➧ RESPONSE GENERALIZATION.)

Stimulus population. A term used in STATISTICAL LEARNING THEORY to refer to the total environment of an organism, from which a particular *sample* may at any time elicit a particular pattern of behaviour.

Stimulus-response psychology. A slightly derogatory alternative term for behaviourism, based on the view that behaviourists attempt to reduce all human and animal activity, including mental life, to complex chains of stimulus and response. (*But* ➧ BEHAVIOURISM.)

Stimulus set. In an experiment, the tendency of an individual to concentrate on the stimulus he is expecting to receive, rather than on the response he is supposed to make. Compare RESPONSE SET.

Stimulus trace. A lingering reaction in the nervous system following a stimulus. The concept was employed by Hull in his theory of learning.

Stimulus word. In a reaction time or word association test, the word presented to the subject to elicit a response word.

Stirrup. One of the AUDITORY OSSICLES and sometimes known as the stapes. The stirrup rests against the membranous oval window of the cochlea.

Stochastic. Relating to events whose probability of occurrence changes continuously.

Stochastic models. Theories, particularly applied to learning, which assume that behaviour can be predicted on the basis of probabilistic models. (➧ STATISTICAL LEARNING THEORY.)

Stocking anaesthesia. Hysterical loss of feeling in the leg. (➧ GLOVE ANAESTHESIA.)

Stoic. Someone able to stand pain without complaining.

Storage capacity. A term drawn from communications and information theory. A memory or other storage system is measured in terms of the maximum number of items (words or BITS) that it can hold.

Story-recall test. Test of memory or intelligence in which the subject is told a simple story and asked to recall it later.

Strabismus. Squint: failure of eyes to align properly on the object being fixated.

Strata theory. Any theory of personality or the mind which assumes a subdivision of personality characteristics, some being 'deeper' or less accessible than others. Freudian theory is an example.

Stratified sample. Breaking a society or population into a number of groups (according to, say, social class) and then taking a representative sample from each group. The final pooled samples are said to resemble the whole more accurately than taking a sample of equivalent size from the population at large. It is a technique commonly used in market research, Gallup polls, etc.

Stratton's experiment. A famous experiment on perceptual learning performed by G. N. Stratton in which the subject wore spectacles which rotated the RETINAL IMAGE so that the visual field appeared upside down. In due course learning took place and the field appeared 'normal'; a further period of upset and reacclimatization occurred when the spectacles were removed.

Stream of consciousness. The ongoing 'stream' of continuous processes making up conscious experience; a term coined by William James.

Strephosymbolia. Perceiving things reversed, as in a mirror image.

Stress. A state of physiological or mental strain of a chronic rather than an acute nature. Modern views of stress tend to centre around the theory first put forward by Hans Selye in the early 1950s. Selye described stress as a specific physiological reaction to threat or danger, which manifested in the symptoms known as the general adaptation syndrome (GAS). This itself evolved through three phases – a short-term state of alarm, a longer-term phase of resistance to the alarm, and finally a collapse of resistance which might feature dramatic symptoms such as those involved in a 'nervous breakdown'.

Stress interview. Situation in which the interviewer tests the interviewee's capacity to cope with emotional strain caused by aggressive questioning.

Striate body. ➧ CORPUS STRIATUM.

Striate muscle. The musculature of the body can be classified roughly into muscles under voluntary control and those which are involuntary. The former are striped in appearance and are known as the striate muscles. Involuntary muscles are known as smooth muscles.

Striatum. ➧ CORPUS STRIATUM.

Striped muscle. ➧ STRIATE MUSCLE.

Stroboscope. Device for illuminating an object with a series of bright, rapid flashes. In stroboscopic illumination, moving parts of a machine may appear stationary provided that the strobing is in phase with the machinery's rhythm.

Stroke. Damage to the brain caused by a ruptured blood vessel.

Strong Vocational Interest Blank. One of the most widely used American tests for VOCATIONAL GUIDANCE.

Stroop test. Test of cognitive flexibility featuring a set of coloured cards incorrectly labelled – e.g. the blue card is labelled green. The subject must name the actual colour of the card when it is presented to him, and the test measures the degree to which he is capable of ignoring the *written* label.

Structuralism. An approach to psychology which argued that the central area of study should be the *structure* of the mind and the mechanisms of cerebral and mental processes, rather than their *functions*. It is generally associated with the pioneering work of Wundt. Contrast FUNCTIONALISM.

Structure. The enduring form and composition of a complex system or phenomenon. Contrast with FUNCTION, which is a process of a relatively brief duration, arising out of structure.

Structured interview. An interview featuring a planned series of questions with a specific area of discussion.

Structured psychology. ➧ STRUCTURALISM.

Structured stimulus. A precisely defined stimulus which can be easily discriminated from the background and has a definite pattern.

Study of values. Sometimes known as the Allport-Vernon-Lindzey study, it is a test of the range of interests, attitudes and values of an individual. It consists of a two-part multiple choice questionnaire, easily administered.

Stupor. A state of greatly reduced mental responsiveness with only partial consciousness.

Stuttering. A common speech disorder featuring the rapid repetition of words or parts of words, generally at the beginning of a sentence. For some reason it is far more common in males than in females. Stuttering is generally equated with stammering, but some people use the latter to refer to the blockage of words rather than to their repetition.

Stylus maze. A small experimental maze, generally printed on paper, through which the subject traces a path using pencil or stylus.

Subception. ➧ SUBLIMINAL.

Subconscious. The word is sometimes used interchangeably with UNCONSCIOUS, but actually has a quite different meaning. The *un*conscious, if one accepts the psychoanalytic definition, is a distinct and partly autonomous segment of the mind with motives and goals of its own. It does not yield up information readily to the probings of the conscious mind. The *sub*conscious on the other hand refers to processes which are on the edge of attention or not subject to conscious attention at that particular time. In fact Freud used the word PRECONSCIOUS to denote these processes in order to distinguish them from those in the unconscious mind.

Subcortical. Relating to all nervous structures and activity which occur in tissue below (or more accurately, *other than*) the cerebral cortex.

Subculture. A culture within another, sharing a number of the major system's rules and attitudes, but also offering others unique to itself.

Subcutaneous. Beneath the surface of the skin.

Subdural. Below the outer layer or dura mater of the nervous system.

Subject (S). The individual in a psychological experiment who is in some way the object of study.

Subjective. Personal; relying upon interpretation by an individual; relating to a private as opposed to a public world. The word is sometimes used to imply unreliability. Contrast OBJECTIVE.

Subjective colour. Colours perceived by the individual when the necessary wavelengths of light are not present or illuminating the retina. Fechner's colours and Benham's top are good examples.

Subjective psychology. An approach to psychology which relies almost exclusively on introspection or personal experience.

Subjective sensation. A feeling or experience which is not brought about by direct external stimulation. A good example is the bright spots of light or colours often seen when the eyes are closed in a darkened room.

Subjective test. Any test which has no formal system of scoring and which relies on the opinion of the examiner. Contrast OBJECTIVE TEST.

Subjectivism. The view that the only reality is a personal one; also refers to a tendency to judge or perceive the world exclusively in terms of one's own experiences or motivation.

Sublimation. One of the main mechanisms of ego defence according to Freud's psychoanalytic theory. Sublimation consists of the channelling of unacceptable desires or impulses into acceptable or positive activity – the classic example being the transfer of sexual energy into creativity or general industriousness. (➧ DEFENCE MECHANISM.)

Subliminal. Relates to any activity occurring below the level of awareness or perception. The phrase subliminal perception, sometimes known as subception, refers to a state of responsiveness to a particular stimulus which is not accompanied by conscious awareness that the response has been made. The topic had an experimental vogue in the 1950s and is associated with the controversy over so-called PERCEPTUAL DEFENCE.

Subliminal learning. Learning which has taken place without the individual having been aware of it. (➧➧ LATENT LEARNING.)

Subliminal perception. ➧ SUBLIMINAL.

Subliminal stimulus. A stimulus or a pattern of stimuli too weak to arouse awareness.

Submissiveness. Tendency to yield to the demands of others; opposite of dominance.

Subnormal. Below the normal; most commonly used in connection with IQ.

Subset. Something totally contained within a larger unit; one set is a subset of another if each member of the first is also a member of the second.

Subshock therapy. A mild form of insulin coma therapy where the patient retains consciousness throughout treatment. It is used to relieve anxiety and tension states.

Subsidiation. The series of subgoals or steps that have to be reached before a final goal can be achieved.

Substantive states. A term used by William James to refer to individual moments or 'focusing points' within the STREAM OF CONSCIOUSNESS – e.g. the objects or things one attends to or thinks of.

Substitute formation. Psychoanalytic term for the process of replacing one course of action, motive or attitude with another which is for some reason more acceptable. Substitute formation is a 'normal' and 'rational' strategy which the neurotic individual, however, is generally unable to adopt.

Substitution test. Test of intelligence or reasoning where the subject has to substitute one set of symbols for another – as in deciphering a simple code.

Subtest. Segment of a major test.

Subtraction method. Used in reaction time experiments where one subtracts the time taken to perform a previously measured task from the time taken to perform a compound task which *includes* the first task. The figure remaining is taken as a measure of the time devoted to the other part or parts of the compound task.

Subvocal speech. Tiny movements of the mouth or vocal cords which represent a sort of miniaturized version of speech, but which do not lead to the production of audible speech. Subvocal speech often takes place before the *act* of speaking, and at one time it was actually equated with thinking by early behaviourists such as J. B. Watson. (➧ MOTOR THEORY OF CONSCIOUSNESS.)

Successive approximation method. An approach to conditioning which involves first rewarding *any* kind of behaviour which approximates to the desired response, and then gradually reducing the range of rewarded behaviour until only the exact response required is being emitted. (➧➧ OPERANT CONDITIONING.)

Successive contrast. ➧ SIMULTANEOUS CONTRAST.

Successive practice method. Used in studying TRANSFER OF TRAINING. One takes a measure of the time it takes for a particular group to learn a task *B* on its own, and compares it with the time taken for a second group to learn task *B* after another task *A* has been learned. Gains or losses in learning time are assumed to be a function of information transferred from task *A* to task *B*.

Successive-reproduction method. Measure of long-term memory which involves the subject reproducing the learned material on a number of occasions, each separated by a considerable lapse of time.

Succubus. ➧ INCUBUS.

Suckling. The feeding behaviour in the infant; may also refer to an infant before it has been weaned.

Sudoriferous glands. The sweat glands.

Sufficient reason law. The view that, given enough information, it is in principle possible to discover the cause of *any* event.

Suggestibility. Tendency to be readily influenced by SUGGESTION and believed by some people to be a general personality character.

Suggestion. Any process designed to cause an individual to lower or blunt his critical faculties and accept information coming from another source without criticism, doubt or argument. At the heart of the phenomenon lies the fact that human beings learn from infancy onwards to absorb a good deal of information presented to them by their environment and also by other people 'on trust' and without laborious verification or checking procedures. This of course simplifies decision-making considerably. The rules for deciding what may or may not be safely taken on trust are fairly basic and include such factors as the previous reliability of the information source, its status within the society, its 'power' or 'authority' relative to the receiver, etc. Techniques of suggestion therefore, which include all forms of advertising, most political argument and of course the subset of phenomena involved in hypnosis, seek to sidestep an individual's critical faculties by presenting material in the guise of information that may be taken on trust, and thus be accepted without question. (➧➧ HYPNOSIS.)

Suicide. Taking one's own life. In most societies, suicide remains one of the ten most common causes of death.

Sulcus. One of the shallow grooves on the surface of the cortex.

Sullivan, Harry S. (1892–1949). American psychiatrist who developed a psychoanalytic theory which represented a major deviation from the Freudian position. He replaced the concept of the libido by introducing *two* basic needs – for security and for satisfaction.

Summation. The total aggregate of a series; in physiology, refers to the activation of a neural cell by input from two or more other cells when input from only one would have been below its response threshold. When the stimuli follow each other rapidly in *time* this is known as *temporal* summation; when they occur at the same moment but impinge from different locations, this is *spatial* summation.

Summation curve. Plot of a cumulative frequency distribution.

Summation tone. ➧ COMBINATION TONE. heard when two other tones, differing from each other by over 50 Hz, are presented together. The summation tone is the sum of the two frequencies.

Superego. One of the three main divisions of the mind according to the psychodynamic theory of FREUD – the other two being the ID and the EGO. Broadly speaking, whereas the id consists of instinctive desires and behaviour patterns, the superego is made up of all restraining forces learned by the individual in the course of his social evolution – those forces or 'programs' in other words which strive to mould instinctive ways of behaving so that they do not clash with social realities. The superego consists mainly of parental commands and guidance, plus 'moral' programs drawn from religious or cultural teaching and of course those drawn from experiences at school, etc. The combination of these modifying factors might be likened to the CONSCIENCE, and not surprisingly the superego finds itself in more or less constant conflict with the id. (➧➧ PSYCHOANALYSIS.)

Superior colliculi. The anterior pair of the four bodies known as the corpora quadragemina.

Superior intelligence. Referring to an individual scoring over 120 on the STANFORD-BINET TEST (roughly 15 per cent of the population).

Superiority feeling. Chronic tendency to form exaggerated ideas as to one's own powers or abilities. Compare INFERIORITY COMPLEX.

Superior oblique. One of the extrinsic eye muscles – the pair which turn the eye downwards.

Supernatural. Not being subject to natural laws.

Supernormal. Above the normal but not to the extent of being supernatural.

Superstition. An irrational or partially rational belief which is maintained in the face of contrary evidence. Superstition is normally associated with primitive mystical or religious beliefs, but it is reasonable to apply it to *any* long-term irrational belief – e.g. slavish devotion to individual political systems or even fallacious scientific ideas. Experimental demonstration of superstitious behaviour patterns in animals has been claimed – pigeons, for example, may continue to peck at a button which once yielded rewards even when the button now delivers punishment.

Supination. Assuming the supine posture.

Supportive therapy. An approach to psychotherapy in which the main role of the therapist is to give emotional support in a time of crisis until such time as the patient is confident enough to attempt to tackle his problems directly.

Suppression. Blocking of activity; in psychoanalytic theory, it refers to the conscious and voluntary blocking of unwanted ideas or behaviour patterns. The emphasis here is on conscious blocking; contrast REPRESSION. (➧ DEFENCE MECHANISM.)

Suppressor area. Segment of the cortex whose function appears to be to inhibit activity in some other segment.

Supraliminal. Above threshold. Contrast SUBLIMINAL.

Supraliminal differences method. ➧ MEAN GRADATION METHOD.

Suprarenal glands. More commonly known as ADRENAL GLANDS.

Surdity. Deafness.

Surface colour. Colour which is perceived as a property of the surface of something, as opposed to colour which appears inherent in an object, e.g. as in a gem. Contrast FILM COLOUR and VOLUME COLOUR.

Surface structure. ➧ TRANSFORMATIONAL GRAMMAR.

Surface trait. In personality testing, certain traits are relatively easy to identify and test but are possibly misleading because deeper SOURCE TRAITS are more representative of the individual's true personality.

Surgency. A term used by R. B. Cattell to describe a personality trait associated with cheerfulness and sociability. Contrast DESURGENCY.

Surrogate. A substitute; someone who stands in place of another. (➧➧ MOTHER SURROGATE.)

Survey. Generally refers to some technique, usually highly structured, of group observation or questionnaire sampling. It is one of the major methods of gathering data in the social sciences. (➧➧ METHODOLOGY; EXPERIMENT.)

Survey test. Test of group (as opposed to individual) behaviour, activity or achievement.

Survival value. Relating to a trait, characteristic or pattern of behaviour likely to ensure the survival of the individual or his species.

Suture. A surgical join; a close union between neighbouring bones as in the skull.

Sweet. One of the four primary TASTE qualities (the others are sour, salt and bitter).

Swindle's ghost. ➧ PURKINJE AFTER-IMAGE.

Sydenham's chorea. ➧ ST VITUS'S DANCE.

Syllogism. A deductive argument which features two premises and a conclusion, the problem being to determine whether the conclusion is valid given only the two premises. For example, given the premises (a) all birds can fly, and (b) swans are birds, the conclusion is that swans can fly.

Syllogistic thinking. ➧ DEDUCTIVE REASONING.

Sylvian fissure. ➧ LATERAL FISSURE.

Sym-, syn-, sys-. Prefix drawn from the Greek meaning with or together.

Symbiosis. Refers to an harmonious relationship between two biological organisms – sometimes so profound that neither can survive without the other.

Symbol. A thing taken to stand for something else or represent it. In information theory the word has much the same meaning as sign.

Symbol-digit test. ➧ SUBSTITUTION TEST.

Symbolic process. Sometimes used in behaviouristic literature to denote thinking or problem-solving behaviour.

Symbolism. All the processes involved in the use of symbols. The topic is of great interest to psychologists because it underlies the whole basis of language, of representational thought processes, and also of perception. According to the various theories of psychoanalysis, symbolism is also richly involved in the dream process, where it signals the nature of repressed material, and (according to Jung) in mythology and most forms of artistic expression. (➧➧ SEXUAL SYMBOLISM.) Perhaps the most significant fact, however, is that man appears to be unique among the animals in the creative use of symbols both to communicate with other members of his species on an immediate basis, and also to communicate over a longer period through written or pictorial languages.

Symbolization. Psychoanalytic term for the process by which repressed material in the unconscious is transferred into symbols and thereby allowed expression in acceptable form.

Symond's Picture Study Test. Form of the THEMATIC APPERCEPTION TEST (TAT) specially designed for adolescents.

Sympathectomy. Surgical severing of part of the sympathetic nervous system.

Sympathetic ganglia. Nerve centres of the sympathetic nervous system which are distributed down and on either side of the spinal cord.

Sympathetic nervous system. ➧ AUTONOMIC NERVOUS SYSTEM.

Sympathin. A hormone secreted by nerve endings within the sympathetic nervous system. It is similar to adrenalin in its action.

Sympathy. Ability to respond to another's expression of emotionality. Compare EMPATHY.

Symptom. Functional abnormality which indicates the presence of a disease or disorder.

Symptom formation. ➧ SUBSTITUTE FORMATION.

Synaesthesia. Transfer of qualities from one sense into representational form in another – e.g. perceiving a colour when a particular musical note is heard, etc.

Synanon. A drug rehabilitation programme with many of the characteristics of ALCOHOLICS ANONYMOUS.

Synapse. Junction point at which two neurones come into contact and across which a signal is passed from one to the other. The nature of transmission across thc synapse was long a mystery, and while the mechanism is still not definitely understood it is known, thanks to the work of Eccles and others, that it is basically chemical rather than electrical. A number of synaptic transmitters are known, of which the most common is probably acetylcholine.

Synaptic knob (or bauton). Growth or excrescence on the axon of a neurone in the region of a SYNAPSE. The bouton is the point at which the chemical transmitter is emitted to bridge the synaptic gap.

Synaptic resistance. Tendency for a SYNAPSE to act as a barrier to the passage of a nervous impulse. Such resistance presumably serves the purpose of damping down random activity or noise in the nervous system as a whole.

Synchronicity. Rather vague theory put forward by JUNG as an alternative to the theory of CAUSALITY. Jung argued that there were a great many 'significant' or non-random events occurring in the universe for which no causal explanation could be discovered, and that this suggested an inherent principle of non-randomness quite independent of causality. Like many of Jung's ideas, the concept is intellectually intriguing but resists practical application or logical development. The word has a separate meaning within Argyle's theory of social skills.

Syncope. A brief loss of consciousness; a faint.

Syncretism. Childlike thinking in which events, not causally related in the accepted sense of the word, are nevertheless assumed to be linked. The term is central to Piaget's theory of child development.

Syndrome. A pattern of symptoms which strongly indicate a disease or disorder; may also imply a pattern of responses in a test which indicate a particular personality type – not necessarily abnormal.

Synergic. Relating to forces or activities which work together and assist each other.

Synesthesia. ➧ SYNAESTHESIA.

Synonym-antonym test. Test in which words are presented in pairs with the subject stating whether they are similar or opposite.

Syntactic aphasia. APHASIA in which individual words may be spoken or understood correctly, but grammatical sense is lost.

Syntality. The overall characteristics of a group as regards its motivation and general activity; roughly analogous to PERSONALITY in the individual.

Syntax. The structure of language.

Synthesis. Combining parts to form a meaningful or functioning whole.

Synthetic speech. Words or speech sounds produced by a machine.

Syntonia. Personality trait characterized by being in more or less continuous harmony with the environment and with other human beings.

Syntrophy. The state of being more or less constantly in harmonious relationships with others.

System. A self-contained unit, whether physical (as with a machine) or idealistic (as with a model or theory).

Systematic. Relating to a system or having its characteristics.

Systematic error. A constant error, often introduced by the process of data collection or analysis; bias.

Systematized delusions. A set of false beliefs which nevertheless have self-consistency. It is characteristic of some forms of paranoia.

Systemic. Relating to a system, in particular the living body.

Systemic sense. That part of the sensory apparatus which detects changes taking place within the internal organs of the body.

Systems theory. Any system can be considered as being made up of various sub-systems, or in turn as itself being a sub-system of some more embracing unit. Systems theory concerns itself with studying the interrelationships of such systems and sub-systems.

Systole. Contraction, especially of the cardiac muscle which pumps blood out of the heart.

Szasz, Thomas S. (1920 –). American psychiatrist best known for his campaign against the hospitalization of psychiatric patients against their will.

Szondi test. Test featuring a set of forty-eight photographs of faces of people suffering from various psychological disorders, which the subject must rank according to their relative attractiveness to him. The test was supposed to have diagnostic value, but its reliability is dubious.

T

t. The ratio of a particular statistic to its standard error; also the abbreviation for time passed.

T data. Data obtained from tests.

***t*-distribution.** ➧ *t*-TEST.

T groups. ➧ SENSITIVITY TRAINING.

T-illusion. ➧ HORIZONTAL-VERTICAL ILLUSION.

T-maze. A simple binary choice maze shaped like a T.

t-test. Test of particular usefulness in experimental psychology in deciding whether the means of two sets of data are significantly different. The *t* test measures the significance of a mean deviation against the standard error.

Tabes dorsalis. ➧ LOCOMOTOR ATAXIA.

Taboo. Term for anything forbidden, but in psychology has come to imply anything banned from consideration or use because of religious or social pressures. FREUD argued that taboos arose because of conflicts between instinctual forces which led to the most potent or 'desirable' of the instincts being repressed.

Tabula rasa. Literally a clean slate. LOCKE argued that the mind of a child was a *tabula rasa*, on which all experiences came to be written, thus constituting memory.

Tachistoscope. Device for presenting visual stimuli briefly at controlled levels of brightness and exposure time.

Tachycardia. Abnormally rapid heartbeat.

Tachylalia. Very rapid speech.

Tacit. Not openly stated but designed to be readily understood.

Tactile. Relating to touch. (➧➧ HAPTIC.)

Tactile agnosia. Loss of ability to recognize things by touching them.

Tactile circle. Area of skin within which all touch stimuli are perceived as being one.

Tactual. ➧ TACTILE.

Tail. In statistics, the ends of a frequency distribution.

Talbot-plateau law. A given quantity of light thrown on the retina in a continuous stream is perceived as being indistinguishable in brightness from the same quantity of light when projected as an intermittent stimulus – provided that the frequency is so rapid that flicker is not seen.

Talent. An innate ability. Compare GIFTED and SKILL.

Tandem reinforcement (TAND). A particular type of reinforcement which depends upon two separate units of behaviour being successfully completed.

Tantrum. A violent burst of temper.

Taphophilia. Abnormal preoccupation with graves, cemeteries, etc.

Tapping test. Psychomotor test which requires the subject to tap at particular speeds, according to a schedule.

Taraxein. A protein supposed to be present in the blood of schizophrenics and which may inhibit the action of a particular cerebral enzyme.

Tarchanoff phenomenon. ➧ GALVANIC SKIN RESPONSE.

Tartini's tone. ➧ DIFFERENCE TONE.

Task. Behaviour required of an animal or person in order to achieve a goal. A task is normally a fairly complex act or set of acts, rather than a single movement. (➧➧ DEVELOPMENTAL TASK.)

Taste. One of the major senses, scientifically known as gustation. Taste is mediated by chemically sensitive cells grouped in clusters within the taste buds, which themselves are most commonly located in the tongue, gums and pharynx. A relatively feeble sense in man, taste is heavily dependent on the activation of smell (olfactory) receptors, and if these are knocked out of action – as in a heavý head cold – the taste sense practically disappears. It is generally agreed that there are four dimensions of taste – sweet, sour, salt and bitter.

Taste bud. Tiny structure packed with chemically sensitive cells and located in the papillae or folds of the tongue and other parts of the mouth.

Taste tetrahedron. Graphic representation of the relationship, between the four basic tastes (sweet, sour, salt and bitter) which places them on the four corners of a tetrahedron.

Tau effect. Peculiar illusion involving the interaction of spatial and temporal factors. If three lights are flashed successively in different spatial locations and if the time interval between the second and third is greater (less) than that between the first and second, the spatial distance between them is judged to be greater (less) than between the first two. The effect also occurs with equivalent patterns of stimuli when the skin is touched. The reverse phenomena is known as the Kappa effect. Here, if one is asked to judge the time interval when the spatial distance between the stimuli really *is* varied then the greater (lesser) distance is judged to have had a greater (lesser) time interval than the lesser (greater) spatial distance between the stimuli.

Taxis. Tendency for an organism to move towards or away from a particular stimulus. (⧫⧫ TROPISM.)

Taxonomy. The scientific classification of animals according to their physical and genetic relationships. The principal subdivisions, in descending order from the general to the specific, are kingdom, phylum, class, order, family, genus, species and race.

Taylorism. One of the first systems (1903) attempting to increase business efficiency and productivity, named after its originator, F. W. Taylor.

Teaching machine. A device for presenting instructional material automatically in the form of a series of simple tests with multiple choice answers, the correct choice in each case allowing advance to the next question and incorrect choices leading to explanations and retesting. With the development of relatively inexpensive electronic machinery in the 1950s there were great hopes for teaching machines as cheap adjuncts to orthodox education, but they failed to live up to their initial promise. The main reasons for this were, first, the poor level of motivation they aroused in pupils after the novelty had worn off, and, secondly, the limited and rather stilted range of alternatives offered at each choice point. Current interest has shifted from teaching machines to computer-aided instruction or learning because of the very much more pliable and sophisticated programs that are available – though at present at arguable cost-effectiveness. (⧫⧫ PROGRAMMED INSTRUCTION.)

Tegmentum. ⧫ BRAIN.

Tele-. As a prefix, means long distance.

Teleceptor. A distance receptor – e.g. the eye, ear.

Telegnosis. A rare term used in parapsychology to denote any kind of knowledge gained paranormally at a distance. It would include telepathy, clairvoyance, etc.

Telekinesis. A parapsychological term meaning the moving of an object by paranormal means – i.e. without touching it or using any physical instrument.

Telencephalon. The front part of the forebrain, containing the cerebral hemispheres, the corpus callosum and other important structures. In evolutionary terms the telencephalon is the most recently developed part of the brain and tends therefore to handle most of the so-called 'higher' aspects of brain function. (➧ BRAIN.)

Teleology. The study of purposes or goals; the belief that living organisms can only be properly understood in terms of their purposes.

Telepathy. Communication between minds without the aid of the known senses. Telepathy is one of the supposed faculties of the mind (including clairvoyance, precognition, etc.) given the group name of EXTRA-SENSORY PERCEPTION, and studied experimentally by parapsychologists. Evidence for the existence of telepathy is considered to be weak (though not completely dismissable) by most scientists. (➧ PARAPSYCHOLOGY.)

Telephone theory. A theory of hearing which likens the ear and auditory mechanisms to a telephone receiver which merely relays information to the brain where all auditory analysis takes place. (➧ FREQUENCY THEORY.)

Teleplasm. ➧ ECTOPLASM.

Telestereoscope. STEREOSCOPE whose lens system gives an exaggerated sense of depth.

Teletactor. Device used as an aid for the totally deaf, by translating speech sounds into tactile stimuli, generally sensed by the fingers.

Telic. Relating to ends, goals or purposes.

Telodendron. Filament-like structure at the end of an AXON.

Temperament. A person's predisposition towards emotional responsiveness; not, however, a term considered to be particularly useful in modern personality theory. The idea of a temperament inherent in all humans was first put forward by the Greek philosopher Galen, who produced a quasi-physiological theory based on the four 'basic' body fluids or humours – blood, phlegm, black and yellow bile. These in turn led to four 'basic' temperaments – sanguine (warm and affectionate), phlegmatic (unresponsive), melancholic (depressed) and choleric (short-tempered). Modern research into temperament with newborn infants suggests that characteristics of temperament appear at the very earliest stages of development – e.g. an irritable overactive baby is more likely to preserve this temperament into adulthood.

Temperature senses. Receptors lying in the skin and body surface which respond to heat and cold. That there *are* heat and cold sensitive receptors seems to have been established, but there is disagreement about the nature of the physiological mechanisms which underlie them.

Temperature spot. A spot on the skin which is particularly sensitive to temperature stimuli.

Temporal. Relating to time.

Temporal lobe. Segment of the cerebrum situated in front of the occipital lobe and just below the lateral or Sylvian fissure. There are, of course, temporal lobes on both sides of the brain, with the speech centre being located in the left lobe of right-handed people and some, but not all, left-handed people. (➧ CEREBRAL HEMISPHERES.)

Temporal maze. Maze problem which involves the subject in learning a *sequence* of moves (e.g. make two turns right, then two turns left, then alternating left and right) rather than responding to specific spatial cues (e.g. go left at the red mark, right at the blue, etc.).

Temporal summation. ➧ SUMMATION.

Tendermindedness. A concept introduced by William James to define a personality dimension characterized by an idealistic, optimistic, somewhat emotional approach to life and its problems. James also proposed the contrasting dimension, toughmindedness – referring to individuals of a practical, realistic and often pessimistic frame of mind. The concept has since been elaborated by Eysenck.

Tendon. Type of tissue which connects muscle to bone.

Tendon reflex. Muscle contraction induced by stimulation of a tendon.

Tension. In physiology, refers to the state of strain which exists in a contracted muscle.

Tension-relaxation dimension. One of the three dimensions of feeling or experience as postulated by the pioneer experimental psychologist, Wundt. (➧ TRI-DIMENSIONAL THEORY.)

Teratology. The scientific study of congenital biological malformations and mutations.

Terman, Lewis M. (1877 – 1956). Pioneer of intelligence testing, best known for his studies of gifted children and for his revision of the Binet-Simon intelligence test, later known as the STANFORD-BINET.

Terminal bulb. ➧ SYNAPTIC KNOB.

Terminal depression. Feeling of dejection, depression or any climax which may follow the completion of some major task or the solution of some long drawn-out problem.

Terminal sensitivity. The maximum sensitivity that an organism can experience.

Territoriality. The tendency for an animal (or even a human) to seek out and demarcate territory exclusively for its own use or that of its immediate social group.

Test. Any standardized set of questions or sequence of tasks to be performed which is designed to measure behaviour, ability or knowledge. The word also has a special meaning in logic (where it refers to anything which checks the validity of reasoning) and in statistics (where it refers to anything which assesses the significance of a statistic). Tests may be *un*standardized – as in those given informally by a teacher in a classroom – when they are counted as being applicable for a specific group but may not be for a different one. (⧫⧫ STANDARDIZATION.) Psychologists generally categorize tests under the headings of (a) group and individual, and (b) verbal and performance.

Test age. An individual's rating in terms of age on a test; his score on a test which has been standardized in age units.

Test battery. ⧫ BATTERY TEST.

Testes. The organs in the scrotum which generate semen which contains the male sex cells; the testicles.

Testosterone. Primary male sex hormone produced by the testes.

Test profile. Chart which graphically illustrates performance on a variety of tests.

Test scaling. Assigning values or weightings to particular tests by trying them out on a sample group.

Tetanus. Rhythmic contraction of a striate muscle; also the disease lockjaw caused by the tetanus bacillus.

Tetrachoric correlation. Refers to a correlation between two variables, each of which is continuous, normally distributed and expressed as two classes. For example, a correlation between height (tall-short) and intelligence (bright-dull).

Tetrachromatism. Theory of COLOUR VISION which is based on the assumption that there are four primary colours.

Texture gradient. An important clue in distance perception: the further away a visual pattern is from the observer, the denser and more tightly packed its elements appear to be.

Texture response. A particular type of response met in RORSCHACH TESTS where the subject attaches special importance to the texture of the inkblot.

Thalamic theory. ➧ BARD-CANNON THEORY.

Thalamus. The major relay centre between the cortex and the incoming sensory nerves. The thalamus lies below the cerebrum and is involved in basic responses to sensation and also to pain.

Thalidomide. A tranquillizing drug which produces malformations in the foetus when taken by pregnant women.

Thanatology. The study of death, or more specifically the personal and social problems of an individual facing death.

Thanatophobia. An abnormal and obsessive fear of death.

Thanatos. A term used by Freud in some of his later theorizing to refer to a supposed death drive or unconscious death wish which was constantly at odds with the life instinct (EROS). Thanatos is one of Freud's more controversial concepts.

Thematic Apperception Test (TAT). A widely used projective test developed by H. A. Murray. The subject is presented with a drawing of an enigmatic or ambiguous nature, one of a set of thirty, generally involving one or more humans, and is asked to make up a story to fit the picture. As with all projective tests, the resulting narrative is supposed to contain elements of the individual's problems or anxieties. (➧ PROJECTIVE TESTS.)

Theory. A principle or hypothesis which allows one to understand the relationship between particular facts, and also allows predictions to be made about future circumstances.

Therapeutic. Having value as a THERAPY.

Therapy. The satisfactory treatment of an illness or disorder.

Therblig. A name used by ergonomists to describe a segment of a complex act; the word is roughly Gilbreth (its originator) spelt backwards.

Thermalgesia. A disorder in which warm stimuli are perceived as painful.

Thermalgia. A sense of burning pain, also known as CAUSALGIA.

Thermanaesthesia. Lack of sensitivity to thermal (warm or cold) stimuli.

Thermoreceptor. Receptor sensitive to heat or cold.

Thermotropism. Tendency for an organism to orient itself according to the temperature of its surroundings.

Thinking. A word used extensively in psychological literature, but seldom explicitly defined. It seems that its main characteristic is the use, by the brain, of symbolic processes, and in particular the conscious, deliberate use of such processes. is it then reasonable to speak of *unconscious* thought in the Freudian sense of the phrase? The answer to this is entirely a matter of how one cares to define thought – if one insists on consciousness being a necessary factor in any thought process, then one needs a new word to describe unconscious symbolic processing.

A novel and perhaps helpful new approach to the problem has arisen, rather surprisingly perhaps, from computer science. Recent technological developments have raised the question as to whether, in principle, a computer or machine could be said to be capable of thought, and if it could, how one could ever determine whether it was thinking or not. The current view seems to be that a computer could be said to be 'thinking' if one were able to converse with it (at a distance) for a reasonable period of time and yet not know whether one were talking to a machine or to a human. Such a definition adds weight to the view that it is the conscious symbolic processing that we are really talking about when we use the word thought, and that *unconscious* processing requires a new and separate word.

Thinking type. ➧ RATIONAL TYPE.

Thoracic cavity. The chest cavity, containing the lungs, heart and oesophagus.

Thoracico-lumbar division. Anatomical name for the sympathetic nervous system.

Thorax. Part of the body between the neck and abdomen.

Thorazine. The trade name for chlorpromazine.

Thorndike, Edward Lee (1874 – 1949). American psychologist best known for his pioneering work on animal behaviour, including the invention of special apparatus for testing the intelligence and learning ability of animals (➧ PUZZLE BOX; TRIAL AND ERROR.) He was also a pioneer educational psychologist.

Thorndike-Lorge list. A list showing the relative frequencies of occurrence of 30 000 English language words.

Thought. ➧ THINKING.

Thought reading. Obsolete expression for mind reading or telepathy. More commonly used today to refer to magicians' or mentalists' tricks. (➧➧ MUSCLE READING.)

Thought transference. ➧ TELEPATHY.

Three component theory. ➧ TRICHROMATIC THEORY.

Threshold. The lowest amount or intensity of a stimulus which is sufficient to produce a response. It is also known as a limen. Thresholds are usually classified as being either absolute (AL) or difference (DL), the former being the value at which a stimulus is just *detectable*, the latter being the value which is just large enough to allow it to be *discriminated* from another.

Thurstone, Louis Leon (1887–1955). American psychologist and pioneer in intelligence testing. He was one of thc first workers to employ techniques of FACTOR ANALYSIS in studying the nature of intelligence.

Thyroid. Endocrine gland with important roles in controlling the metabolic rate.

Thyrotropin. Pituitary hormone which itself determines the secretion of the thyroid glands.

Tic. Involuntary muscle twitch.

Tic douloureux. Intense burning pain of the face.

Timbre. The quality of a particular sound or pattern of sounds which makes it unique; tonal quality.

Time. One of the major dimensions of existence. The nature or 'reality' of time is a philosophical question at heart, but from a psychological point of view one can say that time is a subjective experience associated with the observation of a sequence of events. Perhaps the topic would not be of particular interest to psychologists were it not for the fact that the passage or flow of time seems to vary according to the kind of activity one is performing. For example, if a given task is frequently interrupted, the time taken to complete it will appear longer than if one can apply oneself to it continuously. Similarly if one is highly motivated to complete a task (and presumably is able to concentrate attention on it without interruption) then it seems to be completed quickly. Another factor affecting the perception of long periods of time seems to be age – the older one gets, the more rapidly things seem to go by. Some drugs may also affect time perception, the stimulants lengthening it, the depressants shortening it (with some exceptions). Apparently at odds with these findings is the common subjective experience of depressed individuals that time passes extremely slowly. Oddest of all, perhaps, is the finding that under conditions of sensory deprivation, time passes much more quickly – possibly because intervals of sleep occur without the subject being aware of them.

Time and motion study. An aspect of ERGONOMICS; the systematic investigation of a pattern of work, concentrating on the sequences of movements involved in the work, and the relative time spent on each. The aim is to see if overall task efficiency can be raised by eliminating wasteful movements or altering their sequence.

Time error. One of the so-called 'constant errors' in psychophysics which features misjudgement of the properties of objects as a function of their position in time; for example, if two identical sounds are presented in sequence, the first is usually judged to have been louder. This is known as a positive time error, while the reverse phenomenon is known as negative time error.

Time sample. Sampling of behaviour by recording activity occurring within a given period of time.

Time sense. The ability to make accurate judgements about the passage of time.

Time-sharing. A concept important in modern computing where time-sharing computers divide their effort amongst a large number of users 'at the same time'. In fact, their switching is so rapid that the users believe they are receiving the undivided attention of the computer at all times. The concept is of interest to psychology because of the possibility that the brain is itself a time-sharing computer, switching its attention rapidly over a vast number of tasks 'at the same time'.

Tinnitus. Ringing in the ears when not caused by external stimulation.

Tissue. Any collection of living cells having similar structures.

Titchener, Edward B. (1869 – 1927). A former pupil of Wundt who became a leading exponent of structuralism and a pioneer of experimental psychology in America.

Titular leadership. Headship. (➧ LEADERSHIP.)

Token reward. Rewarding an animal or person with something which has no immediate reward value but may subsequently be exchanged for a reward. (➧ SECONDARY REINFORCEMENT.)

Tolerance. The ability to withstand unusually large doses of a drug without suffering physiological or psychological harm. In sociology, the term refers to a liberal or 'non-interfering' attitude of mind.

Tolman, Edward Chace (1886 – 1959). American psychologist who attempted to develop a model of learning (purposive behaviourism) which blended elements from the traditional behaviouristic view and the Gestalt school of psychology.

Tolman's learning theory. A theory formulated by the behaviourist Tolman, who felt that the essential behaviouristic model of learning was too naive and constricting. Tolman argued that it was hopeless to attempt to explain animal behaviour in terms of learned sequences of muscle movements and that some account would have to be taken of the fact that an animal, say, running a maze learned the significance and 'meaning' of certain signs and cues. This is also known as purposive behaviourism. (➧➧ MEANS-END CAPACITY.)

Tonal attribute. A characteristic of a tone, e.g. its pitch, volume, loudness, etc.

Tonal bell. A schematic model – roughly bell-shaped – on which can be plotted the various tonal attributes and their interrelationship. It has the same kind of relationship to sound as does the colour pyramid to vision.

Tonal brightness. The density of a TONE.

Tonal gap. A range of insensitivity to TONE or pitch.

Tonal island. A range of sensitivity to TONE or pitch between two TONAL GAPS.

Tonal pencil. A diagram which allows the relationship of pitch and volume to be graphically represented.

Tonal scale. The range – between 15 Hz and 20 000 Hz – to which the normal human ear is sensitive.

Tonal volume. The 'spread' or space-filling quality of a TONE. An organ has high and a flute low tonal volume.

Tone. A sound consisting of a periodic vibration. A pure tone is a sound made up of waves of one frequency only.

Tone deafness. Lack of ability to discriminate between TONES; lack of sensitivity to pitch.

Tone variator. Apparatus used to produce pure TONES.

Tonic. The basic note which seems to act as the focus of a piece of music; also an adjective, relating to TONUS.

Tonic immobility. A prolonged state of immobility or rigidity adopted by many animals when threatened; also known as feigned death.

Tonicity. ➧ TONUS.

Tonometer. Device for measuring pitch and for producing TONES.

Tonoscope. Device for analysing complex sounds by converting sound waves into light and thus making them easier to inspect.

Tonus. The state of low-level contraction which exists in all muscles even when inactive, and which serves to maintain them in a state of readiness.

Topalgia. Highly localized pain.

Topectomy. Minor surgery to the frontal cortex, somewhat less drastic than lobotomy, and used to reduce symptoms of mental illness.

Topography. In psychology, any attempt at mapping the mind, brain and brain functions.

Topological psychology. Any approach to psychology which attempts to explain behaviour in terms of the dynamic interaction between an organism and its LIFE SPACE. The best known system of topological psychology was that put forward by Kurt Lewin. (⧫⧫ FIELD THEORIES.)

Topology. The study of those properties of things and their interrelationships which are not affected by distortion. For example, a hole retains its property of 'holeness' no matter how its *shape* is distorted.

Torpor. A state of sluggish responsiveness.

Torsional. Twisting.

Totem. Something which is held as being symbolical or representative of an individual or a group; totemism is the belief in a particular totem which serves to unite a society and give it a sense of cohesion, protection and purpose.

TOTE units. TOTE is an acronym for test-operate-test-exit which, according to a theory put forward by Miller, Galanter and Pribram, corresponds to the four basic units of any behavioural activity. TOTE units were proposed as slight elaborations of the behaviouristic model of the reflex arc.

Touch. Any sensation involving either contact or pressure.

Touch spot. Small area of the skin particularly sensitive to touch.

Toughmindedness. ⧫ TENDERMINDEDNESS.

Toxaemia. Blood poisoning.

Toxic. Relating to poisons.

Toxic psychosis. Psychotic state induced by a poison.

Trace. Any change in the nervous system brought about as the result of learning (⧫⧫ ENGRAM). A trace is also the residual image on a cathode ray tube.

Trace conditioned response. The response induced when a conditioned stimulus is first followed by a blank interval and *then* by reinforcement.

Trachea. Windpipe.

Tracking. Following a moving target by constantly making appropriate adjustments.

Tract. Nerve bundle.

Training analysis. A complete and thorough PSYCHOANALYSIS conducted by a skilled analyst and designed to have two goals:

1. To give the trainee insight into his own problems and motivation.
2. To teach him the principles of analysis so that he may in due course assume the role of therapist.

A training analysis is counted as being a necessary prerequisite for practising orthodox psychoanalysis.

Trait. A long-term personal characteristic whether learned or inherited.

Trance. A state of relatively prolonged dissociation from external stimulation with an apparent reduction in consciousness. No satisfactory physiological index of a trance state has been found; and in fact the EEG of individuals in hypnotic trance does not vary from that of the relaxed, fully conscious brain. The word is also sometimes used for the apparently dissociated state entered into by spiritualistic mediums.

Tranquillizer. Any one of a class of drugs with a relaxing, calming effect on the emotions, but not producing sleep unless in heavy doses. They are usually divided into two classes – the antipsychotics (which alleviate the symptoms of psychoses, e.g. largactil) and the anti-anxiety agents (used in minor mood disturbances, e.g. librium).

Transaction. Human behaviour seen as an interplay between an individual and his environment.

Transactional theory. A theory first advanced by Ames to the effect that all perception is a learned reaction as the result of constant interaction with the environment. Particularly striking evidence for this view can be seen in such a situation as the AMES ROOM.

Transcendental meditation (TM). An approach to relaxation and 'psychological self-awareness' popularized in the West in the 1960s by the Maharishi Mahesh Yogi. There is some evidence that through TM individuals may acquire a short-term measure of control over autonomic functions such as brain waves, heart rate, etc, though its value as a long-term aid to relaxation is uncertain.

Transection. A cut made across the long axis, as in severing a nerve.

Transfer (of training). Learning one particular task and by doing so passing on information or habits which affect the learning or performance of a subsequent task. Transfer may be positive (when the material transferred helps the second task) or negative (when it hinders it). (⧫⧫ SUCCESSIVE PRACTICE METHOD.)

Transference. In the course of undergoing psychoanalysis, patients often form a deep, partially conscious, emotional relationship with the therapist. According to psychoanalytic theory what is happening is that the patient begins to see the therapist in the role of a parent (or some other close and significant figure) and thus transfers the emotions normally reserved for this person onto the therapist. In the first phase of transference the feelings are largely positive and the patient may even believe that he or she is in love with the analyst; in the second phase – generally taken by analysts as a sign that therapy is proceeding satisfactorily – the transference is negative and the patient will express aggression and often hatred for the other. Unless the analyst is incautious enough to return these emotional overtures (if he does a state of 'counter-transference' is set up which greatly interferes with the treatment), the transference will in due course dissolve and the analysis should then draw to its natural close. (⧫ PSYCHOANALYSIS.)

Transformation. A change in a mathematical formula which does not, however, involve a change in its content or value. In psychoanalysis, the term refers to a change in feelings into an 'acceptable' form so that they can be transferred from the unconscious to the conscious mind.

Transformational grammar. Since the work of Noam CHOMSKY, linguists have paid increasing attention to the 'deep structure' of sentences as opposed to their 'surface structure'. In a classic example, the sentence 'Flying planes can be dangerous' reveals its surface structure, but its deep structure may be either 'Planes can be dangerous when they fly' or 'It is dangerous to fly planes'. Transformational grammar attempts to determine the relationships between such deep and surface structures. (⧫ PSYCHOLINGUISTICS.)

Transmission. Any kind of exchange of information from one point to another, whether this implies the passage of a nervous impulse, the passing on of characteristics through the genes or the handing down of cultural traditions from one generation to another.

Transmitter. Whatever it is that originates a signal and encodes it for an information channel.

Transmitter substances. Hormones which assist neural transmission in a living system – perhaps the best known being acetylcholine which assists the bridging of the synaptic gap. (⧫ SYNAPSE.)

Transmuted score. A score which has been transformed from one kind of scale to another.

Transorbital lobotomy. A psychosurgical technique consisting of partial ablation of the prefrontal area. Access to the brain is through the roof of the bony socket of the eye. (➧➧ FRONTAL LOBOTOMY.)

Transorientational approach. Refers to an approach which may draw from two or more theoretical sources.

Transparency. Relates to something which can allow light to pass through it without significant diffusion.

Transposition. Repositioning elements within a series; also used in learning theory to refer to the ability of a subject to transfer a principle learned in one situation to another. For example, if a monkey is taught to choose the larger of two circles to get a reward, it will choose the larger of a different pair on a subsequent occasion even if it has never seen either of the second pair before.

Transsexualism. A term used to refer to the belief, by an individual, that he or she is in reality a member of the opposite sex.

Transverse. Lying across, or at right angles, to something.

Transvestism. Strong desire or compulsion to dress in clothes belonging to the opposite sex.

Traube-Hering waves. Fluctuations in the pulse which are supposed to be related to changes in the level of attention.

Trauma. A state of shock, whether physical or psychological, induced by an unpleasant incident or injury.

Traumatic psychosis. Psychotic condition brought on by brain damage.

Traumatophobia. Abnormal fear of being injured.

Tremometer. Device for measuring degree of body or limb TREMOR.

Tremor. Repetitive, uncontrollable muscle movements.

Trend. Tendency to behave in a particular way.

Trend analysis. Series of measurements made to determine if there is any change taking place in a phenomenon.

Trepan. ➧ TREPHINE.

Trephine. Device for cutting holes in the skull.

Treppe. When a muscle is given a series of brief shocks of equal strength, it responds with a series of increasingly powerful movements.

Trial. One complete response or sequence of responses in a single experiment.

Trial and error. A concept introduced by Thorndike to explain the strategy apparently underlying animal behaviour in learning. Typically, when confined to a PUZZLE BOX the animal makes a series of movements, more or less at random, but one or more of which will ultimately help it to escape. Thorndike argued that *all* learning proceeded on this basis – the successful responses being rewarded and thus learned or established, the unsuccessful ones being unrewarded and failing to be learned. Trial and error learning is supposed to be more or less automatic, with the animal being unconscious of what it is doing or how it is actually effecting the escape or achieving its goal. (➧ INSIGHT.)

Tribe. Social group united through a common language, shared territory and often a collective name.

Trichotillomania. Compulsive hair pulling.

Trichromatic theory. Any theory of COLOUR VISION based on the existence of receptors capable of detecting three primaries.

Trichromatism. Normal colour vision as based on the trichromatic theory.

Tridimensional theory. Refers to Wundt's original thesis that there are three dimensions of feeling – pleasantness/unpleasantness, excitement/depression and tension/relaxation.

Trigeminal nerve. The fifth cranial nerve, serving the sensations of the face, mouth, nose, teeth and also the motor function of the muscles of mastication.

Trigeminal nucleus. Cluster of nerve cells in the pons which gives rise to the trigeminal nerve.

Trireceptor theory. The theory that the retina is equipped with three different types of receptor, responsive to three primary colours.

Tritanopia. ➧ BLUE-YELLOW BLINDNESS.

Trochlear nerve. The fourth cranial nerve, serving the superior oblique muscle of the eyeball.

Troland. A unit of measurement of retinal illumination.

Tropism. An orienting response, generally involving movement, by an organism to a particular source of stimulation – e.g. phototropism is the tendency to move (or grow) in response to light.

True score. An ideal score representing a measure which is totally free of error. The closest approximation to a true score is normally taken to be the mean of the largest possible sample.

Truism. Statement which is so self-evidently true that it is barely worth stating.

Truth drug. Refers to any drug which lowers inhibition or causes a confused state of mind which may lead the subject to reveal confidences. One of the best known is sodium amytal.

Tumescence. Swelling or expansion of an organ.

Tune. A series of notes which constitute a melody.

Tunnel vision. Loss of vision in the periphery of the retina.

Turner's syndrome. Disease caused by the individual having one fewer chromosome than normal. There are abnormalities in the primary sex characteristics. Contrast KLINEFELTER'S SYNDROME.

Twilight vision. ➧ SCOTOPIC VISION.

Twin. Two infants born in the same pregnancy. Uniovular or monozygotic twins are caused when an already fertilized ovum splits and copies itself, the resulting twins being identical. Dizygotic twins are born when *two* eggs are fertilized in a single act of conception, the resulting twins of course being no more alike (other than in age) than any other pair of sibs.

Twin studies. Studies relevant to the problem of whether a particular characteristic or factor is inherited or learned. Identical twins are known to share a common genetic background being formed from a single fertilized ovum. In studying, for example, the effect of heredity on intelligence one can observe the performance on IQ tests of such twins when raised from birth in different backgrounds; if heredity is the dominant factor then the twins' IQs should barely differ. Twin studies have also been employed notably in considering the aetiology of schizophrenia and other illnesses suspected of having a major hereditary component.

Two aspect theory. ➧ DOUBLE ASPECT THEORY.

Two-factor theory. Refers to Spearman's theory of intelligence which held that all intellectual behaviour reflects two factors or components, the first a fundamental or *general* (the G FACTOR), the second a SPECIFIC ABILITY (S factor) relevant to a particular intellectual task. (➧➧ FACTOR ANALYSIS.)

Two-point discrimination. The smallest separation of two points on the surface of the skin which allows the brain to detect that there are in fact two separate stimuli. (➧➧ VIERODT'S LAW.)

Two-tailed test. In statistics, one of a number of tests which allow one to assess whether the NULL HYPOTHESIS has been rejected or not. If one has no reason to suspect directionality in the data, then the two-tailed test is more powerful than the one-tailed test; the latter is applied if one suspects directionality.

Tympanic membrane. The eardrum.

Type. A category or class of things whose unity is determined because they share some specific characteristic. The word may also refer to a person considered to be particularly representative of a class, as in personality theory.

Type one error. When testing for the significance of results two errors are possible, depending on the level of significance set. Type one error occurs where the NULL HYPOTHESIS is rejected when it is true – e.g. if the significance level of .01 is chosen, the null hypothesis is rejected in 1 per cent of all cases where it is true. Type two error occurs where a null hypothesis is accepted when it is false.

Type two error. ➧ TYPE ONE ERROR.

Typology. The study of types and the methods of classifying them.

Typrosine. Amino acid found in most proteins.

U

U test. Non-parametric statistic used to indicate whether the differences between means of unmatched groups are significant. (⧫⧫ MANN-WHITNEY TEST.)

Ultrasonic. Relating to wavelengths beyond the limit of human hearing.

Ultraviolet. Refers to light with a wavelength shorter than 390 nm.

Uncertainty interval. ⧫ INTERVAL OF UNCERTAINTY.

Unconditioned inhibition. A phrase used by Pavlov to refer to all forms of inhibition which are not acquired by learning or CONDITIONING.

Unconditioned response. Any reflex or response which occurs to a specific stimulus and which has *not* been previously learned or conditioned. In the classic Pavlovian experiment, the response of salivation when food is presented to a hungry dog, is a typical unconditioned reflex. Conditioned reflexes are those generally acquired through association with an unconditioned stimulus. (⧫ CONDITIONING; PAVLOV.)

Unconditioned stimulus (UCS). A stimulus that serves to provoke an unconditioned reflex or response. In the classical Pavlovian experiment, the food that elicits salivation in an animal.

Unconscious. As a general term, the unconscious could be said to constitute all those mental processes which take place without the individual being aware of them. However, this definition is really too broad to be helpful as it bundles together all kinds of phenomena ranging from those cerebral processes which control, say, digestion to the numerous subtle and enigmatic facets of unconscious motivation, desires and conflicts.

Although one feels that it should always have been obvious that there were mental processes other than those involved in consciousness, the idea of the unconscious runs counter to the mood of much religious and moral philosophy. The reason for this is that consciousness, mind, soul, etc., all imply that man is, through the exercise of his rational, conscious self, in principle in total control of his destiny. Perhaps this partly accounts for the vigorous objections that faced Freud's views on the unconscious which seemed to suggest that 'conscious' man was *not* in total control of his behaviour, and therefore presumably could not be held responsible for many of his 'immoral' actions. Actually, contrary to popular belief, Freud did not discover or 'invent' the unconscious, but merely drew attention to the potency of its role. But he was the first to suggest explicitly that the conscious mind could get access to the material in the unconscious by inspecting the material of dreams and other phenomena. Today few psychologists deny the existence of powerful unconscious processes operating in mental life, though by no means all accept the Freudian model of the interplay between the conscious and unconscious forces. (⧫⧫ FREUD; DREAMS; PSYCHOANALYSIS; SUBCONSCIOUS.)

Unconscious memory. According to psychoanalysis, memories that have been pressed into the unconscious mind because they are either offensive or threatening to consciousness.

Unconscious motivation. Motivation whose origin, and possibly even operation, is not consciously known to the individual. The idea of unconscious motivation is central to almost all psychoanalytic theories.

Unconsciousness. Not the same as the unconscious; the state of unconsciousness exists when no consciousness is present at all – as in deep sleep.

Underachiever. Someone who fails to measure up to the performance expected for his age or educational level. Contrast OVERACHIEVER.

Understanding. The process of becoming aware of the relationship between things or of their meaning.

Undifferentiated. Relates to tissues, including nerve fibres, which have not developed to the point of specialization.

Undoing. One of the main mechanisms by which, according to Freud, the EGO protects itself against conflict or anxiety from within the unconscious. In many ways undoing is the most extreme and irrational defence mechanism and is assumed to be brought into play more or less as a last resort. The mechanism involves a ritual attempt at eliminating some past action which is the source of guilt or anxiety. A classic example is Lady Macbeth's ritual handwashing. Obsessive-compulsive neuroses are supposed to be examples of this ego defence mechanism. (⧫ DEFENCE MECHANISM.)

Ungestalt. A term used in GESTALT PSYCHOLOGY for anything which resists integration, or cannot be formed into a whole.

Ungrouped scores. Scores not yet divided into classes.

Uniaural. Monoaural.

Unicellular. Refers to organisms consisting of only a single cell, e.g. the amoeba.

Unilateral. One-sided.

Unimodal. Refers to data which when plotted show only one mode.

Uniovular twins. ➧ IDENTICAL TWINS.

Unipolar neurone. A nerve cell which has a single pole. Contrast BIPOLAR NEURONE.

Unique factor. In factor analysis, a factor found in only one test.

Unique trait. The statistical term for a trait which has a zero correlation with other traits.

Universal complex. The psychoanalytic term for a COMPLEX which arises because of conflicts involving a basic instinct, e.g. sex, hunger.

Universal language. ➧ LANGUAGE UNIVERSAL.

Universal symbol. A symbol assumed to have the same underlying meaning for everyone; roughly equivalent to an archetypal symbol.

Universal trait. A trait present in all members of a group.

Universe of discourse. Everything that is relevant to a particular discussion.

Unlearning. Attempting to eradicate a learned habit by practising an alternative behaviour pattern.

Unreadiness principle. One of the laws or principles of learning put forward by Thorndike; if a conducting unit is not ready to be activated, conduction by it is 'unsatisfying'. Most of Thorndike's principles turn out to be circular in their argument.

Unreality feeling. Feeling of psychological detachment or of the unreality of one's surroundings; can be a precursor to epileptic fits.

Unsociable. Avoiding the company of others.

Unspaced learning. ➧ MASSED PRACTICE.

Unstable. Unpredictable and erratic.

Unstriped muscle. ➧ SMOOTH MUSCLE.

Unweighted. For a number of reasons data sometimes have to be weighted (multiplied by correction factors) before being merged with others. The original raw data are then termed unweighted. (➧➧ WEIGHTING.)

Uranism. Obsolete term for HOMOSEXUALITY.

Urban's tables. A set of tables used in evaluating the results of psychophysical experiments.

Urethra. The channel leading from the bladder to the outside of the body.

Urethral erotism. A psychoanalytic term for sexual pleasure achieved by stimulation of the urethra or from urethral function of some kind.

Urning. Male who plays the role of the woman in homosexual relationships.

Urolagnia. Sexual excitement associated with the process of urination.

Use law. ➧ LAW OF EXERCISE.

Uterus. The organ in which the embryo develops.

Utilitarianism. The philosophy that the rightness or wrongness of something is best measured by how useful that something is.

Utility. Practical value; in biology, the value of something in maintaining or promoting life.

Utricle. A small sac in the vestibule of the inner ear which contains receptors sensitive to head movement.

Uvula. The fold of skin that hangs down from the soft palate.

V

V factor. Verbal comprehension factor in an INTELLIGENCE TEST.

Vacuum activity. A term used in ethology to refer to a pattern of behaviour occurring apparently in the absence of the appropriate stimulus.

Vagina. The passage leading from the uterus to the outside of the body.

Vaginismus. Strong and sometimes painful contraction of the vaginal muscles which may prevent intercourse.

Vagotomy. Severing the VAGUS nerve.

Vagotonia. Overactivity of the VAGUS nerve.

Vagus. The tenth cranial nerve which passes down to the stomach and plays a major role in controlling the parasympathetic system.

Valence. Whatever it is about something that makes it psychologically compelling or attractive. The concept is employed in LEWIN'S THEORY.

Validation. Checking the truth of something by a systematic process; establishing whether a test actually measures what it sets out to.

Validity. The degree to which something is true; the degree to which a test measures what it sets out to. All psychological tests developed for a particular purpose are subjected to validational procedure before being used. (♦♦ CONSTRUCT VALIDITY; FACE VALIDITY.)

Validity coefficient. An expression of the degree to which a test is valid – i.e. measures what it sets out to. This is measured by the correlation between the test and some variable accepted as the 'criterion'.

Valium. The trade name for diazepam, a tranquillizer; one of the benzodiazepines.

Value. A quantitative measure of some kind; the worth of something.

Value judgement. A subjective assessment based on the worth or value of something rather than on its objective characteristics.

Value system. The set of values accepted by a particular society, group or individual. Compare BELIEF SYSTEM.

Variability. The state of being subject to change; in statistics, refers to the degree and nature of the scatter of values in a sample.

Variability coefficient. The measure of variability in a distribution given by dividing the standard deviation of the sample by the mean of the sample and multiplying by 100.

Variable. Literally, anything that can be changed or altered; in psychology, has a special meaning in connection with the design and analysis of experiments. Here a variable is some factor which may be changed in order to discover the effect on another factor, or a factor which may or may not change as the result of the presence or absence of another factor. In the first case we are talking about an experimental or INDEPENDENT VARIABLE, in the second about a DEPENDENT VARIABLE.

Variable error. Any error which creeps into an experiment more or less as the result of conditions during the experiment – e.g. boredom or practice effects. Compare CONSTANT ERROR.

Variance. Statistical term for the square of the STANDARD DEVIATION. It measures how widely the results are spread about the mean.

Variation. Any difference; in biological terms refers to a particular change in the appearance or behaviour of a species whether caused by environmental or genetic factors. Compare MUTATION.

Variety. Subdivision of a species.

Vascular. Relating to blood vessels.

Vasectomy. Surgical severing of the tubes that run from the testes to the penis.

Vasoconstriction. Constriction of a blood vessel.

Vasomotor. Relating to changes in the capacity of blood vessels.

Vector. Roughly speaking, a line of force; more specifically, any physical quantity which can be described in terms of the two factors of magnitude and direction. The term is also used by Lewin to denote factors which cause behaviour to be directed towards a particular goal. Contrast BARRIER.

Vector psychology. A general theory of motivation put forward by Kurt Lewin which attempts to relate behaviour to 'fields' or 'life vectors'.

Vegetative. Relating to those parts of the nervous system concerned with background physiological activity – respiration, digestion, metabolic processes, etc.

Venereal. Relating to sexual intercourse.

Ventral. Relating to the front of something; opposite to dorsal.

Ventricle. A cavity or chamber in one of the body's organs.

Verbal. Relating to words, both written and spoken.

Verbalism. Preoccupation with words at the expense of the meaning that lies behind them; verbosity.

Verbal learning. The acquisition of verbal skills, whether written or spoken.

Verbal mediation. ➧ MEDIATING PROCESS.

Verbigeration. Meaningless repetition of words.

Vergence. Turning movements of the eyes.

Veridical. Approximating to reality. The term is also used in parapsychology of dreams which seem to have a special significance, or which correctly foretell the future.

Verification. Attempting to prove or disprove some hypothesis by the use of objective methods.

Vermis. The part of the cerebellum which lies between the two hemispheres.

Vernier acuity. A measure of the capacity of the retina to resolve very fine lines – as on a finely calibrated vernier scale.

Vertebrata. The class of animals equipped with backbones.

Vertex. The top or peak of something.

Vertical group. In sociology, a group where members are drawn from at least two social classes. Compare HORIZONTAL GROUP.

Vertical-horizontal illusion. ➧ HORIZONTAL-VERTICAL ILLUSION.

Vertical mobility. A sociological term for the ability of an individual to move from one social class to another.

Vertigo. An illusion that the world is revolving around one. The term is sometimes also used for phobic-type panic associated with heights or unusual visual perspectives.

Very severely mentally retarded. ➧ MENTAL RETARDATION.

Vesicle. Sac-like organ containing fluid.

Vestibular senses. The sensory mechanisms located in the vestibule of the inner ear which concern themselves with maintaining balance and detecting change in the movement of the head.

Vestibular system. The whole of the neural and physiological mechanisms involved in maintaining balance and detecting movement of the head.

Vestibule. The part of the inner ear which lies between the cochlea and semicircular canals and which contains the utricle and saccule. These latter bodies are equipped with minute hairs sensitive to changes in head position. (♦♦ SEMICIRCULAR CANALS.)

Vestigial structure. Part of the body which once served a function (in the past of the species) but which no longer has one, e.g. the appendix in humans.

Viable. Capable of life.

Vicarious. Relating to something which stands in place of something else.

Vicarious learning. Learning something while in the course of attending to something else. In social theory, the term particularly refers to the (generally unconscious) learning of behaviour.

Vicarious trial and error (VTE). Symbolic trial and error: when an animal is faced with a choice point in a maze or some similar problem, it will often scan the alternatives before making a decision. That this should be thought of as unusual activity reflects the extreme attitude of the behaviourist position of the 1930s, when the idea that the animal could be 'internally' or 'symbolically' processing information was considered shockingly unscientific. To overcome the problem of inferring that the animal might even in the most rudimentary way be 'thinking' about the problem in front of it, the harmless phrase vicarious trial and error was introduced. Today the phrase has historical rather than practical value.

Vienna School. The followers of Freud in the early days of psychoanalysis.

Vierordt's law. The TWO-POINT DISCRIMINATION threshold on the skin is lower on the limbs than on the trunk of the body.

Vigilance. A state of relatively high attention and concentration on a particular task. The term is roughly synonymous with arousal.

Vigotsky test. A test of concept-formation ability, featuring the sorting into classes of blocks of various shapes, sizes and colours.

Vincent learning curve. A plot of group learning which allows one to compare the learning curves of different subjects. The technique is to divide each subject's curve into the same number of segments and then average the results.

Vineland Social Maturity Scale. A test for social maturity designed for children and young adults. (⧫⧫ BRISTOL SOCIAL ADJUSTMENT SCALE.)

Violet. The colour perceived when the retina is stimulated with light of a wavelength of approximately 400 nm.

Viraginity. Overt, man-like behaviour in a woman.

Virilism. Male secondary sexual characteristics appearing in a woman.

Virility. Sexual potency in the male; possession of normal primary sex characteristics in a man.

Virulent. Having the qualities of a virus; extremely poisonous.

Viscera. All the organs encased in the abdomen and thorax.

Visceral. Related to the viscera; sometimes used to imply 'emotional'.

Visceral learning. Conditioning or training of the autonomic nervous system – blood pressure, heart rate, skin resistance, etc. The term has come into use in connection with interest in BIOFEEDBACK. (⧫⧫ TRANSCENDENTAL MEDITATION.)

Visceral sense. Relates to all sensations coming from the VISCERA.

Viscerogenic. Originating in the VISCERA.

Viscerotonia. ⧫ SHELDONIAN THEORY.

Visibility coefficient. Measure of the relative visibility of light of different wavelengths to a standard.

Visibility curve. Plot of the relative brightness of light of different wavelengths.

Visile. Used to denote someone whose mental imagery is largely visual. Compare AUDILE.

Vision. One of the main mechanisms by which animals gather information from objects and events distant to their body, and in the case of many animals, including man, the most important of the main senses. The sense is mediated by the EYE which is sensitive to light in the range (roughly) 400-750 nm. (⧫⧫ PERCEPTION; RETINA; COLOUR VISION.)

Visions. Hallucinations or subjective visual experiences generally of a religious or revelatory kind.

Vista response. A particular response met in Rorschach testing where the subject describes shaded areas of the blot as being 'in depth'.

Visual acuity. The capacity of the eye, or more precisely the RETINA, to resolve fine detail in the visual field. The performance of the retina is quite remarkable, being capable of responding to stimulation from a single photon, and detecting lines whose width, when projected on to the retina, are less than the diameter of a single receptor. This high level of visual acuity is believed to be maintained not only by the extreme sensitivity of the cones and their density of packing in the central area, the fovea, but also by the eye's natural ultra-fine tremor. This tremor serves to project an image across a wide array of receptors, thus providing a kind of background scanning to feed extra information to the brain. Visual acuity at a rather less microscopic level is measured in terms of the individual's ability to read letters on a special chart (Snellen chart), and 'normal vision' is the ability to read a particular set or line of letters at 6 metres – 6/6 vision. If the individual can read another row of letters from 6 metres which the person with normal vision can only read from 3 metres, then his visual acuity is better than average and he is said to have 6/3 vision. On the other hand, if he can only read a row of letters from 6 metres which the person with normal vision can read from 18 metres then he is below average with 6/18 vision.

Visual adaptation. The capacity of the retina to change its level of operation in response to changes in the visual environment. The best examples are dark and light adaptation.

Visual agnosia. Failure to recognize common visual objects, normally associated with brain damage.

Visual angle. The angle, measured in terms of degrees or minutes of arc, subtended (formed by opposite extreme points) by the image of an object projected on to the retina, and upon which the size of the retinal image depends.

Visual axis. A straight line running from the centre of the fovea to the point of fixation.

Visual cliff. Apparatus used in checking whether animals or young children have natural depth perception. It normally consists of a sheet of thick glass set into a table-like structure with an opaque surround. The animal or child is placed on the opaque border, and the test is to see whether it will crawl out over the glass – the assumption being that if it has depth perception it will be alarmed at the 'cliff' revealed through the transparent glass.

Visual cortex. Those parts of the cerebral cortex, specifically the occipital lobes, devoted to the receipt of information from the visual senses and the associated processes of perception.

Visual displacement. The deviation of the eyes from the normal position when they fixate any object.

Visual field. The extent of visual experience at any single fixation (compare FIELD OF REGARD); the three-dimensional space in which visual objects are located.

Visual fixation. Bringing the eyes into the position where the image of an object is focused on the central portion of the retina.

Visual illusion. Mismatch between information presented to the retina and the perceptual response made by the brain. (➧➧ OPTICAL ILLUSION; ILLUSION.)

Visual induction. The effect on the perception of one area of the visual field by the changing of stimulation in another. (➧➧ CONSTRAST.)

Visual motor Gestalt test. ➧ BENDER GESTALT TEST.

Visual organization. A term used in GESTALT PSYCHOLOGY to refer to the way in which the visual field appears to divide itself into 'meaningful' recognizable units.

Visual perception. The processes occurring in the brain by which visual sensory information is integrated, classified and related to previous experience. This should be carefully distinguished from visual sensation. (➧➧ PERCEPTION.)

Visual purple. ➧ RHODOPSIN.

Visual righting reflex. Automatic orienting response of the head in response to changes in visual fixation.

Visual type. ➧ VISILE.

Visual yellow. ➧ RETINENE.

Vital capacity. The maximum volume of air which can be exhaled after a single full breath.

Vitalism. The philosophy that living organisms are physical, material things possessed of a special quality or 'life force' which makes them essentially different from non-living things. The vitalistic position, which has been losing ground steadily in biology and physiology over the past century, is basically a form of DUALISM.

Vital statistics. Data concerning the birth and death rates in human populations.

Vitality. Having the power to remain alive; hence vigour, energy, etc.

Vitamins. Substances which play an important role in the body's metabolism but which are not themselves synthesized in sufficient quantities by the body and must be absorbed in food.

Vitreous humour. Jelly-like transparent substance which fills the space in the eye between lens and retina. (⧫⧫ AQUEOUS HUMOUR.)

Vocabulary test. Test designed to assess the range of words with which a subject is familiar and which he understands.

Vocal cords. Those parts of the larynx which can produce speech sounds.

Vocalization. The deliberate production of sounds by the vocal cords.

Vocal register. The range of pitch which the vocal cords can produce.

Vocational aptitude test. Test which indicates whether an individual is suited to a particular job; specific abilities, interests, motivation and personality are among the factors measured.

Vocational guidance. One of the most practical and important fields in applied pyschology – an attempt, by sets of tests and personal interviews, to determine what jobs are likely to be suitable for an individual in terms of his (a) motivation, (b) basic ability, (c) intelligence, and (d) personality.

Vocational interest blank. ⧫ STRONG VOCATIONAL INTEREST BLANK.

Vocational selection. Job selection based on vocational guidance tests.

Voice key. Device which operates a switch in response to the human voice.

Volar. Related to the palm of the hand or the sole of the foot.

Volition. Conscious, deliberate control of one's activities and behaviour; relating to the 'will'.

Volley theory. A theory of hearing put forward by Wever and Bray which suggests that the sensitive fibres in the basilar membrane react in groups, sending 'volleys' of impulses to the brain. Alternative HEARING THEORIES stress that these fibres respond in a continuous way. (⧫⧫ WEVER-BRAY PHENOMENON.)

Volume colour. Colour which appears to be associated with the three dimensionality of an object, as opposed to being merely a surface feature. (⧫ SURFACE COLOUR; FILM COLOUR.)

Voluntarism. The philosophy that the will is the ultimate determiner of events, in contrast with the deterministic position. (⧫ DETERMINISM.)

Voluntary. Relates to anything performed at will.

Voluntary muscles. Those muscles under voluntary control – the striped muscles.

Von Kries theory. ⧫ DUPLICITY THEORY.

Voyeur. Someone who gains his or her main sexual gratification by watching the sex acts of others, people undressing, etc.

Vulva. The female external genital organs.

Vygotsky test. ➧ VIGOTSKY TEST.

W response. In RORSCHACH TESTS, a response which is based on the whole of the inkblot.

Waking centre. Part of the reticular activating system supposed to control wakefulness.

Waking dream. A vivid, hallucinatory experience generally occurring around the time of going to sleep or while waking from it. This is also known as hypnagogic or hypnopompic imagery.

Wallerian degeneration. The disintegration of the myelin sheath which encases the main trunk of some neurones.

War psychology. Can refer to attempts to study the reasons why man makes war, but more usually refers to the application of psychological knowledge and methodology to warfare. Participants in wars have always realized that an enemy may be intimidated, and thus have his readiness to fight sapped, by appropriate displays of aggression and fearlessness – a technique perhaps unconsciously borrowed from animals.

Charging into battle with shrill cries, bizarre body covering or paintings and so on are probably the earliest applications of psychological warfare, but these have been considerably refined in the twentieth century, with less emphasis being placed on battle itself and more on attempting to erode one's enemies' confidence prior to battle. Propaganda of this kind varies from leaflet raids, pointing out the hopelessness of resistance, to subtler and possibly two-edged tactics – such as the Japanese pamphlets distributed to Australian soldiers in the Second World War which implied that American soldiers were seducing their wives and daughters while they were fighting in jungle swamps. Psychological techniques have also been brought into play in the interrogation of prisoners, including the notorious technique known as BRAINWASHING. At a less objectionable level psychologists are employed in devising and administering tests used for selecting personnel, officer training, etc., and in studies of the effects of fatigue on combat effectiveness. Much ergonomic research has also gone into instrument layout in tanks and aeroplanes, and the physical design of small arms and light artillery.

Warm spot. Small area on the skin especially sensitive to warm stimuli.

Wasserman test. Test for the presence of syphilitic infection in the blood or cerebrospinal fluid.

Watch test. Test of auditory sensitivity which involves holding a ticking watch at a given distance from the listener.

Waterfall illusion. Distortion of the visual field experienced after a moving pattern, similar to that of a waterfall, has been viewed for half a minute or more. The distortion takes the effect of an apparent flow of the visual field in the opposite direction to that of the waterfall. (⧫⧫ FIGURAL AFTER-EFFECTS.)

Watson, John Broadus (1878 – 1958). One of the most influential figures in the history of experimental psychology and one of the pioneers of behaviourism as a scientific discipline. In the first two decades of the century Watson seized on the work of Pavlov and expounded the view that psychology could only hope to advance by an objective, as opposed to an introspective, approach. At the same time he argued that words like mind, thought, etc., clouded our understanding of psychology rather than helped it. While his original views are now seen to have been hopelessly simplistic, his general approach has had a lasting impact on Western psychology and remains strong through the experimental and theoretical work of B. F. Skinner. (⧫ BEHAVIOURAL; SKINNERIAN PSYCHOLOGY; MOTOR THEORY OF CONSCIOUSNESS.)

Wave. Cyclic movement of particles which pass their movement on to other particles, thus causing a wave pattern to advance.

Wave amplitude. The height of a wave from tip to trough.

Wave frequency. The number of times the tip of a wave passes a particular point in one second.

Wavelength. The distance between the tips of two waves.

Wave of excitation. The passage of electrical activity through living tissue.

Waxy flexibility. A condition seen in a certain form of schizophrenia (catatonic) when the patient remains relatively immobile, the limbs staying in any position in which they have been placed.

WAY technique. A form of projective test in which the subject has to write down three brief answers to the question 'Who are you?'

Weaning. The process of changing an infant from breast or bottle feeding to solid food. The term is also used in psychoanalysis to describe the process of persuading patients to give up their habits or obsessions.

Weber's law. Weber's law, which is one of the few moderately reliable 'laws' of psychology, states that the JUST NOTICEABLE DIFFERENCE between two stimuli is a constant proportion of the intensity of the stimuli. Put another way, the more intense the pair of stimuli, the greater the difference between them must be before it is noticeable. Weber's law breaks down at extremes, but it is expressable in a simple and generally useful formula:

$$\frac{\Delta I}{I} = K$$

Wechsler-Bellevue scale. Obsolete version of the WECHSLER ADULT INTELLIGENCE SCALE.

Wechsler Adult Intelligence Scale (WAIS). One of the best known and most satisfactory tests of general intelligence, standarized for adults and older children. The test has a high level of retest reliability. The Wechsler Intelligence Scale for Children (WISC) is an intelligence test standardized for children from 5 years to 15 years 11 months old.

Weight. Relative significance of a test item, determined by correlating the item score against the test score.

Weighting. Determining the relative influence each item or score should have in determining the total score; individual items are given proportional values according to their signficance and are then known as weighted scores.

Weigl-Goldstein-Scheerer test. A test of concept-formation involving the sorting of blocks according to their colour and shape. (➧ CONCEPT FORMATION.)

Weismannism. The view that the genetic structure cannot be modified by environmental changes, other than by the purely random effects of mutation. Weismannism is essentially in harmony with the Darwinian theory of evolution and contrasts with Larmarckianism.

Weltanschauung. One's philosophy of life as a whole.

Weltschmerz. Sentimental sorrow about life, the world and the state of mankind.

Wernicke's area. Part of the brain believed to be the centre for recognition and comprehension of spoken words.

Wertheimer, Max (1880 – 1943). German-American psychologist with a major interest in perception and in creative thinking. He was one of the trio, including Köhler and Koffka, who formed the Gestalt school which was so influential in psychology in the 1930s and 1940s. (➧ GESTALT PSYCHOLOGY.)

Wetzel grid. A device for plotting height, weight and age and establishing norms of development from their interrelationships.

Wever-Bray phenomenon. If the main organ of hearing, the cochlea, is physically stimulated it responds by emitting a burst of electrical energy. It is not clear why this activity occurs, but it is not the nervous impulse *per se*, and seems to be some phenomenon associated with the inner mechanisms of the cochlea itself. (➧➧ VOLLEY THEORY.)

Wheatstone bridge. A device for measuring changes in electrical resistance in a circuit.

White matter. Those parts of the nervous system which are covered with myelin sheath and have a characteristic white colour. Cell bodies themselves are greyish – hence GREY MATTER.

White noise. Random noise which tends to have a featureless quality.

White space response. In RORSCHACH TESTS, a response which concentrates on those parts of the card *not* featuring blots or parts of blots.

Whole method. An approach to learning which requires the subject to learn the material as a whole and not in a series of chunks (➧ PART METHOD.)

Whole response. ➧ W RESPONSE.

Wholism. ➧ HOLISM.

Whorfian hypothesis. A theory advanced by the linguist B. L. Whorf to the effect that cultural and behavioural differences between social groups are a function of their linguistic differences. This opposes the traditional view that the differences that actually exist between societies lead in turn to variations in their language.

Wiggly block test. A test of spatial apprehension and manual dexterity in which the subject has to assemble a block cut up into a series of parts by a wiggly line method rather than the usual straight-line segmentation.

Wild Boy of Aveyron. A famous but controversial FERAL CHILD studied in France by Joseph Itard.

Will. The process involved in the conscious control of human thoughts and behaviour. The notion of will as a separate entity has passed out of use in psychology because it tends to propagate the unhelpful dualistic view that mind and body are distinct and different facets of man.

Will factor. That aspect of personality which concerns itself with purposeful behaviour.

Will therapy. A form of psychotherapy introduced by Otto Rank and based on the idea that a patient should come to terms with the fact of his own birth and separation from his mother's womb and hence achieve independence of the will.

Will to power. Drive to dominate others. The concept is central to the Adlerian theory of personality. (➧ ADLER.)

Windmill illusion. An apparent sudden change in the direction of rotation of a spoked wheel.

Wing test. A common test of musical ability. (➧➧ SEASHORE TEST.)

Wish fulfilment. A psychoanalytic term for any attempt at gaining whatever it is that one wishes or desires, whether by real practical means or, more commonly, by fantasies. Freud believed that the raw material of DREAMS consists of attempts at wish fulfilment, though some of the wishes are heavilydisguised to avoid alarming the dreamer.

Witchcraft. Attempting to control some aspect of the world by the use of secret magical techniques.

Withdrawal. Removing oneself from a source of tension or frustration. The term also refers to COITUS INTERRUPTUS.

Withdrawal symptoms. Major physiological and psychological disturbances which follow the weaning of an individual from a drug to which he has become addicted.

Wolf child. ➧ FERAL CHILD.

Woodworth personal data sheet. A test with over 100 Yes/No items, developed by R. S. Woodworth as a screen for neurotic patients.

Woodworth, Robert Sessions (1869 – 1962). American psychologist whose career spanned the formative years of psychology. He was the author of a classic textbook *Experimental Psychology*.

Word association test. A form of test pioneered by C. G. JUNG in the early part of the century and designed to highlight psychologically sensitive areas which were at least partially repressed by the patient. A list of words, some neutral, some emotionally loaded, was presented to the subject who was asked to give an immediate 'unthinking' response. The nature of the response and the reaction time to each word was noted, with bizarre responses or excessive reaction times being taken as indicating 'troublesome' repressed material.

Word blindness. ➧ ALEXIA. The term is also sometimes used, incorrectly, for DYSLEXIA.

Word-building test. Test in which the subject has to manufacture as many words as he can out of a given number of letters.

Word count. Table of the relative frequency of words in the language, e.g. the Thorndike-Lorge list.

Word deafness. Auditory aphasia: inability to understand spoken words because of some form of brain disorder.

Word salad. Garbled, nonsensical speech associated with schizophrenia.

Word-span test. Test to see how many words an individual can recall of a list which has been presented once.

Working mean. An assumed mean.

Working through. An approach to psychotherapy in which the patient goes over and over the problems and difficulties which led him to seek therapy, in the hope of gaining insights into his condition or possibly 'dramatizing' the problem away.

Work-limit test. Test of the relative length of time different subjects take to perform the same task.

World test. PROJECTIVE TEST for children in which the child is given a set of toy objects, models, etc., and asked to construct a scene or 'world' out of it. The final effort is studied for clues as to the nature of his problems.

Writing accent. Characteristics of an individual's handwriting which allow it to be recognizable and discriminable from others.

Wundt's illusion. Apparent bending of two parallel lines as the result of other lines crossing them. (⧫⧫ HERING ILLUSION; BOLLNER ILLUSION.)

Wundt, Wilhelm (1832 – 1920). Considered by many to be the founder of modern psychology, Wundt established an experimental laboratory in the 1870s in Leipzig. He was the leader of the structuralist school and the teacher of most of the individuals who were later to dominate psychology for half a century.

Wurzburg school. A nineteenth-century school founded by Kulpe which concentrated on 'mentalistic' phenomena such as judgement, volition and 'imageless thought'.

X

X axis. The horizontal axis or abscissa of a graph.

X-O test. An early attitude test in which the subject crossed out or circles an item depending on his interests.

Xanthic. Yellowish.

Xanthocyanopsia. Partial COLOUR BLINDNESS featuring normal or even heightened sensitivity to yellow, but no perception of red or green.

Xanthopsia. Heightened sensitivity to the colour yellow caused by certain forms of poisoning.

Xenoglossia. 'Speaking in tongues': the babbling of apparently foreign languages while in a mystical or trance state.

Xenophobia. Abnormal fear of foreigners or strangers. Compare ETHNOCENTRISM.

Xi. The POINT OF SUBJECTIVE EQUALITY (PSE) in psychophysics.

Y

Y axis. The vertical axis or ordinate of a graph.

Year scaling. Measuring intelligence or other abilities on the basis of the norm for a particular age. For example, if a child has a mental age of eight, he is counted as being one year 'younger' than a child whose mental age is nine – irrespective of the chronological ages of either.

Yellow. The colour perceived when the retina is stimulated with light of approximately 580 nm wavelength.

Yellow spot. ➧ MACULA LUTEA.

Yerkes-Bridge scale. A modification of the early Binet intelligence tests.

Yerkes-Dodson law. States that strong motivation will interfere with the learning of a complex task but improve the learning of a simple task.

Yerkes, Robert Mearns (1876 – 1956). Pioneer of the experimental study of animals in psychology and founder of the Yale primate laboratories in Florida. He also pioneered mass intelligence testing – notably the First World War ARMY ALPHA TEST.

Yoga. School of Hindu philosophy which teaches depersonalization techniques as aids to achieving spiritual unity.

Young-Helmholtz theory. The most famous and durable theory of COLOUR VISION, requiring the existence of three distinct types of receptors.

Z

Z-score. ➧ STANDARD SCORE.

Zeigarnik effect. Discovery that subjects are more likely to remember details of tasks which were interrupted experimentally in mid-course than those they were allowed to complete.

Zeitgeist. The spirit or mood of the times.

Zen. Japanese pronunciation of the Chinese word *Ch'an*, meaning meditation; a basic feature of the Buddhist religion.

Zero correlation. Correlation showing no relationship between variables.

Zero-order correlation. Direct correlation between two variables with no attempt to remove the contributory effect of other variables. Contrast PARTIAL CORRELATION.

Zoanthropy. The belief that one can become an animal.

Zoetrope. Obsolete term for STROBOSCOPE.

Figure 32. Zollner illusion.

Zollner illusion. A striking illusion involving the apparent bending of parallel lines.

Zooerasty. Having sexual intercourse with animals.

Zoology. The scientific study of animal life.

Zoomorphism. Interpreting human behaviour in terms of animal behaviour. Compare ANTHROPOMORPHISM.

Zoophilia. Abnormal attraction for animals.

Zoophobia. Abnormal fear of animals.

Zurich school. The name given to the followers of C. G. JUNG.

Zygote. A fertilized sex cell.

Guide to Further Reading

General

E. Hilgard, *Introduction to Psychology*, Harcourt Brace Jovanovich, 1971.
G. A. Miller, *Psychology: the Science of Mental Life*, Penguin, 1977.

The brain and nervous system

S. Rose, *The Conscious Brain*, Weidenfeld & Nicolson, 1973.
D. E. Wooldridge, *The Machinery of the Brain*, McGraw Hill, 1963.
A. R. Luria, *The Working Brain*, Penguin, 1973.

Sensory physiology

F. A. Geldard, *The Human Senses*, Wiley, 1972.
J. J. Gibson, *The Senses Considered as Perceptual Systems*, Allen & Unwin, 1968.
R. F. Thompson, *Foundations of Physiological Psychology*, Harper & Row, 1967.

Experimental psychology

J. W. Kling and L. A. Riggs, *Woodworth and Schlosberg's Experimental Psychology*, Holt, Rinehart & Winston, 1971.
S. Miller, *Experimental Design and Statistics*, Methuen, 1975.
C. Robson, *Experiment, Design and Statistics in Psychology*, Penguin, 1975.

Animal psychology

W. H. Thorpe, *Learning and Instinct in Animals*, Methuen, 1963.
K. Lorenz, *King Solomon's Ring*, Methuen, 1966.
W. C. McGrew, *An Ethological Study of Children's Behaviour*, Academic Press, 1972.

Perception

R. Gregory, *Eye and Brain*, Weidenfeld & Nicolson, 1972.
R. Gregory, *The Intelligent Eye*, Weidenfeld & Nicolson, 1970.
R. N. Haber, *Contemporary Theory and Research in Visual Perception*, Holt, Rinehart & Winston, 1970.
B. Lloyd, *Perception and Cognition*, Penguin, 1972.

Learning and memory

I. M. L. Hunter, *Memory, Facts and Fallacies*, Penguin, 1970.
K. H. Pribram (ed.), *Brain and Behaviour*, vol. 3: *Memory Mechanisms*, Penguin, 1969.
E. R. Hilgard and D. C. Marquis, *Conditioning and Learning*, Appleton-Century Crofts, 1966.

Cognition

J. Turner, *Cognitive Development*, Methuen, 1975.
J. Greene, *Thinking and Language*, Methuen, 1975.
J. S. Bruner, J. J. Goodnow and G. A. Austin, *A Study of Thinking*, Wiley, 1956.

Motivation

P. Evans, *Motivation*, Methuen, 1975. (NB poss. reprinted with new title, *Personal and Social Motives*.)
C. L. Stacey and M. F. de Martino (eds.), *Understanding Human Motivation*, Howard Allen, Cleveland, Ohio, 1963.
D. E. Berlyne, *Conflict, Arousal and Curiosity*, McGraw Hill, 1960.

Brain and nervous system in action

P. Nathan, *The Nervous System*, 1969.
I. Oswald, *Sleep*, Penguin, 1970.
E. L. Hartman, *Functions of Sleep*, Yale University Press, 1974.
S. G. Lee and A. R. Mayes (eds.), *Dreams and Dreaming*, Penguin, 1973.

Maturation and early development

W. A. Marshall, *Development of the Brain*, Oliver & Boyd, 1968.
H. McGurk, *Growing and Changing*, Methuen, 1975.
T. Bower, *The Perceptual World of the Child*, Fontana, 1977.
D. Stern, *The First Relationship: Infant and Mother*, Fontana, 1977.

Development psychology

E. Rayner, *Human Development*, Allen & Unwin, 1975.
J. Sants and H. J. Butcher (eds.), *Developmental Psychology*, Penguin, 1975.
I. J. Gordon, *Readings in Research in Developmental Psychology*, Scott Foresman, 1971.
Bruner *et al*. (eds.), *Play*, Penguin, 1976.

Applied psychology

A. Anastasi, *Fields of Applied Psychology*, McGraw Hill, 1970.
H. J. Eysenck, *Fact and Fiction in Psychology*, Penguin, 1970.
H. J. Eysenck, *Sense and Nonsense in Psychology*, Penguin, 1970.
P. Trower, B. Bryant and M. Argyle, *Social Skills and Mental Health*, Methuen, 1978.

Psychology of communication

R. C. Oldfield and J. C. Marshall, *Language*, Penguin, 1970.
O. U. Team, *Language and Education*, Routledge & Kegan Paul, 1972.
Martin *et al*., *Understanding Children Talking*, Penguin, 1976.
J. Lyons, *Chomsky*, Fontana, 1970.

Social psychology

R. Brown, *Social Psychology*, Free Press, 1973.
E. Aronson, *The Social Animal*, W. H. Freeman, 1976.
E. Aronson, *Readings for the Social Animal*, W. H. Freeman, 1976.
M. Argyle, *Social Interaction*, Tavistock Publications, 1973.
J. Radford and R. Kirby, *The Person in Psychology*, Methuen, 1975.

Abnormal and clinical psychology

H. R. Beech, *Changing Man's Behaviour*, Penguin, 1969.
R. Kirby and J. Radford, *Individual Differences*, Methuen, 1976.
A. Anastasi, *Psychological Testing*, Wiley, 1968.
M. Rutter, *Helping Troubled Children*, Penguin, 1976.
J. A. C. Brown, *Freud and the Post-Freudians*, Penguin, 1969.

Relationship of psychology to other disciplines

R. S. Woodworth and R. M. Sheehan, *Contemporary Schools of Psychology*, Methuen, 1965.
R. Ornstein, *Psychology of Consciousness*, W. H. Freeman, 1973.
F. George, *The Brain as a Computer*, Pergamon, 1973.

Guide to Further Reading

M. J. Apter, *Computers in Psychology*, Wiley, 1973.

C. E. M. Hansel, *ESP: a Scientific Evaluation*, McGibbon & Kee, 1966.

B. B. Wolman (ed.), *Handbook of Parapsychology*, Van Nostrand Reinhold, 1977.